Hispanic Marketing

Connecting with the New Latino Consumer

Second Edition

Felipe Korzenny

Betty Ann Korzenny

Routledge
Taylor & Francis Group

LONDON AND NEW YORK

Second edition published 2012
by Routledge
2 Park Square, Milton Park, Abingdon, Oxon OX14 4RN

Simultaneously published in the USA and Canada
by Routledge
711 Third Avenue, New York, NY 10017

Routledge is an imprint of the Taylor & Francis Group, an informa business

First edition published by Elsevier Inc. 2005

British Library Cataloguing in Publication Data
A catalogue record for this book is available from the British Library

Library of Congress Cataloging in Publication Data
Korzenny, Felipe.
   Hispanic marketing: connecting with the new latino consumer / Felipe Korzenny,
   Betty Ann Korzenny.—2nd ed.
      p. cm.
   Includes bibliographical references and index.
      ISBN 978-1-85617-794-8 (alk. paper)
   1. Hispanic American consumers.
   2. Consumer behavior—United States.
   3. Target marketing—United States.
   I. Korzenny, Betty Ann, 1933–   II. Title.
   HF5415.33.U6K67 2012
   658.80089_68073—dc22   2011009929

ISBN: 978-1-85617-794-8 (pbk)
eISBN: 978-0-08096-278-8 (ebk)

Typeset in Times
by MPS Limited, a Macmillan Company, Chennai, India

Dedication

There are people who have contributed much to our inspiration and quality of life. Here we mention their names. Just note that some are human and others are almost human.

Rachel Korzenny, John Griffis,
David Griffis, Mark Griffis,
Andrew Griffis, Ceci Griffis,
Daniela Griffis, Andrea Griffis,
Chris Griffis, Alex Griffis,
Anna Griffis, David Griffis Jr.,
Robert Millhouse, Miriam Korzenny,
Annet Forkink, Dutchess,
Profeta de España, Chincate Sin Par,
Sugar, Spice, Dulce, Canela,
Micio, Boomer, and a nice school of fish.

Contents

Acknowledgments

There is no question that the most deserving of acknowledgments are the Latinos that live in and contribute to the US. They are our inspiration.

The work reflected in this book owes gratitude to many institutions and people. Florida State University provided a much needed Sabbatical to Felipe in order to concentrate on writing. Steve McDowell, Chair of the School of Communication, and Larry Dennis, Dean of the College of Communication and Information, provided support and encouragement. The students that have been in our graduate and undergraduate courses during the past 8 years have been a great resource for discussion that have brought about ideas and concepts reflected in this book.

The Center for Hispanic Marketing Communication at Florida State University, which we founded, has provided the opportunity for many of our students and collaborators to produce concepts and materials that enriched this book. We should mention the names of Holly McGavock, Maria Gracia Inglessis, Antonieta Echezuria, and Natalie Kates, as examples of those who have distinguished themselves in their efforts to advance our field of work and inquiry. The Center's advisory board comes from different aspects of industry and represents prestigious companies. Many advisory board members deserve explicit mention because of their valuable contributions to our efforts. Geoff Godwin of Emerson Climate Technologies has been a dedicated leader and donor. Others who have made special contributions to further the cause of the Center include Frank Ross of Coca-Cola, Mark Lopez of Google, Rudy Rodriguez of General Mills, Isaac Mizrahi of Alma DDB, Rochelle Newman of Walton Isaacson, Cesar Melgoza of Geoscape, Jorge Ortega of NewLink America, Aldo Quevedo of Dieste, Luis Vargas of Winn-Dixie, Armando Martin of Xledge, Charles P. Garcia, CEO, Garcia Trujillo, Joe Zubizarreta of Zubi Advertising, and Tony Suarez of Suarez Enterprises.

In a very central place are the agencies and institutions that worked with us in producing the case studies for this volume. Here is the list of organizations/companies and agencies which contributed the case studies featured in this book.

Organizations/Companies	Agencies
Allstate Insurance Company	Captura Group
American Family Insurance	The San Jose Group
AOL Latino	
AT&T	Dieste
California Milk Processor Board	Grupo Gallegos
Emerson	
Energizer Holdings, Inc.	Grupo Gallegos
General Mills	Casanova Pendrill
Heineken USA, marketer and distributor of Tecate and Tecate Light	Adrenalina
Honda	ORCI
Illinois Bureau of Tourism	The San Jose Group
Largest Health Care Insurer in Florida	
Lexicon Marketing, LLC	
Liberty Tax Service	Español Marketing & Communications, Inc.
McDonald's	Alma DDB and d expósito & Partners
MyLatinoVoice.com/Mi Apogeo Inc.	
State Farm	Alma DDB
T-Mobile	Conill Advertising
Toyota Motor Sales	Conill Advertising
US Cellular	The San Jose Group
Volkswagen of America, Inc.	CreativeOndemanD
Walmart	Lopez Negrete Communications

The collaboration of Melanie Courtright and her team at DMS Insights has been fundamental in the presentation of new and original data in this book. They have been great people to work with.

We thank Amy Laurens, our editor, for her enthusiastic support of our vision for this edition, and Karthikeyan Murthy, our project manager, who has patiently worked through all the details of its production.

We want to also thank our many colleagues and friends in industry and in academia that have collaborated with us over the year and without whom this book would not be possible. To all these great people and to the amazing industry to which they belong: Thank you!

Introduction

The work on this book started in the 1970s when Felipe was a graduate student at Michigan State University. It is the product of much work that has taken place since then in the company of Betty Ann Korzenny. We both have been immersed in the US Hispanic community and market for a long time. We have seen the US Hispanic market evolve and have witnessed changes in assumptions and in the identity itself of the people that conform it.

Our first book on this subject was published in 2005. So many factors have changed in such a short period of time that a publication in 2011 exhibits substantive differences in content and approach. The similarities in the treatment of the topic are useful because they have shown to help readers become immersed in the consumer mindset of the Latino culture.

In 6 years we have witnessed major economic downturns and changes in the attitudes of many Americans toward Hispanics and immigrants. Many of these changes have been unfortunate but have contributed to the emergence of a new identity and to a new social cohesion among Latinos. It seems like many of the ups and downs of the economy and social trends have crystallized and resulted in a NEW LATINO CONSUMER IDENTITY. Hence the new subtitle of this book.

Further, the processes of acculturation and assimilation have become more complex on one hand and on the other they have become less important in how we look at Hispanic consumers in the US. Several chapters in this new treatment of the subject deal with these issues. As the Latino population of the US matures and becomes more native than immigrant, the way in which we study it has to change. One thing, however, remains the unifying factor that makes pursuing this rich market feasible and productive, and that is the Hispanic culture that is shared at the most intimate levels of being. Here is where the opportunity resides.

This book is organized as the content calls for priorities. First is an understanding of the market with its idiosyncrasies and richness, including issues of culture, language, and psycho-socio-cultural phenomena. Then the book proceeds to deal specifically with cultural insights that make a difference. These are the kernels of cultural connection that allow marketers to establish links with many Latinos simultaneously. These are precisely the elements that make marketing to Hispanics rewarding and profitable.

This book further explains how many of these insights can be obtained and the numerous issues that need to be considered in attempting to better understand the market via research. As a corollary, this volume talks about the Hispanic marketing industry and concludes with important trends of online Latino behavior.

We believe that by establishing the cultural foundations of the market and then exploring the more specific applications we enable the marketer to think about the issues and avoid following prescriptions. It is not likely that any prescriptions will serve the marketer well. There are no "dos" and "don'ts", it is the marketer who has to have the mental tools to judge when and how a strategy or tactic has the possibility of success. That is why specificity is at the end and not at the outset.

The reader should also keep in mind that while this book does analyze data and quotes statistics from the US Census and other sources, its main objective is not to describe the market. The main objective of this book is to serve as a conceptual framework for thoughtful marketing action based on a deep understanding of Latino culture. If the reader becomes a better cultural interpreter and is able to look at Hispanics in a more informed and empathic way then we will have achieved one of our most important goals. This is a book about enabling strategic thinking for marketing to Latinos.

We encourage our readers to continue the conversation with us. The blog at http://felipekorzenny.blogspot.com and our e-mail addresses of fkorzenny@gmail.com and bkorzenny@gmail.com can be used for this purpose. We look forward to an extended dialogue.

Chapter 1

CULTURAL MARKETING: A NEW UNDERSTANDING

From International to Intra-National Marketing

The role of culture in marketing has become salient over the recent past as brands have global strategies and local implementations.[1] Marketers have generally had an easier time thinking about international localization of their brands than localization for diverse ethnic groups within a country. The case of the US Hispanic market is perhaps prototypical in that it is by now the most visible case of intra-national localization in the world. Many countries around the world are now realizing that the diversity of their own immigration is creating more diversity than ever conceived before. Countries like England, Switzerland, Australia, New Zealand, and many others are being forced to address multiculturalism as a central dynamic. Marketers in many of these countries are starting to question whether they need to use different approaches to reach consumers beyond demographics and their cultural heritage. The case of the US Hispanic market may serve as an example of the complexities of intra-national localization.

Marketing to Hispanics in the US has become prototypical because of the sheer size of the market, over 50 million people in 2010, and also because of a unique cultural and linguistic heritage. This homogeneity in background has made Hispanic marketing possible, productive, and lucrative. Still, there are many marketers in the

1

US who cannot see how culture can work in their favor, or against, depending on their approach.

Why Is Culture Underestimated in Marketing?

Cultural understanding can enrich the activity of marketers in significant ways. Yet, few marketers have incorporated the concept of culture in their day-to-day thinking and planning. Culture is an idea, a construct, a phenomenon, that many people in marketing talk about; but grasping the elements of culture to apply in all aspects of marketing has remained largely elusive. One of the main drawbacks has been that the meaning of the concept of culture is complex. It is easy to tell this by listening to the way people use the term: culture can mean what educated people "have" when they talk about history, the opera, and museums. Or culture can mean foreign or radically different groups of people.

Most humans are socialized in relatively homogeneous environments and that makes culture more difficult to grasp. Many cultures around the world are quite homogeneous internally. The Japanese tend to come from a specific ethnic group, tend to prefer not to intermarry, and make it very difficult for anyone not born from Japanese parents to become a citizen of Japan. The Japanese, then, share a great amount of accumulated experience among themselves. They can sometimes speak without words because situations speak for themselves and generate common understandings.

Cultural homogeneity is perhaps best illustrated by the Japanese. Many other nations around the world also have cultures that are homogeneous to some extent, but with the high level of mobility in contemporary society, generally there are diverse cultural influences within most societies.

The US Anglo-Saxon Germanic protestant-dominant heritage has made for a relatively homogeneous centrally visible culture. It has a central set of beliefs, values, cognitions, behavior, and overall ways of living that are relatively consistent. The stamp of hardworking middle-class protestant America is everywhere in every town of the US. Americans are known the world over for the productivity of their workers, and for the numerous and innovative products they manufacture, enjoy, and export. Yes, there is variability within the culture; however, anyone around the world can identify the American character and the American way of doing things in almost every commercial communication, product, and official message.

In addition to productivity, Americans in the US tend to have a communication style that is identifiable and supported by a strong underlying value in the culture. In the US there is a preference for heroes, spouses, politicians, bosses, and religious leaders to be straightforward and plainspoken—to "tell it like it is." Some of the most respected and beloved cultural leaders have illustrated this norm: Clint Eastwood, John Wayne, Harrison Ford, Ronald Reagan, Abraham Lincoln, Harry Truman,

Walter Winchell, Elizabeth Cady Stanton, Gloria Steinem, and Walter Cronkite to name a few. This is an aspect of American culture that has been revered at home, and sometimes caused misunderstanding and resentment in communication across cultures, not only with other countries but with diverse groups within the US as well.

This relative homogeneity is an asset to American culture. It has created a craving for the glory of the ideas, style, and products of US society. However, it is so valuable that many US marketers, who are themselves generally part of the mainstream-homogeneous culture, have a very difficult time understanding that people from other cultures could be different. Even more surprising is the notion that a group of people within the US who have become a very large and important market could be of a substantively different culture. In the case of this book it is the US Hispanic market. While in this book we will largely concentrate on US Hispanic culture, the implications for marketers can be extrapolated to other cultural groups in the US, and also to other diverse societies around the world.

The goal of this book is to encourage marketers to think about how Latinos differ culturally from the rest of the consumer base in the US. It is about encouraging better communication between marketers and US Hispanics. This book is not about marketing to individuals but about marketing to a cultural group. That is the only sense in which a specialized approach, like this, makes sense. Marketers at the forefront of their discipline understand that increasingly marketing is about one-on-one relationships, not about mass messaging as in the past. Still, understanding the culture allows for targeting efforts more accurately than by starting from scratch with every individual consumer. For example, understanding how women think differently from men helps establish more productive consumer relationships with them. The same is true about Hispanics and other culturally distinct groups. The individual is the most important target; still, that individual belongs to groups of different sizes. One of the most important and largest groups people belong to is their culture. That is, the culture they were born in and shared by their loved ones.

The Nature of Culture

The heritage that humans carry with them through history is culture. A culture generally is understood to be the cluster of intangible and tangible aspects of life that groups of humans pass to each other from generation to generation. The reason why cultures have endured the passing of time is that they have provided survival value to founders of the cultures. For example, Jews and Muslims do not eat pork or seafood without scales because at a certain point in history, eating those organisms was very dangerous to human health. The custom endures to this day, even though the danger has greatly subsided. Elements of culture that had great survival value at some point in history continue to be important even after they lose their practical utility.[2] These elements of culture that may have lost their practical utility continue to have emotional value for a long time. So, even when someone is fully competent in the English language, the Spanish language, even if infrequently used, has strong emotional and cultural value. The following is an anonymous quote from a 24-year-old Hispanic man born in the US who responded to one of our surveys:

Spanish is my mother tongue and it is the tongue of my mother. Spanish is still the language which I feel most clearly speaks from my heart. It calls out from my childhood.

What I mean is that it encompasses my sense of identity by its sound and rhythm, and the fact that it is the language which I speak to my family with.

It speaks not of the identity which I project in public now, but rather of my personality and sense of self since birth. When I speak in Spanish, I feel I speak from my soul.

Here one can clearly observe that it is not the utilitarian aspect of the Spanish language that makes the use of the language important. It is the emotional value that makes the difference. Marketers should not be blinded by the notion that eventually everyone blends into a homogeneous culture. The dual identity this young man speaks about is powerful. Connecting with him in Spanish has value that goes much beyond pragmatism.

TANGIBLE CULTURE: OBJECTIVE CULTURE

The tangible or objective aspects of culture are the most commonly known. Those are the artifacts and designs for living upon which cultural groups depend for everyday life. They include foods, buildings, attire, music, preferred colors, statues, urbanization, toys, and all the other aspects that an archeologist would be able to classify as forming part of a particular culture. An example of objective culture in a typically mainstream American cultural scenario might be a fall football game at a Big Ten university. A game with a profusion of home team colors, hotdogs and popcorn, cheerleaders bouncing up and down and making human pyramids, a mascot figure with an oversized fake head and upper body, the crowds doing "the wave," and the team heroes slamming blocks into the opponents and passing the pigskin for a touchdown. A more day-to-day example is that of the coffee break at the office, when people stop at a particular time for a pause in their routines. Another example is hanging an American flag outside the home door or window on the fourth of July. And, of course, there is nothing like seeing a 1957 Thunderbird in mint condition.

Examples of Hispanic Objective Culture

Hispanics of Mexican background are known to eat "Mexican food." In the US, Mexican food typically is known to include items such as enchiladas, tacos,

Figure 1.1 Alebrije.

burritos, fajitas, chiles rellenos, and a few other items. Dishes not as well known in the US include sopes, chalupas, arracheras, sabanas, mole, pozole, menudo, papatzules, cochinita pibil, and so on. Although Mexicans eat many foods not necessarily associated with Mexican food, those just listed tend to be characterized as being part of the heritage of the peoples of Mexico. Clearly, we should assume that there are many complexities even within one country, where regional cuisine can be quite different from one part of the country to the other.

The typical "Spanish" look of many homes in Latin America—with stucco walls and Spanish tile roofs, painted white or in varied pastel colors—is clearly associated with Hispanic architecture. The internationally successful *alebrijes* (as seen in Figure 1.1) are fantasy figures that reflect the rich surrealistic imagination of Mexico and other Latin American countries.

The style of dress of the Mexican Tehuana, India Poblana, Andean Quechuas and Aymaras, and so on, and the overall taste for style and colors differentiate Hispanics. Common trends in typical dresses include very colorful designs. More modern versions tend to be sexier than US versions. The sense of femininity and masculinity found in Latin American dress styles tends to be markedly different from the US. Men tend to dress more formally and women tend to dress so as to emphasize sexual attributes. Clearly, dress varies most markedly with socioeconomic class and occupation.

These more evident objective aspects of culture symbolize the tip of the iceberg whose most substantive mass is *subjective* and below the surface. Objective culture is generally evident to our senses and relatively easy to grasp. The handshake is an objective aspect of culture. In some cultures we shake hands, in others we bow, and still in others we embrace each other. In the metaphor of the iceberg, the submerged and subjective aspects of culture are not evident but they strongly influence how we

Figure 1.2 Cultures are like icebergs.

perceive most aspects of life (see Figure 1.2). That is why in market research we like to go "beyond the surface," and many times that which lies behind the surface is a cultural tendency that we can consider a true insight.

INTANGIBLE CULTURE: SUBJECTIVE CULTURE

Those more subjective aspects of culture can be represented by the submerged part of the iceberg. Because most people share basic needs and values, many marketers tend to minimize cultural differences. They argue that overall, the same stimulus should have the same meaning for non-Hispanic consumers as for Hispanics because "we are all human after all."

The differences become obvious after conducting research and checking for the accuracy of the assumption of similarity. For example, a beverage marketing professional had the impression that the famous rum Captain Morgan could have great potential among Hispanics. Hispanic male consumers, however, reported in the research that they were not just unfamiliar with the brand—they felt the imagery associated with Captain Morgan, the pirate, represented domination and exploitation. Clearly, an image that appears cool to Anglos can be interpreted in a totally different way by people with a different historical experience.

Wendy, the famous secretary in older commercials for Snapple, was found to be humorous and representative of the outspoken New York stereotype to Anglos. For Hispanics, however, Wendy was meaningless and irrelevant. This was because the cultural experience of Hispanics does not include this overweight woman with her brash New York accent.

Red Dog, a beer that was popular among non-Hispanics some time ago, was advertised with ads portraying an actual male dog which was very assiduous in the pursuit of female dogs. The marketers in charge of that particular ad had a very difficult time believing that Hispanics could not relate to an ad for beer containing dogs as main characters. Unfortunately for the marketer, dogs generally do not enjoy the prestige and reputation with Hispanics as they do with Anglos. That is because the less-affluent masses of Latin America have more basic priorities than caring for and feeding dogs. Further, Hispanics typically do not identify with dogs the way that young Anglos do. Thus, that Red Dog ad was not effective in conveying the appeal of the beer, and the marketers had to go back to the drawing board. If the team in charge had had a better understanding of the inner workings of the culture they could have anticipated that their ad did not translate as desired in the Hispanic mindset.

Individualism is generally praised by non-Hispanic White Americans, and manifestations of this value are abundant in advertising for automobiles and many other products. The idea is to confirm for the consumer that differentiating oneself is important. An example is the image of a driver being self-sufficient driving by him/herself, and confidently speeding toward the horizon. The value for collectivism among Hispanics has been portrayed as a group onboard a family car with the tagline "all onboard." It is the subjectivity of the interpretation that makes one portrayal relevant to one group and not to another.

The differentiation between objective and subjective culture is parallel to the contrast between denotation and connotation. Denotation is generally a more public and agreed upon type of significance, while connotation is generally the more profound and often hidden meaning of an object or symbol. The connotation contains the experience of people with the object, thus it is more subjective. The denotation of chair is an object that one can use for sitting, the connotation can be the feeling of warmth associated with that type of chair during childhood. Subjective culture then is more connotative and a lot more dependent on the experience of the people forming a specific culture.[3] In a more relevant sense a flag from a Latin American country is expected to generally denote that specific country, but its connotation is the experience that people have had with the country and the flag itself. That is the set of beliefs, values, and attitudes associated with the country and its symbol.

There are many subjective aspects of culture that can make critical differences in the effectiveness of advertising. They include beliefs about the world, attitudes, values, ways of interpreting and perceiving the world, and other mind constructs shared by the culture. These aspects tend to be deeply rooted in the psyche of Hispanic consumers and closely interconnected with their emotions. A lack of attention to these cultural aspects can mean the difference between a powerful ad, and either an ineffectual, or worse, an aversive ad for the intended Hispanic audience.

Two case studies which illustrate the power of subjective culture in connecting with Latino consumers are The San Jose Group—American Family Insurance Case Study and the Conill—T-Mobile Case Study, both of which can be found at the end of this chapter. In the case of the former, The San Jose Group (SJG) discovered through their qualitative research that Hispanic consumers view their possessions as more than material necessities, but as fruits of their labors that protect their dreams, their families, and their world. Based on this understanding, SJG created the Batazo campaign in which the American Family Insurance agent is shown protecting the family from the results of a damaging baseball hit by their son. Thus, the collective entity of the family, its well-being and reputation, all important on a subjective level, are shown to be preserved by the help of their insurance company, American Family Insurance.

In the Conill—T-Mobile Case Study, T-Mobile and Conill, the Company's advertising agency, recognized that Latinos made up a large portion of consumers who were prevented from getting cellular phone contract plans with the best rates and services because of their credit ratings. Hispanics with this issue were generally more recent immigrants who spoke mostly Spanish. Through intercept interviews in Spanish, Conill learned that these Latinos experienced embarrassment when trying to acquire cellular phones when they were rejected because of their poor credit rating. What was particularly at issue for Hispanics was the challenge to their sense of pride—pride in their rich personal history and their character. Conill developed their PagoFlex campaign based on the idea that T-Mobile understood the unique circumstances of these Hispanic consumers. They appealed to their Latino target group's sense of pride as upstanding citizens and offered them the Flexpay program to address their credit needs.

Deeply Held Beliefs

Beliefs about the nature of the world are particularly relevant in differentiating cultures. For example, Hispanics are more likely than Anglos to believe that nature and the supernatural control their lives. This is very much in contrast with the Protestant belief that humans can control the world around them. Although the majority of Hispanics would endorse the notion that destiny controls or influences their lives, generally Anglos would state that they believe they can shape their future and that destiny does not hold sway.

The marketer, then, needs to understand that advocating "being in control" with a particular product is likely to take a substantive amount of reeducation and persuasion. Ideas like "you can plan for your retirement" are likely to be confronted with objections about the difficulty of sacrificing for an uncertain future. Why not enjoy today's life if the future is not in our hands? Saving is a sacrifice, and to sacrifice, one must hold the belief that one will reap the benefits of such sacrifice. Besides, tradition has influenced Hispanics to believe that their children are expected to take care of them in their old age. If the older folks took care of the kids for so many years, why could they not expect reciprocity?

Knowing these aspects of culture can prevent communication failure, save money, and assist marketers in concentrating on the issues that are more specific to a particular problem. There is no reason that marketers need to rediscover these issues over and over again. Acting on erroneous cultural assumptions is extraordinarily wasteful, and often can be avoided early in the conceptualization of advertising strategy. Understanding the cultural foundation ought to be a prerequisite for anyone who is given a budget to serve a group of culturally distinct consumers.

Here the marketer should realize that understanding beliefs based on culture takes more than hiring a member of the culture to explain the dynamics of these ways of thinking. Being a member of the culture does not make one a cultural expert. Understanding cultural beliefs requires primary and secondary research. Examples of conceptual questions are: What are the beliefs associated with leisure? What are beliefs Latinos hold regarding the role of motherhood? What are beliefs associated with going to bed at night? These contextual and conceptual questions can help understand how Hispanics will relate to certain travel experiences, purchasing products for the family, or consuming beverages at night.

Behavioral Orientations: Values and Attitudes

Beliefs are closely related to the values and attitudes consumers hold. If we believe that our children ought to support us in our old age, then we have a value for family cohesiveness, and a positive attitude toward family reciprocity. At the same time, we would devalue individualism or "each one is on his own in this world," and have a negative attitude toward products that replace family dependence. Table 1.1 provides examples of Hispanic beliefs that are associated with certain values and attitudes.

Attitudes are predispositions to act in certain ways, and these are highly cultural since "people's attitudes are developed and expressed as behavior in a context that

TABLE 1.1 Hispanic Beliefs, Values, and Attitudes

Beliefs	Values and Attitudes
What my friends buy is good for me	Collectivism, the group is more important than the individual
Stay with a brand you know rather than switching around	Loyalty, fear of the unknown, risk avoidance, a sense of reciprocity
Please children by buying them what they want	Being a good mother, giving kids what she did not have growing up, compensating for a past of poverty
Live for today because tomorrow is uncertain	My life is in God's hands, fatalism, little control over the environment
Having your own business is the best way to work	Value for independence and preserving family lifestyle and cohesiveness

is social."[4] Thus understanding cultural ways of behaving can help understand attitudes toward products, ideas, and so on.

Values are deeper internal guides that mediate between the person and the world and also largely emerge in the social context.[5] Values have to do with desirable ends and go beyond specific situations. They guide the evaluation and choice of behaviors, and have a hierarchy in people's minds.[6] Thus a value for collectivism is deeply rooted in a culture in which individuals depend on each other for survival and peaceful coexistence. People that hold more individualistic values are likely to come from cultures where interdependence is no longer as important as the reliance on institutions.

Meaning: Interpretation and Perception

The meaning we attribute to actions, objects, and symbols has to do with how we perceive and interpret these stimuli. Perception is said to be a combination of sensory input and the interpretation of that input.[7] Thus, if Latinos feel that dogs are lesser creatures, seeing a dog is interpreted based on that cultural baggage. The sensory input is the dog and the interpretation is that dogs are lowly beings. Perception, then, is the interpretation of the sensory input. The sensory input can be exactly the same for two or more people but each individual is likely to interpret it differently based on their past experience. Culture is based on a very large amount of common past experience. Culture shapes how we interpret a great variety of items in the physical world of objects and in the social world of people. Culture goes beyond individual experience to be the shared experience of large groups of people over time.

Clearly, for the purposes of this book, perception has a most central role. The way in which members of different cultures interpret the same stimuli is one of the most common problems in marketing. For example, having credit in the US is a very important asset and credit cards are seen as instruments of social mobility and well-being. But large numbers of Latin Americans have been educated to think that credit is shameful. Only those who cannot make it on their own have to rely on credit. Further, credit has many potentially negative consequences. Thus the same stimulus of a credit card can be interpreted in vastly different ways by members of different cultures. The Anglo-Saxon Germanic perspective on children is to help them grow up and become independent as soon as possible. Children for Hispanics, however, are perceived as a continuation of oneself and important to keep around for as long as possible. The same items of knowledge evoke different interpretations across cultures. That is why becoming adept in understanding different ways of seeing the world by different cultures is so important for marketers to succeed.

Culture Is like Water for Fish

Marketing to Latinos or any other culturally diverse group is complex because even members of those cultural groups have a difficult time articulating how they are different. Think of fish in the water, a part of their existence which is completely taken for granted. The water is a constant to the fish, like the air is for those of us who live outside the water. In the same way, culture is a constant for its members. It is hard for them to articulate how they are different because it is just the way people are. Only the trained individual can articulate the differences, which is why relying on someone to do cultural marketing just because he or she is Hispanic may be ill informed. In fact one does not need to be a member of a specific culture to do a great job marketing to that culture. What matters is to understand the culture, including the language, well, in combination with astute marketing savvy.

Our experiences color most aspects of life. A Hispanic born in the US is likely to overemphasize the importance of the market segment that he or she represents if he or she is not well trained in scientific and cultural thinking. Increasingly, academia and business have been recognizing the importance of the study of culture in business, and particularly in consumer research.[8] Some MBAs now pursue anthropological studies, and some anthropologists now pursue business training and opportunities.

The emergence of academic programs, like the Florida State University Center for Hispanic Marketing Communication and other programs and courses around the country, bring to the forefront the recognition of the study of marketing and culture. Other educational examples include the program of Our Lady of the Lakes University, which in collaboration with the local San Antonio Chapter of the American Marketing Association started offering a Bachelor of Business Administration with a concentration in Hispanic marketing in fall 2007. DePaul University offers a Multicultural Marketing concentration that students can include within their Marketing Major. Columbia College in Chicago offers a course in Hispanic Marketing.

Parallel efforts that are not directly focused on marketing but relevant to it include the Center for Spanish Language Media at North Texas University in Denton, founded in 2006; the Institute for Hispanic and International Communication at Texas Tech University in Lubbock; the Center for the Study of Latino Media & Markets at the School of Journalism and Mass Communication, Texas State University-San Marcos.

These programs and this book attempt to provide a perspective that delves into the intersection of marketing and culture. The purpose of these efforts is to make culture salient in as objective a manner as possible within the framework of marketing, so that an individual's personal experience is not what determines how the marketer views culturally based marketing. Basically what this type of training and education does is to make the "water" evident.

How Different Are Cultures Among Themselves?

How much of a difference makes a difference in cultural marketing? This is a very ambitious question, and is explored in this book. Initially, to establish basic knowledge, some overall principles will be discussed. Cultures do have commonalities and do overlap, and it is important to recognize this. Cultures are not unique enough such that members can unequivocally be classified as belonging to one culture or the other.

Part of the explanation for this has its roots in statistical thinking. There are several measures of central tendency. The mean or average is the addition of all scores in a distribution divided by the number of scores. The median is the value of the score precisely at the point below which and above which 50% of the cases fall. Finally, the mode is the most frequent score in a distribution. The mode, then, is the most intuitive measure of central tendency to characterize a culture. That is, it represents the most common set of individuals in a culture. Those people that are more like each other in a culture become the common denominator or the modal personality of the culture— they become the representatives of that culture. Others can be very different, and in many cases, more representative of another culture than of the culture in which they claim they are members.

This is possible because distributions, as cultures, overlap. The famous normal distribution or Gaussian curve is the graphical representation of most natural phenomena including things like weight, age, height, and so forth. Most natural phenomena distribute themselves normally with very few cases in the extremes and the majority of the cases toward the center, like in Figure 1.3. This can be the representation of one culture.

Figure 1.4 illustrates the overlap of cultures and shows how central tendencies differentiate cultures overall.

As these figures show, there will be a relatively small number of individuals that will share more cultural aspects with others of another culture and thus will not be typical of their own culture. Individuals that are closer to the center of the distribution

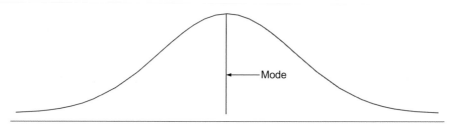

Figure 1.3 Gaussian curve of normal distribution.

Figure 1.4 Cultures as overlapping normal distributions.

are more typical and they are more similar to those who occupy the mode—it is all relative. It is important to point out that this degree of similarity with or difference from typical individuals in a culture is across many dimensions and not just one. That is because there are many cultural traits including beliefs, attitudes, values, behaviors, and preferences. Each of these constitute clusters of variables, thus cultural similarity is along many dimensions.

Marketers' Unease with Cultural Marketing

As the reader may have concluded the boundaries of cultures are not as easy to delineate as we may want in managing marketing across cultures. A lack of firm delineation creates "angst" in most of us because we would love to grasp the nature of cultural bounds. We tend to favor certainty. This problem is not that different from the uncertainty that marketers typically face in dealing with market segments, but they are more used to that uncertainty than with cultural ambiguity. And this is because most marketers have not been trained to see cultural traits, but rather demographics, lifestyles, and category and brand-related behaviors. The latter are correlated with cultural tendencies but they do not strongly overlap.

One skill that helps marketers deal with this anxiety, besides cultural knowledge, is the psychological trait known as *tolerance for ambiguity*.[9] The more a marketer is able to tolerate blurred lines and to abstract essential elements, the better he or she can be in marketing to a different cultural group. This tolerance leads to the patience needed to unpeel the various levels of cultural nuance, and creates a powerful tool for successful cross-cultural marketing.

If the marketer looks for quick closure on important decisions, he or she is likely to make mistakes when dealing with another culture. The marketer needs to spend time analyzing quantitative and qualitative data in order to form a set of initial impressions. Then he or she needs to formulate hypotheses as to what different approaches would work best with Hispanics as compared with non-Hispanics. Testing these hypotheses becomes a critical exercise that takes involvement and work with members of the culture.

This anxiety is not abnormal—all feel it when they enter the unfamiliar—but we need to learn to live with this anxiety when crossing cultural boundaries. It is a part of the world we live in, and as individuals as well as marketers, we have enormous opportunities to grow with what we can learn.

How to Ask Cultural Marketing Questions?

There are better and worse questions in cultural marketing. This book justifies the need for a cultural approach to Hispanic marketing as key to this capability.

- Instead of asking "How can we translate our ad so it reaches Hispanics?" the marketer should learn to ask "What will be the right motivational appeal to emotionally reach Hispanics?"

- Instead of asking "Can our general market campaign be effective with Hispanics?" the marketer should ask "Is there one positioning that can work with Hispanics and non-Hispanics, or would different positioning be more relevant and effective?"
- Instead of asking "Do we have to put a Hispanic in our ad to reach Hispanics?" the marketer ought to start asking "What are the elements of cultural identification that I need to have in my ad?"
- Instead of asking "Should we market to un-acculturated Hispanics?"[10] the marketer should start considering that acculturation is only one variable among many that need to be considered when marketing to Hispanics. Thus the question should be "What characterizes Hispanics who are most likely to enjoy my brand?"

These are just some examples of ways of asking that illustrate the benefits of a cultural approach to Hispanic marketing. Although overall marketing knowledge will always be important and relevant to everyday marketing practice, asking culturally appropriate questions can be more important.

Many marketers find themselves intimidated by the black box of Hispanic culture and desperately look for any answer that will alleviate their fear of failure. They are frequently under pressure to put together marketing strategies and ad campaigns, often with tight budgets. It is precisely a knowledge base about the culture, accompanied by a critical perspective that will prevent failures. No one has all the answers about how to market anything. However, that lack of certainty is even more pronounced when crossing cultural boundaries.

When marketing across cultures, the marketer should:

- Suspend judgment
- Learn to live with uncertainty
- Question any quick answers and remedies
- Be a first-hand analyst of cultural information
- Learn about what questions are more likely to lead to usable answers

A Combination of Disciplines: A Psycho-Socio-Cultural Approach

Marketing is about gaining favor. Marketing is the science of making others fall in love with your products, services, and ideas. Love is the fundamental center of marketing. Historically it was more of a persuasion endeavor but it has gradually become the art of establishing relationships with consumers. This evolution is due to the increased skepticism elicited by the manipulative image that the industry had created for itself. Another factor contributing to the evolution of marketing as a relationship-oriented discipline has been the increased use of research to inform marketing decisions. The more marketers know customers the more they identify with them and the more they attempt to meet their needs and expectations. Further, the advent of new interactive technologies is increasingly making it possible for consumers and marketers to literally interact virtually.

When marketing to consumers from other cultures, making them fall in love with our products, brands, and ideas becomes challenging. If establishing interpersonal human relationships is difficult with members of our own culture, establishing those relationships with members from other cultures is many times more difficult. And that is because we lack sufficient information to make sense of who they are and how to relate to them.

Predicting Behavior Is at the Core of Marketing

The amount of information needed to market across cultures is larger than when marketing within cultures. Charles Berger and Michael Burgoon, in their edited 1995 book, *Communication and Social Influence Processes*, explain how uncertainty reduction is part of relationship building.[11] Marketing and communication are effective when they make accurate predictions. When the marketer accurately predicts how consumers will receive a product they succeed at product design. When they accurately predict how consumers will react to their commercial message about a product they succeed in their communication.

To be effective, marketers need to behave like dedicated lovers or good friends. They need to gather information about the other person so that they achieve their objective of establishing a relationship. By accumulating evidence they can position themselves better to be liked and accepted. In the cross-cultural case, there is much more evidence that needs to be collected to achieve these ends.

There are different types of information that individuals may need to collect in order to reduce uncertainty[12]: psychological, societal, and cultural. These domains overlap, as can be seen in Figure 1.5.

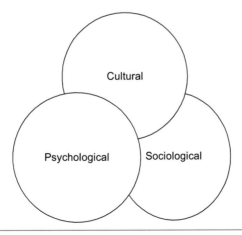

Figure 1.5 The overlap between psychological, sociological, and cultural domains.

The overlap suggests that there is a correlation between psychological, socio-logical, and cultural domains. As discussed earlier, the modal personality is what characterizes a culture, thus it is not surprising that these domains overlap and mutually influence each other. The overlap becomes more obvious when we think of human characteristics as ascending in order of abstraction as they go from psy-chological to sociological and to cultural. The unit of analysis in the psychological domain is the individual, the unit of analysis at the sociological level is the group, and at the cultural level the unit of analysis is the aggregate of social groups that have a common view of the world.

Within the same culture the amount of information that needs to be collected is relatively small because it is almost a constant for most members of the culture, who are socialized from childhood or for a large portion of their lives within it. In any culture there are different social classes, social structures, and norms, and most marketers and communicators will have to collect some sociological informa-tion, for marketing both within and across cultures. This type of sociological infor-mation is largely demographic, and also includes social norms regarding specific situations.

When working within one culture the psychological information will probably be the most challenging. Understanding the idiosyncratic aspects of individuals, as marketers know, can be demanding. This psychological information usually is referred to as *psychographics*. The marketer working within a one-culture situ-ation aggregates some sociological data and much psychological data in order to make accurate predictions. For example, the target for a particular product could be women heads-of-household, ages 28–40, with at least one child under 18 living at home, who enjoy arts and crafts and tend to be heavily home and family oriented. They tend to be "other oriented," and enjoy being there for others.

In the cross-cultural case, the arrangement of these dimensions changes. The marketer in this case is more likely to have some psychological and perhaps socio-logical information, but very little cultural information. Thus the ability to make predictions decreases dramatically. Not only does the marketer require an under-standing of demographics and psychographics, but also needs *culturegraphics*.

The problem with culturegraphics is that they are less accessible to the marketer via direct data collection. The marketer can always do a survey to find out who uses the product, how, when, for what reasons, and can even explore the appeal of a line extension. The marketer can ask lifestyle and psychological questions. But ask-ing questions about culture is difficult, as we discussed earlier, because people have a hard time talking about the intricacies of their own culture. The marketer with total initial ignorance about the culture of the audience of interest tends to ask poor questions that lead to relatively useless information. Since the culture of a group of people is an aggregate set of experiences, the marketer needs to have some sense of what these consumers are about given their heritage.

Continuing with the case of the marketer who is unfamiliar with another culture, he or she may want to sell his or her product to female heads-of-household, ages 21–45, preferably with children at home, who are dedicated homemakers, enjoy catering to their family, and are highly collectivistic Hispanic consumers. For example, if the products to be marketed are refrigerated dough products, the marketer is likely to make many mistakes. The first one is approaching Hispanic women without understanding that their culture has a bias toward perceived freshness. Further, many Hispanics have a negative bias toward frozen and refrigerated products because they believe that food that comes directly from nature is better for them and their family. In addition, most of these consumers have not seen, used, or purchased these types of products, so they have a vacuum of information regarding the category. Thus, if the marketer decides to pursue these consumers, he or she would need to study the target with questions informed by cultural knowledge. Then, he or she would need to approach the marketing problem with knowledge of the stamina needed to succeed in this market.

Many marketers not used to marketing to members of other cultures balk at the notion of having to educate a new customer base. That may be a warranted attitude but the situation is not much different than when their brand has had to educate non-Hispanics in the past. But when marketing to their own culture, marketers seem to have a false sense of confidence that allows them to take more risks. Cross-cultural knowledge and understanding has the purpose of reducing uncertainty and anxiety in the marketer. With less uncertainty and anxiety, the marketer, similar to the lover, is more likely to take risks in courting a new market.

Cultural Knowledge Improves Accuracy

Many predictions are likely to be in error in the cross-cultural case. Let us illustrate the need for cultural understanding with a relatively simple anecdote. A beer manufacturer needed to understand who among Hispanics were their customers, and what media they used. Knowledge about media preferences was to be used to inform a media plan. The questionnaire originally was formulated in English and omitted the genre of Ranchera music. The questionnaire was translated into Spanish using the term Country Music as Ranchera music. When the marketers viewed the percentages along the margins of the original English-language questionnaire, they wrongly concluded that Hispanics were listening to American Country Music in large amounts.

For those reading this example, the misunderstanding may not be obvious. Ranchera music is a typical type of Mexican and Latin American music very different from Country music, even though it is literally "country music." It is very different in its sound, language, lyrics, and artists. The confusion between Country and Ranchera could be obvious only to someone who has a basic understanding of the culture. And this example is just a very simple instance of the large complexity that marketers have to work with when navigating at the interface of two cultures.

Social Class Interacts with Culture

Many marketers ask if they can successfully bring ads from Caracas, Bogota, Buenos Aires, or Mexico City to the US and use them to communicate successfully with US Latinos? The question has much apparent merit. Just think, if one could use the same ads from Latin American countries in the US, this would constitute great savings. The assumption that these markets are equivalent may come from the following logic: Mexicans in the US make up over 67% of all US Hispanics. If Mexicans are the majority and they come from Mexico, then they come from the same culture as those in their home country, thus they should react similarly in Mexico and in the US.

What is missing from this logic is an understanding of the dynamics of social class across cultures. Imagine a gathering of physicians from India, Mexico, Denmark, the US, and Japan. Will they be able to communicate among themselves? Most likely they will be able to communicate very well. That is because most have Western education, and most likely they all have lived or spent time in the US. Further, they are affluent and cosmopolite. They value similar aspects of life. They likely aspire to be examples of Western success.

The lower middle classes and working classes of these countries are more likely to be much more different among themselves in their own country than the physicians. Further, the physicians are most likely to have more difficulties communicating with the lower middle and working classes of their own countries than with physicians from other countries. The social distance between the upper and lower classes of most countries is larger, in many cases, than the social distance of the upper classes of diverse countries among themselves.

Further, migration patterns are not independent from socioeconomic class. Migrants from Mexico and Central America to the US tend to be generally from the working class. These are people that come to the US to get a major break in their financial situations and lifestyle. Many of these migrants to the US were subsistence farmers and factory workers in their countries of origin. They did not have the economic capacity in their own countries to access packaged consumer goods to any large extent. Fundamentally these are people that become consumers when they come to the US.

Their more affluent counterparts in their countries of origin are not as likely to migrate to the US because they can enjoy a relatively comfortable life at home. The migration pressure is so much stronger on the poor. These less-affluent individuals have not had as much access to manufactured goods before coming to the US. The commercial messages designed in Mexico City target those who have the resources to purchase manufactured products. They do not target the poor and the disadvantaged.

Messages in Mexico can be high on image and low on information because they are communicating with a commercially experienced audience. Here in the US, however, the masses of consumers, particularly newer immigrants, need communications that are high on information and low on image. This is because many are relatively inexperienced as consumers and eager to learn the basics about products. This is one important reason why ads from Mexico City are not likely to be as effective here as they were there.

Consider that less than 30% of Mexico's households make US$10,000 or more per year. The 70% below this income level, in the bottom of the distribution, are the ones more likely to migrate to the US. They have very different perspectives on life, and that is what marketers need to work with. The marketer is not just dealing with a national culture but with a set of experiences heavily characterized by poverty. These are people who are willing to risk everything to improve the standard of life for themselves and their children. They generally do not come to the US with middle-class perspectives and experiences. The majority of migrants to the US from Mexico and different parts of Central America tend to have little formal education, and many times their first language is not Spanish but a language native to the continent such as Maya, Quiche, Zapoteca, and Nahuatl.

When coming to the US, these consumers go through a transformation in their ability to deal with the world economically. This transition, many times, is very difficult and frustrating. A large number of these migrants are young men who have left behind their parents, siblings, spouses, children, and everything that is dear to them. When they arrive in the US, their main need is to learn the ways of the new culture. Ads from the big cities advocating the use of products with ethereal images emanating from cosmopolite advertising agencies in Mexico City or Buenos Aires have little to do with the lives of these people.

The New Hispanic and the American Experience: Another Difference

Culture Shock

Another important reason why ads from Latin America are unlikely to work with US Hispanics is that after the process of immigration, culture shock, and adaptation to the new society, Hispanics in the US become different from those in their countries of origin. It would be unrealistic to expect that Latinos would remain unchanged after the enormous effort of immigration. Values, perspectives, tastes, preferences, beliefs, and attitudes do change as people confront a new culture. The literature on culture shock illustrates the painfulness and transforming experience of the immigrant. The culture shock experience induces the individual to reevaluate his/her original culture and to question the host culture. According to Paul Pedersen[13]

Culture shock is a meta reaction both to strangeness and to the awkward feelings provoked by strangeness in an escalation of anxiety. In that way, culture shock resembles any example of rapid social change.

Pedersen also conceptualizes the process of culture shock in four key steps: (a) the honeymoon stage when migrating individuals are ecstatic to have accomplished their move to another culture and have great expectations for the future; (b) the disintegration phase when reality starts to weigh on the individual and the person realizes that one's ways of behaving do not work in the new environment and he/she starts blaming him/herself for not doing well; (c) a reintegration state in which one comes to terms with the new reality and starts to become functional in the new setting but anger is externalized and blamed on others in the host society; and (d) the autonomy stage in which the person creates a new and more balanced perspective and is able to more objectively deal with the host culture and is able to enjoy life while becoming increasingly functional in the new setting.

Most Hispanics have either experienced culture shock or have seen their parents or grandparents experience it. They are not the same people that stayed in the country of origin, they are changed individuals with a new common experience of being different in a new cultural setting. Thus marketing messages that work in the metropolises of Latin America should not be expected to be effective in the US. The target audience has evolved and has become different.

The Risk-Taking Immigrant

Another element that makes the American experience different for Hispanics is that those who immigrate to the US are generally risk takers who are willing to go through much suffering in order to achieve their goals. This new Hispanic American is generally more entrepreneurial than counterparts that decided to stay behind. Those who immigrate put a strong value on success and are willing to sacrifice much in order to improve their lives.

A New Hispanic Identity

The combination of these personal characteristics and the process of culture shock result in a common set of experiences that make Latinos in the US different from those in Latin America. An emerging new Hispanic/Latino identity has been brewing and taking shape. A way of thinking, feeling, and behaving has been emerging and taking root. There is now a pride associated with being Latino[14] in the US. Thus, Hispanics/Latinos represent an emerging cultural force. We will discuss this further in the pages that follow. The emphasis here is that being Latin American is not the same as being Latino in the US.

THE CHALLENGE FACING THOSE WHO MARKET TO HISPANICS

Marketing, advertising, and communications geared to this cultural group need to take into consideration the information and lifestyle needs of these large numbers of diverse people. Marketers face interesting challenges since, of course, there is ample variability among Hispanics in the US. There are those who are relative newcomers to the US, and there are those who have been in this country for many generations. Even among those who have relatively recently moved to the US there are different levels of education, experience, and consumer sophistication. Further, once migrants become established, their perspective on the world changes. They become more sophisticated consumers than they were a few years before.

So, how is the marketer supposed to establish a target when it can be quite heterogeneous in experience? Clearly, a common denominator has to be established to make sense of the complexities of the US Hispanic population. Overall, the US Hispanic consumer will be relatively unlikely to relate to ads from metropolitan areas in Latin America, as we discussed in the previous section. Socioeconomic differences, culture shock stages, and the self-selection of those to migrate will generally complicate the decision on what strategies to use even when attempting to connect with relatively new immigrants. Coordinating a campaign that addresses the diversity of new immigrants and the diversity of those who have been established in the US is clearly more complicated. There are definitely cultural tendencies that make the US Hispanic market targetable. There is homogeneity within the heterogeneity of this important cultural group.[15]

ARE LATINOS A TARGETABLE MARKET?

It is true that the US Hispanic market is complex, and there are specific variables that make it quite desirable to marketers. It is true that some marketers unrealistically have attempted to reach the Hispanic market as a homogeneous whole and have failed. It is also true that many smart marketers have specifically targeted segments of the Hispanic market with much success.

Magnitude

Latino growth has exceeded the expectations of most observers and analysts. The Bureau of the Census estimates that there are now about 50,000,000 Hispanics in the US. That is five times the size of the official size of the market in 1980.

And, of course, those figures do not say everything about those who have entered and continue to live in the US without official documentation. For the 2000 and 2010 Censuses, the Bureau of the Census exerted an unprecedented effort in trying to appeal to undocumented immigrants to be counted. Officials of the Census deserve great credit for that effort. Nevertheless, it would be illogical to think that a majority of people who live in this country without documentation would complete official Census forms. Thus, it can be safely assumed that there are many more Hispanics in the US than the official figures suggest. The problem is that no one knows exactly how many.

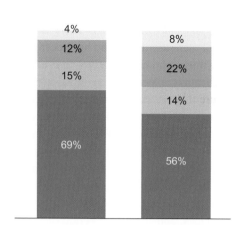

Figure 1.6 Distribution of children by race/ethnicity, 1990 and 2008. *Non-Hispanic; 2008 estimates for Whites, Blacks, and others are for those who identify with only one race. *Source: US Census Bureau and National Center for Health.*

The Office of Immigration Statistics of the Department of Homeland Security states that in 2002 alone, 1.1 million deportable aliens were located in the US; in 2008 the number was down to about 800,000 people.[16] Further, between 1981 and 2000 there were almost 27 million deportable aliens located, and over 90% of them were Mexican. Conservative estimates by the same office are that in 2008 there were 11.6 million undocumented individuals in the US, of which at least 8.7 million were from Latin America.[17]

If the 8.7 million minimum figure of undocumented persons living in the US in 2008 were close to accurate, the total population would have been well above 50 million of Hispanics in the US that year. No one really knows what the total number of US Hispanics is, but a very conservative estimate is that in 2009 there were at least 50 million of them. That makes the US Hispanic market the second largest group of Hispanic background in the world, after Mexico which in mid-2009 had 109 million people. At about the same time Spain had only an estimated 47 million inhabitants, placing it as the third largest Hispanic country in the world. All other Spanish-speaking countries in the world had smaller populations in 2009 according to the Population Reference Bureau.[18]

Now, a population of over 50 million Hispanics, affluent in comparison with the rest of Latin America, becomes a very desirable aggregate of consumers. Clearly, not all Hispanics are the same, and the entire Hispanic population is not necessarily the target of almost any one product or service. Still, the specific segments within it can be substantive and very lucrative. According to the Population Reference

Bureau there were in 2008 16 million Hispanic children in the US.[19] That is 22% of all people 18 years of age and younger in the US. This percentage is disproportionate since all Hispanics in the same year made up 15% of the population. That is an outstanding opportunity for marketers of diapers, formula, baby food, wipes, youth apparel, music, etc. Figure 1.6 from the Population Reference Bureau illustrates the trend.

The numbers within specific segments justify marketing efforts directed to Hispanics. Clearly, there are other aspects that need to be considered.

Buying Power

The Selig Center for Economic Growth placed the purchasing power of US Hispanics in 2008 at approximately 951 billion dollars. A conservative estimate according to the same source is that by 2013 the purchasing power of US Hispanics will be 1.4 trillion dollars.

For proportionality, consider that Mexico had the thirteenth largest GDP in the world in 2008 with 1.14 trillion dollars.[20] The spending power of the US Hispanic market in 2008 was close at 951 billion dollars, and larger than all but the fifteen largest economies in the world measured by GDP in US dollars.[21]

The spending power of US Hispanics compared with Latin Americans is outstandingly high. It is disproportionate and it is not surprising that despite hardships immigration to the US from those countries continues. Most Hispanic immigrants greatly improve their standards of living by moving here. As stated earlier, many of these Latin American immigrants become consumers of manufactured goods here in the US. That is something that many of them could not afford in their countries of origin. And here is also where they become a very important target for marketers, precisely because of their spending power.

A COMMON WAY OF LOOKING AT THE WORLD: MOTIVATIONS, PERCEPTIONS, AND BELIEFS

Latinos Are Not a Race

Race is not what makes Latinos different. Most US marketers do not yet understand that Hispanics are not a race. Hispanics can be of any race. They are African Blacks, they are Asian from almost all Asian countries, they are Caucasian, they are Native Americans,[22] they are mestizos,[23] mulatos, and many other races and origins.

Most of the Atlantic coast of Latin America contains people from African backgrounds that were brought to this continent as slaves. In contrast to the US, in many Latin American countries African Blacks melded with the rest of the population, which contains many shades of brown, black, yellow, and white. In Mexico, for example, individuals of African background are simply Mexican. In the US racial differentiation is still quite prevalent, but in Mexico and the rest of Latin America the differentiation between people tends to be made on the basis of socioeconomic class rather than race.

In most of Latin America there are people from China, Japan, and Korea in relatively large numbers. A well-known piece of evidence of their integration in the societies of Latin America is that an individual like Alberto Fujimori, of Japanese background, became President of Peru. Lebanese, Syrian, Jewish, Iranian, and many other Middle Eastern groups are found in most of Latin America. Well-known individuals of Arabic backgrounds include Shakira, a singer from Colombia, and Salma Hayek, an actor from Mexico. Caucasians have occupied prominent places in Latin America for a long time. A prominent case is past President Fox of Mexico. The O'Farrill family of Mexico has been prominent in the media industry of that country.

These examples make the point that being Hispanic is not a race but a common heritage and culture, that is a common Latin American experience. This common background is what makes Hispanics homogeneous in many interesting respects: beliefs, values, perceptions, and orientations derived from a common history that goes back to the shared roots of the colonization of most of Latin America by Spain. The largest country in Latin America is Brazil with approximately 191 million people in 2009. They are not considered Hispanic, but their Portuguese heritage shares many cultural similarities with Spain. But depending on your choice of labels they would be considered "Latinos."

A Rich Common Heritage

Spain contributed to the shared heritage of Latin America through its cultural influence of four centuries, thus influencing how Latin Americans look at the world and their place in it. The complexities of the Spanish cultural heritage and the process of colonization include the following.

- The Catholic religion has dramatically influenced the way of thinking and feeling of the continent. The notions of original sin and guilt permeate the culture and dramatically differentiate Hispanics from other cultural groups. Related to Catholicism is a value for hierarchical relationships, and also a stoic view of life as a suffering experience, *un valle de lágrimas.*[24] Popular TV shows like the *telenovelas* clearly reflect orientations that reflect the notions of sin, destiny, suffering, and anomie.
- Linguistic elements and values are derived from 800 years of Arab domination over Spain. Many aspects of Spanish-language vocabulary can be traced back to the Arabic language. Examples include *zapato, pantalón, camisa, bodega, algebra, café, cero, azúcar, aceite, adobe, ajedrez, mascara, mazapán, momia, talco, toronja, zanahoria,*[25] and many more. Among the many other Arabic influences on Hispanic culture is the notion of Ah-Riba. This concept refers to

the prohibition to collect interest on debt, and scholars debate whether different types of insurance are included in the prohibition of Riba as well.

Hispanic heritage combines these and many other aspects of Arabic culture that have important implications for marketing. If the concepts of "interest" and "insurance" are problematic in the heritage of the culture then it is reasonable to assume that selling on credit and selling insurance to Hispanics would be more difficult than selling the same to non-Hispanics. Then, as will be seen later in the book, the words and language that people use have important implications for the way in which people think.

- Shared values and ways of looking at the world, including:
  - Collectivism as opposed to individualism: The family and the group are more important than the individual. Appeals that include reference groups are more motivational than appeals to the individual. This orientation has implications for the purchases of large ticket items as well as the way in which consumers can be persuaded to appreciate the benefits of a product.
  - Polychronism as opposed to monochronism: The nonlinear use of time or doing multiple activities simultaneously as opposed to doing one thing at a time.[26] Customer service is expected to be polychronic. That is, a customer service representative should be able and willing to address different topics simultaneously and handle requests from different people at the same time. The consumer is likely to use products intended for one specific time during the day, on many occasions throughout the day instead. The idea of insisting that orange juice consumption be studied as a breakfast beverage exclusively may not make sense for Hispanic consumers.
  - Polymorphic opinion leadership as opposed to monomorphic opinion leadership: Opinion leadership on many topics and areas of expertise tends to be concentrated in a few individuals as opposed to having many specialized leaders on individual areas of knowledge.[27] The realtor becomes family counselor, economic advisor, and immigration expert, instead of just being seen as a specialist in his or her own area of expertise. Thus, training of agents in the real estate, insurance, and other industries requires knowledge of these expectations.
  - A sense of fatalism or lack of control over the environment: Human beings seen as subordinate to nature as opposed to being the masters of it.[28] For example, emphasizing product benefits having to do with the control of events and life may not be as convincing as using arguments that talk about family benefits and potential for spiritual growth.
  - Reverence for tradition, older relatives, and ancestors: In contrast to other cultures, Hispanics generally have positive feelings and respect for tradition, age, and life experience. Denigrating tradition in favor of the "new generation" may backfire in marketing communications because Hispanic youth

does not perceive itself to be divorced from its ancestry and history. An example of a mistake in this category of values is an ad for a cereal that showed a grandmother hoarding the cereal because it was so good that she did not want to share it with her family. This ad failed quite dramatically. Consumers stated that a Hispanic grandmother would never hide food from her children and grandchildren. They were offended because they felt the dignity of the grandmother had been insulted.

- Value for introspection and spirituality, and strong faith in the supernatural: The relevance of products and services to enhance human experience as opposed to sheer materialism can be very appealing to Hispanics. Being aware of the spirituality of the Hispanic market can make a strong difference in creative efforts. Lack of sensitivity about these issues can result in very negative consequences.

This discussion emphasizes how culture and its constituent values, beliefs, perceptions, and orientations make the overall Hispanic market targetable. Clearly, specific subgroups must be delineated for effective segmentation. Still, there is a significant core of homogeneity within the heterogeneity of the Hispanic market. Knowledge of this is a clear asset to marketers as they think through their approach to this culture.

The Spanish Language as a Unifying Force

One of the most unifying aspects of the US Hispanic market is the Spanish language, even though it has lately become less central than it had been just a few years ago. The Spanish language still acts as symbolic glue that keeps Hispanics relatively unified. An Argentinean and a Mexican, who are still fluent in Spanish, can communicate with each other with relatively little difficulty. Similarly, a Cuban and a Peruvian are likely to understand each other quite well.

There are regional dialectical language variations in Latin America. These variations tend to concentrate in specific areas. One of the areas of most variability is the nomenclature for food items. Still, most Spanish speakers in the world can communicate quite efficiently with each other. They may ask for clarification of a couple of terms when interacting but they get the overall gist of almost any message regardless of specific Hispanic origin.

There are some who argue that the Spanish spoken in each country is idiosyncratic. That is not more accurate than stating that the Spanish spoken in different regions within any Latin American country has its own idiosyncrasies. In a country like Mexico, the reader will find differences in the Spanish dialect spoken in the Atlantic coast as compared with the Pacific, Mexico City, the northern border states, and the states of the south like Yucatan and Quintana Roo. Still, Mexicans can communicate with each other relatively well. Their communication is as good as the communication between people from New York and those from Georgia, each with their dialectical differences.

The notion that there is a "Walter Cronkite" Spanish is somewhat misleading; there is not unaccented Spanish because there is no dialect that does not have some specific peculiarities. Since Mexico with Televisa has been the dominant source of TV exports to the rest of Latin America, it is true that formal Mexican-broadcast Spanish has become a sort of standard by default. Some people argue that Colombian Spanish is "pure" and most understandable. The disappointing news is that there is no such thing as pure Spanish. Nevertheless, people from Latin America and Spain do understand each other.

The commonality of the Spanish language has been one of the most salient common denominators that make the Hispanic market highly targetable. Things are evolving, nevertheless, and the Hispanic market is becoming increasingly more complicated in this respect. There are Hispanics who are more targetable in English and others who are targetable in Spanish but in English media. In many cases a culturally relevant message strategy is more important than the actual language.

Consider that about 28% of the Hispanic households in the US were classified as linguistically isolated in Spanish according to the 2007 American Community Survey of the US Census Bureau. These were households that did not contain at least one person 14 years of age and older who speaks English "very well." On the other hand according to the same dataset 22% of Hispanic households are exclusively English speaking. Thus almost 80% of Hispanic households use the Spanish language to some extent. The Spanish language, while becoming less indispensable for utilitarian communication, is still present in the vast majority of Hispanic households and its emotional value is likely to persist. The Spanish language is an important part of the culture and constitutes an axle around which the Hispanic culture revolves.

The above figures also suggest that reaching many Hispanic households in English is becoming increasingly possible. Thus, depending on specific target and touchpoint combinations a campaign may need to use both languages in different contexts.

A Spanish-Language Industry Has Facilitated Targeting

For more than 50 years[29] Spanish-language media has been central in reaching US Hispanics who depend on the Spanish language and/or enjoy programming in Spanish. The importance of Spanish-language media grew dramatically in the 1980s and 1990s along with fast growth of the immigrant Hispanic population. Those years were when there was an explosion of immigration to the US from Latin America of those who clearly depended on the Spanish language for basic communication. While today the touchpoints available to reach Hispanics have grown dramatically, Spanish-language media continue to be salient in media planning efforts directed to Hispanics.

TV networks like Univision, Telemundo, Telefutura; radio networks like Univision Radio, La Preciosa, Hispanic Communications Network; newspapers like La Opinion in Los Angeles and El Nuevo Herald in Miami; and magazines like People en Español, Vanidades, and Siempre Mujer are dedicated to reaching Spanish preferring Hispanics. In addition, the spectrum of Spanish-language media outlets has been dramatically expanded over the last few years with multiple cable offerings that include Vme, Galavision, GolTV, Discovery en Español, ESPN Deportes, and many others. The virtual interactive world of the Internet has music offerings like Batanga.com, and there are multiple websites and portals like Terra Networks, AOL Latino, Yahoo! En Español, Mundo sin Barreras, and Univision.com. Later in the book the reader will have the opportunity to explore these offerings more fully.

Readers may wish to take note that the SRDS Hispanic Media & Markets periodical is a very important media planning resource for buyers of Spanish-language media. This is a virtually complete resource regarding media outlets and events locally, regionally, and nationally.

Culture More Than Language Alone

Interestingly, as specialized Spanish-language channels continue to multiply, programming and advertising in Spanish on English-language media has also grown. Jack in the Box has advertised on English-language TV, Vegas has placed ads in Spanish on A&E, Fox Sports, Bravo, Logo, and the Showtime series "Weeds" includes Hispanic actors that sometimes speak in Spanish without English subtitles.

English-language alternatives are complicating the picture that was relatively simple in the past. There are many shows on English TV that do very well among Hispanics in the US. English-language shows with high ratings in 2009 according to Nielsen's National People Meter, Hispanic Sub Sample included: American Idol, Grey's Anatomy, NBA Playoffs on ABC, NBA Playoffs Conference Finals on ESPN, Dancing with the Stars, House, and Heroes.[30] These TV programs are offered here as an example, but clearly, there are multiple English-language outlets in print, radio, and the Internet that are popular among Hispanics as well. For an example in a different category consider that Google diverse sites alone got about 17.5 million unique US Hispanic visitors in the month of May 2009, according to comScore Media Metrix. Four million of those 17.5 million were unique visitors that preferred Spanish.[31]

While Spanish-language media has facilitated specific targeting in the past, the media landscape and the media behaviors of Hispanics have evolved rapidly. Now efforts to reach Hispanics may require more than Spanish-language media alone and a more aggressive exercise in planning for touchpoints that will reach Hispanic targets precisely.

The marketer should not confuse the fact that Hispanics can now be reached through a wide variety of media, with the erroneous conclusion that Hispanics cannot be targeted as a cultural group. Hispanics do represent a very targetable cultural group, but now the culture more than the language alone is likely to be the central consideration.

Geographic Concentration

Geographic concentration is one more of the elements that has made Hispanics a very identifiable and reachable market. California and Texas contain more than 50% of all US Hispanics. Other remarkable areas of great Hispanic concentration are the metropolitan areas such as New York, Miami, and Chicago.

This concentration makes it relatively expeditious to reach large numbers of Hispanic consumers. This tendency toward concentration traditionally has been associated with the pull of family and friends, and work opportunities. Friends and family attract others and that becomes a multiplying and effervescent growth effect.

It should be carefully noted, however, that in the past 15 years there has been an important geographic dispersion movement toward the center of the country and away from the coasts and the southern border. Markets like Minneapolis, Charlotte, Chapel Hill, Atlanta, Las Vegas, and Denver have experienced disproportionate Hispanic growth in comparison with the rest of the country. This trend is likely to continue, but heavy concentrations in specific areas are likely to persist.

Conclusions: A Cultural Perspective Makes the Difference

The intent of this first chapter is to orient you to the philosophy and intent that motivates this book. It is important to understand the statistics and parameters that describe the US Hispanic market. It is more important, however, to understand where Hispanics come from so that the marketer can establish strong links with them.

Clearly, the seasoned marketer will need to know the demographic and psychographic characteristics of the segment he or she wants to reach. As indicated earlier, overlaying culturegraphics makes the connection so much more meaningful when the marketer and the target are from different cultures.

When marketers can look at the Hispanic market from a culturegraphic perspective they add communication intimacy to their strategy. Knowing how members of the culture feel about life, the future, love, death, children, career, art, sex, and so on empowers the marketer to formulate the right questions. Further, the marketer is also in the position to interpret the results of research and tests in light of the culture. This helps make sense of the consumer's perspective. It is looking at consumers with a more holistic approach.

As an example, the marketer of an orange fruit drink may know that demographically his or her audience is composed of kids 5–14 and their mothers. The marketer may know that psychographically these families are active, engaged, and that the mothers are heavily involved in the food and drink choices of their children. If this marketer also understands that culturegraphically these mothers are likely to experience a guilt syndrome derived from their heritage they can add an important dimension to their marketing effort. The marketer can then position the product as a beverage that helps the mother manage guilt in some interesting ways. If the kids drink too much soda the mother may feel that she has not done enough for the nutrition of the children. If, however, she is able to substitute an orange fruit drink for sodas she reduces guilt feelings because she is doing something positive for her kids. This motivational force can be made sense of only with cultural sensitivity; that is, if the marketer understands at least some of the cultural aspects that are related to the marketing problem at hand.

The importance of the cultural perspective should not be lost by marketers as they learn that Hispanics are increasingly bilingual and are exposed to both Spanish- and English-language media. The temptation might be to assume that these bilingual as well as English-speaking Hispanics can be adequately communicated with in the same way as the non-Hispanic market. However, the unique cultural background of Hispanic consumers which differentiates them from non-Hispanics must be taken into account in order to gain their confidence and connection as consumers for the marketer's brand.

In making sense of the Hispanic market, Chapter 2 looks at critical dimensions of the market.

CASE STUDY: THE SAN JOSE GROUP–AMERICAN FAMILY INSURANCE

Company Name
American Family Insurance

Advertising Agency
The San Jose Group (SJG)

Campaign/Advertising Title
Protegiendo tus sueños, tu familia, tu mundo (Protecting your dreams, your family, your world)

Intended Hispanic Consumers
Partially acculturated Hispanic aged 25–54, who is comfortable in English but prefers Spanish, especially in terms of media consumption.

Background
To call insurance companies' Hispanic marketing efforts "competitive" would be an understatement. In 2008, the insurance category was the ninth highest spending

US Hispanic advertising category. Top spenders were national companies that allocated anywhere from \$46 million to \$75 million to Spanish-language network TV alone and enjoyed leadership positions (in sales and share) commensurate with their investments.

However, messaging had been focusing almost exclusively on price. American Family Insurance saw an opportunity to differentiate itself with a brand message that brought the "human element" back into the category. The brand, which has a 19-state footprint and a Hispanic media budget that is just 5% of the leading spending levels, also recognized that it would have to rely on unique messaging and marketing to truly outflank its competitors.

This goal, however, was offset with a challenge: American Family Insurance's low Hispanic market awareness levels. Despite the brand's 16-year history of targeting Hispanic consumers (mostly through direct translations), American Family Insurance still ranked outside of the coveted "Top 4" awareness positions with Hispanics. As its agency partner, The SJG knew it had to help move the needle on awareness and consideration in order to position the brand to (eventually) tackle the larger objective of new acquisitions.

Discovery Process/Research

SJG and American Family Insurance fielded exploratory focus groups and concept testing to better understand the Hispanic consumer's mindset with respect to insurance. Quantitative research was also conducted to set benchmarks for awareness and consideration—key metrics that would be used to assess the success of the campaign.

Equally as important to this research was American Family Insurance's approach toward fostering collaboration among its agency partners, a model that the company's marketing team has baptized as cultural convergence. While SJG was developing its brand strategy for the Hispanic segment, it also had the opportunity to work alongside of American Family's other agencies (general market, Asian-American, and African-American). All agencies were called in to help identify "global truths," or insights that are shared among all of American Family's core target consumers and develop its total market brand strategy. As a result, SJG's focus on the Hispanic segment not only leveraged Hispanic consumer insights, but also drew upon insights that addressed the larger market.

Cultural Insights

SJG knew American Family Insurance had the opportunity to move beyond the price discussion and rehumanize the insurance category. Through its research, SJG learned that Hispanic consumers viewed their possessions as more than just material necessities. Rather, the value of their cars and homes also included the countless hours of hard work and sacrifice required to purchase them. In short, insurance protected the Hispanic consumers' dreams, their opportunities, their family, and their world.

And while price definitely plays a role in the decision-making process, SJG learned that it is not the most important factor. SJG found that there is still a significant education gap on the topic of insurance for the Hispanic consumer, as compared to the general market. Therefore, the Hispanic consumer places a premium on his or her relationship with an insurance agent and more heavily relies on the agent for many things: from navigating the complexities of insurance, to finding the right coverage, to working through the claims process.

When SJG looked at these main factors, it found a strong intersection between the Hispanic consumers' passion points for family, their appreciation for the human side of

(Continued)

the insurance experience, and American Family Insurance's mission of being the most trusted and valued service-driven insurance company in the US. After all, "Family" is American Family's middle name and a critical part of its brand DNA.

Expression of Insights in the Campaign

The hero of the Hispanic campaign was a 30-second TV spot called "Batazo" (meaning "hit," as achieved in baseball). The commercial opens with a father pitching several baseballs to his young son, who is learning how to hit without much luck. When he finally connects with the pitch, the boy sends the baseball soaring—breaking a satellite dish, which then snaps loose, crashes through a window of the home and ultimately plummets down onto the hood of the family car in the driveway, where mom has just appeared. Rather than showing the family get visibly upset or worried, the next scene shows a repaired dish, a repaired window, a repaired car, and an American Family Insurance agent handing a baseball to the boy. The main message: American Family Insurance is there to help—and protect your dreams, your family, and your world.

To optimize the impact of "Batazo," SJG developed a 360° integrated marketing communications program, including in-language tools for agents (print, direct mail, and collateral) and educational collateral for the Hispanic consumer. The campaign also leveraged newspaper and out-of-home advertising to localize the message for agents and included interactive video and banners to reach the growing number of Hispanic consumers online.

But the integration did not stop here: enter the benefits of cultural convergence. Early on in production, SJG and American Family Insurance recognized that the insights driving "Batazo," namely, peace of mind, the concept of family and the role of the trusted

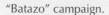
"Batazo" campaign.

advisor, were "global truths" that would likely resonate well with the total market. As such, the "Batazo" concept was tested against internal American Family employee audiences and with external general market consumer focus groups. The verdict: the spot was a total "hit." One test even presented the Spanish spot (to non-Spanish-speaking/non-Hispanic audiences) without the audio track. Even with total silence, every ethnic segment still "got the spot," with enthusiastic laughs, smiles, and nods in all the appropriate places.

As a result, SJG reverse-transculturated "Batazo" into a closely mirrored English-language execution called "Baseball." This version was then incorporated into American Family's general market rotation of commercials, creating a campaign that took "integration" to a new level, complete with a new brand asset that would: (1) connect with its general market audience; (2) create a seamless experience for its Hispanic consumers who view both English and Spanish-language TV; and (3) deliver significant savings in client/agency time and resources.

Effect of the Campaign

The "Batazo" campaign helped to increase American Family Insurance's unaided Hispanic market brand awareness from 11% to 18%, allowing the brand to leapfrog into the #4 awareness position among insurers targeting Hispanic consumers.

Furthermore, the campaign increased brand consideration from 38% to 50%. This means that half of the Hispanic market reported an openness to consider American Family Insurance for their insurance needs because of this campaign.

The results tracked for the "Baseball" were just as rewarding. The commercial came in second in ad recall versus other American Family Insurance English-language spots tested in the previous 10 months—even though "Baseball" had aired for only 1 month. (Most American Family spots run considerably longer.) Lastly, this kind of brand impact came complete with more than $1 million in creative and production cost savings, given SJG's ability to utilize practically all of "Batazo's" core elements to create the "Baseball" version.

Cultural relevance, cultural convergence, brand growth, cost savings—a formula that appears to be a "homerun" for SJG, American Family, and the industry as a whole.

CASE STUDY: CONILL–T-MOBILE

Company/Organization
T-Mobile

Advertising Agency
Conill Advertising

Campaign/Advertising Title
"PagoFlex"

Intended Hispanic Consumers
Credit-challenged Latinos, generally recent immigrants, who were unable to access the favorable rates and services available to subscribers of most major wireless providers'

(*Continued*)

contract plans. Given Conill's budget, they honed in on two key markets with the highest incidences of un-acculturated Hispanics of Mexican origin: Los Angeles and Dallas. Conill chose Los Angeles to be the primary launch market, as it was larger and offered greatest ROI (return on investment) potential. The Dallas launch would follow several weeks later.

Background
Major wireless carriers were restricting consumers with poor credit from subscribing to contract plans that offered their best rates and services. Latinos comprised a large percentage of this demographic, which had to settle for prepaid plans available from second-tier service providers. These services often have limited coverage and were more expensive on a per-call and per-minute basis.

Seeing an opportunity, T-Mobile designed Flexpay, a program for the credit challenged. People who signed up for Flexpay would receive any T-Mobile plan that postpay customers had, but they would pay at the beginning of each month instead of at the end.

Discovery Process/Research
A majority of the credit-challenged Latino consumers were recent immigrants that spoke little or no English. Traditional focus groups would not work as many were legally vulnerable and would avoid such a setting. They needed to be carefully approached in a nonthreatening environment. Conill went with interviewers and carried out live intercepts where their consumers would feel most at ease: local malls, mercados (markets), grocery stores, and bodegas (small shops). The agency asked how these Latinos acquired their mobile phones, and they told about the embarrassment of being rejected because of their credit rating.

The most revealing piece of data was that that these people are not inherently bad debtors; they just did not have a credit history in the US. They were invisible. This meant that they had to pay much more for their calling plan, minutes were more expensive and they often had to leave large deposits to cover the cost of their phone. They came to the US seeking a better life, but were now feeling humiliated and like second-class citizens.

Cultural Insights
Members of the target group had rich personal histories that made them proud. Regardless of anyone's opinion, they knew exactly who they were and that it was their character that mattered. They just did not understand why they were being treated as if they did not know how to manage their money, when in reality; the issue is that they have not had a chance to establish credit in this country. From this, Conill derived that:

Credit challenged Latinos dream of the day when they can stop feeling invisible. A day when an individual's history means more than a credit score.

The Agency decided they would build on this insight by treating them like the first-class citizens they deserved to be. They would know that T-Mobile understood their unique circumstances and supported them.

Expression of Insights in the Campaign
Conill developed a highly engaging and inclusive idea to appeal to the target's sense of pride as upstanding citizens: "You might not have credit, but you do have a history."

The creative executions featured this big idea along with visual elements that showed their progression from their home countries to the US. The message was simple: T-Mobile does not think credit should matter either. What matters is who you are as a person.

In order to reach these cash-driven consumers who lived on a day-to-day basis, the advertising message manifested itself consistently in their environment:

- Out-of-home was placed along their daily routes in public transportation with Bus Kings and bus shelters.
- Lunch trucks with signage, menu cards, and take-one brochures delivered the message to workers at various industrial sites.
- One-sheets in check cashing, Laundromats, money transfer, and bodega locations reinforced the message. Door hangers reached them at home and also gave opportunity for other decision makers and influencers in the family to weigh in.
- Radio was used when our Latinos were most receptive: with heavy-ups during lunch, weekends, and overnight shifts as well as payday roadblocks (when they would have more disposable cash).

Live engagement would also be an important part of this effort. Street teams were sent to T-Mobile-sponsored events like local soccer leagues and jaripeos and beach parties. They wore specially designed uniforms that said "We don't turn our back on you. We don't care about your credit, only your history." Keeping with this theme, custom premiums were given out making fun of traditional credit check applications and showing people how they could use them to have fun. For example, Latinos have a propensity to laugh at themselves even in the face of adversity. Using this, we created mock "Rejected" stamps and credit applications with instructions on how to turn them into paper airplanes.

Effect of the Campaign

From the month prior to campaign launch (September, 2007) to the month after campaign end (January, 2008), the number of monthly activations exceeded expectations, increasing by 40% in Los Angeles and 37% in Dallas. In addition, the base total number of Hispanics signing up for Flex more than tripled in both Los Angeles and Dallas during this same 4-month period. Given our success in the first year, the campaign was extended to run in Houston and Chicago in 2008.

"PagoFlex" campaign.

A ELLOS NO LES IMPORTÓ TU CRÉDITO. SÓLO TU HISTORIA.

A nosotros tampoco, por eso te presentamos PagoFlex.

Ahora recibe todo lo que esperabas.
- Un servicio de primera con una gran cobertura.
- Lo último en teléfonos.
- Elige tu plan.

T··Mobile·

End Notes

[1] See Ted C. Lewellen, *The Anthropology of Globalization: Cultural Anthropology Enters the 21st Century*. Westport, CT: Bergin & Garvey, 2002.

[2] Edward T. Hall, *Beyond Culture*. New York: Anchor Books/Doubleday, 1989.

[3] See for example, Stuart Hall, "Encoding/Decoding." In *Media and Cultural Studies: Keyworks*, Meenakshi G. Durham and Douglas Kellner (eds). Malden, MA: Blackwell, 2001, pp. 166–176.

[4] Michael A. Hogg and Deborah J. Terry, "Social contextual influences on attitude-behavior correspondence, attitude change, and persuasion." In *Attitudes, Behavior, and Social Context: The Role of Norms and Group Membership*, Deborah J. Terry and Michael A Hogg (eds). Mahawa, NJ: Lawrence Erlbaum Associates, 2000, p. 2.

[5] Edward S. Reed, Elliot Turiel, and Terrance Brown (eds), *Values and Knowledge*. Mahwah, NJ: Lawrence Erlbaum Associates, 1996, p. 1.

[6] Shalom H. Schwartz and Wolfgang Bilsky, "Toward a theory of universal content and structure of values: extensions and cross-cultural replications." *Journal of Personality and Social Psychology* 58(5), 1990, 878–891.

[7] Gordon W. Allport, *The Nature of Prejudice*. Reading, MA: Addison-Wesley Pub. Co., 1979, p. 166.

[8] See for example the innovative book by Patricia Sunderland and Rita Denny, *Doing Anthropology in Consumer Research*. Walnut Creek, CA: Left Coast Press, 2007.

[9] Paul Pedersen, *The Five Stages of Culture Shock: Critical Incidents Around the World*. Westport, CT: Greenwood Press, 1995, p. 9.

[10] The reader should consider that there cannot logically be un-acculturated Hispanics or any other type of person. Literally, being un-acculturated would mean that the person has no culture and that is very unlikely unless the person has grown up in the wild without human contact.

[11] Charles R. Berger and Michael Burgoon (eds), *Communication and Social Influence Processes*. East Lansing, MI: Michigan State University Press, 1998.

[12] According to the article by Michael Roloff entitled "Interpersonal influence: the view from between people." In *Communication and Social Influence Processes*, Charles R. Berger and Michael Burgoon (eds). East Lansing, MI: Michigan State University Press, 1998.

[13] Paul Pedersen, *The Five Stages of Culture Shock: Critical Incidents Around the World*. Westport, CT: Greenwood Press, 1995, p. 13.

[14] Not the label itself but a sense of commonality and identification with others who trace their roots in Latin America.

[15] I would like to emphasize that we use cultural group as opposed to segment because there are multiple segments that comprise US Hispanics. What makes them similar is their cultural heritage and cultural behaviors.

[16] Immigration Enforcement Actions: 2008. Washington, DC: Department of Homeland Security, Office of Immigration Statistics. http://www.dhs.gov/xlibrary/assets/statistics/publications/enforcement_ar_08.pdf

[17] Michael Hoefer, Nancy Rytina, and Bryan C. Baker, Estimates of the Unauthorized Immigrant Population Residing in the United States: January 2008. Department of Homeland Security, Office of Immigration Statistics. http://www.dhs.gov/xlibrary/assets/statistics/publications/ois_ill_pe_2008.pdf

[18] http://www.prb.org/Datafinder/Topic/Bar.aspx?sort=v&order=d&variable=109

[19] http://www.prb.org/Articles/2009/latinochildren.aspx

[20] http://www.imf.org/external/pubs/ft/weo/2008/02/weodata/index.aspx

[21] http://www.terry.uga.edu/selig/docs/executive_summary_2008.pdf

[22] Native Americans in this book are any of the peoples considered to be indigenous to the American continent. Many times they are incorrectly called Indians because Christopher Columbus thought he had arrived in India when he discovered the American continent.

[23] This is the resulting mix of Spaniards and Native Americans.

[24] Life is a valley of tears.

[25] Shoe, pants, shirt, warehouse, algebra, café, zero, sugar, oil, adobe, chess, mask, marzipan, mummy, powder, grapefruit, and carrot.

[26] Edward T. Hall, *Beyond Culture*. New York: Anchor Books/Doubleday, 1989.

[27] Everett M. Rogers, *Diffusion of Innovations*, 5th ed. New York: Free Press, 2003.

[28] Florence Kluckhohn (Rockwood) and Fred L. Strodtbeck, with the assistance of John M. Roberts (and others). *Variations in Value Orientations*. Westport, CT: Greenwood Press, 1975.

[29] See http://www.sintv.org/sintv/history.html.

[30] http://adage.com/images/random/datacenter/2009/hispfactpack09.pdf

[31] Ibid.

Chapter 2

THE COMPOSITION OF THE HISPANIC/ LATINO MARKET

It is somewhat unusual that a cultural group becomes a segment and a target market itself. With few exceptions of very specific foods or dress, cultural groups seldom constitute a target. Clearly, marketing Matzo to Jewish people is one of those exceptions. But marketing spaghetti to people of Italian heritage does not make much sense since the consumer base of pasta is much broader than Italians or descendents of Italians.

While it would be absurd to aggregate all Hispanics in one totally homogeneous group, the culture allows for targeting across multiple segments within the overall label categorization. In this chapter we look at what factors make Hispanics relatively homogeneous and distinct. A similar cultural background and common elements in history and life experience makes cultural targeting of Hispanics possible and desirable.

Historical and Cultural Origins of Hispanics

Sharing a common heritage is at the core of being Hispanic. It is not a racial or ancestral lineage but a cultural heritage. That cultural heritage is traced back to the rich history of the Iberian Peninsula, where Iberians, Celts, Phoenicians, Visigoths, Greeks, Carthaginians, Romans, and Arabs created the ethnic and cultural base of **39** the peninsula. The Romans left the indelible seal of Christianity. The Arabs made scientific, architectural, literary, and philosophical contributions. All of these peoples influenced the character and the language of the inhabitants of Iberia. These people eventually left deep marks in the cultures of Latin America by means of conquest, domination, religious conversion, social and sexual contact, intermarriage, and a synergistic mutual influence. Some of these past experiences are loathed and some are cherished, but the process of cultural blending makes what Hispanics are today.[1]

IBERIAN DIVERSITY AND COMMONALITY

The area of Iberia that is currently occupied by Portugal was known as Lusitania, and it was part of a larger conglomerate dominated by Visigoths. Portugal became a separate entity and later on a country, given the mountainous barriers that separate it from the rest of the peninsula. The war against the Arabs, who dominated the Iberian Peninsula for almost eight centuries, further consolidated the identity and relative independence of Portugal. That separation was emphasized as strife against the Arabs continued. Still, the modern countries of Spain and Portugal share much in common in terms of cultural heritage and history despite linguistic differences.

The fact that Portuguese is a different language does not detract from the great similarities that the Portuguese share with the rest of the peninsula. In fact, many regions of Spain have languages other than Spanish as their mother tongue even though Castilian or Spanish is the official language of Spain. Those in Galicia speak Galician, Asturians speak Asturian, Basques speak Basque, Catalonians speak Catalan, Valencians speak Valenciano, and those in the center of Spain have what is commonly known as Spanish as their mother tongue. Interestingly, Galician is very similar to Portuguese. The inhabitants of Iberia have in common a cultural heritage that goes beyond language. Given these historical roots Brazilians and Latin Americans share a large pool of cultural commonality.

THE LATINO MARKET: A HISPANIC HERITAGE

The Romans named the Iberian Peninsula Hispania, and from there the name of the modern nation of Spain derived. Hispanics in the US, therefore, are all those who are descendents from countries conquered or dominated by Spain. These are people who trace their origins to any of the following countries:

Argentina
Bolivia
Chile
Colombia
Costa Rica

Cuba
Dominican Republic
Ecuador
El Salvador
Guatemala
Honduras
Mexico
Nicaragua
Panama
Paraguay
Peru
Uruguay
Venezuela

Of course this includes the people of Puerto Rico and Spain as well. Brazil usually is not included because of its linguistic identity, that is, the Portuguese language. Nevertheless, Brazilians share a large amount of the background that characterizes Hispanic countries.

At this point you may be wondering why Hispanics are sometimes called Latinos, or conversely why Latinos are sometimes called Hispanics. The origin and complexity of labels will be addressed later in this book. For now, the terms Hispanic and Latino are used interchangeably. The Bureau of the Census decided to use the term Hispanic to denote all people who share the background of tracing their roots to a Spanish-speaking country. Those disagreeing with that label came up with "Latino," and that is perhaps more inclusive of anyone from Latin America. Some say it is perhaps too broad. What matters is the use of the labels for simplicity in aggregating people with shared cultural characteristics.

This book will argue and provide evidence that US Hispanics share among themselves a cultural background that makes them relatively homogeneous. In the area of implicit culture, the belief and value systems, thought patterns, and psychological and sociological makeup of the different Hispanic nationalities are surprisingly uniform. Even more evident, the material culture of Spanish-speaking countries exhibits great similarities in architecture, music, poetry, literature, and some aspects of food and dress.

LATIN AMERICAN IMMIGRATION: THE ECONOMIC PUSH AND THE EMOTIONAL PULL

The history of Latinization of the US is long and full of important benchmarks that have characterized the relationships between the US and the rest of Latin America and Spain. The relationship between the US and Mexico has been the closest and most influential.

A famous statement by the prominent Mexican writer Miguel Leon Portilla characterizes the relationship between Mexico and the US: "Poor Mexico, so far from God and so close to the United States." The relationship with Mexico and the rest of Latin America has been colored by power differences. Although there is a profound interest and admiration for some aspects of life in the US, there is also an underlying resentment of the influence the US wields in their countries and lives. The US has been a very important economic magnet that has attracted people from south of the border for many years. Still, the emotional pull of the culture and the social milieu has contributed to the maintenance of customs, ways of life, and ways of feeling and thinking.

Mexico's Proximity and a Moving Border

The arrival of Christopher Columbus in 1492 to the "New World" spread the influence of Spain in most of the North American continent, including the current territory of the US. Mexico held vast territories of the continent. However, it lost more than half of that territory to the US in 1848, including Texas, California, Arizona, New Mexico, Nevada, Utah, and Colorado. The treaty of Guadalupe Hidalgo[2] consummated this loss of territory, marked an end to hostilities between the two countries, and guaranteed the rights of the inhabitants of these states that were previously part of Mexico. The degree to which those rights have been honored by the US has been debated intensively over the years.

Still, those left behind when the border crossed them constituted the first massive contingent of Mexican nationals to live in US territory. Since then Mexico has been the largest exporter of Hispanics to the US. Because of dramatic changes in economic conditions in Mexico around 1980, the official growth of Hispanics in the US has been dramatic and surprising. The official number of US Hispanics in 1980 was approximately 10 million. By 1990 the figure was about 22 million, and by 2010 the official figure was over 50 million. Understandably, official figures are likely to be understated because of the influx of undocumented workers that cross the border between the US and Mexico every day.

Mexicans have made up almost 70% of all US Hispanics for many years. Mexico is likely to continue being the major contributor to the growth of the Hispanic market in the US for the foreseeable future. There are politicians and segments of the American public that condemn Mexican immigration as a danger to the economic stability of the US. Labor unions fear the impact of people that are willing to work for lower wages. Ideological pundits espouse the idea that immigrants who have different values will erode the protestant ethic that has characterized the US. The late Samuel Huntington was the most visible exponent of an ideology that sees a major threat to the US by cultures that are different from the Anglo-Saxon Germanic way of life.[3] The constituencies politicians serve divide them. Some support the legalization and recognition of immigration as part of the engine of US society. Others oppose it on the grounds of national integrity.

Despite this controversy, if all Mexicans left the US, a major crisis would ensue. A 2004 movie produced by Televisa[4] for the US market addresses this specific issue. The movie, "A Day without a Mexican," addresses the hypothetical situation in which all Mexicans disappear for one day with disastrous and distressing consequences. The immigration controversy contains paradoxes that are not being directly addressed. Both sides of the border depend on each other.

The US depends on Hispanics, particularly Mexicans, for the labor that different sectors of the economy demand: agriculture, building, landscaping and gardening, hospitality, janitorial, and many other trades and services. In addition, there are growing groups of professionals and entrepreneurs that energize the American economy. Mexico depends on US Hispanics for many reasons. The most important contributions US Hispanics make to Mexico are money remittances to relatives and friends. In 2008 the value of these remittances was estimated to be about 26 billion dollars by Banco de Mexico[5] but the recent recession in the US and an anti-immigration sentiment have contributed to a decline in remittances to Mexico and other countries. Figure 2.1 illustrates[6] this trend that appears to be bottoming out at the time of this writing.

In the case of Mexico remittances constitute the second largest source of income, second only to the oil industry. As these figures indicate many families in Mexico depend on the remittances from their relatives in the US. The economic crisis in the US has obviously negatively affected the well-being of a large percentage of Mexican households.

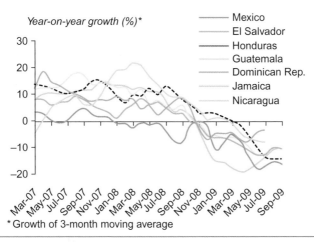

Figure 2.1 Changes in remittances from US to Mexico and other Latin American countries.
Source: Central banks of the respective countries.

The majority of Mexican immigrants to the US trace their origins to agriculture, manufacturing, and other relatively low earning occupations in Mexico. While in Mexico they generally had very limited funds available to purchase other than staples. Therefore, many of these immigrants learn to become full-fledged consumers once they are in the US. This background of inexperience in buying products and services for themselves and their families strongly characterizes patterns of purchase and consumption behaviors in the US. Since these consumers tend to be relatively new to the economy of the US they require information and education to incorporate themselves into the mainstream of US consumption.

A growing number of companies have recognized that the large Mexican population in the US provides an excellent target market for their products.

Tecate, marketed and distributed by Heineken, recognized the potential opportunity of increasing their brand presence with Mexican immigrants, those Spanish speakers who come to this country to work in the lower paying sectors of the economy as described earlier. They selected Adrenalina as their advertising agency to develop a campaign that would focus on the reality of Hispanic immigrant workers' lives in this country rather than just the product itself. Through focus groups and shadowing these men in their daily lives, Adrenalina developed a keen sense of the strength of character these Mexican immigrants embodied in the long hours of hard work involved in their everyday life. Adrenalina recognized a common theme between the character of the Tecate brand and these self-sacrificing Mexican laborers. Their campaign based on this concept, *Tecate. Con Carácter* (Tecate, With Character) is described at the end of this chapter in the case study: Adrenalina—Tecate.

Puerto Rico

Puerto Ricans are American citizens whose culture is more similar to Latin American countries than to the US. The Spanish American War of 1898, when the US took Puerto Rico, Cuba, and the Philippines from Spain,[7] marked the beginning of US control over the Island of Borinquen, as Puerto Rico is known. In 1917 the US granted US citizenship to Puerto Ricans, and in 1952, Puerto Rico was granted Commonwealth status. Important controversies over the political status of the island have marked the US–Puerto Rico relationship into the present. Since World War II, the influx of Puerto Ricans to the US has been important. At the time of this writing, there are almost as many people of Puerto Rican origin in the US mainland as there are in Puerto Rico. According to estimates by the Bureau of the Census, there are about 3.954[8] million residents in Puerto Rico and about 3.9 million people of Puerto Rican origin living in the US.[9] Puerto Ricans in the US constituted almost 9.5% of the US Hispanic population in 2004 according to the American Community Survey of the US Census Bureau.[10]

Puerto Ricans are unique in many ways. For one they can travel freely between their homeland and the US. They are also unique in that most Puerto Ricans have access to consumer products from the US. Thus, they are familiar with the US consumer culture. Ethnically, they represent a variety and an amalgamation of Spanish, Native Americans, and Africans. Since Puerto Ricans in the US have the ability to freely travel between the US and Puerto Rico, they tend to take new consumer trends to the island, and reciprocally they reinforce their cultural roots as they reunite with family and friends via food, customs, music, social relationships, and other important aspects of their native culture.

Cuba

The population of Cuba was a mixture of Spaniard, African Blacks, and Indians early in Cuba's history, scarcely 100 years after the discovery of the island.[11] The Indians were decimated by the treatment they received from the Spanish conquerors and by the diseases these intruders brought. It was a very similar case to what happened to Indians[12] in most of Latin America. Cuba declared its independence from Spain in 1868 but it was never consummated. It was not until 1898, when the US defeated the Spanish in the Spanish American war that the US occupied Cuba. Americans intermittently occupied and maneuvered the politics of Cuba up to the point when they influenced the system to place Fulgencio Batista as president.

During the era of American Prohibition (1919–1933), Cuba developed an important tourism industry, which included prostitution. Batista presided over Cuba and further contributed to the development of casinos, hotels, and bordellos for the enjoyment of Americans. Fidel Castro and his communist revolution obtained strong support from those that were left behind by the tourism prosperity. Fidel Castro became the communist leader of Cuba in 1959.

From 1960 to 1991 Cuba partnered with the Soviet Union and Soviets had a strong presence in the island for those 31 years. Many Cuban children were given Russian names, and the way of thinking of the population at large was strongly influenced by Soviet thinking.

A large number of elite and well-educated Cubans left the island in 1960. A vast majority of them came to the US as refugees from the Castro regime. This sophisticated group of immigrants has been part of the progress and "Latinization" of South Florida. Many other legal and illegal refugees from Cuba have arrived in South Florida since Castro took over. Of particular interest was the Mariel boatlift in 1980 that consisted of about 125,000 Cubans that were allowed to leave Cuba for the US. Castro played rough because among the emigrants he mixed undesirable individuals he released from prisons and insane asylums. The Cuban emigration to the US had consisted of elites at first and then of much less affluent individuals.

The consumer experience of the first immigration of Cubans was characterized by sophistication and affluence. Working-class people, who have known very little about consumer products, have characterized later migrations. Most of these individuals had been touched by Soviet ways of thinking. Because of this social class dichotomy, Cubans in the US do not represent a group of consumers with homogeneous experiences. Some are highly demanding and very knowledgeable about the US consumer culture. Others indicate they want more consumer education and information. According to the American Community Survey of the US Bureau of the Census in 2004,[13] the estimated population of individuals of Cuban origin in the US was over 1.4 million people or 3.6% of the US Hispanic population.

Central America

It is difficult to speak of Central America as if it were a unit even though the US Bureau of the Census and other organizations speak of it as such. It is a conglomeration of countries in a relatively small geographic area. These countries, however, are quite diverse. The Spanish-speaking countries of Central America are Guatemala, El Salvador, Honduras, Nicaragua, Costa Rica, and Panama. Belize is English speaking.

The population of Native American Indians in Guatemala is the largest of any country in Latin America. According to the US State Department over half of the people of Guatemala are direct descendants of Maya Indians.[14] El Salvador, Nicaragua, and Honduras are largely mestizo, like Mexico. Costa Rica is mostly European with a heritage of Spanish, German, and Italian among the most prevalent origins. Costa Rica also has a strong component of citizens of African origin. Panama has the largest population of African heritage among the countries of Central America.

Migration from Central America to the US has been characterized by economic and political need. Many migrants from Central America pass through Mexico. Mexico has had its own illegal immigration problems due to this influx. The largest population of Central Americans in the US is of Salvadorans with more than 1.2 million people, many of whom came as official or unofficial political refugees during the unrest of the 1980s. It is estimated that about half a million Salvadorans came to the US during that time. They have settled mostly in Los Angeles, San Francisco, Washington, DC, and South Florida. Guatemalans constitute the second largest contingent of Central Americans in the US, Nicaraguans are the third largest group. Other Central American country contingents in the US are relatively small. In the aggregate, all people of Central American background accounted for roughly 7.2% of US Hispanics.[15]

South America

If clumping all countries in Central America as a unit is arbitrary, it is even more arbitrary to do so with all of South America. Despite its large magnitude, according to the American Community Survey of the US Census Bureau, in 2004 only 5.5%[16] of US Hispanics traced their origin to South America. This is a small but influential contingent because of their important contributions to Hispanic culture in the US. South Americans are dispersed throughout the US but tend to concentrate in South Florida and in the areas surrounding and including New York State. Some groups have concentrated in specific areas that have become magnets for others from the same country in Latin America. For example, there is concentration of Peruvians in the Bay Area of San Francisco.

Brazil is not heavily represented in the US with about 350,000 people claiming Brazilian ancestry[17] and it is not considered to be a Hispanic country because of its Portuguese background. Still, Brazil was the largest Latin American country in 2008 with over 196 million people.[18] Further, depending on the preference for labels, the term "Latino" would include Brazilians.

The richness of Spanish-speaking South America is beyond the scope of this book. Immigrants from Argentina, Chile, Venezuela, Colombia, Ecuador, Peru, Bolivia, Uruguay, and Paraguay enrich Hispanic life in the US. Because of the distance from the US, immigrants from these countries tend to be somewhat more affluent and educated than those from countries that are closer to the US. More affluent individuals are much more likely to afford travel to the US. And due to education and exposure to international marketing efforts, these consumers tend to be somewhat more sophisticated about consumption than some of their less cosmopolite counterparts.

Dominicans

The Dominican Republic has been a strong contributor of immigrants to the US in recent years. The New York/New Jersey area used to be predominantly Puerto Rican, but Dominicans have increasingly challenged that prevalence. In 2004 Dominicans constituted 2.6% of all US Hispanics.[19] Dominicans share with Puerto Ricans a heritage of Spanish and African backgrounds and many common cultural patterns. Still, Dominicans have the unique idiosyncrasies of their history. Dominicans share their island with Haiti and were dominated by them for a period of time. Dominicans are not US citizens as Puerto Ricans are and immigration is a struggle they share with the majority of other Hispanic immigrants to the US. Dominicans do have a history of exposure to American and global brands, and many come to the US with some knowledge of those brands.

Implications of Homogeneity and Diversity

As indicated in the preceding overview, there are specific tendencies that make the Hispanic market targetable. You also should have become cognizant of the variability that exists in the aggregate of people covered under the label Hispanic.

The homogeneity of the market is due to historical and cultural roots. Hispanics do share a rich history marked by the Spanish conquest of the continent and a struggle for independence. Political turmoil and instability have been omnipresent in many Spanish-speaking countries. That background colors the experience of Latin Americans and their relative distrust in institutions including governments, banks, hospitals, and phone companies.

Religion, language, and many other aspects of Hispanic culture serve as the glue that ties Hispanics together. These represent the commonalities that make Hispanics an ideal marketing target. It is difficult to find many other niche markets in the US that share so much in common.

Clearly, there are dominant tendencies in the market. Mexicans are the vast majority of all Hispanics. They represent the single most relatively homogeneous group within the overall Hispanic market. Many product categories benefit from attracting the interest of Mexicans first. That is one way of acquiring momentum. Still, the marketer needs to remember that even consumers of Mexican origin are not all similar to each other.

There are some whose ancestors were in the current US territory before modern Mexico existed. There are affluent Mexicans that live in Coronado, La Jolla, Houston, and Miami. They do not have a lot in common with the large number of Mexicans that come from more humble backgrounds to start a new and better life from scratch in the US. There are those who are relatively new immigrants that depend on the Spanish language for their understanding of basic aspects of shopping and using products; those who can handle English and Spanish almost interchangeably; and those who are English dominant.

Still, a common Mexican origin provides a very strong point of origin and cultural commonality.

Testing the Assumption of Homogeneity

If a marketer decides to have a national campaign he or she may want to test the assumption that Hispanics are quite homogeneous. In practice it has been found that an acid test is to "talk" with Mexican consumers in Los Angeles and also with consumers of Cuban background in Miami. If the brand, product, commercial, stimulus, and so on produces similar reactions with these two diverse segments, then the marketer can confidently conclude that the object of the research will probably behave similarly across most groups of Hispanics. That is because if the most different segments react similarly one can be on safe grounds assuming that the underlying product or message touches the same cultural chord.

Mexicans and Cubans are as different as Hispanics can be among themselves given their history. If an idea is interpreted and appreciated equally in both markets, the marketer can trust it is a general Hispanic concept. If Cubans and Mexicans disagree, then there is a need for investigating further. The marketer then would need to learn how several of the other subgroups think and feel about the idea under consideration.

Food products and other iconic items that are very specific to a country may not be for widespread dissemination. For example, there is a frying condiment that Cubans, Puerto Ricans, and Dominicans use, called *sofrito*. It would be unlikely that Mexicans would relate to it without some education and persuasion effort.

There was the case of an advertising campaign that used the Aztec calendar as part of the symbolism of the ad. East Coast Hispanics generally rejected the message as being "too Mexican." Clearly, Cubans or Puerto Ricans have very little to do with the Aztecs. This basic cultural sensitivity can be part of the challenge in attempting to reach across Hispanic groups. Also, non-Mexicans tend to resent being lumped with Mexicans because they feel that their unique identity is being neglected. Thus, the marketer needs to make sure that she or he does not make assumptions about homogeneity without checking first.

Nevertheless, there are striking similarities in very complicated cultural beliefs. Through qualitative research the authors have found that beliefs about upset stomach are widely shared among Hispanics. For example, there is the belief that if a food is spoiled or does not agree with the person eating it, it gets stuck in the gut. This is called *empacho*. Consumers from Mexico, Cuba, Puerto Rico, Venezuela, and other countries know about this phenomenon and even agree about the basic treatment for it. Some rub and stretch the skin of the back of the patient and others rub the legs. Still the basic premise is that by stretching and rubbing they release the food that is stuck in the stomach. There are many cultural beliefs like this, which transcend country of origin. The marketer that connects with the consumer at the level of cultural beliefs is likely to reap windfall profits.

GEOGRAPHIC TRENDS

The geography distribution of Hispanics in the US is a function of physical nearness to different parts of Mexico and the Caribbean. The map in Figure 2.2 shows the distribution of Hispanics in 2004.[20]

This distribution and the relative densities have been fairly constant but the actual numbers have increased dramatically. This dramatic increase from 10 million Hispanics in 1980 to over 50 million in 2010, documented by the US Census, has awakened the interest of marketers, politicians, educators, and most other sectors of US society.

The geographic concentration of Hispanics in the west, the southwest, and select areas of the east of the US has traditionally singled out the Hispanic population as a highly targetable aggregate of consumers. Typically, media purchases have tended to be focused on those areas of high Hispanic density.

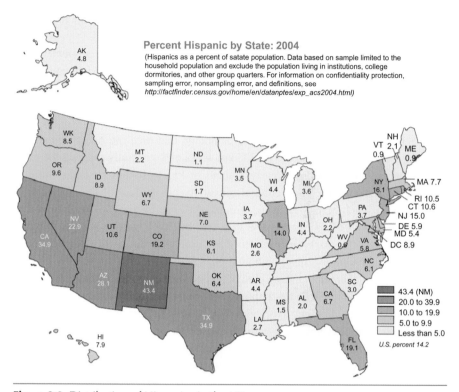

Figure 2.2 Distribution of Hispanics in the US.
Source: US Census Bureau, 2004 American Community Survey, Detailed Tables,
B03001.

But with the growth of the Hispanic population there has also been dispersion as well. Internally, in the US, Hispanics have been exploring new geographies—areas that had not had a strong presence of Hispanics in the recent past. Some of these areas have experienced surprising changes in their Hispanic population. An interesting example of this migration trend, according to self-reports, is that from 1995 to 2000, 160,374 Hispanics reported moving to the state of California, and 505,947 indicated they moved out.[21] This means that more than three times as many Hispanics already residing in the US moved out of California as moved in.

Among the states that have gained Hispanic population is Colorado, which experienced in-migration of 503,409 and out-migration of 388,356. Other states that experienced pronounced gains in Hispanic population include Florida, Georgia, Indiana, Iowa, Kansas, Kentucky, Michigan, Minnesota, Nebraska, Nevada, North Carolina, South Carolina, and Tennessee.

Some of these states have made dramatic gains. For example, from 1995 to 2000, Nevada gained 87,917 and lost only 26,267. North Carolina gained 71,268

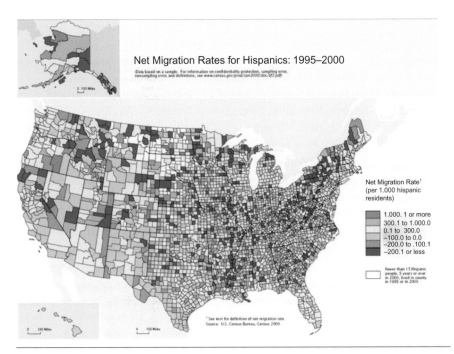

Figure 2.3 Net migration rates for Hispanics by county: 1995–2000.
Source: US Census Bureau, Census 2000.

and lost only 30,197. Regardless of cold winter weather, Minnesota gained 26,137 Hispanics and lost only 11,405. Texas, however, a highly Hispanic state, like California, did not change much according to Census-measured internal migration. New York, on the other hand, gained 67,273 and lost 225,429 Hispanics. These dramatic migratory changes are just for those who moved within the US, not for those that came from abroad during those years. Still, what this internal migration dynamic indicates is that there appears to be an increasing trend toward dispersion of the US Hispanic population.

The map[22] in Figure 2.3 from the US census shows the US counties that experienced gains in Hispanic population from 1995 to 2000. Comparing the map in Figure 2.2 with this one shows that the areas of more pronounced growth are those that were not typically where Hispanics have lived until recently.

2008 Data Confirms Dispersion

Analyzing the American Community Survey of the US Census Bureau for 2008 reveals that there are key states that experienced net in-migration of Hispanics from other states in the prior year. This was the most up-to-date information of what states Hispanics are moving to, and what states Hispanics are leaving behind at the time of the writing of this book. At the top of the gaining list are Texas, Colorado, Utah, North Carolina, Washington State, New Mexico, Oklahoma, South Carolina, Mississippi, Pennsylvania, Louisiana, Virginia, Arizona, Missouri, Indiana, Iowa, Massachusetts, Kentucky, Maine, and Maryland, in that order.

The states with the largest out-migration of Hispanics, in order of loss to other states, were: California, New York, Florida, New Jersey, Alaska, Illinois, Michigan, Rhode Island, Connecticut, District of Columbia, Nevada, Georgia, Ohio, Delaware, Nebraska, and New Hampshire.

These trends appear to confirm the continued dispersion of Hispanics throughout the US to places that were not typically attractive to Hispanics in the recent past, thus continuing the trend documented above. Growth in states like Utah, North Carolina, Oklahoma, South Carolina, Mississippi, and Louisiana seems to uphold the trend that Hispanics are moving to states that offer job opportunities and a reasonable cost of living, even if these states were not atop of the Hispanic agenda in the past.

Those states losing Hispanics to other states are those which have experienced severe economic difficulties in the 2007–2009 recession and/or are also expensive to live in, for example: California, New York, Florida, New Jersey, Nevada, Alaska, Illinois, and Michigan.

This analysis, however, does not include in-migration from other countries. Thus, one cannot conclude from these data that there is no actual Hispanic growth in some states that are losing Hispanics to other states. The problem in conducting this type of analysis is that the American Community Survey does measure people coming in from other countries but not people leaving the country. That is because the US Census Bureau only interviews or administers questionnaires to people in the US.

Table 2.1 contains the state in-migration and out-migration data for 2008 and the net gain or loss.

In conclusion:

1. Hispanics move toward out-migration from states with a high cost of living, like California and New York, and/or experiencing economic downturns.
2. Migration toward states goes along with increasing labor needs. Those states that have experienced population growth have become magnets in the construction, agricultural, landscaping, janitorial, and other service industries. A noteworthy example is Louisiana after the devastation of New Orleans by Hurricane Katrina, where Hispanics have played a key role in the reconstruction.
3. The pressure of increasing Hispanic population growth in the US has also made migration out of centers of high concentration attractive. Areas of lesser Hispanic density present less competition and more opportunities.
4. Increasing pressure from anti-immigrant groups has also contributed to a migration out of states and localities where immigrants feel discriminated against, harassed, threatened, or simply disliked.

TABLE 2.1 State In-Migration and Out-Migration

State	ACS 2008		
	Moved In from Other State	Moved Out to Other State	Net
Texas	119,035	85,153	33,882
Colorado	29,337	19,505	9,832
Utah	14,177	6,432	7,745
North Carolina	30,397	23,061	7,336
Washington	20,878	14,368	6,510
New Mexico	24,256	17,912	6,344
Oklahoma	14,653	8,380	6,273
South Carolina	12,340	7,282	5,058
Mississippi	5,827	1,125	4,702
Pennsylvania	21,896	17,950	3,946
Louisiana	10,070	6,223	3,847
Virginia	21,687	17,885	3,802
Arizona	39,723	35,930	3,793
Missouri	10,553	6,924	3,629
Indiana	11,899	8,411	3,488
Iowa	7,900	4,575	3,325
Massachusetts	14,725	11,929	2,796
Kentucky	6,340	3,577	2,763
Maine	1,994	434	1,560
Maryland	14,296	12,783	1,513
Hawaii	7,629	6,679	950
Minnesota	6,539	5,713	826
Arkansas	6,664	5,943	721
Alabama	6,537	5,822	715
Kansas	11,334	10,762	572
Montana	1,561	1,145	416
South Dakota	1,430	1,022	408
Wisconsin	6,605	6,381	224
Oregon	11,705	11,608	97

(Continued)

TABLE 2.1 (*Continued*)

State	ACS 2008		
	Moved In from Other State	Moved Out to Other State	Net
Idaho	4,563	4,580	−17
Wyoming	2,520	2,632	−112
West Virginia	1,058	1,194	−136
Vermont	739	944	−205
North Dakota	1,008	1,343	−335
Tennessee	9,349	10,034	−685
New Hampshire	1,940	3,039	−1,099
Nebraska	5,520	6,675	−1,155
Delaware	1,296	2,508	−1,212
Ohio	9,272	10,508	−1,236
Georgia	21,714	23,058	−1,344
Nevada	22,138	23,998	−1,860
DC	2,926	4,828	−1,902
Connecticut	10,639	12,659	−2,020
Rhode Island	1,900	4,057	−2,157
Michigan	8,891	11,531	−2,640
Illinois	25,005	30,144	−5,139
Alaska	3,919	13,343	−9,424
New Jersey	22,584	32,615	−10,031
Florida	61,124	74,499	−13,375
New York	37,647	63,629	−25,982
California	76,082	121,089	−45,007

Dispersion also Takes Place in Metropolitan Areas

Further, dispersion has not taken place just across states but also within metropolitan areas. The Pew Hispanic Center in analyzing Census 2000 data reports that 57% of Hispanics lived in Census tracts in which they constitute 7% of the population in the average. Only 43% lived in areas where Latinos were majority, and they constituted a mix of immigrants and US-born Hispanics.[23] This tendency toward national and local dispersion creates interesting challenges for marketers.

TABLE 2.2 Average Percentage of Friends

Group	NHW	AA	A	H
Non-Hispanic White	71.75	6.78	3.63	6.05
African American	19.25	58.43	2.91	6.71
Asian	32.17	6.93	39.71	7.78
Hispanic English	30.81	10.50	6.61	35.95
Hispanic Spanish	11.96	4.63	1.90	59.97

Implications of Geographic Dispersion

The trend toward geographic dispersion of Hispanics is likely to have strong implications for Hispanic marketing in the future.

1. The dispersion of Hispanics among the non-Hispanic population will likely accelerate their influence on the culture of the US furthering the Hispanization of the US. More non-Hispanics likely will have friends, acquaintances, workers, neighbors, mates, relatives, and professional relationships with Hispanics. These associations and relationships will further enhance the mutual influence of both Hispanic and US cultures.

2. The acquisition of English as a second language is becoming a more pressing necessity in these new environments. It cannot be denied that as it happens in most human contexts, Hispanics will seek the companionship of other Hispanics. Still, the opportunity for non-Hispanic contact will increase. Becoming bilingual and bicultural will be a more pressing priority for Hispanics. Table 2.2 from the Florida State Center for Hispanic Marketing Communication, DMS Research, and Captura Group 2009 Multicultural Marketing Study shows a tendency of Hispanics to diversify their friendships.

   The question asked from this sample of almost 2500 respondents nationwide online was "about what percentage of your friends is…?" As can be seen above non-Hispanic Whites have the most homogeneous friendship network in which almost 72% of their friends are like themselves. Hispanics who answered the questionnaire in English had the most diverse friendship network with only 36% of their friends being Hispanic. Hispanics who answered the questionnaire in Spanish were more likely to associate with other Hispanics, but their friendship network was still more heterogeneous than that of non-Hispanic Whites. This highlights the mutual influence between Hispanics and the rest of the population. Thus, marketing efforts need to start gearing up for a social dynamic that is effervescing in the Hispanic marketplace.

3. Having Hispanics less concentrated will force marketers to reach them via media that is not considered to be typically Hispanic. Campaigns on TV, radio,

print, and other outlets will have to be customized to reach Hispanics in Spanish and/or English in places where Spanish-language media is not as accessible as it is in major metropolitan areas.

4. Hispanics likely will preserve their cultural roots due to their cultural pride and the desirability of their bilingual and bicultural skills in many areas. The likely trend is that instead of assimilation, bicultural acculturation is more likely to take place. Still, at the time of this writing there is a strong anti-immigrant sentiment among some segments in the US. This carries the potential of casting a shadow on Hispanic self-esteem. However, as economic conditions improve and xenophobia subsides, the contributions of Hispanics and their importance to marketing are likely to continue to flourish.

Marketers will benefit from revising the assumptions they have made thus far about marketing to US Latinos. They will have to consider the complex dynamics of geographic dispersion and its associated social consequences. Understanding the core of Hispanic culture, however, will continue to be profitable because of the pull of culture on Latinos based on common origins, values, and way of life. There are fundamental differences in the vision of the world held by Latinos as contrasted with their largely Protestant Anglo counterparts.

SOCIOECONOMIC TRENDS

Perhaps one of the most important predictors of culturally based behaviors is the social and economic standing of US Hispanics. Those that trace their origins to the elites of Latin America are very different from those who were the working classes in those countries. And these two extremes are also different from the middle-class Hispanics who immigrate to the US.

The Elite

Latino elites that immigrate to the US constitute relatively small numbers of people. These are those who had done so well in their country of origin that they found it more comfortable and convenient to have their base in the US. Some of them are actually afraid to live in their own countries because of the danger of kidnappings and prevalent crime. Others are simply rich retirees that fondly remember their shopping trips to the US, and eventually make a life of spending their money in the US.

They go back and forth to their countries of origin and live a very affluent cosmopolite existence. They live in places like La Jolla, Coronado, San Francisco, Aspen, Dallas, Houston, Miami, Atlanta, and New York. They are likely to have servants that come from their own country of origin. This is not the subgroup that best defines the Hispanic market in the US; however they are great targets for large investment companies, luxury cars, expensive real estate concerns, and other goods and services that define the affluent elite.

There are many examples of elite individuals and families that did not start out in the US being affluent. Many from different national backgrounds have forged fortunes in the US on the basis of hard work, dedication, and business intelligence. Some have cultivated business that started very small and advanced to become medium and large-size enterprises. Some have become influential and affluent without necessarily owning a business.[24]

An interesting example of a family that became the affluent owner of a business in the US is the Diaz family, owners of Diaz Foods in Atlanta, Georgia. Diaz Foods was founded in 1969 by immigrants from Cuba that had lost everything to the Castro regime and came to the US to start from scratch. They got started doing menial jobs or anything they could work at to support their families. Father and son, Domingo Diaz and Julio Rene Diaz, were able to open their first grocery store called Diaz Market in Atlanta. Their business grew fast and after opening their fifth store they needed a distribution center. This distribution center became Diaz Foods in 1980. Diaz Foods evolved into one of the largest distributors of Hispanic products in the US with estimated sales of $200,000,000 in 2009. Rene M. Diaz, respectively grandson and son of the founders, bought out all shareholders of the company with the exception of his sister and father in 1987, and has led impressive yearly growth (Figures 2.4 and 2.5).

The type of entrepreneurship demonstrated by Rene M. Diaz and his family characterizes many now affluent Hispanics. The latest estimate from the US

Figure 2.4 Rene Diaz, his father Julio Rene, and his mother Ines in front of Calle Cinco, their second grocery store.

Figure 2.5 Rene Diaz in his warehouse.

Department of Commerce is that by 2007 there were about 2.3 million Hispanic-owned businesses generating approximately 345 billion dollars.[25]

The Middle Class

Those from the middle classes who immigrated are also a relatively small group. The middle classes in Latin America are small in each country and tend to be strongly attached to their societies. They do not easily migrate to the US because they leave behind status, prestige, credentials, titles, professional licenses, and so on.

For example, Mexican physicians do not make as much money, in general, as their US counterparts. Nevertheless, they enjoy great prestige and a comfortable lifestyle. If they emigrate to the US they need to obtain their license to practice again, which is a very cumbersome and time-consuming process. The middle-class businessman or businesswoman knows that to get started in the US they need to confront very difficult obstacles. They have much to lose.

The threat of losing status and a sense of stability is what keeps the middle classes anchored to their countries. They do not make the sacrifice to come to the US until economic pressure is so strong in their country of origin that they feel they have no further recourse. Middle-class emigrations to the US from Latin America tend to be defined by economic crises in specific countries. For example, after the economic disaster in Mexico in 1994, there were physicians, attorneys, and others who came undocumented to the US to work in the fields or as construction workers. The economic pressure was too much at that time. When that pressure subsided, however, many of these professionals returned precisely because of the difficulties of obtaining their credentials in the US.

Some of those middle-class members that migrate to the US do extremely well. They perform well because they had a head start in their country. They were provided with entrepreneurial tools and they brought them here. An interesting success story that illustrates the potential of this middle class is that of Lulu's Dessert Corporation.

In 1982 there was a major economic crisis in Mexico. As previously stated these are the occasions when the middle class is willing to take a risk in the US. A cultural custom in Mexico is to consume ready-to-eat gelatins—beautiful and colorful cup-size gelatins that children and adults buy as snacks in bakeries, supermarkets, small specialized stores, and street vendors. Of course, moms also make these gelatins for children's parties and just for healthy snacks.

Maria de Lourdes "Lulu" Sobrino worked for a travel and conventions company in Mexico that failed due to the economic downturn that year. She noticed that ready-to-eat gelatins were not available in the US. She also thought about the fact that the US Hispanic market was growing fast, particularly in Los Angeles. She decided to open a gelatin factory and store in Los Angeles. That was an entrepreneurial innovation. Maria de Lourdes took an opportunity that no one else had seen. She started from nothing, making 300 gelatins per day and having a hard time selling them in her small store in Los Angeles, and now sells 40 million gelatins for 5 million dollars per year. She represents the quintessential case of the middle-class immigrant to the US that becomes a success story. Her photo, along with her large line of products is shown in Figure 2.6.

The Largest Contingent: The Working Class

The working-class contingent is the bulk of the US Hispanic consumer in the US. This is the largest aggregation of people characterized by those who have come to the US, many undocumented, to find a better standard of life. These are individuals who in their country of origin had very little, or nothing to lose by coming to the US.

Many of these immigrants come from subsistence farming backgrounds—people who produce what they consume, and have little extra to sell for money. They come to the US for survival, not for luxury. Many of these are people who could have starved if they had not had the courage to take a risk for a better life. Their attachments to their country of origin are not titles, money, professions, licenses, or material goods, but just their friends and family and their culture. Friends, family, and culture keep them loyal to the land where they had very little. An excellent illustration of the pressures toward migration is the episode of the FX series 30 days titled "Immigration."[26] In this episode Frank George an immigrant from Cuba

Figure 2.6 Maria de Lourdes "Lulu" Sobrino.

becomes a minuteman and volunteered to patrol the Mexico US border, forgetting his own immigrant origins. He got recruited by "30 Days" to spend a month with an undocumented family from Mexico. Those 30 days reveal the hardships that these immigrants experienced and forced them to immigrate without documents to the US. It is not just poverty, but extreme deprivation that drives many of these humble but hardworking people to cross the border without proper authorization.

These are people that might have been factory workers in cities, but who had very little disposable income to enjoy the material life of their environments. Some of them had been domestic servants. Some of them had been occupied in a mixture of agricultural and industrial low-level jobs that barely allowed them to enjoy any of the benefits of a materialistic society.

They come to the US with nothing. Many cross the border by foot confronting oven-cooking temperatures in the desert and risking their lives. Others come with tourist visas and stay.[27] The many that are here already claim others as relatives and obtain immigration permits for them. They arrive with relatively little background and experience regarding consumer products. What they know is taught to them by those who preceded them. Those brands that had done a good job in penetrating the market are perpetuated in the minds of new arrivals. Marketers should notice that establishing early relationships with these immigrants can be very important in establishing brand primacy among these new consumers.

These new arrivals tend to be courageous, generally young men, who have left their mothers, fathers, wives, family, and friends behind in search of fortune. That is a fortune that eludes them in the highly stratified society of Mexico and most Latin American countries. They come to the land of opportunity and take the risk of perishing for it, often being abused and discriminated against once they arrive. Communities find it offensive that these men hang around on street corners waiting for temporary jobs. Most of these young people suffer loneliness and despair. Their hoped-for reward is to make money to go back to their country and share it with their families. They dream of a house and perhaps building a business. The reason so many are willing to take the risk is because they know of many relatives and acquaintances who have made it.

These recent immigrants send money to their country routinely. They live a hellish life for a while with the reward of knowing that their loved ones are enjoying the fruit of their labor. Eventually, the young men start saving money, moving to better occupations, and deciding either to marry[28] or bring the significant women in their lives or wives they have left behind.

These couples start having children. These children are American citizens by law, but not recognized as such until they are 18 years of age. Some of these kids are denied public education because of the illegality of their parents even if they themselves are US citizens. However, generally the children grow up and learn English in school. The Spanish they learn at home tends to be modest because many of their parents did not have the privilege of extended formal education. Also, the majority of these offspring do not obtain formal education in Spanish. They bring the English language home and teach their parents about the world of consumerism in the US.

The parents nurture the dream of going back "home." They continue sending money to Mexico and other countries. They may buy a piece of land, a home, and perhaps a small business in Mexico to be there for them upon their return. The children grow up, and despite their parents' dreams, they prefer to stay in the US. Thus the dream of going back home remains just a dream for many of them. The parents tend to be heavily dedicated to the success and well-being of their children in the US. They sacrifice and pay for their education. Many children of parents who did not finish elementary school become professionals and prosper in the US. These young people become an important component of the future prosperity of the US.

Many immigrants just decide to stay in the US because of tougher immigration measures along the borders. The so-called "war against terrorism" inadvertently keeps many illegal immigrants in the US. Many of them give up their homeland just to avoid having to cross back and forth. These are dangerous and dreaded crossings.

Things could be very different if the US had a migrant worker program that would make the process legal and easier for everyone.

At the end of the first decade of the second millennium the ranks of US Hispanics who come from humble backgrounds appear to continue to grow. Examining the 2008 American Community Survey of the US Census Bureau shows that almost 530,000 Hispanics entered the country that year alone, and those are people who were willing to be counted by the US Bureau of the Census. These consumers start with little consumer knowledge and evolve into the US consumer society as many forces, including their children, lead them to learn to function in the US. This is one area where many marketers have missed an opportunity.

The Hispanic market has a complexity that makes it different from the Anglo-Saxon Germanic market. Marketers have typically assumed that, like in the more individualistic Anglo-Saxon Germanic market, the decision-making unit is the individual. However, in reality and particularly among Hispanics it is the family. Further, these families are likely to have members with different levels of acculturation. Children may be English dominant, the father may be bilingual, the mother may be Spanish preferred. And the grandmother who lives with them is likely Spanish dominant.

Let us think about the instance in which the family decides it is time to buy a new car. The input is going to come from everyone. The kids will have seen ads on English-language TV and may have friends whose father has a car brand X. The father has seen ads in English and Spanish for brand X but he is confused because the ads in English and Spanish emphasize contradictory attributes. The mother's friends have told her that brand X is OK but that the family should consider brand Y. The grandmother definitely goes for brand Y.

If the integrated marketing communication campaign for brand X had made use of a uniform message that took into consideration the different decision-making inputs, the decision would have been X. But since the brand X message was equivocal, the family goes for tradition and purchases Y. This is a brand X missed opportunity due to the marketer's lack of consumer understanding.

INCOME LEVELS: SURPRISE FOR MARKETERS

According to the US Census Bureau[29] in 2008 dollars the income of Hispanics has had ups and downs as has the income of the overall population. In fact the two covary quite well. The correlation between median income of Hispanics and that of the overall population is very high ($r = 0.89$).

The median income of Hispanic households has lagged behind the overall population of the US for a long time and the gap does not seem to be getting better yet. The largest difference since 1980 was in 1996 when the disparity was $14,465 dollars (in 2008 dollars). Since 1980 the smallest gap occurred in 1981 with a difference of $8,573. The latest figures available are for 2008 show a difference of $12,390, a gap similar to gaps in the 1990s. See the historical trends in Table 2.3.

TABLE 2.3 Historical Median Income Data (in 2008 Dollars)

Year	Hispanic	US	Gap
2008	37,913	50,303	12,390
2007	40,165	52,163	11,998
2006	40,346	51,473	11,127
2005	39,668	51,093	11,425
2004	39,064	50,535	11,471
2003	38,629	50,711	12,083
2002	39,618	50,756	11,138
2001	40,820	51,356	10,536
2000	41,470	52,500	11,030
1999	39,730	52,587	12,857
1998	37,371	51,295	13,924
1997	35,617	49,497	13,880
1996	34,033	48,499	14,465
1995	32,069	47,803	15,734
1994	33,647	46,351	12,704
1993	33,580	45,839	12,259
1992	33,976	46,063	12,087
1991	34,982	46,445	11,462
1990	35,660	47,818	12,158
1989	36,752	48,463	11,711
1988	35,606	47,614	12,008
1987	35,058	47,251	12,193
1986	34,398	46,665	12,268
1985	33,328	45,069	11,742
1984	33,539	44,242	10,704
1983	32,680	42,910	10,230
1982	32,515	43,212	10,696
1981	34,755	43,328	8,573
1980	33,961	44,059	10,098

TABLE 2.4 Hispanic and US Median Household Income

Median Household Income	Hispanic%	US%	Difference
Less than $10,000	8.52	7.21	1.32
$10,000–$14,999	6.44	5.43	1.01
$15,000–$19,999	6.79	5.19	1.60
$20,000–$24,999	7.37	5.46	1.91
$25,000–$29,999	6.43	5.07	1.36
$30,000–$34,999	6.61	5.30	1.31
$35,000–$39,999	5.91	4.87	1.04
$40,000–$44,999	5.63	4.92	0.71
$45,000–$49,999	4.95	4.38	0.57
$50,000–$59,999	8.61	8.29	0.32
$60,000–$74,999	10.03	10.50	−0.47
$75,000–$99,999	10.22	12.39	−2.17
$100,000–$124,999	5.54	7.93	−2.39
$125,000–$149,999	2.79	4.38	−1.59
$150,000–$199,999	2.49	4.38	−1.89
$200,000 or more	1.67	4.31	−2.63

The current gap probably reflects some of the social and economic issues that resulted from the downturn of the economy between 2007 and 2009. *But there is uplifting news.* Our analysis of the American Community Survey data of 2008[30] shows that income differences are not evenly distributed in the population as shown in Table 2.4.

This is very revealing because for the majority of consumer products income levels between $25,000 and $60,000 are ideal, and that is the range in which there are more Hispanics. This alone is a very important reason for marketers to pay attention to Latinos.

Clearly, the fact that proportionally Hispanics have more households in the lower end of the distribution and fewer in the upper end is not desirable. Nevertheless, where the sweet spot of most marketers resides, that is in the middle, Hispanics have higher representation. This is surprising and uplifting, and helps to understand that Hispanics are not generally poorer but they are better represented where it counts for marketers.

FAMILY SIZE AND ECONOMIC BEHAVIOR

Because of a larger family size, Hispanics consume greater amounts of products for the home and family. According to the US Census Bureau,[31] in 2008, Hispanic households with five or more people were 21.7% of all Hispanic households. Comparatively, only 8.3% of the overall population had households with five or more members. Further, 60.8% of Hispanic households contained three or more people, while the figure for the overall population was 36.5%. This is a clear opportunity for marketers of products for home and children including food, beverages, diapers and other paper products, home improvement, clothing, telecommunications, travel, and many other categories.

A large family size is a function of two factors. One is the presence of more children due to a pronatal attitude in the culture. The second factor is that Hispanic families are likely to host friends and relatives for extended periods of time. New immigrants tend to establish their residence in the home of someone that preceded them. Sometimes a parent, a sibling, or someone else comes to visit and stays for very extended periods of time. These friends and relatives can sometimes live with a family for years before finding their own way in American society. Some take care of elderly relatives until they pass on. Many Hispanic families still serve as "social security" for elderly, sick, or poor relatives. The concept of family among Hispanics is more inclusive than in the Anglo-Saxon Germanic population. It encompasses members of the extended family, and many times, others. For example, the 2008 Current Population Survey of the US Census Bureau shows that among Hispanics nonfamily households with two or more people are 25% of this type of households while only 17% of the US population.

Sharing a Roof

An additional complication is that many Hispanic families that are in the process of escalating the economic ladder in the US simply join other households. It is common to find two families sharing a rented home for some time. It is also common for families who own a home to rent part of the house to another family.

And it also happens that two or more families apply together for a loan to purchase a home. This latter approach baffles some financial institutions because they are not prepared to deal with this type of transaction. Interestingly, in Mexico and other parts of Latin America it is a relatively common practice to purchase large ticket items by having several families pool resources. Sometimes these pooling families buy a car or home for each of the pool members but do it over time. They may all live in the first home, and then when they have money they raffle who stays in it, and then purchase the second home, and so on. With cars even financial companies facilitate the process by having people start buying their car on installments and they raffle who gets the first, second, etc. over time. This practice is sometimes called a "tanda" or a "vaquita."[32]

These patterns make for complications in understanding some of the consumer behavior of some segments of Hispanics. The income of the household may actually be more than what the nuclear family makes. Relatives that live in the home are likely to contribute in many ways. A tangential issue is that many Hispanics work in jobs that pay cash and thus operate in the underground and unreported economy. Their income may be significantly higher than what they report. Most Hispanics, even undocumented do pay taxes. Many undocumented, however, are afraid to file a return and simply let the refund stay with the IRS. In 2004 the IRS had 1.3 billion dollars in unclaimed returns, and the states with the largest share of the money were precisely where many undocumented individuals live—California, Texas, Florida, New York, and Illinois.[33]

EDUCATION

One of the most important issues facing the US Hispanic market is education. According to the US Census Bureau, Current Population Survey, 2008 Annual Social and Economic Supplement[34] only 62% of US Hispanics 25 years of age and older had completed high school or equivalent. That is compared to 92% percent of non-Hispanic Whites, 87% of the overall population, and 83% of the Black population. In other words, almost 40% of adult US Hispanics had not finished high school by 2008. The educational gap is a challenge that the US needs to address in the near future with determination. As the non-Hispanic White population decreases proportionally, and as it gets older with the bulk of the baby boomers at the forefront, Hispanics and African Americans will be the supporting pillars of the US economy in the future. These two groups will largely bear the burden of supporting the aging non-Hispanic White population. But, without educational attainment, their ability to generate income and advance the causes of the US economy will likely be at a deficit. Politicians and planners would do well to start making strong efforts to elevate the educational level of Hispanics and other groups that suffer from educational deficiencies. The future of the US cannot rest on large constituencies with limited access to education, even though these constituencies are needed for their contribution to the economy.

For marketers, it is important to understand that the future of the Hispanic market will indeed be brighter if higher levels of education are attained. Even if Hispanics need to face limited educational opportunities, marketers will continue to have profitable Hispanic ventures. Still, it is in the best interest of marketers and their clients to contribute to the education of the market. The higher the education that Hispanics achieve, the better the opportunities they will have to increase their income and their consumption of all types of goods. That is why scholarships, mentorships, and other types of educational sponsorships and promotions can be of mutual benefit to Hispanics and marketers alike.

It is paradoxical and interesting that US marketers' interest in Hispanic disposable income seems to be doing more for Hispanics these days than established political and social institutions. It was not until the market became worthy of the attention of marketers that other institutions started attributing importance to Hispanics in the US. This economic power is likely to continue to grow and attract further respect and interest in US Hispanics. As marketers, and sometimes politicians, help elevate the self-esteem of US Hispanics, Hispanics become more important in our society and thus a feedback loop is created. It is the hope of these writers that this feedback loop of increased attention leading to increased self-esteem, and then consequent increased attention, will result in a more vibrant and productive Hispanic population to the benefit of all Americans. Further, as US Hispanics contribute to the Hispanization of America, marketers accelerate the acculturation of Hispanics in a mutual flow of influence and growth.

Two of the case studies presented at the end of this chapter illustrate how very different companies have recognized the education needs of Spanish-speaking immigrants in learning how to become empowered in critical aspects of their lives. In the Lexicon Marketing—Mundosinbarreras.com Case Study, Lexicon Marketing widely known for its English-Language training product, Inglés sin Barreras® (ISB), introduces the web portal Mundo sin Barreras to the Spanish-dominant market. The portal is designed both linguistically and culturally specifically for this market to educate Spanish-dominant Latinos on how to use their computer in the online world.

The Español Marketing & Communications, Inc.—Liberty Tax Service Case Study also focuses on educating Spanish-speaking immigrants, in this case with messages that are totally educationally oriented. While some of their training is related to financial topics, they cover a broad training scope catering to the information needs of Spanish-speaking consumers. Español Marketing & Communications, Inc. supports their client in the multifaceted campaign, *Una Familia Sin Fronteras* (A Family Without Boundaries), which includes such elements as teaching through media, community partners, and seminars.

Conclusions

The overwhelming message on the Hispanic population in this chapter is that this is a substantial segment in this country that marketers will either ignore at the peril of their competitiveness, or take notice of for potentially great benefits to their companies. This chapter has shown that this market is dynamic, changing rapidly in overall numbers and geographic configurations. US Hispanics have continued the trend of geographic mobility; however, that movement now has taken them into areas of states and cities of even lesser Hispanic density than in prior decades. This Latino spread across the US has meant more and more involvement economically and socially with the larger non-Hispanic population and created greater opportunities for its Hispanicization. While Hispanics overall have lower median incomes than the market in general, interestingly, there are now proportionally more Hispanics in the middle-income categories than those in the market overall. These mid-level income segments are often the targets for much of US advertising, yet the buying power of Latinos in these areas may get buried because of the lack of understanding of their buying potential. The growth of the more youthful Latino population in contrast to the shrinking numbers and aging of the non-Hispanic White segment, makes consideration of their education and well-being a central issue for the US—for marketers as well as broader economic and social interests. Latinos will be those who contribute to all of our well-being in the future.

All in all, this chapter clarifies that the characteristics of the US Hispanic market make it an enticing avenue for companies and their marketers. The basic understanding of the historical and demographic materials presented in this chapter provides the framework for considering and approaching the Hispanic market. The cultural commonalities and size of this population segment may indeed make this a market of interest for many brands looking for growth opportunities. However, the Latino market is complex and dynamic, and careful research is required prior to moving ahead. Reaching out to Hispanic consumers with an informed strategy and relevant communication can indeed result in enormous benefits for both the companies that market to them and the consumers themselves.

IMPLICATIONS FOR MARKETERS

- Assess both the broad demographic picture of the Hispanic market and the evolving trends. This market is indeed targetable based on common historical influences and other shared cultural dimensions. However, the savvy marketer will not neglect the reshaping that has occurred in the past few years. Understand how your products, services, and business objectives match specific needs and characteristics of the Hispanic market. Investigate Hispanic consumer tendencies through secondary research to develop hypotheses. Then, test these assumptions by gathering primary consumer data.
- Consider both short- and long-term strategy in planning for the US Hispanic market. Given the demographic overview in this chapter including recent Census date, you can get the picture of where the market has been and is today. In addition, you can develop a vision of where it may be in only 3–5 years. Good strategic planning for your business could include noting demographic

shifts of Hispanics into areas not previously considered worth your attention. Check into changes in the Hispanic market brought about by volatility in the economy which may require strategic adaptation. Note that migration tends to follow demand for workers; dispersion from state to state is influenced by cost of living and the political climate.

- Consider what connecting with Hispanic consumers means for your business, from a cultural perspective. This chapter has presented the common aspects of Hispanic culture derived from the language, religion, and heritage of Spain. Certain products, services, and communication campaigns are likely to fit with these shared Hispanic traditional values and beliefs. Background knowledge about the Latino market gives you an initial opportunity to assess its potential for your brand.

- Do not neglect to take into account educational levels and language preferences. There are large numbers of Hispanic consumers who depend on Spanish for their communication, growing segments which are bilingual, while still others who speak and read only in English. Adapt campaigns to the linguistic and educational needs of your Latino targets. For those who must count on Spanish or English it is obviously important to provide them with communication in their preferred language. Preferences of bilinguals vary and need research assessment. All communication needs to be culturally relevant. Keep in mind that information needs of Hispanic immigrants, particularly the Spanish dominant, are strong. Remember that educational levels and language preferences often vary even within one Latino family unit.

CASE STUDY: ADRENALINA–TECATE

Company
Heineken USA, marketer and distributor of Tecate

Advertising Agency
Adrenalina

Campaign Title
Tecate. Con Carácter (Tecate. With Character)

Intended Hispanic Consumers
Mexican-born males who have lived in the US for less than 10 years

Background
Mexican-born men in the US live a simple existence, often working 18 hours a day, getting by on very little sleep, 7 days a week—all while trying to make a new life in a new country, learning a new language and enduring extensive responsibilities and challenges.

(Continued)

To Americans in general, these men seem to be invisible despite the fact that often they may indeed be the true architects building this nation. They tend to work several jobs in order to earn enough to live in this country and provide a better life for their families in the US and in Mexico.

These men often are blue- and green-collar employees, working for hourly wages in skilled and unskilled labor jobs that most American-born workers will not typically take, toiling in industries including construction, agriculture, manufacturing, processing, and restaurant services.

Generally, the personal rewards for these men are few and far between. Adrenalina has learned through their studies that when these workers do decide to take a break, a cold cerveza, home-cooked meal, and time to reflect on what they have done in order to improve their lives are a fitting way to end a long day—and to begin looking ahead to the start of another day of heavy work.

Even though much of the nation could not run effectively without their contributions to the US labor force, these Mexican male immigrants embody the definition of American working-class heroes. Yet, they often go unnoticed and unrecognized for their efforts. They remain anonymous faces that deliver dinners, maintain offices, and help to build the places in which Americans live and work.

Tecate is manufactured by Cervecería Cuauhtémoc Moctezuma (CCM), Monterrey, Mexico. CCM is a subsidiary of Heineken International following an acquisition announced in January 2010.

When domestic marketer and distributor Heineken USA awarded Adrenalina the Hispanic advertising business in 2007 for Tecate, the brand had yet to make a relevant connection with Mexican consumers in the US who were loyal to the brand in their home country. Three separate advertising campaigns in the 3 years preceding Adrenalina's *"Tecate. Con Carácter"* ("Tecate. With Character") campaign appeared to leave the brand without a definitive personality.

It is the agency's opinion that the previous three campaigns were focused on virtues reflecting the brand, not the consumer. Each campaign focused on Tecate's bold beer taste—something other beers did not offer. Yet, the messaging seemed to Adrenalina to be flat and brand centric, rather than showcasing the common ground and emotional connection shared by the brand and the target consumer.

Tecate sought to find a unique and ownable voice that would speak candidly and sincerely with its core consumer of Mexican immigrant males. In order to connect with these Mexican males, Tecate had to pinpoint attributes that distinctly reflected the brand and the hardworking men whom they wanted to reach.

Discovery Process/Research

Focus groups with Tecate and non-Tecate drinkers in Chicago, Houston, and Los Angeles helped to shed light on an opportunity that was distinctive to this often overlooked newcomer target.

In order to truly step into the shoes of the consumers and understand their world from their point of view, Adrenalina shadowed their every move as closely as possible in order to map the numerous prospective opportunities for connecting and activating the brand with consumers.

The agency accomplished this by following the Mexican males every other weekend during a 1-year period to their first job of the day, and often to their second job

Tecate. Con Carácter (Tecate. With Character) campaign.

after that, as well as in between jobs, at boxing events, via pay-per-view programming, media sponsorships, and while watching TV. They found that it is difficult to imagine how hard these men work until one experiences their 18-hour days firsthand.

Through their research, the agency felt they were able to understand the mindset required to work so hard. These men seemed to Adrenalina to be among the hardest working people known, and that it was their unique sense of values, drive, perseverance, and resolve which pushed them to be "better" men and enhance the lives of their families.

Cultural Insights
Adrenalina's research revealed that Mexican newcomers possess a set of virtues that are widely held but have been seldom acknowledged in national advertising campaigns.

In the agency's estimation, these men work longer hours and plug away in harder, backbreaking jobs that most people in the US would balk at doing for menial pay. They have made many sacrifices along the way, yet they appear to be men who act boldly in the face of adversity. They also drink Tecate because it is the beer that they believe recognizes them for who and what they are: men with character. After dozens of dead ends in their analysis, the agency was able to find a common ground that the Mexican newcomer and Tecate share: *Carácter* (Character).

Expression of Insights in the Campaign
The insight of the shared values of *carácter* (character) was brought to life in a simple and straightforward way. Because it appeared to Adrenalina that no one was communicating to these unique and hardworking men, the agency chose to leverage their

(Continued)

learnings from research and speak to them in a personally relevant way to capture their attention, appreciation, and their dollar.

These vignettes were set in workplaces and everyday situations considered familiar to our newcomer target. Yet these scenarios and the Mexican male's perspective were images and points of view that the agency believed had not been showcased in such a high-profile way by other brands. Thus, the campaign pays homage to the everyday experiences and struggles of the Mexican male who works everyday for months at a time eking out a living in the US, working as a cook in a restaurant kitchen or as a farmer perched on a tractor in the sweltering sun and sending his hard-earned money to family in Mexico instead of spending it on himself. The campaign was showcased in a multimedia effort in major US Hispanic markets including California, where the campaign received the heaviest play, Texas, Arizona, and New Mexico via Spanish-language TV on Telemundo, Univision, and various cable and independent networks, print, radio, and outdoor. Promotional events and sponsorships also supported the rollout.

Through the dual expression of "*Carácter*," and the distinctive places where these hardworking men live and work, the agency attempted to shed light on and to respect the work ethic, values, and drive that push these men ahead every day. This connection is intended to strengthen the consumer's relationship with Tecate.

Effects of the Campaign
Since the implementation of the campaign, the brand's distributor, Heineken USA, has experienced increased sales at a time when the overall industry has remained flat. According to Tecate brewer CCM, the brand sold nearly 20 million cases in between 2008 and 2009. This represents an 8% spike in sales that the agency attributes to the creative advertising and insights gleaned about hardworking Mexican-born males in this country.

CASE STUDY: LEXICON MARKETING–MUNDOSINBARRERAS.COM

Company/Organization
Lexicon Marketing, LLC.

Campaign
www.MundosinBarreras.com

Intended Customers
Spanish-dominant Hispanics in the US

Background
In 2004, Lexicon launched Computación sin Barreras®, a computer learning product designed as a follow-up to their widely successful English-language learning product, ISB, and bundled it with a computer. Computación sin Barreras was designed from the ground up to help first-time computer users understand how to buy a computer, setting it up, and use a computer for basic activities such as going online, and using the Microsoft Office suite of programs. Through the launch and growth of this business line, Lexicon found that there was a high level of demand from the Spanish-dominant

Lexicon Marketing–www.MundosinBarreras.com campaign.

community to "get a computer" but a tremendous gap that the company was filling through their customer service center on how to even set up the computer. Lexicon saw an opportunity to not only help their customers set up their computer, but also to learn about and navigate the online world. They decided to create a Spanish-language portal that would be easy to use for a novice computer user, offer empowering, educational, and life-enhancing content in Spanish, and the opportunity to experience firsthand the social networking tools that the Internet has to offer.

Discovery Process/Research

Lexicon conducted phone and online surveys as well as focus groups with their customer base to better understand their level of knowledge and use of various existing websites and what were perceived areas of need. The company also tested various design and lay-out concepts with the target to optimize the user interface and understand what level of relative importance the target placed on various featured content components. During the soft launch of Mundo sin Barreras, they opened up the site to employees and their friends and family followed by the community at large. During the beta period, the company conducted several rounds of surveys to gain a better understanding of what were the features that Spanish-dominant consumers liked best and least. They also used their analytics package to track visitors and registered users' activities.

Cultural Insights

Given Lexicon's long focus on educating, empowering, and serving the Spanish-dominant community in the US, they undertook this project with a very clear understanding of the target customer. It was challenging to remember what it was like to use a computer for the very first time and how the everyday activities in which most of us

(Continued)

engage, like e-mail, Facebook, or Skype, are foreign to this community. They had to constantly check in to make sure that they were making the site and its tools as easy to use as possible and with the utmost attention to providing support and explanations for all the activities offered. They were also adamant that all content on the site be in Spanish—no hidden English words when you click on a link. Lexicon has seen an amazing revolution since the company launched the site in that it is providing a safe space for the Spanish-speaking community to speak up about the issues on their minds, to share their strong sense of optimism and faith with other like-minded Hispanics-to really be seen and heard for the first time. Hispanics love to share photos of their families, their lives, to connect with others, and get answers to problems or concerns. With its combination of educational content and social networking, Mundo sin Barreras really provides a unique place for Spanish-speaking immigrants to tap into a new network of support as they navigate the sometimes strange waters that are life in the US.

Expression of Insights in the Campaign
Part of the unique things they have done with Mundo sin Barreras is to personify the advice-giving interaction. There are other Spanish-language sites that offer Q & A like spaces, but they are all very impersonal. They have created three "experts" on the site that answer users' questions on immigration, technology, and health and really developed a story and persona around each. For example, they created "Edgar the Geek" as their technology guru who answers people's questions in a very straightforward, easy to understand way. He is a cartoon character but the company also takes a real-life version of him to shows where they teach Hispanics how to use the Internet and its many tools to improve their lives. This has expanded to the point where users help each other and reach out to others in need. Hispanics are social creatures and it is important to bring a human element to everything they do.

Effect of the Campaign
Within 6 months of launch, MundosinBarreras.com has over 5000 registered users and over 65,000 unique visitors a month. It has also created a great deal of interest with brand advertisers who are looking for innovative ways to connect deeply with this community. Brand advertisers are often surprised to learn that the Spanish-dominant community is indeed online and hungry for information in-language.

CASE STUDY: ESPAÑOL MARKETING & COMMUNICATIONS, INC.– LIBERTY TAX SERVICE

Company/Organization
Liberty Tax Service

Hispanic Agency
Español Marketing & Communications, Inc.

Campaign/Advertising Title
Una Familia Sin Fronteras (A Family Without Boundaries)

Intended Hispanic Consumers

First-generation (legal or not) and second-generation Hispanic Americans, who are living and working in the US. Core target consumers are working Hispanics who live outside of the "American Dream"; they are unbanked (holding no basic bank account) or underbanked (having a basic bank account and yet relying on less sophisticated methods for everyday transactions such as check cashing), and have little or no experience with financial services or processes in the US or in their country of origin. Spanish is the primary language spoken (or preferred), and the preferred language for business transactions.

Background

Liberty Tax Service is a rapidly growing tax preparation firm with over 3300 locations in the US and Canada. The founder and CEO, John Hewitt, created an organization with a firm commitment to social responsibility and altruism, and with a sense of responsibility for the communities it serves. Liberty Tax Service is very sensitive to the hurdles and barriers to education and resources that frequently exist in the Hispanic community, particularly for the new immigrant. Rather than targeting Hispanic consumers with a traditional Hispanic marketing program, Liberty Tax Service created a unique Hispanic initiative called *Una Familia Sin Fronteras* (A Family Without Boundaries) that seeks to empower Hispanic consumers, particularly first- and second-generation immigrants, by providing them financial and fiscal responsibility education, as well as other types of education, which will lead them to achieve greater success and well-being.

Through *Una Familia Sin Fronteras*, Liberty Tax Service provides valuable services to the Hispanic community such as free ITIN (Individual Tax Identification Number) applications, free tax education, free small business education, a free Interpreter's Course for its bilingual staff, and many more fiscal and financial educational programs for Latino communities nationwide. Liberty Tax Service also provides a Hispanic Services Seal of Excellence Certification program that ensures that its offices provide bilingual assistance and are knowledgeable about how to properly serve the Hispanic community.

Liberty Tax Service has a Diversity Marketing Department in its Virginia Beach Corporate office. Working with franchise owners throughout the US, in both highly developed and emerging Hispanic markets, as well as with Español Marketing & Communications, the Diversity Marketing team seeks out opportunities to fill the significant education gaps that exist in many areas of financial and health literacy. Franchise owners and staff conduct seminars year-round in Spanish, partnering with Mexican Consulates, school districts, and local nonprofit organizations to teach their clients, constituents, and community members about financial literacy and fiscal responsibility, and providing them with the tools to more easily enter into the mainstream economy of the US and ultimately become responsible financial managers. Additionally, franchisees partner with local and national community outreach organizations to provide Hispanic consumers with important information about other topics and issues that are pertinent to them and their families, such as disease awareness prevention education, proper prenatal care, and much more.

Discovery Process/Research

The members of the Diversity Marketing Team travel to key Hispanic markets in the US, as well as to Mexico, meeting with thought leaders and nonprofit organizations

(Continued)

Una Familia Sin Fronteras campaign–Liberty Tax Service seminar.

to determine key issues of concern and areas where education gaps exist in Hispanic communities. Likewise, they participate in conferences with educators, the Mexican Consulate, and with other community organizations to look for areas where they can provide materials, staff, or outreach to help provide education and resources that are sorely needed. Seminars are always offered in an "open environment," which allows attendees to ask questions throughout the presentation. This enables the presenters to better integrate personally and professionally with the audience. Following each seminar, presenters note questions that were asked about topics that were not covered in the prepared materials. In some areas, the seminar leaders survey the attendees following the seminar, asking them to list three additional topics they feel would be of value to them. Based on these new questions and interests expressed in other topics by the attendees, the Diversity Marketing Team creates new seminars, or revises the materials for an existing seminar, to improve the relevance of and information offered in each seminar. The organic spirit of the Hispanic initiative has allowed the team to grow the program and direct it to best meet the needs of the Hispanic community.

Cultural Insights
The key cultural insight is that first and second-generation immigrants are avid information seekers, but frequently do not have access to resources or information to help them understand the complex financial systems in the US. Additionally, many immigrants first become true consumers after coming to the US, earning enough money, for

the first time in their lives, to get to make purchase decisions and to really have the need to become good money managers. Liberty Tax Service recognizes these consumer needs and resource and information gaps, and is committed to helping provide the resources and fill in the gaps wherever possible, using relevant and comprehensible materials and presentations. Additionally, the Hispanic initiative helps consumers understand how to view their world in terms of "opportunities" instead of "roadblocks"; that is, a free-lance landscaper or an at-home mother who takes care of other children in her home can see themselves as "small business owners" ... and learn how to run those businesses successfully.

Expression of Insights in the Campaign

The Hispanic initiative is a multifaceted one, and the Diversity Marketing team and Español Marketing are constantly searching out partnership opportunities and media opportunities where the company can reach consumers effectively with its educational message. The messaging is completely educational in its orientation. There are no brand-sell messages at all. The company uses media to teach consumers about finan-cial education and fiscal responsibility, as well as creating opportunities for commu-nity partners to interact with consumers and deliver their educational messages. Liberty Tax Service experts is hosting weekly Spanish-language radio shows in 20 markets in 2010 (up from 10 in 2009), informing listeners about important financial issues and inviting them to call in with questions or concerns. Franchisees host Roadside Fiestas on many weekends, inviting community organizations to participate, and creating fun family-oriented environments where kids can enjoy themselves while parents learn about important and relevant topics. Seminars are conducted in locations where Hispanic immigrants are taking adult education classes, learning English, or visit-ing their consulates—making it easy for consumers to trust Liberty Tax Service as a company concerned with their welfare, and making it easy for consumers to attend the seminars. And franchise representatives participate in many grassroots events in the Hispanic communities throughout the US, handing out Jarritos and hot dogs, and pro-viding educational materials and "cute premiums" to interested consumers. In early 2009, a Spanish-language website went live (www.libertytaxespanol.com), and in late 2009, a blog was added to the site where consumers can get all kinds of tax advice in Spanish. Liberty Tax Service provides free ITIN application services (Tax IDs) to consumers who do not have Social Security numbers, so that they can pay their income taxes each year and comply with IRS laws, and teaches these consumers how to be fiscally responsible and how to comply with the laws.

Effect of the Campaign

The need for and belief in the validity of the *Una Familia Sin Fronteras* initiative is evi-dent in the partnerships that Liberty Tax Service is establishing with other organizations who are committed to improving the lives of Hispanics in the US, but who frequently are nonprofit or government organizations who have never partnered with a corporation in the past. *Instituto de Mexicanos en el Exterior* (IME) in Mexico City has sanctioned Liberty Tax Service as a *preferred educational partner* for their 50 consulates and 200+ *Plazas Comunitarias* (Teaching Centers) nationwide. Liberty Tax Service is the first for-profit corporation allowed to partner with the Los Angeles and Saddleback Valley

(Continued)

school districts in their instructional adult outreach educational programs. And Liberty Tax Service is being sought out by universities and professional organizations as a company with expertise in embracing diversity in the workplace, as well as for its culturally oriented training programs used to ensure that Hispanic clientele are provided the tax preparation and educational services they need in the language in which they prefer to communicate. In 2010, Liberty wil be partnering with large School Districts in 21 different markets by providing educational seminars about the Census, entrepreneurship, and fundamental financial and fiscal education, explaining the credit-based economy in the US that is so foreign to many Hispanic immigrants.

And while the Hispanic initiative is clearly noncommercial in its focus, it is obviously having a very positive effect on Liberty Tax Service's business. In 2009, approximately 50% of Liberty Tax Service's franchisees participated in the Hispanic Services Seal of Excellence Certification program, with new members participating on a weekly basis, all fulfilling the required 22-hour certification training course. Through its *Una Familia Sin Fronteras* program, Liberty Tax Service has touched well over 100,000 Hispanics with its free ITIN and educational programs, in 2009 alone.

End Notes

[1] I understand that some readers prefer one label over another. We use Hispanic or Latino indistinctly here for the sheer purpose of aggregating people who trace their origins to Latin America and who now reside in the US.

[2] Treaty of Guadalupe Hidalgo, Encyclopedia Britannica Online, June 25, 2004. http://search.eb.com. proxy.lib.fsu.edu/eb/article?eu=39059

[3] Samuel P. Huntington, *Who Are We?: The Challenges to America's National Identity*. New York: Simon & Schuster, 2004.

[4] The largest and oldest Mexican TV network.

[5] Dilip Ratha, Sanket Mohapatra, and Ani Silwal, *Migration and Remittance Trends 2009. Migration and Development Brief 11*. Washington, DC: World Bank, November 3, 2009. http://siteresources.worldbank. org/INTPROSPECTS/Resources/334934-1110315015165/MigrationAndDevelopmentBrief11.pdf

[6] Ibid, p. 2.

[7] http://welcome.topuertorico.org/history4.shtml

[8] Annual Estimates of the Resident Population for the United States, Regions, States, and Puerto Rico. April 1, 2000 to July 1, 2008 (NST-EST2008-01).

[9] The American Community: Hispanics 2004. American Community Survey Report. Released February 2004, ACS 03. Washington, DC: US Census Bureau, 2007. http://www.census.gov/prod/2007pubs/ acs-03.pdf

[10] Ibid.

[11] "Cuba," Encyclopedia Britannica Online, June 25, 2004. http://search.eb.com.proxy.lib.fsu.edu/eb/ article?eu=127868

[12] In today's vocabulary these would be considered Native Americans, as all the indigenous people of the continent.

[13] Ibid.

[14] See the US State Department Background Note for Guatemala at http://www.state.gov/r/pa/ei/ bgn/2045.htm.

[15] The American Community: Hispanics 2004. American Community Survey Report Released February 2004, ACS 03. Washington, DC: US Census Bureau, 2007. http://www.census.gov/prod/2007pubs/acs-03.pdf

[16] Ibid.

[17] According to the American FactFinder, US Census Bureau, 2006–2008 American Community Survey. The estimate of 350,000 people of Brazilian origin in the US is controversial because the Brazilian Government claims that there are 1.1 million of them according to a New York Times article: http://www.nytimes.com/2007/12/04/nyregion/04brazilians.html

[18] http://www.state.gov/r/pa/ei/bgn/35640.htm

[19] The American Community: Hispanics 2004. American Community Survey Report. Issued February 2007, ACS 03. Washington, DC: US Census Bureau, 2007. http://www.census.gov/prod/2007pubs/acs-03.pdf

[20] Ibid.

[21] Jason P. Schachter, Migration by Race and Hispanic Origin: 1995–2000. Census 2000 Special Reports CENSR-13. US Census Bureau, October 2003. http://www.census.gov/prod/2003pubs/censr-13.pdf

[22] Ibid.

[23] Roberto Suro and Sonya Tafoya, Dispersal and Concentration: Patterns of Latino Residential Settlement. Washington, DC: Pew Hispanic Center, December 2004. http://www.census.gov/prod/2003pubs/censr-13.pdf

[24] See for example the list published by Hispanic Business Magazine each year. http://www.hispanicbusiness.com/top100influentials/?cat=Corporate

[25] http://www.commerce.gov/blog/2010/09/21/hispanic-owned-businesses-grow-more-double-national-rate

[26] See this episode at http://www.hulu.com/watch/56908/30-days-immigration.

[27] Approximately 45% of undocumented immigrants arrive in the US with tourist visas and overstay their permits. http://pewhispanic.org/files/factsheets/19.pdf

[28] Many of these individuals do not necessarily legally marry but they cohabitate and form a family that could last a lifetime. When asked, many of them state they are married just to avoid a longer and less-desirable explanation.

[29] Current Population Survey, Annual Social and Economic Supplements. http://www.census.gov/hhes/www/income/histinc/inchhtoc.html

[30] http://factfinder.census.gov/servlet/DatasetMainPageServlet?_program=ACS&_submenuId=&_lang=en&_ts=

[31] US Census Bureau, Current Population Survey, Annual Social and Economic Supplement, 2008. http://www.census.gov/population/www/socdemo/hispanic/cps2008.html

[32] The word vaquita means little cow because that is the way in which people in small towns used to pool resources to purchase cows.

[33] http://www.bankrate.com/finance/money-guides/irs-holds-1-3-billion-in-unclaimed-refunds.aspx

[34] http://www.census.gov/population/www/socdemo/education/cps2008.html

Chapter 3

THE LATINO ESSENCE OF "HISPANIC"

Making Cultural Identity a Core Marketing Element

CULTURAL IDENTITY DERIVES FROM REFERENCE GROUPS

People are social beings that generally identify with groups they belong to, and sometimes with groups they do not belong to. These can be referred to as belongingness reference groups and non-belongingness reference groups. They overlap many times, but not always. People may not belong to a social group and still use that group as a reference group to derive the criteria and standards they need in making decisions about courses of action or judgments.[1] Usually these are aspirational groups. Individuals may identify with these groups without necessarily being part of them because they serve as role models, or they have similar values, or because they represent success or other reward experiences.

Those in charge of marketing to US Hispanics need to understand the reference groups that Hispanic consumers use for their consumer decision making. Also, a key point is to understand which reference groups Hispanics may use under varying circumstances. This is particularly relevant in the case of US Hispanics who maintain cultural ties with their country of origin, and/or with others like themselves, but at the same time live within the context of the US culture. This multiple cultural affiliation brings about the need to understand when different identities become salient.

81

Humans, in this case Hispanics, may have affinities with multiple cultural groups and thus have diverse cultural identities. Cultural identity refers to the cultural group that individuals use in specific circumstances for selecting courses of action or evaluating ideas or objects. It is conceivable that for certain categories Hispanics may use non-Hispanic role models because these role models are relevant in a specific situation. Thus, when purchasing an automobile a Hispanic may be inspired by a Black colleague that closely associates with his or her own cultural group. In addition, it is possible that an individual may use different cultural reference groups in different situations. Thus, understanding the implications of the interactions of these different reference groups may assist in making sense of cultural consumer behavior. We should note in passing that all consumer behavior is culturally influenced.[2] Otherwise, why would we be attracted to specific car designs or flavors of food? As marketing influences culture, culture should direct marketing efforts.

A Hispanic individual may use the reference group of coworkers when making a decision about insurance, and these coworkers may not be Hispanic at all. That same person may make decisions about reading materials using the reference group of his or her schoolmates even if they are not Hispanic. This person may be influenced by African Americans when on the dance floor. He or she could also order food in a restaurant remembering what his or her non-Hispanic boss likes to eat. This is because reference groups may have different saliency in different circumstances. The extent to which different reference groups become salient in different circumstances has to do with the emotionally perceived links between the situation and the reference group.

The reader, however, must not conclude that when non-Hispanic reference groups are at play consumer behavior will be void of Hispanic cultural influence. This is because culture, like history, lingers in our mind. Thus, a Hispanic manager may be influenced by a non-Hispanic boss to consider the purchase of a BMW because of the prestige of the brand. Still, the Hispanic consumer is likely to have memories and references in his or her mind to how he or she will feel showing up in a BMW at a family gathering. Will he or she be able to fit all his relatives in the car for an outing? While the family as a reference group may not have made BMW part of the consideration set, the consideration of how the family will accept or reject the product will be part of the equation. Thus, the metaphor of a Venn diagram of overlapping reference groups in Figure 3.1 may help explain these influences.

The Venn diagram is a simplified overlap of influences as other inputs will also influence the decision that this consumer will make. For example, the ads he or she has seen which are also cultural manifestations will play a part. Further, the influence of friends and even celebrities are likely to come into play. The point being made here is that even if the introduction of the idea of purchasing a BMW may not come from a Hispanic source, the evaluation of the idea is likely to include

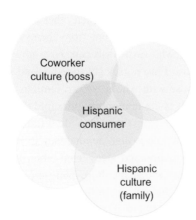

Figure 3.1 Overlapping reference groups.

Hispanic cultural considerations. It is also important to emphasize that while Hispanic culture is likely to be present when Hispanic consumers consider products and ideas, non-Hispanic inputs also need to be taken into consideration. That is because Hispanics in the US do not live in a vacuum or isolated from the rest of society influences.

REFERENCE GROUPS AND THEIR ROLE IN CONSUMER SOCIAL LEARNING

Multiple role models can guide Hispanic consumer behavior. The key to social influence is identification. Albert Bandura's *Social Learning Theory*[3] establishes the conditions under which humans learn behavior from others through observation and modeling. Models that are similar to the observer and those models that have aspirational status are more likely to be emulated. Identification is the process by which an individual emulates the thinking patterns, feelings, and actions of another individual who is the model.[4] This identification is based on perceived similarity with the model, the power or reward ability of the model, prestige, and the competence of the model among other factors.

Homophily: The Importance of Similarity

Perceived similarity, or homophily, is the reason why Hispanics are more likely to identify with other Hispanics. Homophily is the degree to which individuals who engage in communication perceive they share common attitudes, values, aspirations, and beliefs.[5] People sharing a common Hispanic or Latino background, like most human beings, are expected to engage in communication and learn from others who are similar to themselves. This reminds us of the typical scene of the cocktail party in which those who already know each other, and share something in common, are more likely to interact with each other than they are to talk to others they do not know or feel are too different from themselves. That is why affinity groups are popular. Those who own Saab cars have clubs and interact with each other. Those who have Paso Fino horses get together and share their riding experience. We tend to seek those with whom we are familiar and with whom we have certain traits in common. It is the homophily principle that keeps those people who are alike together and separate from those who are different.

A side effect of this principle is that the tendency to interact with others similar to oneself keeps new information and ideas from other people out of the in-group. Thus, homophily tends to perpetuate a culture over time until the network of similar people opens to others from the outside, or the out-group.

Thus, Hispanics are more likely to identify with other Hispanics and to use them as their reference group under many circumstances. If a consumer's cousin purchased a car from dealership A and he or she indicates having had a good experience with the car, then the consumer is more likely to go to dealership A than B. That is because the cousin possesses credibility in the eyes of the consumer. The consumer perceives his or her cousin to be very similar to him- or herself. This similarity provides confidence that the resulting experience will be similarly good. This is why brands and ideas that penetrate a homophilous network tend to spread through it relatively fast. The challenge is how to get access to the homophilous network.

Successful Models and Their Expertise

Similarity is not the only component of social learning theory. Social learning theory also indicates that individuals will emulate behaviors of people they admire. Albert Bandura stated that "the behavior of models who possess high status in prestige, power, and competence hierarchies is more likely to be successful and therefore to command greater attention from others than the behavior of models who are socially, occupationally, and intellectually inept."[6] Thus, Latinos may admire others outside their own "Hispanic" group. These role models could be people who are aspirational because they are successful in different aspects of life and/or their interpersonal attraction.[7] A large number of US Hispanics and/or their predecessors come to the US for economic advantage. Success is an important goal for them. Thus, many Hispanics adopt role models and reference groups that are not Hispanic. Hispanic individuals look up to their bosses, their neighbors, their schoolmates, and others for examples of behavior, and these role models may or may not be Hispanic. Latinos can learn consumer social behavior from both Hispanics and non-Hispanics, and they complement their consumer learning from both.

In the Adrenalina–Tecate Light Case Study at the end of this chapter, the Agency, Adrenalina, and the brand take on an interesting challenge: to understand why Mexican immigrants, who come from a tradition of taste and tasty beers switch to more watery domestic light beer brands when they move to the US. Through ethnographic research in the homes of Mexican immigrants, Adrenalina discovered these men feel that drinking light beer is a more American thing to do. Yet, these young Mexicans report they still would prefer the fuller taste of the beers from their Mexican roots. The "Tecate Light. *Por los que quieren más*" advertising campaign developed by Adrenalina features the interplay between traditional taste preferences as embodied in Tecate Light, and taking on the ways of the US by drinking other light beers. The Tecate Light humorous advertising puts the pull of the traditional Mexican culture in the hands of Mexican parents as they talk disparagingly about the changing preferences of their sons who have immigrated to the US.

Advertising models and portrayals may be more or less aspirational and credible depending on their relevance to the individual. In some cases Anglo role models could be more appealing, and in others Hispanic role models could be more persuasive. There may also be circumstances in which both Hispanic and non-Hispanic consumer behavioral models may strengthen each other as in the case of a communication campaign directed to Hispanics and non-Hispanics alike. The campaign may have appealing Hispanic models in the Hispanic component of the campaign, and appealing non-Hispanic models in other sub-campaigns. These can clearly reinforce each other in the mind of a Latino consumer if he or she perceives all these models to be attractive and relevant. Considering the circumstances under which each of these models can complement or work against each other can be important. This is why a completely separate and distinct Hispanic campaign may not be advisable in many cases, particularly when the consumer may be exposed to dissonant messages about a brand in different media.

Modeling the Behaviors of Even Those Who Oppress

A non-Hispanic reference group can be appealing in some aspects but aversive in others. Understanding this possible ambivalence can be highly instrumental in conducting advertising research. In 2009, 81% of US Hispanics indicated that discrimination is still a part of Hispanics' day-to-day lives.[8] If Hispanics believe that they have been discriminated against in the US, they may be cautious in modeling the behaviors of those who have shown negative behaviors against them. However, discrimination does not come from everyone nor from every group, thus there is plenty of room for Hispanics to find non-Hispanic models that they can relate to and look up to.

Even in cases of overall feelings of being discriminated, the potential for identification is still possible. The social-psychological literature has shown that there are circumstances under which victims identify with victimizers.[9] A notorious example of this phenomenon, which some readers may recall, is how Patty Hearst identified with her captors of the Symbionese Liberation Army and took on their values and behaviors.[10] Under certain circumstances, victims take on the values or beliefs of their victimizers as tragically happened in the Nazi regime, in which Jewish, Russian, and other victims sometimes identified with their victimizers as an adaptation for survival.[11] In terms of consumer behavior it is plausible to imagine that even an abusive non-Hispanic boss can be identified with and consequently become a model for some consumer behavior.

Thus, there is ample opportunity for Hispanics to use non-Hispanic reference groups and role models under certain circumstances. These processes and their surrounding circumstances are an important area of inquiry when investigating cross-cultural marketing.

The Identification of Models in Practice

It makes intuitive sense that Hispanics would more readily identify with other Hispanics. One can hypothesize that ads and testimonials featuring Hispanics should be more impactful than if the portrayals were non-Hispanic. Still, because of the reasons just elaborated above, it is very likely that for certain types of decisions some Hispanics will use non-Hispanic reference groups as well as non-Hispanic individual role models. This is particularly true of the immigrant experience of these Hispanic consumers who are exposed to a constant bombardment of information regarding the accomplishments of those in the larger US culture. Also, these immigrants are surrounded by glamorous images of people who are different from themselves.

For many around the world, the US has been the land of aspirations and the realization of dreams. US Anglo-Saxon Germanic[12] people have been the embodiment of those ambitions. Consequently Anglos can be powerful influences because of their success and aspirational quality. Would a Hispanic that has been able to attain some degree of success in US society be more likely to go to a bank like Banco Popular because of affinity, or to a bank like Bank of America because that is where successful Anglos go? This is not a simple question, and marketers need to address this question taking into consideration the salience of the role models and situations. The dimensions of success/expertise and homophily/similarity are likely to influence which reference group is used for specific consumer decision-making situations. Table 3.1 illustrates potential options.

TABLE 3.1 Situation Importance Scores for Hispanic and Anglo Models

Situation Salience	Hispanic Model	Anglo Model
Success	50	75
Homophily	90	25

The cells in Table 3.1 contain example "importance" scores. Thus, a Hispanic looking to purchase a new home may have a combination of reference group influences in his or her mind. For example, he or she may use an Anglo reference group and assign to it an importance score of 75 on a 100-point scale, because this consumer has seen that Anglos he or she knows have been very successful at purchasing their homes. Nevertheless, this consumer also feels that other Hispanics he or she knows have been successful at getting their home, but not as much as Anglos.

Because of these considerations this consumer assigns an importance score of 75 to Anglos on the "success" criterion, and a score of 50 to Hispanics. When it comes to homophily (or similarity) this consumer feels much more comfortable listening to Hispanics and assigns them a score of 90 because they are very much like him or her. They have gone through the same issues and problems. He or she also feels some homophily with Anglos, but less, and so assigns this cell a score of 25.

In the course of a quantitative study, Hispanics could be asked to assign importance scores to the reference group by the dimensions of credibility: success and homophily. Across many individuals an advertiser would be able to determine what type of role models would be most impactful to the Hispanic consumer of interest.

The main conclusions that the marketer would be able to derive from this set of scores include:

1. A successful Anglo model is likely to be highly appealing.
2. A successful Hispanic model has appeal.
3. Hispanics are most likely to feel similar to the Hispanic model and thus believe that his or her probability of success is higher with company X if Hispanics are portrayed as succeeding in getting mortgages from this company.
4. A communication should indicate that both Anglos and Hispanics succeed when applying for a mortgage with company X, and that Hispanics, like the consumer him- or herself, recommend company X.

These conclusions provide an initial template for a communication with high probability of credibility and increased sales. Notice that this rough template does not include creative nuances of any type. It only addresses the need for both Anglo and Hispanic characterizations of success, and Hispanic characterizations of homophily in connecting with the consumer. The results of this analysis may be counterintuitive to many who have thought for many years that only Hispanic models should be used when selling to Hispanics. In fact, many companies have spent a great amount of resources in trying to find the typical Hispanic for their ads. Many of these companies have tried to find a pan-Hispanic model that can appeal to all Hispanics, others just use someone that "looks" Hispanic.

As the reader may conclude this quest may be a waste of time in many cases. In the first place it is hard to say that there is such a thing as a typical "Hispanic." While many US Hispanics come from Mexico and are likely to have a mestizo background, there is ample variability among them and much more variability among Hispanics in general. Second, the look of the person is less likely to be salient to the consumer than his or her behavior and demeanor. Third, the relevant role models for this particular purchase decision may be a mix of looks, behaviors, and demeanors.

The central take-away here is that the "importance" scores are the ones that determine the inclusion of characterizations in ads. What this perspective emphasizes is that reference groups may vary by their degree of relevance in specific situations in which consumers are expected to make decisions. Also, that stereotypical characterizations may actually backfire.

IDENTITY AND SOCIALIZATION

The social context of our lives defines our identity.[13] It is in the course of social interaction that we acquire a sense of self. This is somewhat paradoxical because in common parlance many individuals argue that they want to be themselves, as if being like the group detracts from who they are. Interestingly, in large parts of Western civilization, like northern Europe, the US, and Canada, what is common is individualism and wanting to be different. So what makes people alike in these societies is the yearning for a unique identity. It is a shared social commonality that in a meta-sense results in individual differences.

Despite the desire to be individualistic there is no way of *not* being part of some group, at least in one's mind. Humans, to be "human," must be socialized in at least one social group. That group or groups become the standard against which the individual compares the rest of the world. In contemporary Western society it is difficult to think of individuals who are socialized in only one social or cultural group, although in isolated communities it may still occur. The place where people are first socialized, particularly if they spend an important part of their youth in that social and geographic location, rarely fades away. The original socialization group continues to be a very important and a unique source of influence for a long time, sometimes forever. That is why one's hometown and family linger in one's mind for the rest of our lives. That is how culture gets perpetuated as well.

Individuals who become socialized in rural, isolated, or socially segregated societies are more likely than others to have one physical cultural reference group. The media, however, may also present reference groups to which people may relate even if these reference groups are virtual. Thus, even if an individual was raised in a remote community, he or she may have built a mental and emotional image of another group that the media portrayed. Thus, soap-opera characters or actors from western films can become relevant reference groups. Clearly, there are other ways in which a virtual reference group may evolve in one's mind like in the case of storytelling. Nowadays, even relatively isolated communities are likely to contain members who have developed many reference groups they have never physically met or interacted with. Online social networks and groups provide opportunities to participate in communities that go far beyond one's immediate environment. As Michael Hogg and Debora Terry state in their book "People's attitudes are developed and expressed as behaviors in a context that is social; it contains other people who are actually present or who are invisibly present in the social norms that define social groups to which we do or do not belong."[14]

Further the sociological literature on the influence of "significant others" provides further support for the importance of diverse people in our socialization: *"It is only through others that we can come to discover ourselves.* Even more specifically, it is only through significant others that we can develop a significant relationship to ourselves."[15] While during our early socialization the family is the most important provider of "significant others," later on "significant others" come from multiple social groups. Clearly, the influence of those closer to us during childhood tends to persist and have a relatively stronger mark in our lives than "significant others" that appear later on. Thus, the transmission of culture has the advantage of being part of that early experience and being associated with "significant others" who are generally held in high regard for a lifetime.

The key issue emphasized in this section is that the identity of Latinos is likely to be influenced by multiple sources. Although the main source of influence is generally the one in which the individual was socialized from childhood, there are other sources that need to be known. Understanding the reference groups that form the identity of specific Hispanic segments is crucial for effective Hispanic segmentation and targeting. For example, what was the motivation of a person for immigrating to the US? Was it to be like those Americans he or she had seen on TV? Or was the motivation to earn some money and return to his or her most important reference group of his or her native social milieu?

Understanding the complexity of reference groups that Hispanics have in mind when looking forward to their next stage in life can be most important. Their decisions are likely to be influenced by the synergies of the confluence of several and important reference groups that may not necessarily be in agreement. As mass marketing gives way to individualized marketing the aspirations and reference groups of Hispanics will need to become more salient in marketing planning. While in mass marketing one has needed to find common denominators, even if somewhat crude, in individualized marketing consumers' behavior, values, and affiliations need to become more precise for the marketer to stay relevant.

In the ORCI–HONDA Case Study at the end of this chapter ORCI and Honda set out to identify through both quantitative and ethnographic research, the younger Latino target for their Honda Civic brand. They discovered an upbeat, full-of-life and confident largely bilingual and bicultural segment which moved between two worlds, the Hispanic and the non-Hispanic mainstream, in their daily lives.

The reference groups which influenced their choices for the Honda Civic came both from their Latino heritage and from their positive experiences as young Latinos in the everyday life of this country. ORCI realized that the Honda Civic cool image from these Latinos' countries of origin and the cool factor of being young and Latino in the US created a powerful combination for their brand. From this amalgamation of cultural identities ORCI developed Honda Civic's "we are driving the future" positioning and their "Guateber" TV advertising.

Shared icons are one of the threads which hold the fabric of a culture together. If members of a culture generally laugh, cry, mourn, and detest various stimuli, they share a common identity as part of that culture. Take the example of the Energizer Bunny® in the Grupo Gallegos–*Energizer*® Case Study, at the end of this chapter. The Energizer Bunny® is an iconic symbol for most Americans from the time they are children; it makes us laugh and connects us immediately to the Energizer brand. However, *El Conejo de Energizer* has not had that iconic status with Latinos. The challenge for the brand and its agency, Grupo Gallegos, was to make that connection between the Energizer Bunny® and Latinos.

Grupo Gallegos selected music, already a strong cultural bond for Latinos, and linked it to the Energizer Bunny® as the fastest route to a high level connection. They used three of the most popular Latino artists recording the longest-lasting songs of their careers—long-lasting like the Energizer Bunny®—in their Pop Goes The Energizer Bunny®, Latin-style campaign. The campaign was successful in increasing brand and specific product awareness, purchase consideration, and preference.

PREDICTABILITY IS CENTRAL TO MARKETING

Those attempting to communicate with Hispanics, including marketers, advertisers, and the media, need to assume stability and predictability in looking at consumer behavior. The assumption of behavioral consistency over time has been necessary for marketing planning to be consistent with traditional marketing practices. In this vein, it has been assumed that the cultural identity of Hispanics is relatively stable and that Hispanics use the people of their own culture as their main reference group in most situations. This is justifiable in the sense that one's culture of origin should have primacy or dominance in many situations.

Still, the empirical question of cultural reference groups is crucial as is the case with most consumer behavior. Even within the realm of Hispanic reference groups the consumer may have different subsets as reference groups. Recent immigrants from Mexico, for example, may have reference groups that are more specific than just Hispanic. For example, the new immigrant may be thinking about how his peers and siblings would approach a purchase situation, even though those peers and siblings may still be in Mexico.

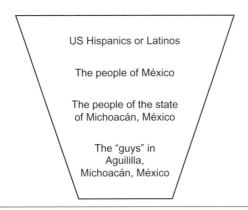

Figure 3.2 Reference group ladder example.

It is common for marketers to ask the question about what kind of models they should put in their commercials; that is, models that Hispanic consumers can identify with. The answer can vary from very specific to very general. The accuracy of a communication effort is likely to increase with a more accurate understanding of the reference groups Latino consumers have in mind when making decisions. An example of a specific reference group ladder in ascending order of abstraction is presented in Figure 3.2.

The marketer can derive more accurate predictions and create more precisely targeted communications at the lower level of abstraction.[16] Nevertheless, it can get very expensive to target consumers at lower levels of abstraction in terms of their reference groups. Thus, a compromise level needs to be arrived at. This compromise will always be troublesome. It is almost like the dilemma between globalization and localization. What is important is that the market researchers need to consider and include in their studies the notion of reference groups. This is so the marketing decision maker can make an informed decision as to how specific or general the reference group ought to be to reach a specific target. Basically, who do you look up to when thinking about buying a new TV set?

LABELS AND IDENTITIES IN MARKETING TO HISPANICS

Questions Influence Answers

In marketing circles it has generally been accepted that the label that people use to describe themselves represents their cultural identity. This may be a necessary condition but not sufficient in the sense that someone may say they are Latino but that may not help predict their consumer behavior. On the other hand if someone we call Hispanic does not consider him- or herself Hispanic in some way, then he or she just does not belong to the classification at all.

People may indicate being Hispanics for many different reasons depending on who asks the question, where the question is being asked, and the purpose of the question. Other things being equal, if an Anglo asks a person of Mexican background what "he is," the person is likely to respond Hispanic or Latino because that is the category that more Anglos are likely to understand and relate to. The reason for using the general label, however, may be related to a desire to avoid negative stereotypes. These authors have heard multiple consumers of Mexican origin state that they answer Hispanic or Latino instead of Mexican because "they [Anglos] don't like Mexicans." Assumed prejudice is a reason for using one label instead of another, and again, that depends on who asks the question.

If the question is being asked in the context of a group of Hispanics of different national backgrounds, then the salient identity would be Cuban, Mexican, or Colombian, as opposed to the more general Hispanic. The context has inherent demand characteristics that make it relevant to use one label as opposed to another.

Further, the purpose of the question can have a strong impact on the response. If the question is for the Census then there is no choice. Hispanic or Latino is the overarching label available. If the question is asked in an application for a grant, scholarship, license, loan, and so on, then marking Hispanic or Latino is very likely because it is common knowledge that preference quotas and Federal mandates provide certain benefits to members of specific classes of persons, in this case, Hispanics/Latinos.

Marketers should be cognizant of these tendencies to avoid misunderstanding what are the reference groups likely to influence Hispanic consumer behavior. In the practice of marketing, the data should provide indications of key influentials in changing or reinforcing behavior, not on whether the consumer uses the term Hispanic or Latino.

Is There a Hispanic Essence?

In contrast with the concept of race, the issue of how to identify a Hispanic or Latino person can only be done subjectively. This means that being Hispanic or Latino is how a person feels about themselves. In fact, the person may never use the term Hispanic or Latino, but some other identification such as country of heritage or origin. The reason why marketers, politicians, and other outreach organizations may want to identify Hispanics is to simplify the task of targeting. Since Hispanic culture has unique characteristics that are widely shared among Latinos, the aggregation has strong money and time-saving equities.

Does it matter whether or not someone is "really" Hispanic? Not important at all, because this type of identity is almost totally subjective. A useful marketing question is, instead, what are salient groups with which these Latinos identify for a particular product category. In short, what is their reference group for that specific consumer instance?

The Question of Labels

Sometimes Hispanics use specific labels to describe themselves and sometimes these same labels are imposed on them. Some examples are as follows:

- The label of the country of origin such as Cuban, Puerto Rican, Mexican, Salvadoran, Argentinean, and so on
- Chicanos
- Raza
- Mexican-Americans
- Latin Americans
- Cubans
- Cuban Americans
- Hispanics
- Latinos
- New Yoricans
- Boricuas
- American

It seems that there are more varied labels for Mexicans because they have constituted the majority group of Hispanics in the US. It should be stated again that in this book the label Hispanic is used to include all people who trace their origins to a Spanish-speaking country. That does not mean that those included necessarily accept the label or that they identify with any Hispanic background at all.

If someone describes him- or herself as Mexican-American, the assumption is that the individual identifies and uses as his or her most salient reference group that which is composed of Mexicans who also feel American. When someone describes him- or herself as Chicano, we expect that the person using that label will be someone whose most salient reference group is that of people of Mexican origin who feel they are not Mexican or Americans, but who have a new identity born from those two. A Boricua is usually a person who thinks of the people of the island of Puerto Rico as their main reference group.

Different labels have different origins. Some of these labels have been born out of convenience and others out of pride. Some have emerged out of political impetus. Sometimes Hispanics describe themselves with the label of their nationality or that of their ancestors. These nationality self-descriptors seem to indicate that the individual using them feels the people of that country are his or her closest cultural reference group.

The use of labels, however, is complicated. Hispanics have been shown to use a different label depending on who asks.[17] So, for example, when an Anglo in Orange County, California, asks a Mexican something along the lines of "What are you?" or "How do you describe yourself?" the person may respond Hispanic or Latino.

When the person inquiring is also Mexican, however, the respondent may be more likely to describe him- or herself as Mexican.

For marketing purposes, it does not really matter what is the absolute label the person uses; what is important is the meaning of the label to that person. If in the preceding case, the term Hispanic and Mexican refer to the same cultural reference group, then the label is not necessarily denoting a substantive difference. If the person, on the other hand, takes great pride in being Mexican, then using the term Hispanic in marketing communications may not be emotionally effective. In many cases, however, the label should not be used at all because there is more of a risk to alienate individuals who do not feel the label is accurate or appropriate. What matters are the symbols and cultural manifestations that are used as reference when the consumer makes purchase decisions. Thus, saying that "Hispanics love product X" may actually be counterproductive, while emphasizing how product X is enjoyed by an important reference group can be very effective.

Hispanic or Latino?

The term Hispanic, as used in the US these days, traces its roots to the US Census Bureau attempt to collectively label all those people in the US who traced their origins to Spanish-speaking countries. This label was instituted in the 1970s, and was first used in the 1980 Census as a general denominator for Hispanics. The US Bureau of the Census definition of Hispanics is:

> *Hispanics or Latinos* are those people who classified themselves in one of the specific Spanish, Hispanic, or Latino categories listed on the Census 2000 questionnaire -"Mexican, Mexican Am., Chicano," "Puerto Rican", or "Cuban" -as well as those who indicate that they are "other Spanish/Hispanic/ Latino." Persons who indicated that they are "other Spanish/Hispanic/Latino" include those whose origins are from Spain, the Spanish-speaking countries of Central or South America, the Dominican Republic or people identifying themselves generally as Spanish, Spanish-American, Hispanic, Hispano, Latino, and so on.[18]

Different Latino constituencies have felt differently about this label. The more politically active segment of the Hispanic community argued and still continues to argue that this label was imposed from the outside and that it represents the roots of oppression from Spain. That is because Hispania was the name of one of the Roman provinces that now constitutes Spain.

These same politically oriented individuals, after much debate, came up with the label "Latino" as better representing the category. Still, the label is controversial because it encompasses almost anyone from a culture with Latin roots. That could be Italians, Romanians, Portuguese, French, and so on.

Despite the controversy, the term "Hispanic" enjoys a small margin of preference. According to a 2008 survey by the Pew Hispanic "36% of respondents prefer the term 'Hispanic', 21% prefer the term 'Latino' and the rest have no preference."[19] Further, according to another survey by the Pew Hispanic Center in 2006 "48% of Latino adults generally describe themselves by their country of origin first; 26% generally use the terms Latino or Hispanic first; and 24% generally call themselves American on first reference."[20]

The question of what label to use to refer to Hispanics is complicated and controversial. The answer depends on who asks the question, under what circumstances, and what is the reference for the question. Identifying the label may be much less important than understanding the cultural frame of mind and reference groups that the consumer uses when evaluating a decision.

How to Identify Latinos

Label Choice as Equivalent of Identity

When conducting research with Hispanics, one of the first chores is to identify those who fall in the category. Subjective self-identification as Hispanic or Latino has been a common way of separating samples of Hispanics from others. But from what we have seen earlier, Hispanics may identify themselves as "Hispanics" because of the person asking, the context, or the purpose of the question. This type of self-identification, however, may not necessarily reflect either the subjective or the objective meaning of the term.

Classification Based on Country of Origin/Ancestry

Another way of identifying Latinos has been to ask people to indicate what country or countries they trace their ancestry to. If they mention any Spanish-speaking country in Latin America or Spain, then they are classified as Hispanics. This is a viable option from an objective perspective. It is a relatively simple alternative that has shown to reliably classify individuals who have roots in Spanish-speaking countries. This approach does satisfy a minimum criterion of objectivity, at least from the point of view of the definition of the US Bureau of the Census. Still this does not tell us whether or not the person actually identifies culturally with that country of origin.

Identifying country or countries of ancestry can be used in combination with more subjective measures such as "how much do you feel an emotional attachment to the culture of [country of heritage]." Further, one could also use another measure such as "how much do you feel an emotional attachment to the United States." This approach then provides an objective and a subjective way of determining not only origin but degree of emotional linkage or identification. The latter two scales could then be represented in a two-dimensional space as in Figure 3.3.

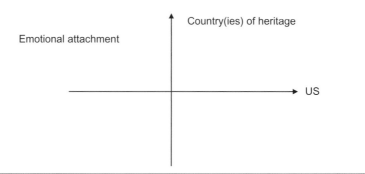

Figure 3.3 Identification by emotional attachment.

Anyone using a scale that places them in the upper part of the space can be considered to still have a minimum degree of attachment to their tradition/culture. Those who mark a scale that places them in the lower portion of the space can be considered to have abandoned their tradition in favor of US or other customs, but not Hispanic. Those people clustering in the upper right-hand quadrant, for example, are those who have strong dual emotional attachments. Those clustering in the lower left-hand quarter are those with weak emotional attachment to both country(ies) of ancestry and the US. The other two quadrants should be obvious in representing strong attachments to either heritage in one, and the US in the other. This classification scheme allows for more subjective measures of cultural identification that can assist in predicting consumer behavior with more accuracy than less discriminating dichotomous measures.

For this type of measurement the authors recommend the use of a 10-point scale in which 0 represents a complete lack of emotional attachment, and 10 represents extreme emotional attachment. No labels should be used to characterize the rest of the points in the scale so as to allow respondents to subjectively differentiate their feelings between the extremes of the scales.

Further Identity/Reference Group Measures

This book suggests that further reference group measures be used to more finely target specific groups of Hispanics. Clearly, this may pay off only when the reference group can be practically refined to achieve a more specific marketing objective. For example, when thinking about new automobiles, the marketer may benefit from knowing who the reference groups are for this category.

The following is a list of ideas for measures that can be used to better define Hispanics according to their identity. Some of the measures are behavioral or "objective" in that they ask for actual actions. The other measures are subjective and deal with identification with aspects of culture.

Objective/Behavioral Measures

- Who are the top two or three people you talk to the most about new cars these days? Please tell us their role in reference to you, for example, are they friends, relatives, coworkers, superiors at work, and neighbors. For each of them please tell us if they are of Hispanic/Latino or not.
- About what percentage of your friends these days is of Hispanic/Latino background?
- About how many hours per week do you spend communicating with people from your country of origin, who are still there?
- About how many hours per week do you spend communicating with people who are of Hispanic/Latino origin, who are now in the US?
- About how many hours per week do you spend communicating with non-Hispanics?

The first item is category and role specific to provide an overall sense of where influence is coming from. The rest of the sample measures assess the degree to which the hometown is behaviorally salient to the individual, and also how much influence is being received by other Hispanics as opposed to non-Hispanics.

Subjective Measures

- How often do you find yourself thinking about the people in your hometown in _____ (country of origin)?
- How often do you find yourself missing your hometown in _____ (country of origin)?
- How important is it for you to celebrate in the US the customs of your hometown in _____ (country of origin)?
- How important is it for you to return to your country of origin to live there once you achieve your objectives in the US?

The above questions constitute examples of items that have been used in different studies in trying to measure cultural identification and saliency of different reference groups. In the area of Hispanic-market research there are no standardized batteries with established validity and reliability, although some can be adapted from the literature in social psychology. In marketing practice the measures used tend to depend largely on the specific needs and objectives of the particular study. Nevertheless, it will be important for the field to develop more standardization than what is now available in the measurement of important concepts such as the ones handled in this chapter.

One important consideration is that while some of the measures above are described as being objective and others subjective they are all self-reports nevertheless. Self-reports are generally subject to shortcomings that include faulty recall, social desirability, and emotional interference. While for objective/behavioral measure it would be better to obtain reports from others who observe the behavior of the individual in question, it is generally difficult and expensive to do so. In addition, the above sample measures can be grouped into one or more indexes that reflect how much individuals depend on different group affiliations for their consumer decision making.

Stereotypes and Identity

Hispanics see images of themselves in media portrayals or when they are told about the stereotypes they belong to. These stereotypes whether they are evident in media programming or used in advertising convey a limited view of the complex characteristics of Latinos in the US.

Stereotypes are also held by individuals and they are talked about and discussed by both Hispanics and others in the wider population. The persistence of stereotypes which become reinforced in conversations or the media tend to impact Hispanics' perceptions of themselves as well as how they believe others see them as part of US society. This is an area in which marketers have impacted Latino identity and continue to hold influence.

STEREOTYPE STAGES

The media has been postulated to have gone through different stages in the portrayal of minorities.[21] At first the media tended to ignore minorities and made them largely invisible. As a second stage, that of ridicule, minorities tended to be portrayed as clowns and buffoons. Third, minorities have been portrayed in both sides of law enforcement, as either thieves or criminals or cops. Last, an era yet to be fully realized is that of respect, in which minorities are portrayed in diverse roles in different walks of life.

Media and other forms of social stereotyping can have important implications in generating reactions by the target, in this case Hispanic consumers.

STEREOTYPES AND THEIR IMPACT ON THE LARGER SOCIETY

One of the typical Latino reactions has been criticism and discontent with Hispanic portrayals, because of their lack of variability and depth. Hispanic consumers who have had the advantage of higher levels of formal education tend to be very critical of stereotypical representations. Many of these consumers tend to feel insulted by the popular Telenovelas, which typically cast Hispanics as rootless elites or suffering servants. Also, they tend to find programs like *Sábado Gigante* bothersome because of the ridicule to which audience members are subjected and because of the very homogeneous characterization of Hispanics as hypersexual or childish.

These are similar to the audiences that took offense to the characterization of Frito Bandito in the 1970s and contributed to its demise. These audiences felt that perpetuating the imagery of Frito Bandito would hurt the public image of Hispanics.

Negative reactions to stereotypical portrayals are not the exclusive privilege of highly educated Hispanics. Many Hispanics with lower levels of education have expressed to these authors their dismay at the cheap and caricature-like quality of many Hispanic characterizations they still find in Spanish-language advertising. When Hispanic consumers compare what they see in the relatively more sophisticated advertising in English-language media with some of the stereotypical ads they still see in Spanish-language TV, they object. These consumers object to the lower quality and refinement of Hispanic representations.

It should be noted, however, that advertising directed to Latino consumers has experienced a renaissance in the past few years. Guided by the discipline of account planning and research, as well as by an increasingly sophisticated industry, Hispanic characterizations are more varied, and have claimed a wider appeal and recognition. The stereotypical ads of a mother with children and husband who praise the qualities of products are slowly disappearing. Marketers have been learning to establish a more ample array of characterizations that help him or her to establish better and more specific links with the Hispanic consumer. These newer characterizations capture Latino consumers in their more realistic variety, as opposed to traditional stereotypes.

Also, the wide appeal that Hispanic culture has had to the overall culture over the last few years seems to support the notion that an era of respect and Hispanic diversity seems to have flourished. Content and advertising geared to Hispanics has resonated with non-Hispanic audiences. Now Latino culture has increasingly become popular and desirable. Hispanics now appear to look at their own portrayals in the media with measured optimism. Because of newer media portrayals Hispanics are beginning to be perceived as sexy, successful, and attractive. Jennifer Lopez, Christina Aguilera, Marc Anthony, Jose Leguizamo, Shakira, Santana, Ricky Martin, Gloria Estefan, and many others have become aspirational not just to Hispanics but to society at large. An era of respect may be on the near horizon.

Stereotypical characterizations can produce limited, inaccurate, and negative homogeneous views of Hispanics. Some stereotypes can also produce positive impacts on society—think of groups of people considered to be attractive, hardworking, and productive.

STEREOTYPES AND THEIR IMPACT ON HISPANICS

A self-fulfilling[22] prophecy is part of the social phenomenon[23] that stereotypes and portrayals can produce. The low self-esteem that many Hispanics have experienced over the years can be traced back to the stereotypes they have seen in the media and also to those that they have heard proffered by others. The images of short, fat, lazy, sleazy, drunken Hispanics cannot have helped Hispanics' sense of pride.

Varied representations of successful Hispanics seem to be infusing Hispanics with a renewed sense of pride. Interestingly this phenomenon is closely related to the courting of Hispanics, in which large companies have engaged. As Latinos feel courted and as they perceive their own images to be evolving for the positive, they testify to a renewed sense of vigor and cultural pride.

We seem to be at the verge of a new era in which the negative stereotypes of Hispanics are turning toward positive images, although immigration issues at the time of writing this book have in some ways impacted this trend. Increasing the positive images of Latinos will be important for the future of Hispanics and for the US society as a whole at a time when Hispanics are growing in size and the Anglo community is shrinking.

Stereotyping is not necessarily negative and not avoidable, and perhaps there is no reason for even trying to avoid stereotyping.[24] It is not the stereotypes that do harm, but prejudice and lack of awareness that stereotypes are generalizations. Generalizations can help or hurt depending on the context and how they are employed. As images in the media and in the social milieu become more diverse and positive, Hispanics are likely to hold increasingly positive auto-stereotypes.[25]

Marketers appear to be in a privileged position in this historical moment with regards to the US Hispanic market. This is a time when courting the Hispanic consumer with positive images can result in product trials and potential brand loyalty. The work of the marketer is part of the acculturation process of US Hispanics. The consumption of products and services contributes to acculturation. Interestingly, marketing approaches that positively portray Hispanics also create a reciprocal positive attitude among non-Hispanics. When non-Hispanics see attractive and appealing portrayals of Hispanics and their culture they start having reasons for coveting Hispanic culture.

Now is the time when media images and ads can profitably cross language media boundaries. It is a time when the Hispanic consumer likes to see him- or herself in both Spanish and English-language media, and also a time when non-Hispanics are more likely to enjoy Hispanic portrayals in English-language media and to be more curious about Spanish-language media images.

At the same time that Hispanics acculturate, non-Hispanics are also acquiring the Hispanic culture as a second culture. Clearly, Hispanics have more urgency to acculturate, but the process has become increasingly reciprocal. Crossover marketing opportunities can now go both ways.

Conclusions

The factors that account for what makes Hispanics "Hispanic" are multiple. Identity is a complex construct that is socially determined, thus Hispanic identity varies with the social context in which the individual interacts. During socialization children acquire long-lasting cognitive, emotional, and behavioral patterns from their initial reference group, largely their family, and these tend to persist. Nevertheless, as the individual navigates through life and interacts with numerous people both in person and virtually, reference groups and significant others multiply. These various groups are likely to have different salience in diverse decision situations.

This chapter has presented a matrix of influences which the Latino consumer brings to a situation, and the importance of taking these into account. Clearly, simplistic stereotyping of Hispanics detracts from the creation of cultural connections with Hispanic consumers. Advertising cannot assume that Hispanic consumers will only relate to other Latinos, or that portrayals in the media need to be homogeneous. These are notions that should be tested for the successful communication of the brand. It is likely that reference groups will vary by product categories.

The chapter also explored social group identification as a function of homophily (the tendency of similar people to affiliate and talk to each other) and success (looking up to others who achieve in the US), and how identity on these dimensions needs to be considered according to the marketing objective. There is a potential impact of a hierarchy of group influences across the socialization process, ranging from hometown, to particular area in the home country, to the entire country of origin, to the new country of residence. Whether a person defines the self as Hispanic, Latino, Mexican, or Puerto Rican is influenced by who is asking the question and what the respondent feels will be the best response in that situation.

As marketers seek predictability about their Hispanic target consumers, they should keep Hispanic identity constructs in mind. Who people think they are strongly impacts their emotions. To address Hispanics as they see themselves can create powerful allies for a company and its products; to address them inappropriately can sink marketing aspirations. It is essential to develop an understanding of Hispanic identity related to a marketing objective, and to use this consumer knowledge subsequently for guidance on marketing decisions.

IMPLICATIONS FOR MARKETERS

- Resist the temptation to assume that all Hispanics primarily use their country of origin belongingness group as the reference for making purchase or adoption decisions. This leads to stereotyping that could dampen consumer interest. Although closeness to one's own people may be the main influence for certain products or services, it is important to check this out with research for your particular marketing objective.
- Clarify the levels of identity that relate to your marketing objective. This means consider whether Hispanic consumers identify with their town or area of origin, their country of origin, their community in the US or their US affiliations when they make decisions regarding your product or service.

- Do not get blind-sided by labels. Thinking about Hispanic, Latino, Chicano, Mexican-American, or Colombian labels may rattle your comfort level, and that could be appropriately so. The key is to find how people themselves consider their identity; how they would prefer to be addressed either directly or strategically. Understanding this self-identification may be the key to their motivation, and the foundation for building a powerful campaign.

- Check out the combination of influences from both homophily groups and success groups in order to build a subtle campaign clearly adapted to your brand. This will aid in discovering your Hispanic target's comfort level regarding a product or service, as well as their aspirations. Reliance on homophily groups may be stronger for those who have immigrated to the US more recently, whereas a tendency toward other non-Hispanic success groups may increase as Latinos become more acculturated over time.

- Use both behavioral and subjective research questions to understand how Hispanic consumers identify themselves related to your marketing objective. It is important to listen not only to who people say they are, but how they tend to behave in identifying with particular reference groups. This takes into account that Hispanics tend to gear their identity answers to who they think is asking the question and why it is being asked and provides a behavioral basis for assessing identity.

- Keep in mind the influence of the mainstream US culture on Hispanic identity. Hispanics have constant exposure to non-Hispanic success models in the media, in the business world, at work, and in various day-to-day settings. They are also exposed to stereotypes of themselves which may blur important and culturally sensitive aspects of their identity. Although Latinos may clearly see themselves as identified with other Hispanics, they also may pick out aspects of their US identity that more directly relate to your brand.

CASE STUDY: ADRENALINA–TECATE LIGHT

Company
Heineken USA, marketer and distributor of Tecate Light

Advertising Agency
Adrenalina

Campaign Title
Tecate Light. *Por los que quieren más* (Tecate Light. For those who want more)

Intended Hispanic Consumers
Mexican-born males who have lived in the US for less than 10 years

Background
Mexican consumers come to the US from a country that embodies flavor, yet something which seems hard to explain happens when they arrive here: they start drinking

domestic light beers. Yet their cultural preference for distinctive tastes just does not seem to fit this pattern.

When Adrenalina was awarded the advertising business for Tecate Light in 2007, the brand previously had struggled to gain sizeable traction in the US, despite its status in Mexico as the No. 1 light beer manufactured by Cervecería Cuauhtémoc Moctezuma (CCM), Monterrey, Mexico. The brewery is a subsidiary of Heineken International following an acquisition announced in January 2010.

For Adrenalina, the strategic and creative communication challenge was to connect Tecate Light on a cultural and emotional level, differentiate itself with consumers, and to break through the already crowded market of domestic light beers dominating more than 50% of beer consumption in the US.

Research
Tecate Light embarked on a dual market campaign strategy in English and Spanish, eschewing the conventional wisdom that all marketing created for US Hispanic consumers must be devised only in Spanish.

Ethnographies in Houston and Los Angeles at the homes of the dual target consumers revealed that newcomer Mexican males often opt for light beer because of its wide availability and because it is a very American thing to do, illustrating their acceptance and adoption of an American lifestyle. Additionally, the agency was able to glean a better understanding for such things as how these consumers dress, live, and acknowledge who they are.

Further study of these Mexican- and US-born male consumers of light beer showed that those with strong cultural ties to Mexico, whether they were native or US born, expected more from a light beer and favored a full-flavored cerveza. Thus, emerged the tag: *"Por los que quieren más"* ("For those who want more").

Cultural Insights
Seeking to gain stronger insights into the confounding decision by Mexican male newcomers to embrace domestic light beer soon after arriving in the US, the agency conducted interviews with target consumers, raising this no-nonsense question: "What the hell happened to you?" The insights garnered via interviews helped to reconfirm and buoy the thinking that humor is a key way to connect culturally and emotionally with the Mexican newcomer consumer. Research also indicated that the use of the recognizable scenario of the family they have left behind in Mexico, peppered with witty language and sharp comedic timing, provides messaging that clearly resonates and taps into the hearts and minds of consumers who yearn for a taste of home.

Adrenalina's research confirmed that these Mexican newcomers tend to remain tethered to Mexico, and the country's cultural influence remains powerfully engrained through their familial relationships and the strong connections with their parents.

Moreover, according to their sons' opinions learned from the research, the Mexican parents of these newcomer consumers represent the idealized tradition and history of Mexico, where mothers and fathers expect their sons to be hardworking men of character who are committed to establishing and building a strong life. These are the Mexican parents who worry their sons will fall prey to the negative trappings of American life.

As described by their sons, these are Mexican parents who do not want them to adopt American culture so strongly that they forget and abandon their roots and the aspirations instilled in them at home. These parents would not want the family name

(Continued)

disparaged—and would consider themselves failures as parents—if their sons were to develop a reputation for living a flavorless life in the US, or anything short of the lives they would have been raised to lead in Mexico. The one thing these well-intentioned parents would find entirely unacceptable, in their sons' estimation, would be for their sons to adopt bad American habits like drinking watered-down domestic light beer.

Expression of Insights in the Campaign

The TV spots are set in the living room of an unassuming Mexican mom and dad, the *"Papás."* The parents of the newcomer target are perched on the couch and talking to the camera. The intent of the creative execution is to establish an emotional connection with the target even though he appears in the TV spot only in a photo. These young Mexican males, recently immigrated to the US, connect culturally and emotionally to the image of the parents' son. This is because they see themselves in the photo being thrust into the camera, Adrenalina contends.

The TV spot begins just as the *"Papás"* receive a picture of their son drinking watered-down American light beer, immediately they question what they did wrong in raising him. Dad says "He didn't learn it from me!" and mom says, "It's all my fault, I made him drink water as a child."

The light-hearted chiding the parents deliver allows the Tecate Light brand to connect with the newcomer by asserting that the son they raised, who they are so proud of, would never, ever, drink American light beer because it lacks the real cerveza flavor that only Tecate Light embodies.

In the evolution of the *"Papás"* campaign, we see the same mom and dad, in the very same living room, continuing to lecture their son on the pitfalls of drinking American light beer.

In another spot, dad tries to convey the difference between Tecate Light and American light beers, comparing a jalapeño with a bell pepper. Mom closes the spot by watering a potted plant with American light beer saying, "And with light beer, you can water the plants."

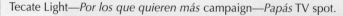

Tecate Light—*Por los que quieren más* campaign—*Papás* TV spot.

In another spot, dad lectures his son about his domestic light beer consumption. He warns him that it is the first step down a slippery slope. "What's next?" he asks: "A piña colada and cantaloupe margaritas?!"

Effects of the Campaign

The *"Papás"* campaign has elevated the comedic Mexican parents as icons for the brand, entrenching Tecate Light's presence as a flavorful light beer for those who want more, according to the Adrenalina; and increasing sales 14% per the 2009 earnings statement for Heineken USA's Dutch parent Heineken NV, a change which the agency believes may be attributable to the campaign.

Additionally, the *"Papás"* campaign has garnered recognition for creativity and innovation from the advertising industry for its insightful and humorous approach, winning two 2009 Advertising Age Hispanic Creative Awards: a gold for best campaign, considered the most prestigious in the TV category, and a silver in the TV category for a sister ad, Tecate Light's *"Papás Medias de Seda"* (*"Papás* Silk Stockings") spot.

CASE STUDY: ORCI–HONDA

Company/Organization
Honda

Advertising Agency
ORCI

Campaign/Advertising Title
Defining a New Generation of Hispanic Car Buyers

Intended Hispanic Consumers
The target for this campaign consisted of young Latino consumers, ages 18–24. Unlike general market consumers whose primary motivation to buy a vehicle from the compact segment is price, Honda Latino consumers within this target segment tend to be young and eager to be seen in a new Civic, according to brand research. The badge value of the Honda brand is strong, almost aspirational, back home in their Latin American countries of origin, and Civic generally carries a certain "cool factor." This is a group, according to the agency, that wants to buy this car; they did not make the choice because they "had to."

Background
In the Fall of 2008, the outlook on the US economy appeared bleak with little on the horizon offering hope for a speedy recovery. Latinos were hit particularly hard by the recession with unemployment reaching 7% and climbing. Subprime borrowers, common among Latino homebuyers, were reportedly devastated as the market bottomed out. The country entered the worst recession in almost 70 years, and it was in this landscape that Honda was preparing to launch the all new 2009 Honda Civic.

Automotive sales in the compact segment were down 8% verses previous year, following years of continuous growth. Toyota was leading the category with the Corolla,

(Continued)

while Ford and Nissan were investing significantly to market the Focus and Sentra respectively.

The compact segment was for the most part targeting entry-level buyers with the intent of building long-term owner prospects for brands overall. The data indicating that the older end of their consumer base was beginning to leave the category. There was little differentiation in the way automakers were communicating to consumers—everything was about price and fuel efficiency.

In this scenario the agency recognized the advantage of being Honda—price and fuel efficiency are in Honda's DNA. When consumers think Honda according to their research, these characteristics come to mind first—especially for the Civic. ORCI's challenge was to identify an insight that would allow them to emotionally connect with consumers to make the 2009 Honda Civic more than just an affordable, fuel efficient compact vehicle.

Discovery Process/Research

In order to learn more about this Hispanic target both demographically and psychographically, ORCI conducted a series of primary and secondary research efforts. They felt it was imperative to speak directly to this consumer in their environment. The agency embarked on ethnographic studies in key Hispanic markets in Texas, California, and Florida. This allowed them to understand the full spectrum of Latinos from coast to coast including the differences and similarities derived from heritage. Focus groups were used to further refine and test concepts. Secondary research included Simmons, Iconoculture, Scarborough, and Polk Data.

Cultural Insights

Research Indicated the Following Scenarios

Living Their Best Moment   The agency discovered that young Latinos, more so than their non-Hispanic counterparts, were in a "magnificent" transitional life stage and having the best time ever. This was not limited to any specific area of their lives. They were for the most part on top of their game in these aspects—education, career, relationships, and family. Additionally, they felt that it was a great time to be Latino in the US. According to the research, they smiled as they heard Spanish everywhere they went … they laughed as they saw lines of non-Hispanics waiting to take salsa classes … they puffed their chests with pride as they listened to the experts declare that Hispanics will elect the next President of the US.

Things Are Bad?   Young Latinos according to these research studies had heard talk about the horrible economy, unemployment, foreclosures and the stock market crashing … it did not seem to slow them down. Those in this research were new college graduates with employers knocking on their doors in need of bilingual candidates; they were preparing to become homeowners and saw an opportunity in the reduced home prices; and they were less likely to have invested in the stock market so they had not been part of the crash. Also, no matter how bad things became, they felt that things were most likely worse back home in their opinions. Their parents came to the US to provide better opportunities, and they were taking full advantage. They saw young Latinos in the spotlight as role models in business, entertainment, and athletics, and took the message to heart that they can accomplish anything they want to. In fact, they were already doing it. They were much further ahead of their parents at this age and felt they had much more ahead of them if they continued to make the right choices and work hard. All in all they felt that things were good.

Both Worlds The agency's conclusion from the time spent with these consumers was that they seemed to be living seamlessly between two worlds: mainstream USA and the Latino environment. They generally spoke English and Spanish every day, and often in the same conversation. They had favorite teams in both Futbol and Football. They would eat dinner with friends at a trendy Asian fusion restaurant downtown and wake up to a breakfast of huevos and chilaquiles in the kitchen with their parents. They mentioned they get their morning news from Fox News Channel and in the evening they tune into Noticiero Univision. The most important part the agency felt is that they seem to do it seamlessly and do not notice nor differentiate between these everyday experiences … it is for the most part how they live and it seems to be very different from Latinos before them. As a result of this research process the agency decided to name them, "Generation Hoy." This is a profile of young Latinos who take advantage of the opportunities they have in mainstream USA without forgetting where they came from—they appear to be grounded in their culture and heritage through their family and friends.

Latino First The trends below provide a snapshot of the mindset of "Generation Hoy"—a generation where there does not seem to be a sole emphasis on being Mexican, Puerto Rican, Argentinean, or Colombian:

- "La Voz"—a unified Latino voice; a community coming together to more effectively take advantage of available opportunities.
- "Pan-Latino"—an umbrella identity that makes a larger impact culturally, socially, and politically.
- "Power in numbers"—as demonstrated by current political results. Hispanics will collectively exert influence on the future of this country.

The Agency's Conclusion ORCI's analysis of this consumer led them to their answer to the question, "Why do young Latinos love Honda Civics?" Their conclusion—The Honda Civic is a true representation of "Generation Hoy."

These young consumers are: Innovators, Leaders, Technologically advanced, Smart, Stylish, Fun. These are all tremendous qualities and when combined they seem to be an exceptional description for anyone or anything.

Positioning The agency concluded that Honda Civic was a brand built on success, leadership, and innovation that was targeting consumers, leading the way and inspiring others with no hesitation. Both consumer and brand were part of a world going through a period of economic uncertainty with political power about to shift. The intersection of brand and consumer in the current marketplace led the ORCI to a positioning of: "We are driving the future."

Expression of Insights in the Campaign

ORCI's positioning "We are driving the future" was created to convey the spirit of the consumer and the reality of the Honda Civic's brand image. This message and accompanying tonality were used to develop the TV ad titled, "Guateber" (Whatever). In this Spanish-language ad which was shown on Spanish-language TV, the agency summarized their learnings and key insights through a portrayal of the consumers' attitude toward life. The agency exemplified this attitude through a simple phrase, "Guateber" (Whatever). The phrase captures the bilingual world in which this target lives. It also portrays their "Guateber" (Whatever) approach to life, not because these consumers do not care but because they care a ton, and as a result they are prepared for whatever comes their way.

(Continued)

Honda—Defining a New Generation of Car Buyers campaign—Guateber TV spot.

Effect of the Campaign
- Civic Hispanic Sales increased 4%[26] in the target markets during the first month of the campaign (non-Hispanic sales were down).
  - All other models in segment decreased (Corolla 17%).
  - Texas markets Civic Hispanic sales + 34%.
- Strategy was embraced by ORCI's media partners. They developed on-air elements to support the advertising. One network allowed ORCI to take over one of their series to create a Honda Civic "Guateber" version of the program for 13 weeks.

CASE STUDY: GRUPO GALLEGOS–*ENERGIZER*®

Company/Organization
Energizer Holdings, Inc.

Hispanic Agency
Grupo Gallegos

Campaign/Advertising Title
Pop Goes The Energizer Bunny®, Latin-style

Intended Hispanic Consumers
Young Hispanic families with kids

Background
Can the Energizer Bunny® translate? (That is, to the Hispanic market.) Grupo Gallegos realized that was a question that, like the Energizer Bunny® himself, just would not stop.

Twenty years of advertising had made the Energizer Bunny® a pop-culture icon, a metaphor for "long-lasting". In a category like batteries, such recognition has given Energizer a huge edge. But not with everyone.

Among Hispanic consumers, *El Conejo de Energizer* had not attained the iconic status he has long enjoyed in the general market. To Hispanics, *Energizer*® was just another battery. *Energizer*® wanted to change that, and they did not want to take another 20 years to do it.

Charged with finding a way to make the Energizer Bunny® a Hispanic-market icon in a short time, Grupo Gallegos resorted to one area of culture where overnight successes happen often: music.

Clearly, according to the agency, traditional advertising alone would not get the job done. They needed a shortcut, a brand lightning strike that would connect *Energizer*® and the Energizer Bunny® to consumers' lives. The intention was to make the Energizer Bunny® into a Latin Pop Star.

Exploiting the core consumer's phenomenal appetite for Spanish-language pop music, the Energizer Bunny® was partnered with three of the genre's hottest artists. Inspired by his example, the bands wanted to create the longest-lasting songs of their careers. And, according to Grupo Gallegos, that made for a cultural sensation, with *Energizer*® at the center of it.

Discovery Process/Research
Using syndicated studies and proprietary data, the agency segmented the Hispanic market and narrowed the focus down to a group of consumers who had two crucial attributes, one behavioral and one attitudinal. They were heavy-duty consumers of batteries, and they were also psychologically receptive to the *Energizer*® brand's fun and irreverent personality.

As the agency dug further into their lifestyle, they found the breakthrough insight, right at the bull's-eye where heavy battery use and fun intersect.

These core consumers were passionate about music. They listened to it daily at many different times throughout the day: in the morning, while working, when exercising, with friends ....

And it does not hurt, of course, that some of the devices playing all that music were running on batteries.

Cultural Insights/An Insight of Note (Actually, Lots of Notes)
With the newfound insight that music could be the most powerful way to bring the Energizer Bunny® into consumers' lives, the agency laid out the approach: bring the irreverence of the Energizer Bunny® and the concept of "long-lasting" into consumers' lives by using something they are totally engaged with, music.

The goal was to have music communicate the brand idea and make the core message relevant to the consumer segment. Music would connect the brand directly to the consumer, and advertising being just the icing on the cake ... something that makes consumers reach out to *Energizer*® ... not the other way around.

With that, the briefing conducted by the agency quickly morphed into a creative jam session.

"How about the longest song in the world?" someone offered. Blank stares.

"Okay, so how about the longest solo in the world?" another suggested. Glass.

(Continued)

Finally one of the creatives asked what CD was playing.

"Camila," someone said.

"So," the creative guy said, "what if we take the TV budget, pay Camila to record the longest song of his career, and give it away for free?"

Every face in the room lit up. Within minutes, the planning team led creatives and media people to map out the whole campaign: Take three of the hottest artists in Latin music, have them "get together with the Energizer Bunny®" and create their longest songs ever—songs exclusive to *Energizer®*—and offer them as free downloads to feed the fans' insatiable appetite for new products from their favorite artists. The agency would build a microsite as the one place to download the music, and would use advertising to drive traffic to the site.

Expression of the Insight in the Campaign

The three artists they would go after were identified. Within weeks the three bands were in the studio to record the longest songs of their careers.

The songs were not *Energizer®* jingles; they did not mention batteries, electronics, or the brand name. Thematically, however, all three songs were closely linked to brand's core essence: long-lasting power. Elvis Crespo recorded "Don't Stop" (total running time—6:16), Conjunto Primavera created "Everlasting Love" (5:19), and Camila recorded "Eternal Love" (6:00).

Meanwhile production was underway on the microsite, Energizer.com/SigueYSigue (Spanish for *Keep Going®*), and on TV commercials that asked the provocative question, "What happens when your favorite band gets together with the Energizer Bunny®?"

The campaign started working before the site even launched and the advertising broke, and as suspected, the sheer magnitude of the artists' star power ignited the PR effort that multiplied the effectiveness of the effort. News outlets appeared to explode with the news. The agency found that blogs seemingly throughout the Spanish-speaking world were atwitter with speculation about the songs to come.

Effect of the Campaign

- Within 60 days results had surpassed the annual goal of 200,000 unique visitors to the microsite, the only place where the songs could be downloaded.
- Blogs monitored across the Web posted links to the site.
- Radio stations in many Spanish-speaking countries including South America directed listeners to the site.
- Consumers created, on their own, more than 40 cover videos of the songs and posted them on YouTube, where they were watched over 70,000 times.
- The artists' MySpace pages reported on the *Energizer®* recording deals and included links to the videos and TV spots, garnering another 235,000 views.

The effort also included "guest appearances" of the artists and the songs. The artists appeared to embrace the tongue-in-cheek spirit of the campaign, appearing on the top-rated music shows in the Hispanic market to perform their songs and give interviewers the inside story of the influence of the Energizer Bunny® on their music. In some cases, entire shows were dedicated to *Energizer®* and to the artists' long songs.

An independent study corroborated the campaign's power. From October 2007 to September 2008 the campaign registered:

- 44% increase in total brand awareness for the *Energizer® Ultimate Lithium* product.

Pop Goes The Energizer Bunny®, Latin-style campaign—Camila star power.

- 88% increase in future purchase consideration for the *Energizer® Ultimate Lithium* product.
- 150% increase in brand preference for the *Energizer® Ultimate Lithium* product. During the same period, increases for overall *Energizer®* brand were also seen:
- 12% increase in total brand awareness for *Energizer®*.
- 29% increase in future purchase consideration for *Energizer®*.
- 107% increase in brand preference for *Energizer®*.

And the Energizer Bunny®? According to Grupo Gallegos he was on his way to attaining iconic status among Hispanics.

End Notes

[1] Theodore D. Kemper, "Reference groups, socialization and achievement." *American Sociological Review* 33(1), 1968, 31–45. http://links.jstor.org/sici?sici=0003-1224%28196802%2933%3A1%3C 31%3ARGSAA%3E2.0.CO%3B2-W

[2] Elke U. Weber and Christopher K. Hsee, "Culture and individual judgment and decision making." *Applied Psychology* 49, 2000, 32–61.

[3] Albert Bandura, *Social Learning Theory*. Englewood Cliffs, NJ: Prentice Hall, 1977.

[4] Albert Bandura, "Social-learning theory of identificatory processes." In *Handbook of Socialization Theory and Research*. David A. Goslin (ed.). New York: Rand McNally & Company, 1969, pp. 213–262. http://des.emory.edu/mfp/Bandura1969HSTR.pdf

[5] Everett M. Rogers, *Diffusion of Innovations*, 5th ed. New York: Free Press, 2003.

[6] Albert Bandura, *Aggression: A Social Learning Analysis*. Englewood Cliffs, NJ: Prentice Hall, 1973, p. 70.

[7] Ibid.

[8] 2009 Yankelovich Multicultural Marketing Study in collaboration with Burrell Communications and Felipe Korzenny, Director of the Center for Hispanic Marketing Communication at Florida State University. Chapel Hill, NC: The Futures Company, 2009.

[9] Jody M. Davies and Mary G. Frawley, *Treating the Adult Survivor of Childhood Sexual Abuse: A Psychoanalytic Perspective*. New York: BasicBooks, 1994.

[10] Philip G. Zimbardo, Ebbe B. Ebbesen, and Christina Maslach, *Influencing Attitudes and Changing Behavior: An Introduction to Method, Theory, and Applications of Social Control and Personal Power—Topics in Social Psychology*, 2nd ed. New York: Random House, 1977.

[11] Martin S. Bergmann and Milton E. Jucovy (eds), *Generations of the Holocaust*. New York: Basic Books, 1982, p. 300.

[12] As in other chapters our use of Anglo-Saxon Germanic is usually abbreviated by the referring to Anglos, for short.

[13] Peter L. Berger and Thomas Luckmann, *The Social Construction of Reality: A Treatise in the Sociology of Knowledge*. New York: Anchor Books, 1990.

[14] Deborah J. Terry and Michael A. Hogg (eds), *Attitudes, Behavior, and Social Context: The Role of Norms and Group Membership*. Mahwah, NJ: Lawrence Erlbaum Associates, 2000, p. 2.

[15] Peter L. Berger and Brigitte Berger, *Sociology: A Biographical Approach*. New York: Basic Books, 1975, p. 62.

[16] Ibid, p. 68.

[17] Generalization based on multiple qualitative observations by the authors.

[18] http://quickfacts.census.gov/qfd/meta/long_68188.htm

[19] Jeffrey Passel and Paul Taylor, "Who is Hispanic." A Report of the Pew Hispanic Center. Washington, DC, May 28, 2009, p. 4. http://pewhispanic.org/files/reports/111.pdf

[20] Ibid.

[21] Bradley S. Greenberg and Jeffrey E. Brand, "10 minorities and the mass media; 1970s to 1990s." In *Media Effects Advances in Theory and Research*. Jennings Bryant and Dolf Zillmann (eds). Hillsdale, NY: Lawrence Erlbaum Associates, 1994, pp. 273–309.

[22] Also called the Pygmalion effect.

[23] James L. Hilton and William Von Hippel, "Stereotypes." *Annual Review of Psychology* 47, 1996, 237–271.

[24] Yueh-Ting Lee, Lee J. Jussim, and Clark R. Mccauley (eds), *Toward Appreciating Group Differences*. Washington, DC: American Psychological Association, 1995, p. 3.

[25] J.W. Berry. "A psychology of immigration." *Journal of Social Issues* 57(3), 2001.

[26] R.L. Polk.

Chapter 4

LANGUAGE CONSIDERATIONS IN MARKETING TO US HISPANICS

Language and Culture Overlap

Many marketers and advertising executives still talk about language and culture as if they were two separate entities, as if one could exist independent of the other. Many educational institutions teach language as if it were an isolated code—as if by learning words and syntax rules one would be able to put together any possible thought into the empty vessel that language is supposed to represent. Almost as if a language were just something to be practiced and learned in a vacuum.

Language, however, is not an empty vessel and it does not live in a vacuum. For example, Esperanto, the supposedly ideal universal language, has not become popular among peoples of different countries because this language is disconnected from its social context. As humans evolved into what we are now over millions of years, we use sounds along with pointers and objects to share experience. Human experience and language are not separate from each other. They are fundamentally connected at the most intuitive level. It is the presence of language that makes the transmission and survival of human cultures possible.

The connection between language and culture is similar to the way in which memory and emotion are linked. People are more likely to recall experiences that have some emotional value to them. In a parallel way, language gets shaped and

113

acquires rich meaning as humans associate experiences with words, sentences, poems, books, and so on.

Language has been hypothesized to be an innate ability of humans. Sociolinguist Noam Chomsky[1] coherently argues that humans can distinguish acceptable word sequences from nonacceptable ones with little or no formal learning. Humans may have a universal capacity for language, but the specific words and content of the language are not universal as the experience of human groups in different geographies and conditions varies substantially.

Languages are made of words and syntax. The syntax is the set of rules for assembling words, or the lexicon in a language. Words are the product of experience. Words may have roots that can be traced to other languages. Still, words are tied to the experience of a group of people. If the referent for a word has positive connotations it is because the experience of a people with that word has been generally positive.

An example of a word that has roots in a different language but that has a specific emotional connotation for the culture that adapted it. The word *mariachi*, which refers to a musician, a band of musicians, and to a genre of Mexican music, comes from the French word for marriage or *mariage*. Allegedly, these were the musicians who played at weddings in the Mexican state of Jalisco. The French had a strong influence on Jalisco. The root of the term *mariachi*, however, has relatively little to do with the term the way it is now used by Mexicans and others who refer to that type of music or musicians. The word *mariachi* evokes strong Mexican nationalism and pride. The emotion associated with the word *mariachi* has more to do with the experience of Mexicans while listening to mariachis and mariachi music than with any reminiscence of the French influence over Mexico in the 19th century. Mariachi music evokes colorful events, great food, and music that speak loudly of the pain of love, love of the fatherland, the joy of living, and the pain of dying. The typical Mexican scream that accompanies mariachi music is a sound associated with both pain and joy simultaneously. And this is just one word. Talk about mariachis with Mexicans and the term alone is likely to evoke an emotional response.

Although there are some words in any language that are similarly enunciated and that have a similar meaning across cultures, the majority do not. An example of such similar words are the archetypical mother, mamá, ima, mutter, and so on, which all stand for the same referent "mother" and sound similar when spoken. Also, these words generally have an emotionally charged connotation that is positive. These are basic words that speak of our common human heritage and mammalian condition. Many of these almost universal words are onomatopoeias in that they resemble the sound of what they represent. In this case it is the sound of a baby drinking milk from the mother's breast.

Onomatopoeias are a useful example of the connection between language and human experience. Intuitively, we understand that these words are linked to human life. More abstract words that are not connected to their referent by similarities are also linked to experience, but the connection is less obvious and they are more culture bound. For example, certain types of worms have been a source of food and nutrition to a cultural group. *Gusanos de maguey* (or cactus worms) hold a positive connotation contained in the social experience of many Mexicans. For members of another culture the thought of eating cactus worms can be revolting. Words are not neutral universal equivalents but conveyors of shared experience. In a very powerful way words carry the meaning of the practice of a culture. A culture represents the sets of tools that a human group assembled over time in order to preserve the physical, intellectual, and spiritual integrity of its members. One of these tools is the language that this group managed to use in order to maintain cohesion, share experience, allow for coordination, enable self-defense, and preserve continuity of the group over time.

The relationships between language and culture present complexities beyond the lexicon of a language. Words are not the only carriers of cultural experience. Sentences, phrases, sayings, proverbs, poems, books, and other linguistic manifestations are associated with cultural experiences. Proverbs like *al que madruga Dios lo ayuda*[2] are difficult if not impossible to translate. This difficulty is due to the cultural experience accumulated behind the phrase. In addition, the way in which we emphasize and enunciate words can carry cultural meaning as well.

Language synthesizes the richness and texture of human interaction. A people whose culture shares a sense of fatalism use words and expressions that help suggest the experience of fatalism. In such cultures one typically hears expressions like "If God wills," because the members of that culture doubt their self-efficacy and ability to alter the course of events. But fatalism is not an arbitrary construct. Groups of people who have been subjected to much uncertainty and oppression in their history are fatalistic for a reason. Their experience taught them that they could not overcome the forces of the supernatural, and their language and expressions reflect that. Language in its diverse forms is like the container that holds or reflects the experience of people.

MARKETERS SHOULD APPROACH LANGUAGE CHOICE PRAGMATICALLY

Language is an adaptive mechanism that serves us, but in some ways also enslaves us. Our language expands horizons or limits them. Some languages are said to be better for the communication of affection and love than others. Language, then, is not the simple tool we learn in school for when we have to talk to others who use that language. Language encompasses the accumulated and collective evolution of human groups. Learning a language is more than pairing a term of a known language with a term of a new language. That is why it can be argued that marketing to Hispanics in Spanish and with an understanding of their culture can be very important in specific cases. It is important to highlight that not all Hispanics would prefer to receive and process communications in Spanish. In some cases an understanding of the culture may be more relevant and powerful than simply communicating in Spanish.

In many cases the use of the Spanish language will be important in signaling to Hispanic consumers that the brand is interested in their business. Also, the use of even just a few words in Spanish can communicate respect and help elevate the self-esteem of the Hispanic consumer because his or her ancestral language is featured. Also, the most obvious use of the Spanish language is to engage with individuals that feel more comfortable in Spanish or who have little understanding of the English language. As the dynamics of the Hispanic market in the US becomes more complex, the choice of language clearly depends on the following factors:

- The need of the consumer to be communicated in the Spanish language because otherwise the communication would not be properly understood or processed.
- The context can be very important as it would be somewhat awkward to use either Spanish or English in certain situations. For example, having an English-language ad in a telenovela[3] would be somewhat illogical as the audience for the telenovela is most likely expecting the content to be in Spanish. Clearly, the marketer ought to use his and her judgment to achieve the desired effect. In some cases, for example, placing a Spanish-language ad within English programming can attract attention and signify to the consumer a sense of his and her special importance to the brand. Just one example of this is what Vehix. com, an automobile shopping site, has done. They placed Spanish-language ads within English-language content in the Washington DC area in Spike, Nick at Nite, FX, and Sci Fi, among others. That effort was based on their research indicating that many Hispanics with English-language proficiency are watching English-language TV.[4] One of the appealing characteristics of this approach is that the ads stand out quite a bit, particularly for Hispanics. On the other hand there has usually been a backlash, even if small, from those who do not believe any language other than English should be spoken in the US. Parallel executions in entertainment content include Spanish-speaking utterances and dialogues in the ShowTime program "Weeds," in which characters communicate in Spanish occasionally and there is no translation offered. In this latter effort, the Spanish language is part of the story and also is likely to signal a sense of affiliation or identification to Hispanic consumers.
- The use of Spanish for emotional connection. With the Spanish language being so intertwined with the culture, a few expressions or words can help connect with consumers. Clearly these language expressions need to be relevant and well placed.

- The use of English with Hispanic cultural insights in order to connect with Hispanics who prefer or understand English well. As stated in Hispanic Market Weekly[5] "Dos Equis' English-language 'Most Interesting Man In the World' campaign has attracted both non-Latino and Hispanic youth and young adults through an active presence on English-language broadcast and cable television."

The use of English within Spanish advertising or programming has not been common as yet, but it is likely to be a development to watch, particularly as more and more Hispanics are becoming proficient in the English language. This use of the English language in the context of Spanish-language content has been slowed down by the lack of receptivity that Spanish-language media has had for such communications. Also, there is the somewhat justified assumption that if the consumer is watching or listening in Spanish, the advertising should be in Spanish as well.

In sum, the use of Spanish and English will likely become more intertwined with time. As the growth of the US Hispanic market is increasingly driven by births as opposed to immigration, and as educational levels of Hispanics increase, both languages will likely be used in specific ways for strategic purposes. The assumption that marketing to Hispanics is supposed to be in Spanish is not tenable anymore. That is not to say that marketing in culture, regardless of language, is still and likely will be for a long time what makes it efficient and effective to market to US Hispanics.

A NEW DIALECT OF SPANISH AND ENGLISH FOLLOWS A NEW IDENTITY

A dialect is the usage or vocabulary that is characteristic of a specific group of people.[6] As Hispanics become increasingly acculturated in the US, their use of language will likely become increasingly hybrid in casual settings and interactions. Thus, certain words in Spanish will be interspersed with English, and some English words will be adapted into the Spanish-language context. As part of the experience of Hispanics in the US, a new identity and a "way of speaking" will become more standard and accepted. This will likely happen in a parallel way to what happened to Yiddish and Hebrew words that now are somewhat standard in English parlance.

In colloquial settings Hispanics will likely use a mix of Spanish and English to better convey emotion. The experience of being Hispanic in the US will be reflected in this new dialect that has been incubated since the times of the formation of the US as a country, but recently accelerated by fast Hispanic growth. In a way, this will become the new dialect of US Hispanics. This will be a dialect that reflects what it means to be Latino in the US cultural context. The growth of this new dialect will be influenced by pragmatism, context, and pride. Later in this chapter we will address more specifically Spanglish and code-switching in more depth.

Translation Is Harder Than it Appears to Be

"Traduttore, traditore" is a popular Italian dictum stating that translation generally betrays the original. A typical question from many marketers reaching out to US Hispanics has been: "Can I just translate my English ad into Spanish?" This question seems justifiable because if the answer is affirmative, the economies of scale that could be realized through translation would be substantive.

Given this discussion of the relationship between language and culture, the immediate intuitive response is that translation is not likely to work. Even if it were to work it would not work as well as if the original communication were designed to reach the intended recipient in Spanish in the first place. It is very difficult for a translation to do justice to the original for the reason that the cultural elements in the original communication were not designed with the second culture in mind. While some simple communications may be successfully translated with little detriment to the original intention, most of the time there are substantive barriers to success.

The cultural nuances of a message originally encoded in English are generally unlikely to be replicated in Spanish. And even if replicated in Spanish, the relevance of the message is likely to suffer. If advertising is by nature an art of persuasion and psychological connection, then most translations are likely to suffer from lack of cultural relevance. Many times, depending on the translation effort, the translation can actually deform the message and sometimes alienate the consumer. An interesting and humorous example is the translation of the Mad Mariner website into "Marinero Loco" that features some stereotypical translations that are very much word by word dictionary efforts like translating Diesel Ducks into "Patos Diesel."[7] It is not that these efforts are necessarily wrong, but they are likely to have the unintended effect of alienating the very audience they are supposed to please.

Translation is an ongoing area of debate in Hispanic marketing. Regardless of how precise a translation can or should be, the results are many times not what the source of the message intended. Some of the issues follow.

Professional Translations

Federal and state governments in the US certify interpreters and translators. Those who qualify for the distinction of certification are definitely meritorious individuals. Nevertheless, even with certification, translators and interpreters bring biases to the interpretation situation. One bias is the notion that one's version of the language is the "correct" version.

A proficient interpreter or translator from almost any Spanish-speaking country in Latin America will utilize language that is technically correct. Most likely their work is worthy of the Royal Academy of the Spanish Language.[8] However, despite adherence to established language standards, intended meanings of a communication may not be conveyed and the intended audience may be baffled by the text. The problem with translations by certified translators is that they give a false peace of mind to the marketer, and lead him or her to believe they have done their communication job.

It is not that certified or uncertified translators are unqualified to do their job. The issue is that they cannot do the job because the job is not one of translation but of cultural adaptation. It is the original cultural message that counts, not the language code in which it is cast.

Further, there is an elitism implied in most professional translations. The notion of correctness creates noise between the marketer and the consumer. Only a consumer-oriented translator/interpreter could aspire to do justice to the marketing objective of the marketer. Most consumers, including Hispanic consumers, have relatively low levels of education. There is no doubt that educational levels do compound the communication problem.

The most crucial gap between the consumer and the message generated by the translator is that the intended meaning is not likely to be there. The marketer would need to thoroughly brief the translator as to the intention and objective of the communication. In addition, the translator would need to have a sense of how the audience will interpret the message. Sociolinguistic and anthropological research needs to be conducted to understand how consumers are likely to understand a message. At a minimum, marketers need to conduct focus groups or in-depth interviews with the target audience to test their communications, and ideally the translator should be listening. Without being made aware of this issue marketers are unlikely to think of it because a good translation should be "good" right? Unfortunately, most of the time "good" is not good enough from a consumer perspective. This is particularly true in cross-cultural marketing efforts because the marketer and the consumer likely come from different cultures. Even in the case when the marketer is Hispanic, he or she may come from a different social class and thus not be able to anticipate how the consumer will interpret his or her communications.

Unfortunately, there is no real solution to this paradox of translation. It is generally a losing proposition. The problem becomes more evident when thinking about communicating a message in English to Hispanics. Then, it is not the "code" *per se* that gets in the way. In this instance, it is the cultural insights that need to be evident in the message for the consumer to connect.

The idea that cultural insights can be more powerful than the use of language *per se* compounds the issue as to why it is hard for translations to work. If a translation could magically transmit the intended cultural meaning that would be ideal. Unfortunately there is no mechanism that can achieve such a feat.

Translation, Confusion, and the Reason Why

Many marketers arrive at the conclusion that they must translate all their materials to be consistent and to serve their Hispanic constituencies. Their conclusion is very understandable. They want to serve their Hispanic customers and wish to do a good job, but there are several problems in attempting this.

An overall recommendation is that, instead of translating, documents should be prepared in Spanish from scratch, if Spanish is the language that specific customers require. Further, the level of Spanish and vocabulary to be used needs to be appropriate for the Hispanic consumer that will be served. As stated earlier, translations are rarely transparent and culturally informed to connect with the consumer at the appropriate level.

If generating messages in Spanish from scratch is not possible and translations are required, then the translations must be of high quality and adapted to the specific type of consumer. Many Hispanic consumers have indicated that often they prefer to read materials in their "poor English" rather than reading a confusing and contrived translation. If the translator does not clearly understand the objective of the translation, he or she is not likely to communicate the message appropriately through translation. Here is where the translator may need to resort to "cultural adaptation" to make the message relevant. Cultural adaptation consists of understanding the intended message and then casting it into the second language as opposed to achieving a literal translation.

TRANSLATION VERIFICATION

To fully adapt the translation to the Hispanic consumer, the marketer should not stop at the translation stage, but take one further step to verify that the translation achieves the intended meaning. This is what we have called "translation verification."[9] It consists of submitting an original and its translation to a panel of literate bilingual individuals from different Hispanic countries of origin. The panel is convened in a central location and is provided with both the English- and the Spanish-language versions. Individuals are then asked to discuss and debate the translation in terms of changes that are required in order to achieve the communication objective; changes that would improve the understandability of the message; and changes that would be nice but are not necessary to achieve the intended meaning.

Translating technical materials generally is not advisable. If writing for computer scientists, IT personnel, and others who have a high level of technical expertise, translating into Spanish (and many other languages) tends to make the reading of the materials more complicated. Most of these individuals generally have been trained in English. Translations of technical terms are either very difficult or impossible.

Thus the translation winds up being an interesting version of "Spanglish" that few people, if any, could understand expeditiously. This is an extreme case, because it is assumed that the document is highly technical and the reader is very sophisticated regarding the technology in question. Many times high technology companies assume that by providing the translation they are doing a service to the reader when in fact the English version is generally more likely to be read.

SEMI-TECHNICAL TRANSLATIONS

Translating semi-technical text is very tricky and more difficult than expected. Imagine a brochure dealing with "How to obtain a home loan," or "How to open a brokerage account," or "How to use your new VOIP[10] phone." Much of the terminology either does not exist in Spanish or the consumers are very unlikely to know it. One solution frequently utilized is to place the original word in English next to the translated term. A preferred solution is to explain the "meaning" of the intended message with common terminology. This is very difficult, however, because the translator must know the marketing issue and have the intention to do justice to the message. Again, a cultural adaptation that starts off by encoding the message originally in Spanish, and that avoids technical terms, would be most desirable. Translating words such as equity or escrow into Spanish are likely to confuse many consumers, even many of those with higher levels of education. Thus, the translator that sits at his or her desk with a dictionary and restates the message in Spanish is likely to be creating a confusing and often useless message.

Then there is the issue of connotation. The term "mortgage" is one of those particularly complex terms. If translated as *hipoteca*, the consumer may be turned off, even if this term is possibly the most accurate translation. This is because the marketer, the translator, or both may not have considered the emotional charge of *hipoteca*. Here is where consumer understanding impacts translations and consumer reactions. In many parts of Latin America a *hipoteca* is a course of last resort. When someone is in dire straits they may resort to taking a *hipoteca* on their home. But that is generally seen as a negative course of action because one endangers the patrimony of one's children. Also, it means that the borrower is not doing well. Almost the opposite to what happens with Anglo consumers in the US. If they get their mortgage they are starting a prosperous life. A more positive term in Spanish would be *prestamo*, or loan. A home loan would not have the negative connotation of a mortgage. Knowledge of how language is interpreted is something that few marketers, and translators, tend to consider. It is not only that technical terms need to be cast in commonly used terms, but that emotionally charged terms need to be replaced with those that are more appropriate to achieve the goals of the communication.

What Language(s) to Communicate In?

Marketers often need to decide whether or not they need to communicate their message to US Hispanics in Spanish, English, or both. To make this decision some marketers conclude it is a good idea to conduct focus groups to find out the answer. The typical approach is to conduct groups with consumers that prefer Spanish with those that can go either way, and with those who prefer communicating in English.

The reader would expect the answer to be self-evident—those who prefer Spanish would want materials in Spanish, those who can go either way would have no preference, and those who prefer English would express a preference for English. However, things are more complicated because these consumers live in a unique social world.

In this type of research it has been most common for respondents to state they would prefer bilingual materials. And this is across all language preference groups. Hispanic consumers argue that bilingual materials are important to them for several reasons, including:

- The typical Latino Household tends to contain individuals who are Spanish dominant, bilingual, and English dominant. Thus, a bilingual piece would serve the different levels of language proficiency and preferences in the household. This is a very important and symptomatic aspect of US Hispanic households. The marketer is seldom selling to an individual but rather to a household with different levels of language skills and preferences. Further, these consumers have large extended families with which they share communications of interest. Thus, if they want to share with others, a bilingual piece is also useful.
- Those who prefer Spanish express an interest in the English translation in order to learn the vocabulary in English, and the ones who prefer English tend to be interested in refreshing or learning Spanish, and those who are bilingual like the idea of comparing. A bilingual item, then, provides a learning experience.
- And, there is an overall distrust of translations. Thus having a bilingual communication helps the consumer make sure they have a way to verify that the translation they are reading is adequate.

The use of language by Hispanics is complicated because their sociocultural environment is complex. Consumer insights are crucial for effective outreach and communication design. Language adaptation, as in the case of communicating with US Hispanics, is not a simple matter of deciding if the message should be in Spanish. It is a matter that requires thoughtful consideration of the context where the materials will be made available, for example, the home, work, and so on; and the nature of the communication, for example, technical, entertainment, and so on; and the needs and skills of the intended targets. The issue is becoming increasingly complex because many more Hispanics have become proficient in English, and many have not learned or used Spanish. Thus, the marketer may need to decide if the communication would best reach the target in English, but to demonstrate a sense of affiliation and respect may want to use some Spanish within the English context. Or, he or she may ponder if a bilingual piece is most likely to satisfy the requirements of the targeting effort? Clearly, in some cases a Spanish-language piece can be required, particularly when the target prefers Spanish and the social milieu is also Spanish speaking.

LANGUAGE AND THOUGHT

Can you think without words? Close your eyes and try to think without words. Close your eyes and try to articulate thoughts and ideas and see if you can do it without words. Some people say they can think without words but most have a hard time assembling ideas in their minds without verbal aid. In general, most humans would agree that language plays a part in their thinking even if not exclusively.

Thought and language are parallel. Thoughts are formed of words and other symbols, or representations, and these are linked by rules. That is what logic is about. That is why we can distinguish between sound thoughts and conclusions and faulty thoughts and conclusions. This is similar to the way in which we can judge if a sentence is correct or incorrect. People talk to themselves and call that process thinking. The more abstract the thinking process the more likely it is to be verbal. Words are symbols or abstractions that represent generalizations and concepts. Higher order thinking involves concepts that are difficult to cast in any other way but in language.

Edward Sapir and Benjamin Whorf, early in the 20th century, advanced the notions of linguistic determinism and relativism.[11] They argued that language determines the way people think, and that because of this determinism, members of different cultural groups would think and perceive the world relative to their language. Thus, the experience of members of different linguistic groups or cultures would be different enough so that their thinking and their way of perceiving the world would not necessarily converge, and that constitutes linguistic relativism.

Sapir and Whorf's theory has been highly controversial and widely debated. There have been tests and revisions of this theoretical approach. Still, one of the main conclusions is that even if the language we speak does not determine the way we think, the language we use does have an influence on the way in which we organize information. This would be a softer interpretation of the main tenets of the Sapir–Whorf hypothesis.

A key problem with linguistic determinism in an absolute sense is that there is no way to test the proposition that language determines thinking. That is because there is no way to observe thinking without language. The "strong" statement of the theory is considered to be a tautology like determining which came first, the chicken or the egg.

The softer version of the proposition, tested in several contexts[12], talks about how the language we speak influences what we choose, how we organize information, and what we are more likely to remember. Bruce Kodish calls this phenomenon neuro-linguistic relativity.[13]

Because of this phenomenon of neuro-linguistic relativity language must be a consideration in marketing efforts to Hispanics. Even those Hispanics who speak English fluently are likely to be influenced by the language of their home and ancestors, if they grew up with it to some extent. Certain categories of experience, emotion, and knowledge are likely to be affected by the language used by the advertiser. So it is not just whether Hispanics can understand English or not, but whether their neuro-linguistic programming will predispose them emotionally to react differently if communications are in Spanish as opposed to English. The influence of the language used does not necessarily need to extend to the entire message but perhaps to key terms, words, and expressions that will account for more basic, emotional, reactions.

WHEN TO MARKET IN SPANISH?

Even in the case of when Hispanics are fluent in English, but still hold on to some of their linguistic heritage, the use of some Spanish can be very important to establish the connection. It is not the same thing to say to someone "you are very kind" as it is to say "*usted es muy amable.*" The two expressions are equivalent in terms of translation, but not in terms of emotional value. The term "amabilidad" literally translated into English means something close "lovable," much beyond what kindness can convey in English. Telling someone he or she is "amable" conveys not just the concept but the feelings associated with it.

The images and connotations that are evoked by one language are likely to be different from those evoked by another language.[14] Many of these images are the concepts that cultures use to perpetuate themselves. The concept of fatalism, for example, can be found in the colloquial Mexican expression *valemadrismo*. This expression is not really translatable, and it is generally understood only by those who were raised in the context of a specific way of thinking. *Me vale madres*, is a vulgar expression that connotes the frustration of repeated failure and the inability to shape one's life. It is like Aesop's fable of the fox and the unripe sour grapes. The expression reflects an attitude and view of the world that is unique to a set of cultural circumstances.

In a study conducted by e-mail in 1999 on the subject of acculturation, it was found that the Spanish language provided Hispanic consumers with specific perceptions of self. The study quotes a 24-year-old Hispanic born in the US:

Spanish is my mother tongue, and it is the tongue of my mother. Spanish is still the tongue which I feel most clearly speaks from my heart. It calls out from my childhood. What I mean is that it encompasses my sense of identity by its sound and rhythm, and the fact that it is the language which I speak to my family with. It speaks not of the identity which I project in public now, but rather of my personality and sense of self since birth. When I speak in Spanish, I feel I speak from my soul.[15]

This testimonial, also mentioned in Chapter 1 regarding the nature of culture, emphasizes the emotional quality of the Spanish language for the individual. It describes how the language relates to a sense of self. Perhaps most importantly it refers to the duality of identities that this bilingual speaker relates to. Each language and hence each identity has a different domain. Language differentiates the public and the private selves. Spanish best characterizes, according to him, his private or more personal sense of self even though his English expression is excellent.

LANGUAGE AND OUR DIFFERENT SELVES

Language, Culture, and Identity

The symbols imbedded in the Spanish language conjure images, thoughts, and emotions that are different from those evoked by the English language. A large part of the difference can be accounted for by culturally accumulated experience. Karl Jung spoke of the collective unconscious, conceptualized as a repository of human experience.[16] That common experience is composed of the experiences of many groups of people over time. If the experience of humanity is accumulated in our biological heritage, then these are parts of different cultures that become salient when in a similar cultural context. A different part of oneself is awakened when interacting in a different culture.

Recent studies by David Luna, Torsten Ringberg, and Laura A. Peracchio[17] support the idea that people who are bicultural respond differently to concepts when presented in Spanish or when presented in English. Monocultural individuals who are bilingual, on the other hand, respond the same way to concepts regardless of the language in which they are presented. They found that Latinos associated femininity with self-reliance when the message was in Spanish, and with other-dependent when the message was in English. What these researchers showed is that culture influences perceptions of stimuli and ideas, and that bicultural individuals think differently depending on the language they use. In this sense the link between culture, language, and identity becomes strongly associated.

It is common to hear travelers talk about how they discover new parts of themselves when experiencing another culture and/or speaking another language. This line of reasoning explains why one language would be more or less effective in conveying images and experiences than another. That is because the aggregated part of human experience in the collective unconscious can be better evoked or made relevant within a specific language. That is the language in which the experience was learned. Perhaps that is why popular wisdom has characterized different languages as reflecting different approaches to life. Italian, French, and Spanish are said to be languages of love, whereas German and English tend be characterized as languages of work and efficiency.

Language then becomes not just a filter or an influencer of thinking and experience but part of being and behaving differently in different cultures. Advertising and marketing in Spanish, when dealing with those who prefer the Spanish language, touch realms of experience that could not be touched in English. The phrase *caminante no hay camino, se hace camino al andar*[18] evokes images of nostalgia and fatalism that can hardly be conveyed in English. Using this well-known phrase to communicate the virtues of an automobile could be highly effective. The effectiveness would come from the familiarity with the phrase. Most of the impact of the phrase, however, has to do with the cultural imagery associated with the meaning; that is, lack of clear destiny because destiny is made as one lives. This way of talking and thinking finds affinity among Hispanics. The Anglo-Saxon view of control over the environment is in sharp contrast with fatalism. Living life as we evolve with it conveys a sense of harmony with the universe, not of dominance.

In simple (but transcendental) phrases like *caminante, no hay camino, se hace camino al andar*, cultures encode their archetypes and communicate them to other members of the culture. This is an important way in which language influences the way in which the marketer and the communicator can establish relationships that go beyond the surface.

These pieces of cultural thought reflected in sentences are like memes.[19] Memes are ideas or pieces of knowledge that for different reasons spread through societies and become part of them. They are basic units of cultural continuation and reproduction.[20] Some ideas find better receptivity in certain cultures because they are compatible with existing beliefs and they evoke emotional reactions that favor their diffusion.

Advertising, marketing, and communication across cultures largely depend on their ability to reach out and conjure in the minds of recipients the images intended. To do this, the symbols must find resonance among customers. These symbols that replicate themselves are memes.[21] And they are heavily dependent on language, much like poetry depends on the language in which it is cast for its appeal.

The Cultural Importance of the Spanish Language

Some evidence supporting the importance of the Spanish language to Hispanics can be found in the national study of Hispanics conducted in the context of the

Yankelovich's *MONITOR® Multicultural Marketing Study* of 2009. In that study Hispanics were asked to Strongly Disagree, Disagree, Agree, or Strongly Agree with the statement "The Spanish language is more important to me today than it was just five years ago." Among those who indicated preferring Spanish for communication in every situation the percentage agreeing or strongly agreeing was 69%. Among those preferring English the percentage was 68%, and for those who said they had no preference the percentage was 67%. Despite language preferences this national sample of individuals 16 years of age and older reported the increasing importance of the Spanish language in their lives. In the same study, when Hispanics were given the same scale as above to agree or disagree with "I appreciate it when businesses communicate with Hispanics in Spanish" the percentages agreeing or strongly agreeing were even higher than above. A total of 97% of those preferring Spanish in every situation agreed with the statement strongly or very strongly, and even 83% those preferring English similarly agreed. A 93% of those with no preference also agreed or strongly agreed. These results are pretty overwhelming in support of the importance of the Spanish language regardless of language preference. Still, these are self-reports and they do not provide direct evidence regarding effectiveness.

Nevertheless, these findings serve as partial substantiation of the claims made here. According to these findings, the Spanish language is appreciated even by those who are able to comprehend the message in English. The marketer who takes the trouble to understand the Hispanic consumer and to identify the memes and archetypes that best connect with him or her will be most effective. Language plays an integral part in this effectiveness. In many cases the Spanish language will be effective, particularly for those cases in which language and cultural experience are strongly linked.

In a related vein, advertisers should note the language that they use in their communications will likely be interpreted differently by bicultural individuals depending on the language being used. The meanings associated with words and concepts will likely be processed differentially depending on the language used given different cultural meanings. This issue will be further discussed below.

When to Target in Spanish

One of the reasons for reaching out to those Hispanics who either depend on or prefer the Spanish language is that many of them tend to be geographically concentrated in neighborhoods. The notion of the *barrio* or neighborhood where Hispanics concentrate is common and newcomers find in these neighborhoods a feeling of comfort, like a home away from home. They tend to concentrate in specific areas where the language and consumer environment is favorable to their needs and meets their expectations. Also, the largest concentrations tend to exist in specific states, even though we have seen a tendency toward dispersion earlier in the book. Latinos have traditionally concentrated in urban areas and in a few states, and these are the states with the largest concentration of households who are linguistically isolated in Spanish according to the 2009 American Community Survey of the US Census Bureau.[22] Linguistically isolated households are those where there is no person aged 14 years or over who speaks *only* English and where no person aged 14 years or over speaks a language other than English speaks English "Very Well." Table 4.1 shows that the US states with the largest Hispanic concentrations have substantive segments of linguistically isolated people who speak Spanish at home.

Based on 1-year estimates of the American Community Survey 2009, approximately 70% of Hispanics speak Spanish at home. Also, estimates from the 2009 American Community Survey show that about 54% of those who speak Spanish also speak English "Very Well" or "Well." And that approximately 77% of all Hispanics speak only English or speak it "Well" or "Very Well." This suggests that there are important pockets of US Hispanics who can still be profitably targeted only in Spanish. It also suggests that growing numbers are becoming increasingly proficient in English and that language strategies will become more important as bilingualism becomes prevalent.

The Health Information website—Florida Saludable Case Study, at the end of this chapter, describes a Spanish-language health information website for Florida Hispanics. This largest health-care provider in the State of Florida with a Spanish-speaking population across the state of approximately 20% (see Table 4.1) provides online health information in the Spanish language as well as in culturally

TABLE 4.1 States with Largest Hispanic Population and Linguistic Isolation

State	Hispanic Population	% Hispanic	% of Households Linguistically Isolated
CA	14,342,000	39	26
TX	9,952,000	40	26
FL	3,956,000	21	30
NY	3,247,000	17	29
AZ	2,100,000	32	22
IL	1,694,000	13	26
NJ	1,671,000	19	29
CO	923,000	19	26
GA	838,000	9	32
NM	809,000	16	15

relevant ways, to inspire the trust of Latino consumers and to attract and keep them as members. Their aim is to reach out to the numerous Floridians who either depend on Spanish or prefer to receive information in Spanish even if they do speak English.

The meaning of health is particularly bound to a person's native culture. Health care is an area in which language and cultural experience are linked on a basic survival level. Ways of taking care of one's own health and the health of the family are learned early in life, and for Latinos are tied closely to the Spanish language and their Hispanic heritage. The Florida Saludable Case Study illustrates how the largest health-care provider in Florida supports critical information needs of Spanish-speaking Latinos, and demonstrates commitment to the Latino community through culturally informed content.

Consumers that communicate in Spanish share many perspectives on life and the products they need. They are easy to target in Spanish because they are exposed to Spanish-language media more than to English-language media. Spanish-media outlets generally have been less complex and less expensive to purchase than English-language media. Thus geographic concentration and highly targeted and relatively inexpensive-media channels make for a very good marketing "deal."

According to the Advertising Age 2009 Hispanic Fact Pack with data from HispanTelligence, the research arm of Hispanic Business, total national Hispanic media ad spending in 2008 was over 4 trillion dollars. Also, from the same publication, expenditures by giant consumer products company Procter & Gamble on Hispanic media were of almost 200 million dollars (data from TNS Media Intelligence). Clearly, as these numbers suggest, there is still a strong case for targeting specific groups of Latinos in Spanish. Because of the need or preference of Latino consumers, and/or because of the emotional link that the Spanish language provides to the culture for them, targeting Hispanics in Spanish may serve to build a brand relationship.

In the Emerson—Blue Selecto Case Study at the end of this chapter, Emerson initiated the use of Spanish in the prompts of its programmable Blue Selecto Thermostat intended for the Spanish-speaking or bilingual Hispanic homeowner. It launched Spanish–English bilingual advertising for this innovation which was targeted toward Hispanic contractors who sold to Hispanic homeowners. The company conducted qualitative research with the intended audiences, but decided against quantitative in order to keep their product confidential and be first to market. In the process of this launch they learned a lot about their company's readiness for this market, and reaped the benefits of unintended consequences for their initiative. While product sales did not escalate as quickly as they expected, Blue Selecto Thermostat in Spanish spawned growth in sales to Latin America, increased sales and loyalty of US Hispanic contractors, and moved the company into new online and social marketing areas.

The Increasing Case for English

The reader should consider that as the experience of Hispanics in the US is increasingly in English or bilingual/bicultural, the effectiveness of English in connecting with these consumers is likely to increase over time. The fact that the Spanish language has emotional value for even those Hispanics who are fluent in English does not mean that the effectiveness of Spanish is or will be universal.

The logic is parallel to that of the Spanish language as a cultural experience. As Hispanics increasingly experience their lives in English or a mixture of English and Spanish, the English language or dialectical adaptations thereof will consolidate as powerful communication tools. Consider the language spoken at home by the ability to speak English 2009 estimates according to the American Community Survey of the US Bureau of the Census shown in Table 4.2.[23]

Based on these estimates, the percentage of US Latinos that speak English only, "well" and "very well," according to their own reports is 77%.[24] Further, 63%[25] indicate they speak only English or speak it "very well." Thus English is becoming prevalent among US Hispanics. While these estimates are likely to contain errors inherent in the type of data they come from, the main concern will continue to be the willingness of undocumented Hispanics to answer these questions. Still, regardless of a likely undercount of undocumented, the figures are highly revealing of the evolution of language among US Latinos. In addition, 84% of Hispanics agree or strongly agree that "all immigrants should learn English if they plan to stay in this country," according to the 2009 Yankelovich's *MONITOR® Multicultural Marketing Study*.

The reader should consider, however, that when we talk about the English language, we are talking about a specific experience of Hispanics living in an English-language environment. Since language is not an isolated code, the new identity, and the new cultural experience constitute the culture of Hispanics developing a way of living that integrates the English language. Consider that according to the same 2009 Yankelovich's *MONITOR® Multicultural Marketing Study*, 97% of Hispanics

TABLE 4.2 Language Spoken at Home by Ability to Speak English and Spanish

Speak only English	10,218,938	24%	
Speak Spanish at home and:	32,538,981	76%	Of these 76%
Speak English "very well"	16,880,836		52%
Speak English "well"	6,099,733		19%
Speak English "not well"	6,111,727		14%
Speak English "not at all"	3,446,685		8%

agree or strongly agree with the statement "I feel very proud of my Hispanic American background." Because of this complex identity, understanding the emerging culture of Hispanics in their new cultural environment will be crucial in order to connect with them. It would be a mistake to conclude that since Hispanics are using the English-language code they are just part of a mass culture, if such exists. That is not the case. The Hispanic American culture is evolving and it comprehends the overlapping ellipses of Hispanic heritage, the Spanish language, the English language, and the experience of being Hispanic in the US (Figure 4.1).

The Case Study: MyLatinoVoice.com at the end of this chapter describes a website which speaks to the intersection of these ellipses. The website is in English but its content relates directly to the experience of being Latino in the US, indeed it is focused on providing a new voice for this large online target of English-speaking Latinos. In 2008 the website launched as MiApogeo.com (translation—My Apogee.com) but the company discovered that their target preferred the tagline in English of "My Latino Voice" for the website name. Their users felt that the use of Spanish in the site name suggested just another Spanish-language website which did not meet their interests. These users according to MyLatinoVoice.com are truly leading the American Latino experience, and their website is intended to speak to that audience in all its complexity.

While marketing in Spanish is likely to continue being relevant, depending on the specifics of the marketing problem, it seems that marketers may have overlooked interesting English-language opportunities. Consider the following archetypical narrative that pertains to recent Hispanic immigrants to the US.

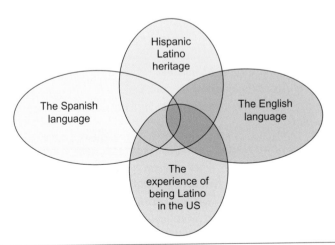

Figure 4.1 Overlap of Hispanic heritage, Spanish language, English language, and experience of being Hispanic in the US.

Maria Hernandez arrived in the United States 15 years ago when she was 20 years old. She came illegally from Mexico to join her boyfriend, Juan, who had come two years earlier, and already learned a lot about how to live in the United States. Juan taught Maria much about what products to purchase, and where, and introduced her to new customs he developed in those two years. Juan and Maria soon had a baby girl, Martha.

When Martha was three years old she got twin brothers, Mario and Miguel. At seven years of age Martha and her younger brothers spoke the Spanish their parents taught them. Martha also learned English at school and when playing with kids in the neighborhood. The kids watched Spanish-language TV with their parents in the evening, but during the day they watched English-language shows. They learned a lot from those shows, including a lot of their English. Juan and Maria both worked and earned a good enough income to qualify for a home loan. They purchased their first home. That was one of their dreams.

Juan and Maria thought they would like to have some of the abuelitos (their own parents and the grandparents of Martha) join them so they could enjoy their company, but also they could help by being at home with Martha and her two brothers while they were at work. Soon the household was composed of two parents, two grandparents, and three children. Each of them had a different level of proficiency in English and in Spanish.

The decisions about what to eat, what to drink, what movie to see, what car to buy, and many others were made by means of family discussions. Since they all shared the consequences of most purchases, all had an interest in the decisions. The kids became very important in product decision making because they were the best informed about what is available in the market place. When Martha turned 12 and her brothers 9, they had an important influence in at least 60 percent of the purchases relevant to the family. Their parents and grandparents listened to them with respect because these kids just "knew more."

Maria and Juan also tended to indulge their kids quite a bit because they wanted the children to enjoy what they did not have when they were young. In many ways these kids grew up prematurely by US standards, but they grew up happy and loved. When the kids were teens they wanted what all teens want except that they felt proud when Hispanic stars became popular and the Americans would look up to Hispanics.

These kids grew up in a cultural conundrum but with pride. In their early adulthood they became good citizens and in many ways reclaimed a lot of their Hispanic heritage that had been somewhat diluted during their teen years. Some enlightened marketers that understood the trajectory of this archetypal family did well with the millions of families like them.

This narrative illustrates that even new immigrants soon find themselves in a household where both the Spanish and English languages are forced to live together. Different generations and different language abilities coexist. Therefore, this scenario of the Hispanic household presents yet another cue to marketers that language decisions, Spanish, English, or both, should be taken only after informed consideration.

Given the above scenario, a compatible positioning in English and Spanish would be important so that members of the family receive compatible messaging about a brand. When the family gets together to discuss purchase decisions the input they bring to the "table" should be compatible regardless of whether the input was in English or Spanish. Thus, the case for communicating in English and Spanish with these typical emergent families is also evident. For some members of the family the input in Spanish will be most accessible, and for others the input in English will be better understood.

The importance of children as guides to the consumer information environment of the home cannot be neglected. These young people are exposed to a mix of touch-points that need careful consideration, and they can be in Spanish, English, or both.

Another element in the narrative that should be highlighted is that men are more likely to be influential in the decision to purchase household products than non-Hispanic men. Often neglected, these men are likely to come to the US before the women they pair with. They are more likely to acquire consumer preferences that they pass on to their female counterparts.

The above also brings about the controversial and complicated issue of Spanglish or code-switching. A discussion on that important topic follows.

Can the Marketer Use "Spanglish" or Switch Codes?

There has been much talk about the use of "Spanglish" to establish rapport in communicating with US Latinos. The term has been used by Hispanics for a long time to refer to the common practice of mixing the lexicon of both Spanish and English in the same sentence, or to adapt English terminology to the Spanish language. Mixing words or sentences of both languages generally is known in academic circles as code-switching. Spanglish has also been used to refer to code-switching. Spanglish in a narrower, and perhaps more precise sense, is a special case consisting of transforming English-language words into Spanish-sounding ones, even if the original meanings from English are lost.

Let us look at some examples, starting with code-switching:

"Oye Juan, traeme la calabaza (Hey Juan, bring me the pumpkin), because my Mom wants to cook it," and "here I come mi hermano (my brother)." Another example of code-switching would be "Querida mother I am ready to finish la escuela" (dear mother I am ready to finish school). In these examples Spanish and English are mixed in one sentence, and uses of both languages are correct.

Examples of Spanglish, in its narrower sense, would be:

"Voy a vacunar la carpeta" (I am going to vacuum the carpet). This would be generally stated in Spanish as "voy a aspirar la alfombra."

"Soy un picador" (I am a cotton picker). Interestingly here the speaker uses a word generally used in the context of bullfights, but after converting "picker" into what he thinks is Spanish uses the bullfighting term for something that has nothing to do with it. Spanish speakers would usually say "piscador de algodón" instead.

"Necesito filiar la aplicación" (I need to fill out the application). This would normally be stated as "necesito llenar la solicitud."

"Me prestas una corita" (can you lend me a quarter). Here "corita" is used instead of "quarter" because "corita" sounds like Spanish to the speaker.

These examples are adaptations of English vocabulary into Spanish despite the fact that the expressions can be considered illogical and even offensive to formally educated Spanish speakers. In these cases English words are converted into a code that resembles Spanish that technically it is not.

In common practice switching codes between Spanish and English, and adapting words from English into Spanish, happen together. Spanglish, in its more general sense tends to be used to denote both practices.

The use of code-switching or Spanglish among US Hispanics is widespread for different reasons:

■ Lourdes Torres discusses the use of code-switching in the growing body of US Latino authored literature as a reflection of Hispanic life in the US: "Increasing numbers of Latino/a immigrants, and the US/Mexican border means that code-switching in literature is not only metaphorical, but represents a reality where segments of the population are living between cultures and languages."[26] Further, she also argues that the use of code-switching seems to be a way of asserting one's identity as a different user of the English language. It seems like code-switching is both a reflection of daily life with its spontaneous speech pattern, and also a way for Hispanic speakers to distinguish themselves in a quest for identity. In this respect it is interesting to observe the experience of young Hispanics raised in the US. They find themselves learning the Spanish of their grandmother and generally have no formal education in Spanish. Most of their verbal life is in English, but they do get together with other Hispanics and bring in terms from Spanish as they become relevant and emotionally satisfying.

- Language users acquire vocabularies relevant to specific situations or contexts. So, for example, the language of the family includes vocabulary about food, cooking, family love, role relationships, home, garden, pets, and so on, and this vocabulary is very likely to have been acquired in Spanish. On the other hand the language of work and school, including technical terminology and vocabulary about peer relationships and other relevant language clusters are likely to be learned in English. Then, when the Hispanic consumer gets together with Hispanic coworkers, he or she speaks in English but introduces Spanish-language terms when referring to family and other home and emotional issues. When at home, with family, this consumer is likely to speak Spanish but mix some English when referring to work or friends outside the home.
- Many Hispanics who come to the US for economic opportunity have had relatively little formal education. Many are not fully fluent in Spanish and are functionally illiterate. For some the Spanish language can be a second language, since their first language could have been of American Indian origin like Otomi, Zapotec, Mayan, Quiche, Quechua, Aymara, or any of the many other native languages of Mexico, Central, and South America. For some of these individuals communicating in Spanish can be as difficult as communicating in English. In these cases mixing Spanish and English has more to do with not having enough vocabulary in any one language and they mix English and Spanish to make do in different situations. Terms are converted into Spanish and words like "application" becomes *aplicación*, "truck" becomes *troca*, "pitching" becomes *pichear*, a "quarter" becomes a *cora*, to "eat lunch" becomes *lonchear*, and so on.
- In many circumstances, after years of living in the US, even those Hispanics who have had more formal education mix terms of the "other" language when speaking in one of them for the sake of saving energy, as Zipf's law would predict.[27] It becomes just too difficult to build complete sentences in one language as one retrieves terms from different repositories in the neural mass.

None of these scenarios are pure cases because they can combine and juxtapose depending on the circumstances. Also, some form of Spanglish has been used in Latin America and Spain for many years as the result of the adoption of cultural and consumer products from the US.

A WAY OF COMMUNICATING: CAN WE MARKET TO HISPANIC YOUTH IN SPANGLISH?

Many marketers have been advised that to reach young Hispanics they should communicate with them in Spanglish. That creates anguish and uncertainty on the part of Anglo marketers who generally do not understand this phenomenon. They hypothesize that if young Hispanics mix English and Spanish, advertising directed to them should emulate their communication style. This makes sense. Part of the problem, however, is that there is no Spanglish *per se* as a distinctive language. It is a way of speaking, not a formal language with a defined vocabulary and syntax. While there appear to be certain rules for code-switching in general, there are not specific rules associated with Spanglish specifically. The rules associated with code-switching are that basically the grammar of the main language used in the communication takes precedence. Thus if a communication is mostly in English, then the few Spanish-language words within it would generally follow English syntax.[28] Thus "I am going to build you a beautiful casa" would be correct and most usual, and "I am going to build you a casa beautiful" would be unusual and considered incorrect.

The prolific Mexican scholar Ilan Stavans, currently at Amherst College, pub-lished a book entitled *Spanglish: The Making of a New American Language*. For him, Spanglish is the result of the meeting of the Hispanic and Anglo worlds.[29] Stavans espouses the reasonable perspective that languages evolve and change like other living organisms. He defines a large number of terms that are used as Spanish terms but are based on English roots. The English and the Spanish languages will continue to evolve to recognize the existence of each other as a result of the inter-action of the cultures. Ilan Stavans uses the term Spanglish in its broader sense to include both the intermixing of English and Spanish and the transformation of English words into Spanish-sounding terms.[30] It is difficult to argue that Spanglish is a language because it does not have a discernable syntax that rules how and when the words from both languages are to be mixed, or when an English word should be made into Spanish-sounding term. Still, those who use Spanglish in its broader sense do produce understandable expressions that people with similar experiences can relate to.

The answer to marketers that ask if they can communicate to Hispanic youth in Spanglish is not without caveats. If well achieved in commercial messages, Spanglish can be a communication style in which Latino youth can see their own image and values because "An individual's choice of language signals a specific social identity and/or belonging to a particular community."[31] But it has to be spon-taneous and emanating from those youth themselves, and not from a copywriter that tries to fake the code.

The drawbacks of communicating in Spanglish include a strong potential back-lash from those who have been formally educated in Spanish and who think that Spanglish is a perversion. A further potential backlash may come from English speakers who may be offended by having Spanish vocabulary in an English-language message or programming context. The 2009 Multicultural Marketing Study of the Center for Hispanic Marketing Communication at Florida State University, DMS Research, and Captura Group,[32] found that for those people who are online the acceptance of Spanish-language ads on English TV is low, with Hispanics being the most favorable, followed by Asians (Table 4.3).

TABLE 4.3 Enjoy Seeing Ads in Other Languages on English-Language TV

I Enjoy Seeing Ads in Other Languages on English-Language TV				
Groups differ at ≤0.05				
Ethnic Quotas	Non-Hispanic White	African American	Asian	Hispanic English	Hispanic Spanish
Means	1.10	1.98	2.29	2.62	3.40
Total cases per group	487	472	488	513	337

Please indicate how much you agree or disagree with each of the following statements (From 0 = completely disagree to 5 = completely agree).

The means on the zero- to five-point scale reveal that the popularity of ads in other languages on English-language TV is low, particularly for non-Hispanic Whites who are the most critical and still the majority of viewers of English-language TV. Thus there is reason for marketers to be cautious when mixing languages in a context that is likely to be frequented by non-Hispanics. These scores confirm parochialism of the larger American culture, and also highlights the rejection of challenges to the dominance of the English language.

Marketing practice does call for using language that the audience can relate to, thus using code-switching or Spanglish in its broader sense, can be a powerful tool promoting identification with a brand. The danger is that, as is the case with most media, spillage may result in a backlash by others who are also important targets for the same brand. Marketers may attempt to do more specific targeting both with their messaging and with their choices of media channels to attempt to prevent criticism. Or they may simply use more subtle ways of signaling bilingualism with just a few Spanish words in an English message, or a few English words in a Spanish message. An example of the use of a few Spanish words in an English-language context is the "Right For Me" in the "Yo Soy El Army" campaign of the US Army.[33] In this ad a young Latino man is attempting to get consent from his parents to join the army. In the 2006 Super Bowl, Toyota advertised its hybrid Camry model with the use of Spanish and English words intermixed. In this ad a father and his son converse mostly in English interjecting a few Spanish words as a metaphor for the hybridism of being bilingual and that of a car that is powered by electricity and gasoline.[34] These subtle uses of code-switching are unlikely to alienate non-targeted viewers and still connect well with the target.

Another consideration that marketers can use in their thinking about using Spanglish is the recent research by David Luna and Laura A. Peracchio.[35] They have conducted experiments that document that when the language switch is from the majority to the minority language, product evaluations are lower than when the switch is from the minority to the majority language. They have also found, however, that when the attitudes toward the minority language are salient and positive then the switch from majority to minority language produces higher product evaluations than the alternative of switching from minority to the majority language. This line of research suggests that marketers ought to know their Latino consumer well enough to understand if their attitudes toward Spanish are more positive than their attitudes toward English when switching languages in their advertising. Clearly, this research is not without limitations as most research is. The samples used by the authors are small and specific to certain geographies and country of origin backgrounds. Further, the generalizability of the findings can be questioned due to the contrived nature of the experiments conducted. Still, this line of research suggests that how Spanglish is used can affect product evaluations.

It is interesting that an article in NPR's Youth Radio is titled "Spanglish the new Ad Lingo."[36] It argues that to reach young Hispanics marketers are now speaking to them using their own style: "What's los mas caliente trend in advertising? In many media markets its Spanglish, that muy útil mashup of Spanish and English that's become común to millions of Latinos."

HOW SOCIOPOLITICAL CONDITIONS MAY INFLUENCE LANGUAGE TRENDS

Speaking Spanish in the US has become increasingly valuable over time. While English will continue to grow as the main language of Hispanics, particularly those who are born and form their lives in the US, the Spanish language is likely to also flourish. That is because of the relatively constant replenishment of immigrants, and because of the cultural–emotional value of this ancestral code. There are, however, developments that can hurt the prestige of the Spanish language and hurt the potential benefits of bilingualism, for example:

- A potential major turn to conservatism in the US that would punish Hispanics, as happened before the 1980s, for speaking Spanish and ostracize them for preserving their culture. In the past 30 years Hispanics have become salient in US society because more and more Americans have neighbors, friends, and relatives who are Hispanic. An increasing drive toward recognizing and nurturing multiculturalism has also flourished, but it has ups and downs. If conservative nationalistic tendencies reemerge, then the Spanish language will likely go back in the closet. In the 1960s you could find Hispanics in Los Angeles who would avoid speaking Spanish for fear of being marginalized, even though they were marginalized anyway. Richard Rodriguez, a well-known Latino writer of Mexican origin, gives an interesting example of that need to avoid being ostracized. In his autobiography he speaks of the way in which his youth was punctuated by discrimination.[37]
- The increasing drive to make US borders more secure has the side effect of keeping many undocumented immigrants from Latin America away. The

obstruction of border flows, added to increased xenophobia and parochial-ism has reinforced negative attitudes toward "foreign" languages, particularly Spanish. American youth and most Americans still value diversity and will probably continue to do so. There are, however, outspoken and powerful minori-ties that are capitalizing on the fears of Americans to further their antiforeign agenda.

Forces that will likely reinforce the use of the Spanish language in the US include:

- A roots-type phenomenon that is influencing many Hispanics to reclaim their heritage including the language. This is a trend toward retro-acculturation by which Hispanics who are established in the US for two, three generations, and beyond, feel a drive to reengage with their Hispanic culture because of its revi-talization in the US. These are also the individuals who would encourage their children to reclaim their ancestral cultural identity.
- An interest on the part of non-Hispanics to have an insider's view of Hispanic culture and an interest in communicating with Latinos in Spanish. The number of college students taking Spanish is on the rise. A Modern Language Association study in 2007 found that more than 820,000 students at US Colleges and Universities were taking Spanish. That represented an increase of over 10% from 2002, constituting more than 50% of all foreign-language enrollments at these institutions.[38] Further, tolerance for diversity appears to be growing at a fast pace. A study of the Pew Center for the People and the Press released in early 2010 indicates that the vast majority of Americans aged 18–49 support interracial marriages.[39] While this growing tolerance for diversity may not necessarily be reflected in tolerance for foreign languages, it likely contrib-utes to it.
- The value of being fluent in Spanish to both Hispanics and non-Hispanics because bilingualism pays better when it comes to jobs and other opportunities.

That Spanish is likely to grow and continue to be salient in American life seems obvious. That has little to do, however, with the fact that Latinos value the English language and those who are not yet fluent in it will continue to learn it. Bilingualism, both for Hispanics and non-Hispanics is a likely future. That is because language and cultural isolationism is becoming less tenable and desirable.

Conclusions

The one thing that has become increasingly clear about the use of language by US Hispanics, be it Spanish and/or English, is that it is in a state of flux. As the US Hispanic population is changing demographically, socially, and individually, their language use is evolving. This chapter presents a model of four overlapping ellipses to give a sense of the language and cultural interactions going on for US Hispanics (Figure 4.1). The Spanish language, English language, Hispanic cultural heritage, and the Experience of being Latino in the US, in Figure 4.1, impact one another to create a unique and challenging communication environment which marketers need to address. The marketer's challenge is to grasp the needs of their target for English, Spanish, or bilingual communication, recognizing the power for their brands if they get it right, and the risks involved in failure.

The temptation is to take a mechanical approach to the problem; that is, to look at the difference between languages as a matter of words, and conclude that the use of good translations often from English to Spanish will straighten out the whole confusing dilemma of how to address Hispanics. However, this chapter clarifies that language and culture are tied to one another, and that words are not "empty vessels" but carry meanings of a group's shared experiences loaded into them over time. Indeed, a "good" translation is not a word-for-word transliteration by a credentialed expert, but a cultural adaptation based on common understanding of the meaning of a message by the Hispanic target group.

Again, to come to a reasonable marketing approach it is necessary to look at the use of language and its impact on Hispanic consumers. This chapter cited statistics indicating that approximately 77% of US Latinos in 2009 speak English only, "well" and "very well." And, of those who speak Spanish at home, over 70% say they speak it well or very well. With this increasing English-language use, the question then becomes whether to market strictly to that Spanish-speaking segment in the language they speak at home, take a new direction and go after those who already are or are becoming English speakers, or go bilingual and face the challenge of maintaining one brand identity and associated messages in two languages.

To answer that question, a marketer may decide to target the Hispanic household as a unit. In one Latino household different generations may use Spanish or English almost exclusively, or both languages depending on whom they are conversing with in and outside of the household. Children often navigate between Spanish and English, bringing ideas learned in English into the household. Many companies, such as those in telecommunications and pharmaceuticals, have recognized this fact and have created bilingual communications that serve all members of the household.

Another way marketers can clarify language decisions is to look at the meaning that becomes attached to words and ideas in either Spanish or English, for Hispanic consumers. Depending on the topic, US Hispanics may have learned their vocabulary in either Spanish or English. Topics that are close to their socialization experience in their home country typically are carried in the Spanish language; those that are related to what they have learned in their lives in the US, which include many consumer products, tend to be associated with English. Marketers may then find it useful to look at their marketing objective and decide whether they should use the emotion-laden Spanish language to appeal to Hispanic consumer motivations, or the more functionally oriented English language to underscore relevance to their lives in the US.

In targeting Latino consumers who code-switch between English and Spanish or use Spanglish mixed in with English, marketers should tread carefully. Only close contact with the consumer target group for a code-switching or Spanglish message can yield a credible and motivating outcome. Since the language structure in these cases or lack thereof is full of uncertainties, there is ample opportunity for blunders. On the other hand, the modification of language based on the influence of Latino heritage and US culture may carry a special bond for particular groups such as young people or those in dual language situations. Understanding the changes that these diverse cultural and language interests bring about among US Hispanics and the groups in which they work and live present a constant challenge for successful marketing.

IMPLICATIONS FOR MARKETERS

■ Do not assume you can just translate English to Spanish in order to include Latinos in your marketing communications. Language carries the cultural power of tradition, loyalty, pride, success, and yearning. Without cultural sensitivity your message will likely fail to resonate with this rapidly changing market.

■ Be aware that translation of materials can be an important element of relevant bilingual communication. Think of translation as "cultural adaptation" versus word-for-word more academic approach so that the intent of the communication comes through in both languages.

■ Always check the translation with intended Spanish-speaking consumers to make sure that what they hear or read is what was intended. For a national campaign that will cover several Hispanic countries of origin, make sure through research that the Spanish terminology used is common and understandable to all groups.

■ Consider carefully whether your product or service initially was introduced to Hispanic consumers in Spanish or English. Vocabulary in Spanish regarding soap or coffee may have strong emotional associations as part of growing up with these products in their countries of origin; however, vocabulary regarding banking or computers may be familiar only in English from their experience in the US.

■ Be aware of the huge potential of the English-speaking Hispanic market. However, remember that the cultural experience of a Latino living in the US will influence the emotional appeal of your message even in English. Therefore, craft your English-language messages from a within-culture perspective based on solid research with Latino consumers.

- Approach language choice pragmatically. Consider: the context of where the communication will be introduced, the nature of the message, and the language needs and associated skills of the target.

- Be open to the potential that both Hispanics' cultural pride based on their heritage and their success orientation in the US may support the use of either Spanish- or English-language media or both for your marketing objectives.

CASE STUDY: HEALTH INFORMATION WEBSITE—FLORIDA SALUDABLE

Company/Organization
Largest health-care insurer in Florida

Campaign/Advertising Title
Florida Saludable

Intended Hispanic Consumers
Members, prospects, individuals, and small groups

Background
The Hispanic website (www.FloridaSaludable.com) is part of the health insurers continued efforts to attract the Hispanic market. Through creating a culturally relevant website, the insurer is able to:

- Improve the reach, service, and influence in the Hispanic Market.
- Build brand value, loyalty, and positive word of mouth within the Hispanic market.
- Inform and educate consumers who depend on Spanish for interactions, as well as those who could transact in English but prefer Spanish.

Discovery Process/Research
A variety of research tools were used to determine website design and execution. Among them, the health insurer used a leading acculturation model to narrow down which segments of the Hispanic population to target the site's content to. Both primary and secondary qualitative and quantitative research methods were also used to supplement the acculturation model to determine culturally relevant design features such as health and wellness articles and a multimedia library featuring topics of interest to Hispanics, intuitive navigation menus, online tools, and information sharing applications (e.g., article rating and sharing, blogging, site visitor-populated calendar of events, doctor and agent finders, product shopping, and so on). Concept and usability testing with the target market revealed that culturally relevant site would have colors and imagery that are warm and appealing as well as content delivered in a friendly and engaging way.

Cultural Insights/Expressions of Insights in the Campaign
Based on the insurer's research efforts and experience with Hispanic Floridians, it was determined that the website's target market is seeking relevant health information

from a trusted source that focuses on their culture, community, and language. For example, research shows that Hispanics respond well to content delivered in a "telenovela" format (Spanish soap operas); therefore, this design concept was used in article development. Article topics were also selected to inform visitors about well-known Hispanic health issues such as diabetes, high blood pressure, heart disease, and so on. Through this effort, the insurer seeks to earn the Hispanic consumer's trust by becoming their preferred source of health and wellness information, thus establishing a long-term relationship with this audience. This website will also provide the insurer a foundation for testing new ideas and evolve their understanding of Hispanic Floridians.

Effect of the Campaign

The insurer measures the effectiveness of the site with the following metrics: utilization—number of site visits and lead conversion rate, visitors who visited once, visitors who visited multiple times, number of views per visitor, time spent viewing each page, and number of visits to the online provider directory. They typically receive around 700–800 visits a month, and the most visited pages are the product pages and home remedies. To date, the site has been performing on track with its success metrics.

Florida Saludable website.

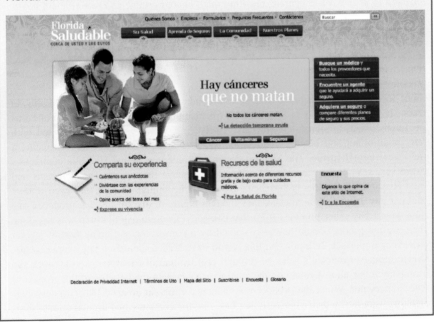

CASE STUDY: EMERSON—BLUE SELECTO THERMOSTAT

Company
Emerson

Advertising Agency
Brenalt Sabatino Day

Campaign Title
Blue Selecto Thermostat—"Happy Home"

Intended Hispanic Customers
Spanish-dominant homeowners and Spanish-dominant or bilingual air conditioning and heating contractors

Background
As homeowners in the US become more energy conscious, the sales of programmable thermostats continue to rise. Programmable thermostats, unlike mechanical thermostats with dials and on/off switches, allow consumers to program desired temperatures for specific times of the day. The home's heating or cooling system then responds according to their energy savings and comfort preference. Because programming involves text prompts and commands, language becomes a factor in the homeowner experience. Even a basic programmable thermostat with a 2" × 2" screen can be filled with many words or abbreviations. For those whose primary language is not English, thermostats can be difficult to program and operate, resulting in an uncomfortable and less-efficient home. Given the growth of Hispanics in the US, Emerson decided to develop a thermostat with Spanish language on the screen, and launch it with an advertising campaign targeted specifically toward Hispanic contractors selling to Hispanic homeowners.

Discovery Process/Research
Product
Four focus groups with homeowners were conducted in Los Angeles and Miami. In each city, one group was in Spanish with Spanish-dominant homeowners and one was in English with bilingual homeowners. Twelve interviews were also conducted with air conditioning and heating contractors. Most of the interviewees were Hispanic, a few were non-Hispanic. The Spanish-dominant homeowners and Hispanic contractors were very receptive to the idea of a Spanish-language thermostat. The bilinguals and non-Hispanics were less enthusiastic. However, the bilinguals said that even if they did not buy a Spanish thermostat, they thought highly of a company that produced one and would buy other products from that company. Quantitative research was not done because the product could be easily copied by a competitor and being first to market was very important. In hindsight, this would have helped identify a key channel issue. Since most of Emerson's sales go through professional distributors to contractors, the company relies almost solely on the contractor to explain the benefits of the product to the homeowner. When the product was launched Emerson learned that Hispanic contractors were not in their core customer base and the company had limited relationships

with them. Because quantitative research requires larger sample sizes, the company might have recognized this issue if they struggled to get an appropriate number of contractors.

Advertising
Advertising was tested with homeowners and contractors. Multiple concepts were produced and were tested qualitatively. The "Happy Home" was preferred by research participants. The participants then gave further feedback on language, message, context, and images. They improved the advertising significantly.

Cultural Insights/Expression of Insights in the Campaign and the Product
The "Happy Home" capitalized on cultural insights uncovered in the qualitative research. For example, Emerson learned that Hispanics over indexed on preference for cozy, harmonious households. If Spanish-speaking people can control their thermostat more easily because it is in Spanish, then the home will be more comfortable and family members will be happier.

There is also a business to business message in the ad. The headline, *"If your customers speak Spanish, shouldn't their thermostat speak Spanish too?"* reminds businesses that their customers will prefer this product to an English one because the product and their customers both speak Spanish. Finally, the campaign was bilingual so that it could appeal to Spanish speakers and non-Spanish speakers alike. In the research, Spanish-dominant participants supported bilingual advertising.

Effect of the Campaign and the Product
Although initial sales in the US have been slower than expected, there have been several positive results from the advertising campaign and Spanish language–focused product.

- *First, sales of the product are growing faster than expected in Latin America.* Not only is this the first Spanish-language thermostat in the US, it is the first to be introduced in Latin America.
- *Second, executing a campaign targeted specifically for the Hispanic market developed **their** (Emerson's) competency in emerging areas such as social media and online advertising.* For the first time, Emerson saw blogging activity about their product in publications beyond their traditional air conditioning and heating space. The company was reaching the homeowner, but their channel to market was slow to react.
- *Finally, because Hispanic homeowners are more likely to be second- or third-generation Hispanics, the acculturation process has reduced the need for a Spanish-language thermostat in the US. However, sales of English-language thermostats to the Hispanic contractors servicing these markets have grown.* The loyalty to Hispanic contractors Emerson was trying to develop with this product and campaign has been successful because the company made an effort to address their needs.

(Continued)

Emerson Blue Selecto Thermostat—"Happy Home" campaign.

CASE STUDY: MYLATINOVOICE.COM

http://www.mylatinovoice.com

Company/Organization
MyLatinoVoice.com/Mi Apogeo Inc.

Campaign/Advertising Title
Development of MyLatinoVoice.com as a product truly by and for the acculturated US Latino audience

Intended Hispanic Consumers
Acculturated and English-dominant online users

Background
Mi Apogeo Inc. was created as an online media company to develop properties that targeted the younger, acculturated, and English-dominant US Latino (the fastest growing demographic in the US Latino and general market segments). In 2008, it launched MiApogeo.com—now MyLatinoVoice.com—and WikiLatino.com (now its own site but still a channel within MyLatinoVoice). The sites were developed as an offering for the acculturated Latino market, that is, for the English-surfing Latino user. According to the AOL CyberStudy 2010, Hispanic respondents indicated that on the Internet:

- English-language messages tend to be favored by all demographics and life stages.
- English-language sites are perceived as more comprehensive, detailed, and useful than Spanish-language counterparts across all levels of acculturation and life stages.

MiApogeo.com made use of the English language but with a Spanish name to create user affinity. Mi Apogeo's research has shown that the Spanish language, and specifically, peppering English with Spanish words, is a point of affinity for Latinos, even for those not fully fluent, according to 2007 Mi Apogeo focus groups. Research also indicated that the Latino audience wanted:

- A positive website, where Latinos celebrated their success instead of the usual focus on only their challenges as a community (thus the name Mi Apogeo, which means "My Apogee," highest peak of success, apex).
- A website where their "voice" could be heard, which led to the tagline "My Latino Voice." Thus, the site was named "Mi Apogeo … My Latino Voice." This naming also helped to communicate that the site was in English, which Mi Apogeo by itself did not. The developers were convinced that their target audience would ignore a Spanish-language online product.

Discovery Process/Research
Research included focus groups, surveys, and direct engagement of users. Mi Apogeo surveyed mostly qualitatively through focus groups and Q&A short online surveys of their target users across the country. They included local markets as well as family, country of origin diversity. Surveys also included age and lifestyle diversity (e.g., college students as well as 30 "somethings," Afro Latinos and Gay Latinos). Mi Apogeo wanted its research to represent many subcommunities, which it found that others in this space had not usually included in their research, specifically, Afro Latinos and Gay & Lesbian Latinos as well as religious affinities (Latino Jews and Latino Muslims).

(Continued)

Cultural Insights

Given their research and direct engagement with their US Latino audience, Mi Apogeo believes that Latino culture is alive and well in the US, but that Latinos are now living the "American Latino" experience, which greatly differs from the new immigrant experience. The American Latino audience appears to them to be truly American with a cultural affinity to their Latino roots. The fusion of many cultures—their collective countries of origin, the mainstream American culture, and even other affinity communities such as African Americans—seemed to have created a very distinct US Latino identity. Mi Apogeo users indicate that they are proud of their heritage but generally identify as "American" first and that their Latino identity has become more of a "pan-Latino" one versus a country of origin designation. Even if they say "I am American, but my family is from Guatemala," they overall define themselves as "Latinos."

The website has found that this audience is English dominant, especially in online media usage. They seem to generally not read or write Spanish, and even for those who can, the content in most Spanish-language sites is not perceived as relevant to them. They prefer English-language sites and use these exclusively. However, they indicate that they crave a Latino connection to their music, food, and shared personal stories. My Latino Voice has found that these simple three things represent the most popular content on-site.

Expression of Insights in the Website

The site was originally launched as Miapogeo.com with the tagline "My Latino Voice." Mi Apogeo's user feedback and research indicated that these Latino users were so English-dominant online (reading and writing Spanish is much different from

MyLatinoVoice.com website.

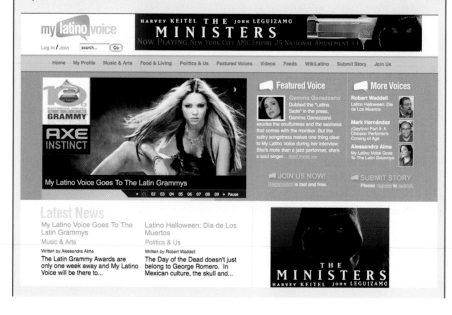

the spoken language) that they had automatically started calling the website "that My Latino Voice site." As a result, Mi Apogeo Inc. rebranded and relaunched their site as MyLatinoVoice.com, with an upgrade to requested functionalities, like news feeds and video, as well as the use of the name the Latino audience most connected to. This change also facilitated better SEO (search engine optimization according to ranking in the search results).

Technology as well as content for the target US Latino user was developed specifically with "My Latino Voice" reflecting the target's need to "be heard." To accomplish this, the website features user-submitted content (news and information, entertainment, lifestyle, and politics) and social a community, where users can create profiles (with Facebook and Twitter links) and can contribute to WikiLatino.com, the company's proprietary "Latino Wikipedia." The site is constantly evolving based on direct user feedback and requests.

Effect of the Campaign

The site rebranded as My Latino Voice in August of 2009, a year and a half after the original launch. The rebranding has made a significant impact on all key metrics and the site's ability to build awareness. Traffic as of March 2010 has almost quadrupled and the brand now has significant "buzz" as *easy to remember, easy to find.*" It is drawing high-quality contributors as evidenced on the site, which yields relevant and quality stories, as well as media partners. The site is now on call by major events brands in the market, for example, Latin Grammy's, Latin Billboards, Film Festivals, CNN's "Latino in America" series, and has well-known advertisers, for example, Virgin Mobile, Doritos, McDonalds, and Universal Music.

The brand and site have also attracted strategic alliances, including the most recent, with Maya Entertainment, a filmed entertainment company that shares a common vision—to celebrate Latino voices and talent in the US Latino film and TV space. My Latino Voice has assumed marketing and sales responsibilities for www.latinoreview. com, a Maya site, and as of March 2010, this My Latino Voice partnership delivers over half a million unique users per month, making My Latino Voice one of the most popular and the fastest growing online communities dedicated to the American Latino audience in the US.

Despite their Latino focus, the site's online statistics also indicate a growing number of non-Latino mainstream users, as "things Latino" become part of the American mainstream and popular culture. Due to this ongoing evolution, the site has created a new site tagline: "My Latino Voice. The American Experience. The Latino Point of View."

End Notes

[1] Noam Chomsky, *Knowledge of Language: Its Nature, Origin, and Use.* New York: Praeger, 1986.

[2] Roughly translated as that who wakes up early gets help from God.

[3] Telenovelas are a genre of TV programming very similar to "soap operas" but with a unique fatalistic and emotional flare.

[4] See Jose Antonio Vargas, "Spanish ads on English TV? An experiment." *The Washington Post*, Tuesday, May 31, 2005. http://www.washingtonpost.com/wp-dyn/content/article/2005/05/30/AR2005053000978. html

[5] http://www.hispanicmarketweekly.com/featureArticle.cms?id=2436

[6] http://wordnetweb.princeton.edu/perl/webwn?s=dialect

[7] See http://www.marineroloco.com/.

[8] http://www.rae.es/rae.html

[9] Mike Durance and Felipe Korzenny, "Focus groups for translation equivalence among Hispanics." *Marketing News* September, 1989.

[10] Voice Over Internet Protocol.

[11] John A. Lucy, "Language diversity and thought: a reformulation of the linguistic relativity hypothesis." In *Studies in the Social and Cultural Foundations of Language: No. 12*. Cambridge: Cambridge University Press, 1992.

[12] Bruce I. Kodish, "What we do with language—What it does with us." *ETC: A Review of General Semantics* 60(4), 2003.

[13] Ibid.

[14] Alfred H. Bloom, *The Linguistic Shaping of Thought: A Study in the Impact of Language on Thinking in China and the West*. Hillsdale, NJ: L. Erlbaum Associates, 1981, p. 73.

[15] Felipe Korzenny, "Acculturation vs. assimilation among Hispanics: e-mail self-reports." *Quirk's Marketing Research Review* November 1999, 50–54.

[16] Avis M. Dry, *The Psychology of Jung, a Critical Interpretation*. London: Methuen, 1961.

[17] David Luna, Torsten Ringberg, and Laura A. Peracchio, "One individual, two identities: frame-switching among biculturals." *Journal of Consumer Research* 35(August), 2008, 279–293.

[18] "Walker there is no road, you make the road as you walk." This is part of a well-known poem by the Spanish poet Antonio Machado born in 1875.

[19] Aaron Lynch, *How Belief Spreads Through Society*. New York: Basic Books, 1996.

[20] Richard Brodie, *Virus of the Mind: The New Science of the Meme*, 1st ed. Seattle, WA: Integral Press, 1996.

[21] Betsy D. Gelb, "Creating 'memes' while creating advertising." *Journal of Advertising Research* 37(6), 1997, 57.

[22] http://factfinder.census.gov. Here we reported American Community Survey estimates for the 5 years culminating in 2009. The total population data comes from the 2010 estimates of the Current Population Survey. http://www.census.gov/hhes/www/cpstc/cps_table_creator.html

[23] These estimates are based on a total population of Hispanics of almost 43 million, according to the 2009 American FactFinder using 1-year data from the American Community Survey of the US Census Bureau.

[24] As a percentage of the total of almost 43 million Hispanics estimated by the ACS in 2009.

[25] Based on the total of 43 million, again.

[26] Lourdes Torres, "In the contact zone: code-switching strategies by Latino/a writers." *Melus* 32(1), 2007, 75–96.

[27] Colin Cherry, *On Human Communication: A Review, a Survey, and a Criticism—Studies in Communication*, 3rd ed. Cambridge, MA: MIT Press, 1978.

[28] The context or main language is called the matrix language and the other is called the embedded language. See: David Luna, Dawn Lerman, and Laura A. Peracchio, "Structural constraints in code-switched advertising." *Journal of Consumer Research* 32(3), 2005, 416–423.

[29] Ilan Stavans, *Spanglish: The Making of a New American Language*. New York: Rayo, an Imprint of Harper Collins Publishers, 2003.

[30] http://www.npr.org/templates/story/story.php?storyId=1438900

[31] David Luna and Laura A. Peracchio, "Advertising to bilingual consumers: the impact of code-switching and language schemas on persuasion." *Journal of Consumer Research* 31(4), 2005, 760.

[32] This study was conducted online with respondents 18 years of age and older across the US in March 2009.

[33] See the ad at http://www.usaac.army.mil/sod/download/tv/archive/Right%20For%20Me%20(30%20 seconds).MOV.

[34] http://blog.thecar.com.my/commercial-ad/toyota-hybrid-camry-commercial-ad

[35] David Luna and Laura A. Peracchio, "Advertising to bilingual consumers: the impact of code-switching and language schemas on persuasion." *Journal of Consumer Research* 31(4), 2005, 760–765.

[36] http://www.youthradio.org/oldsite/wtnw/wtnwadlingo.shtml

[37] Richard Rodriguez, *Hunger of Memory: The Education of Richard Rodriguez: An Autobiography.* Toronto: Bantam Books, 1983.

[38] Press release of November 13, 2007. http://www.mla.org/pdf/release11207_ma_feb_update.pdf

[39] Report available at: http://pewresearch.org/pubs/1480/millennials-accept-iinterracial-dating-marriage-friends-different-race-generations.

ENCULTURATION, ACCULTURATION, AND ASSIMILATION: A BICULTURAL HORIZON

Chapter 5

Latin Americans and Asians on the Rise

Legal immigration to the US experienced marked changes in the recent past. Immigrants from Europe have been replaced by immigrants from Asia and Latin America as shown in Table 5.1.[1] More recent data shows that these trends continue. In this table[2] the reader can see that immigration to the US from North America (including Mexico, Central America, and the Caribbean)[3] combined with South America constitutes almost half (44%) of all legal immigration to the US, and that trend has grown in the last decade.

Table 5.1 also shows that legal immigration from Mexico accounts for about half of the total immigration from North America to the US and it has been on the rise. Legal immigration from Asia in 2008 reached 35% of all legal immigration. The combined legal immigration from Latin America and Asia is close to 80% and that suggests important changes in the configuration of the cultural landscape of the US.

UNDOCUMENTED IMMIGRATION

The growing trends of immigration from Latin America, and particularly Mexico, even without considering undocumented immigration strengthens the US Hispanic

153

TABLE 5.1 Legal Permanent Resident Status by Region and Country of Birth: 1999–2008

Persons Obtaining Legal Permanent Resident Status by Region and Country of Birth: Fiscal Years 1999–2008

	1999	2000	2001	2002	2003	2004	2005	2006	2007	2008
Total	644,787	841,002	1,058,902	1,059,356	703,542	957,883	1,122,257	1,266,129	1,052,415	1,107,126
Africa	36,578	44,534	53,731	60,101	48,642	66,422	85,098	117,422	94,711	105,915
Asia	198,918	264,413	348,256	340,494	243,918	334,540	400,098	422,284	383,508	383,608
Europe	92,314	130,996	174,411	173,524	100,434	133,181	176,516	164,244	120,821	119,138
North America	270,719	338,959	405,638	402,949	249,968	342,468	345,561	414,075	339,355	393,253
Oceania	3,658	5,105	6,071	5,515	4,351	5,985	6,546	7,384	6,101	5,263
South America	41,444	55,823	68,484	74,151	55,028	72,060	103,135	137,986	106,525	98,555
Mexico	147,402	173,493	205,560	218,822	115,585	175,411	161,445	173,749	148,640	189,989

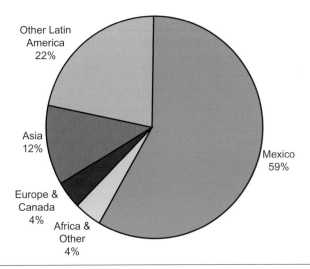

Figure 5.1 Estimates of unauthorized immigrant population by region and country of birth, 2008.
Source: Pew Hispanic Center estimates, 2008, based on March Supplements to the Current Population Survey (CPS).

market. Current estimates of the undocumented population of the US show that there are about 12 million undocumented people living in the US. The following chart in Figure 5.1 from the Pew Hispanic Center provides estimates of the composition of that figure.

About 7.2 million people are estimated to come from Mexico, and 9.7 million from Latin America in general. While these estimates are likely to be underestimates they are the most reliable figures available at this time. Thus, between documented and undocumented immigration Latin America contributes the largest contingent of new Americans.

Births Versus Immigration: The New Equation

Nevertheless, the US Bureau of the Census documents that the increase of the US Hispanic population is now due to births rather than immigration as was the case in the past 40 years. Table 5.2 contains data from the 2008 American Community Survey of the US Bureau of the Census. It documents the nativity of US Hispanics.

While the figures in Table 5.2 are unlikely to include all undocumented individuals, it provides directional guidance as to the developments in US Hispanic growth. All Latinos in the US under 18, males and females were at the time of the study 34% of the population, an impressive proportion that further emphasizes the youth of this market. Within those under 18 years of age, a staggering 91% were

TABLE 5.2 Nativity of US Hispanics

Sex by Age by Nativity—Hispanic or Latino Population	Estimate
Total	46,891,456
Male	24,212,122
Under 18 years	8,220,903
Native	7,490,109
Foreign born	730,794
18 years and over	15,991,219
Native	7,176,917
Foreign born	8,814,302
Female	22,679,334
Under 18 years	7,830,965
Native	7,153,178
Foreign born	677,787
18 years and over	14,848,369
Native	7,260,473
Foreign born	7,587,896

native born, and that provides a good indication of what type of growth to expect in the near future. Sixty-six percent of the population were those 18 years of age and older. Among that older segment 53% were foreign born. While foreign born are still the adult majority, the obvious likelihood is that they will suffer further declines in favor of their native-born counterparts.

These patterns of nativity and immigration have important consequences:

■ Newcomer immigrants need to adjust to a new cultural and social situation. Immigrants experience a loss of identity and social structure that they need to rebuild in the host country. They experience culture shock as we explained earlier in the book. This happens until immigrants rebuild enough of the structure they need and until they acquire enough tools from the second culture.

■ The US as the receiving country absorbs new cultural patterns and becomes increasingly diversified. This growing diversity structurally involves other US Hispanics and non-Hispanics who become enmeshed with Hispanic immigrants as neighbors, relatives, friends, and coworkers, and learn new ways of doing things. Therefore there is a give and take that affects both newcomers and those who are here.

- Immigrants influence their countries of origin when they send information, and share cultural values, expectations, and money to relatives and friends. This flow of influence encourages or discourages further migration to the US, depending on the economic situation, and creates a feedback loop that affects future trends.[4]

- Those born in the US influence their parents and grandparents and guide them in their decision making. They become the cultural guides of their elders.

- Having more US-born Latinos is likely to represent the emergence of a new identity that has some roots in Latin America and some in the US, but more importantly the deepest roots become those of being Latino in the US. That experience, the ways of perceiving the world, ways of thinking, ways of relating, and ways of feeling are at variance with what their parents and grandparents taught them and also at variance with the receiving culture. And as we will see below, the attitude of the receiving culture toward these new generations of Hispanics will shape their adjustment and ultimately the way they feel about themselves.

Two shifts are powerfully evident. On one hand there is a dramatic change in the profile of immigrants to the US. On the other, the growth of the Hispanic population is most likely to come from within the US going forward. In the process of Hispanics forming a new identity and learning to be consumers in the US, they are also influencing marketing practice. A feedback loop of influence highlights the importance of understanding how Hispanics enculturate and acculturate as they create meanings to form a new way of being in the US.

MUTUAL CULTURAL CHANGE

Latinos in the US represent a large-scale case study of mutual cultural change. Immigration to the US is the first step of change. The immigrant must adapt to the new cultural environment and the receiving society adapts to the immigrants as well, in different ways. As the adaptation experience of immigrants continues they become part of the new society through cognitive and behavioral modifications. Their children claim unique identities, and the receiving society learns to like some aspects the immigrants contribute and reject others.

Immigrants

There are different reasons why cultures evolve and change. Immigration is one of the most common cases of cultural change. This process involves large amounts of stress that come from the attempt to cope with uncertainty and lack of cultural support systems.[5] It is important to emphasize the amount of emotional and physical turmoil that immigrants experience because that struggle characterizes Hispanic life in the US.

The scene of Hispanic men standing on street corners waiting for a pickup truck to take them away for a day's work is a different experience depending on the onlooker's perspective. For many of the local residents these men are an eyesore that they would like to have vanish. They do not like those poorly dressed men hanging around their neighborhood. They are considered a particular nuisance on weekends when these men have nothing to do but get drunk and sit around public places to talk about their loneliness. They look bad, smell bad, and many residents wish they would go away.

To those who hire their services for the day, these men are hard workers willing to do more work than anyone else and for less money. They are a blessing because they can get landscape, agriculture, and construction jobs done fast at reasonable prices; and these men do not object to doing more work. The more work the better for them, and they let their short-term employers know this.

They are generally honest and create a congenial work culture wherever they are. They smile, sing, joke, and have fun doing heavy work. It is difficult to find better workers. So, when manual work piles up the only thing one needs to do is go pick up a few "Mexicans" for the day. "Mexicans," in many locations where Mexican labor is abundant, has become the generic term for workers, pretty much like Kleenex has become the generic term for facial tissues.

The experience of these men is different. They have left behind their friends, their girl friend/wife, many times their children, their mother and father, relatives, and pastor. The images of those they care for stay vivid in their minds, day after day. They came to the US to earn money to send back home. Many of the families of these workers would not survive without the support they receive from *el otro lado*.[6] After muscle-breaking work during the day, many hours under the sun, and nostalgia in the soul, these men face emptiness at the end of the day. They have nobody to go to, no real home, and, most of the time, they have nothing to do when they are not working.

Some cry in the loneliness of their evening for those they left behind. Others get drunk with the other men anywhere they can sit and have some relaxation. Most can barely communicate in English, and some do not speak Spanish either. Many of those from Oaxaca, Yucatan, and other regions of Mexico and Central America do not speak Spanish or English. They speak Mayan, Zapotec, and other native languages. These men are real oddities to Anglos and also to their Spanish-speaking counterparts. But they strive and they work, and eventually they succeed at making some money and becoming residents of the US, or they return to their homeland defeated by the loneliness and nights of anguish and tears.

While this initial immigration experience is not the only one that immigrants undergo, it does represent an important segment of Hispanic first contact with the US. It illustrates the give and take that occurs as individuals from one culture attempt to become adjusted to living in a second culture, even if the conditions vary. This is one stage in the cultural adaptation process that marketers need to understand as new immigrants represent an important target for specific types of products and services. A marketer that understands the emotion and sensitivity involved in this process can better communicate his or her product or service benefits and create long-term brand equity and related loyalty.

Becoming Settled, Having Children, and Making the US Home

Large numbers of US Hispanics have come over the years as migrant workers and/ or undocumented work seekers. The ones that are able to overcome the urge to give up and return have tended to form families, establish businesses,[7] climb the occupational ladder, and work for a better future. Most have considered the US adventure a temporary episode in their lives and have thought they would return "home" after attaining some degree of success. The dreams to return "home" tend to vanish after a while as the sense of home has shifted along with roots, and clearly the anchors that children represent.

Many of these families have struggled to learn the language, improve their standing, and rear children that will make them proud. Some of the kids intermarry with non-Hispanics. The families and their kids become friends with non-Hispanics, and also become the next door neighbors. They teach their customs to non-Hispanics, and they, in turn, learn about multiple aspects of life from their non-Hispanic counterparts. Many prosper, and many are impeded in their aim to establish a new home by their lack of documentation.

While many non-Hispanics embrace these newcomers, others see them as burdens to society and low-cost competition for US jobs. While some politicians cater to them hoping to get their votes, others vilify them and try to exclude them from US society. While some savvy marketers understand the economic and social power of Latinos, others ignore them as historical blips. Ultimately, the ambivalence of society reinforces the sense of a new identity. It becomes clear that they are not "from here and not from there" anymore. As children grow and become a driving force in the economy marketers try to elucidate the folkways of these new consumers. The kids know they are different even when they do not want to be. And many develop an important sense of pride in their difference, but the difference is not being like their parents but a unique cultural product.

The Synergy of Cultures in Contact

Like most social processes, the adaptation to a new culture and the emergence of a new identity involve at least two parties. One is the contingent of Hispanics adapting as they become part of the host culture. The other is the host culture also adapting to a large and powerful incoming group.

This interplay has no known end state, but both sides merge in interesting ways. As the non-Hispanic White segment of the population grows older and its ranks shrink, Latinos become one of the powerful driving forces of the new society. Some of their customs, beliefs, and ways of being become part of the overall culture. Thus interestingly some of the simple things of life become part of the fabric of the overall society. Ketchup becomes overshadowed by salsa in terms of dollars volume, and very close in units sold, according to Information Resources in 2007.[8] It has been reported that tortillas now outsell white bread in the US. While that assertion is difficult to confirm it is interesting that in 2003 The San Jose Mercury news reported that according to the Tortilla Industry Association, tortillas have 32% of the market for all types of bread, compared with 34% for white bread, and that tortilla sales have been reported to have grown by about 10% a year.[9]

American society is adopting and adapting Hispanic customs as the prevalence of Hispanics, and their importance in society increases. Gourmet cuisine in the US is being recreated by Mexican and other Latin-American chefs. Avocado, papaya, chipotle, jicama, mango, plantains, yucca, tomatillos, quinoa, pomegranate, mole, and many other flavors are now integral parts of the American gourmet repertoire. The chefs diffusing these innovations have come through the ranks and made it big in the culinary scene. Photographers for *Loft*, a glossy high-end magazine that used to be published in Miami, got into the kitchens of many restaurants in New York and found that "everything good in New York—be it French, Italian, Chinese or Hindu—is cooked by Mexicans" and called it "Guey Cuisine."[10] Curiously "guey" is a colloquial, somewhat demeaning, way in which Mexican men who know each other will address each other. The term is said to be equivalent to "buddy," or "dude."[11] Thus, by an interesting twist of cultural contact the taste buds of the US are awakening at the hands of immigrants, or children of immigrants.

The interplay and mutual influence is enormous. Many genres of Latin music are now part of the American mainstream. On October 10 and 12, 2009, PBS broadcast a special entitled "Latin Music USA: It's Gonna Move You." This event was clearly directed to the general public and currently has its own website.[12] Further, the reader has surely observed the renaissance of tango in the American music scene along with the celebration of salsa, Latino rap, and Latin and Brazilian Jazz. John Storm, a scholar who has studied the influence of Latin-American music on the US, states that "not only does the standard [US] repertory contain a significant representation of tunes of Latin-American origin or inspiration, but the whole rhythmic basis of US popular music has become to some extent Latinized."[13]

Further, English-language TV has been including Spanish-language themes and/or content in advertising and also in programming. In 2007 Vegas ran ads in Spanish on A&E, Fox Sports, Bravo, and Logo.[14] VH1 has produced Latino content with "Viva Hollywood" and "My Antonio." The Showtime series "Weeds" includes Latino talent who often speak in Spanish without offering subtitles in English. The mutual influence of cultures is both because of the importance of the emerging Hispanic group and its youth becoming central in the culture, and at the same time non-Hispanics finding aspects of Latino culture appealing. We could continue citing examples like the curious emergence of Dulce de Leche as an ice cream flavor phenomenon in recent times. By now the reader gets the point that the process of cultural influence is a two-way street. And those who regret what they call the foreign invasion of Hispanics, while at the same time they eat massive amounts of Mexican food, and have their homes built and maintained by people of Mexican and Central American origin, should realize that they also have been irreversibly influenced.

BELONGING TO A CULTURE DOES NOT MEAN UNDERSTANDING IT

Definitions of culture vary widely.[15] A compromise definition of culture is the sets of designs for living that human groups pass on from generation to generation. These designs for living are both objective and subjective.[16] Objective culture consists of the external manifestations of culture that can be observed in food, dress, architecture, speech codes and patterns, interior décor, gestures, and so on.

Subjective culture consists of less-concrete elements. These include values, beliefs, attitudes, ways of perceiving the world, social cognitions, norms, and so on. These subjective aspects are harder to pinpoint than the external or objective aspects of culture. Nevertheless, subjective culture can have profound effects on the ways in which people make choices and behave.

Subjective culture is what our parents taught as a way of perceiving objects, the world, and the cosmos, and that is in turn what they learned from their parents. This perceptual set includes notions of what is right and wrong, and also of who is in our in-group or out-group.[17] This part of culture is metaphorically fluid because subjective culture for humans is like what water is for fish. The fish can hardly be aware of the water because the water is constant. Humans very rarely are aware of their subjective culture because it is constant and most often imperceptible. It is like the operating system of a computer. Subjective culture runs in the background. It is the program that we live by, what we value, what appeals to us, what turns us off, what makes us sad, and in general characterizes our way of being.

Just because someone is a member of a culture does not mean that he or she is aware of its subjective aspects. That is why marketers who assume that by hiring a Hispanic brand manager, they are hiring someone that automatically understands Hispanic culture are committing an error of judgment. Members of cultures are not necessarily experts on their own culture. A false assumption that naïve members of a culture make is that all other members of the culture are just like them. Many of the fiascos in Hispanic marketing happen just because of this. A more "Americanized" marketer assumes most Hispanics are like him- or herself, and a more Spanish-dominant marketer assumes most Hispanics share his or her perspectives. Almost anyone who studies Latino cultural patterns and becomes involved with the culture, and is a savvy marketer, can do well in marketing to Hispanics. Clearly, someone who has been brought up in a Hispanic family and studies the culture is likely to have an edge just because they can recognize patterns they have experienced. Nevertheless, there are many marketers that these writers know who are not Hispanic but who have done a great job in connecting with Hispanic consumers because of their cultural understanding. A great combination for successful contemporary marketing is the study of anthropology, marketing, and consumer behavior.

How Do We Learn Culture: Enculturation, Acculturation, and Assimilation

LEARNING A FIRST CULTURE: ENCULTURATION

This term has been defined in varied ways.[18] There is general consensus, however, that enculturation is the learning of a first culture. This is the process that all humans born into a social group experience. They become part of their culture by learning the folkways, mores, values, orientations, and perceptual patterns of their social milieu. Enculturation tends to be very enduring and imperceptibly influential in our lives. Most people who have been raised in a particular culture tend to preserve aspects of it even if they spend only a few years in their original culture. The native culture a person experiences tends to leave an almost indelible pattern in the cognitive, emotional, and behavioral framework of people. The reader can probably think of someone he or she knows who is still "very Argentinean," "very Mexican," or "very Cuban" even if that person has been in the US culture for many years.

The compelling force of enculturation affects the way in which immigrants adjust to the second culture. Many Latinos, when they first immigrate to the US, tend to believe that they will go back home when they achieve their economic or professional goals. Many avoid becoming citizens of the US for some time because they feel they would be betraying their country of origin, or because of their emotional attachment to it. Almost exactly half (49%) of those who have been in the US less than 10 years state a desire to return to their country of origin, and more impressively 49% of all Latino immigrants say that their country of birth is their "real homeland."[19] Thus, enculturation imbues a strong loyalty to their country and the social lifestyle these individuals leave behind. The passing of time makes the return increasingly difficult. Those who give birth to children in the US find it particularly difficult to return "home" because the children insist on staying in the US.

ACQUIRING A SECOND CULTURE: ACCULTURATION AND ASSIMILATION

The Interplay of Individual and Society

John Berry[20] presents a heuristic paradigm in which he considers the degree to which individuals value keeping their original cultural orientation, and the degree to which they find it valuable to maintain a relationship with the second culture. Those individuals who wish to preserve their culture and also relate to the second culture "integrate." Those who do not value preserving their original culture and value the relationship with the second culture "assimilate." Those who value their culture and do not care for the second culture tend to "separate." And, finally, those who do not value either culture become "marginalized."

Since there has been a strong movement toward cultural preservation and identity assertion it is likely that Latinos at this time are most likely to integrate. Some, particularly those who feel alienated from US society, tend to remain separate, but few seem to assimilate or to remain marginalized. That is because most tend to value their culture of origin, or their enculturation. Berry also addresses the reciprocal approaches that the receiving culture adopts to relate to immigrants. Individual integration has its societal parallel in multiculturalism, in which the immigrants' culture is valued and society wishes to respect that cultural difference. Multiculturalism is the result of society accepting those who are different and proud to be so. Assimilation is the social parallel of the melting pot phenomenon in which the larger society accepts those who give up their original culture. If society respects the culture of the immigrants and does not wish for them to mix the result is segregation. This is what at the individual level means separation. Finally, when society finds no value in the culture of the immigrant and does not wish to have them integrate the result is exclusion. This is what at the individual level parallels marginalization.

In sum, immigrant integration corresponds to multiculturalism in a larger societal framework. Individual assimilation matches the melting pot from a larger society perspective. Separation corresponds to social segregation, and individual marginalization matches social exclusion. Berry's paradigm emphasizes that it is both the attitude of the immigrant and the attitude of the receiving culture which result in forces that affect the way in which both immigrants and the receiving society behave. Marketers, in their efforts to connect with consumers, can consider that accepting the differences of Latinos promotes their harmonic integration in a multicultural society. This process elevates self-esteem and when paired with brand attributes, it can create long-lasting brand relationships.

At the time of this writing the so called "immigration debate" is acrimonious and it is hard to predict how the larger society will behave toward immigrants in the near future. Nevertheless in the past 30 years or so there has been a tendency by the majority of US society to embrace diversity, and the cultural esteem of Hispanics has been elevated by wider acceptance and respect. Greater and more visible Hispanic achievements have contributed to this increased acceptance. The likely outcome is that integration in a multicultural framework is the trend of the future. Most Hispanics have no reason for forgetting their original culture at this point. Hispanics appear to see more social and economic value in preserving key elements of their heritage. But let us not make the mistake to think that such preservation is a copy of what Latin Americans experience in their countries, it is the preservation of the synergistic cultural identity of being Latino in the US.

Acculturation as a Process

"How groups and individuals orient themselves to and deal with this process of culture contact and change" is considered acculturation.[21] Assimilation is one of the possible outcomes of the acculturation process when individuals do not feel an attachment to their original culture and attribute strong value to the host culture. Another outcome of the acculturation process can be biculturalism or integration to the host culture. That can happen when the individual holds his or her original culture in high esteem and also appreciates the host culture. As discussed earlier, the host culture also plays an important role in how individuals acculturate. If they are valued by the host culture, and this host culture also values diversity, then multiculturalism takes place. The receiving culture plays a very important role in how immigrants feel and behave, and how they adapt or fail to adapt to the new society.

The Conill–Toyota Motor Sales Case Study at the end of this chapter describes the advertising campaign of the Toyota Tundra directed at Mexican-born Hispanic males intending to buy a full-size pickup. Toyota faced strong competition from other major US brand trucks that had already acquired brand equity for their toughness in Mexico. Conill, their US advertising agency, developed their "Tundrazo" campaign based on the communication concept and tagline: "Tundra, as strong as the man who drives it." Then they supported the campaign with traditional Mexican events, sports, and music, all intended to connect the US Mexican male target to the Toyota Tundra. "Tundrazo" charreadas, "Tundrazo" Mexican music tours, and traditionally oriented integrated media communications were implemented to link the Tundra and the "jefe" (meaning strong leader in Spanish) who drives it. Toyota and Conill tapped into the emotional need for position and power of those acculturating to life in another culture.

Biculturalism, a subset of multiculturalism, is not necessarily a transitional stage between one culture and the other. It can be a semi-permanent state in which individuals find themselves. Thus, bicultural individuals are precisely the elements of a new identity. Many marketers, researchers, and thinkers have thought that the bicultural would eventually assimilate, but that is not necessarily the case. What we are observing is an emerging Hispanic identity that is bicultural in a synergistic way. There is not absolute biculturalism because elements of two cultures are not just mixed with elements of the other culture. Elements of both cultures start to blend, in an interaction sense, so that a new identity develops that is different from the original cultures. This is something that needs further research and understanding. What is the new identity that Latinos are claiming in the US?

Figure 5.2 illustrates how biculturalism consists of enlarging the cultural repertoire of an individual, whereas assimilation keeps the repertoire constant by replacing one culture with another.

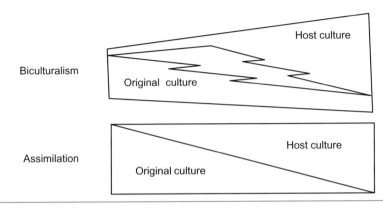

Figure 5.2 Biculturism and assimilation.

In the illustration of biculturalism, the jagged center is an attempt to represent the resulting uniqueness of the synergy of the two cultures coming together. It is the result of the interaction of both cultures.[22]

The marketing of many products and services to Hispanics is contributing to the building of capabilities in their second culture, while acknowledging the need to include elements of the first culture to maintain comfort level in this transition. Biculturalism appears to be now the most prevalent strategy used by Hispanics in order to deal with cultural change in this new society. Those who are relatively new to the US understand the need to learn the second culture. Those who in the past had abandoned their Hispanic orientation are now reclaiming it themselves or through their children as part of a "roots" phenomenon that has swept the US. This is sometimes called retro-acculturation. This seems to be happening because it is now a more positive experience, in general, to be Hispanic in the US. Despite remnant and lurking prejudice and discrimination, the overall balance of Hispanic experience in the US is now more positive than it had been at other points in time.

The Alma DDB: State Farm Case Study at the end of this chapter describes an advertising campaign for Hispanics with a strong cultural affinity to their country of origin whether they were Spanish dominant or bilingual. The aim was to increase the bond between State Farm and young Hispanics by tapping into cultural roots and their dreams of success in this country. The advertising campaign, La Banda del Pueblo, featured a regional Mexican band struggling for success in the US portrayed in a reality show–type advertainment. Alma DDB created an 8-week reality series supported by TV, Internet, CDs, and concerts to involve the Hispanic target with the band as its members took advantage of their "big opportunity." The Alma DDB–State Farm campaign is symbolic of a company which understands the struggle of those who work against odds in their process of acculturation to a new culture. It was used successfully in this case to build emotional affinity with Latinos who still maintain a strong connection to their heritage and to increase positive perceptions of State Farm as a helping hand.

Are These Immigrants like Their Predecessors?

Many marketers continue to ask the question of whether Hispanics will undergo the same experience as their counterparts from Europe experienced in the 1800s and early 1900s. These marketers seem to think that if immigrants will eventually assimilate, then there is no reason to bother with their transitional stages. It is commonly known that immigrants from Europe eventually assimilated. They, however, had different immigration goals than those of today's Hispanics. European immigrants wanted to escape famine, violence, and turmoil. Many wanted to forget their bitter past. While that may be true for some Hispanics it is not so for the majority.

While many Latino immigrants wish to make the US their new home, they maintain emotional and behavioral links with their country of origin.[23] In addition, regardless of attempts to control undocumented immigration it is unlikely that it will stop completely and that, along with legal immigration, it continues to refresh the ranks of Latinos. Many communities become heavily Hispanic, and remaining Hispanic is increasingly easy and achievable. Still, most Hispanics understand very well that their economic and social future depends on being able to succeed in US culture. Thus being bicultural becomes a most attractive outcome.

Biculturalism and Bilingualism Are Advantages

Some think of bicultural Hispanics as those who merge the best of both worlds. They are said to have the opportunity to select attributes of both cultures that they appreciate. Those who become bicultural, as opposed to assimilated, seem to have a more complex view on life. Those who appreciate both cultures are more likely to have offsprings that appreciate diversity. The complexity of new bicultural societies like Quebec in Canada and US Hispanics makes biculturalism a way of being and not just a state of transition. There are studies that have documented both negative and positive aspects of bilingualism. The balance, however, appears to be positive.[24]

It seems obvious that individuals who look at the world from more than one perspective would have an advantage over those who do not. Bilingualism, unfortunately, has been the label loosely applied to many who are not only not bilingual but rather functionally illiterate in one or both languages. The fact that someone says a few words in Spanish and a few words in English does not make him or her bilingual. When someone has the necessary competence to communicate in an articulate and effective fashion in one language and another, then that person can be said to be bilingual. These are the individuals who are socially advantaged by having a dual communication perspective and cultural outlook.[25] A notion that derives from this line of reasoning is that if more Hispanics become increasingly educated in both English and Spanish, they will likely make increasingly important contributions to US society.

This will contradict the negativism that many ethnocentric writers have publicized when reflecting on the impact of Hispanic growth and bilingualism in the US.[26]

Not from Here and Not from There: Third-Culture Individuals

After crossing cultures, belonging to the original or host cultures becomes difficult. Some Latinos in the US are often quoted as saying *ni soy de aquí ni soy de allá*, or "I am neither from here nor from there." That is part of the experience of cultural change. As immigrants move from one culture to another they find that their culture of origin becomes more and more distant. Unfortunately the second culture, for many, is also elusive. The reasons why the second culture is not eagerly adopted include the following.

■ The individual rejects the second culture for not having the qualities he or she misses from the first culture. For example, the person may dismiss the second culture as a cold and unfriendly culture and may justify being in the US for the economic advantage but not for the customs. The justification of economic benefit seems to compensate for the suffering of culture shock and lack of social integration, thus the individual can rationalize being in the US without integrating into the larger society. The theory of cognitive dissonance appears to explain this phenomenon. If the salient element for immigration is economic gain, then that helps the individual justify why they are here without having to think or feel affinity for the second culture "I am here because I need the money."[27]

■ The individual aspires to be part of the second culture, but this receiving culture may not welcome the immigrant as he or she may be perceived as having a different set of standards and behaviors. In this situation the incoming person may develop a "sour grapes" syndrome and express disdain for the second culture even though he or she originally wanted to be part of it. This can result in separation or segregation. Clearly, a combination of this and the above reason is also a likely explanation for not wishing to belong.

The problem is that even when one remains marginal, separate, or segregated, one also loses touch with one's first culture. The condition of being different or marginal is known as the "third-culture" phenomenon. Research conducted with children of expatriates show that these children, even after they are adults, tend to feel most comfortable associating with others who share the third-culture experience.[28] All those who "are not from here and not from there" share something important. They share being different, marginal,[29] with the salient identity of not belonging. This is a phenomenon that has not been widely recognized but that should help explain why there are communities of expatriates who do not mix well with their host culture.

"Third culture" is a concept that stands for the result of immigration without full assimilation in the receiving culture. Many Latinos, for example, after immigrating to the US, find themselves affiliating with others who have had similar experiences, both in their native country and in adapting themselves to living in the US. In a paradoxical way, when they go back to their country of origin they find out they do not belong anymore. Their friends and relatives in their native land accuse them of speaking "funny," dressing different, behaving arrogant, being richer, and so on. Interestingly, in the US they are also accused of speaking "funny" and being different in many ways. These people do not fit in their original culture nor do they belong to the new culture. They become members of a "third culture." The third-culture phenomenon becomes more pronounced among marginalized young people. They experience adolescence rebelling against their parents and also society at large. They wind up having a unique identity.

The Chicano movement of the 1960s is a relevant example of this third-culture phenomenon.[30] It was a movement of Mexicans in the US in search for a new identity associated with strong social and political tendencies. Nuyoricans, Puerto Ricans raised in New York, are also a salient example of people who have experienced a struggle for identity. "The experience of being in between, so deeply familiar to Puerto Ricans in the United States, thus harbors the possibility of an intricate politics of freedom and resistance."[31]

Marketing to members of a third culture demands a different way of thinking. Communicating with groups of people who are in search of identity requires sensitivity to their needs in their duality and struggle for identity. US media directed to Hispanics has incorrectly assumed that US Hispanics would continue to relate to imagery and ideals of their countries of origin. It has not been until recently that these media began to recognize that reaching Hispanic consumers in the US requires more than showing what Mexicans watch in Mexico City, or Venezuelans watch in Caracas. A new generation of shows has started to represent the life experience of Hispanics in the US in its search for a new way of being. Marketers and media who recognize this evolution are more likely to connect and establish lasting relationships with new Latinos. In advertising, the positioning of products also needs to address this emerging identity. Selling products to consumers as if they were still in Michoacán or in San Salvador would be irrelevant.

A New Hispanic/Latino Identity

While many Latinos do not appreciate the terms "Hispanic" or "Latino," and forgive the paradoxical statement, a pan-Latin-American identity seems to be emerging. As immigrants from different parts of Latin America have experienced the marginalization inherent in being part of a third culture, they share more in common. The labels are debatable, but the sense of identification with others that share Latin-American roots seems to be growing. The pan-Latino phenomenon occurring in New York[32] seems to be spreading to many other areas of the US.

Marketers should consider that while a single label is not likely to please everyone, a new emergent way of being needs to be investigated. How are pan-Latino consumers evolving in the US marketplace? What ideas, lifestyles, values, and other factors are relevant to them? How can they be better targeted and engaged? These are emerging questions that market research ought to inform.

SEGMENTING HISPANICS BY ACCULTURATION PHASES

Marketing generally segments consumers in order to more accurately develop products and customized marketing programs directed to relatively homogeneous types of people. The introduction of Integrated Marketing Communication (IMC), however, has challenged the idea that consumers need to be aggregated in relatively large segments. More extreme IMC advocates endorse the idea that new marketing approaches should be based on one-on-one customization and not on segments. Some speak of aggregations of individuals as opposed to segmenting a population.[33] This is because new technologies permit the customization of products and messages. For example, if you are a customer of Amazon.com you are your own segment. Your purchase history identifies your profile and Amazon.com tries to target you with offerings that match your unique profile. Still, the majority of marketing organizations still feel that having rough aggregates, or segments, of consumers who share some elements in common is an effort saving device while waiting for individual customization to become more feasible.

There are different ways to segment customers.[34] Many segmentation approaches rely on demographics. Others rely on demographics and psychographics. Still others use behavioral data to create segments of customers who exhibit similar behaviors. Clearly, if a segmentation approach is not pragmatically oriented to the needs of the marketers it can be useless.

Linear Segmentation

In the practice of marketing to Latinos there have been several efforts to segment Hispanics. One of the most common approaches in segmenting Hispanic consumers has consisted of a linear division of Hispanics into categories like Spanish dominant, transitional, and English dominant. Clearly, Spanish-dominant consumers exhibit certain common behavioral patterns associated with their language behavior. Those called transitionals or partially acculturated are those who are supposed to be between cultural worlds. Then, those who are English dominant are supposed to be those who have technically assimilated. This approach has the weakness of assuming that acculturation is a progressive process that goes from being "completely Hispanic" to being completely immersed in the US Anglo culture. This perspective points to the end process of acculturation as being assimilation and does not allow for the emergence of a new identity or biculturalism. This oversimplified perspective has been widely used and marketers have assumed that all those in one of these large categories show very similar behaviors, without further exploring the nuances that may make subgroups substantially different from each other.

Acculturation Segmentation in Two Dimensions

Clearly, there are variables in addition to language dependence that influence how people behave. In the mid-1990s, based on the psychological literature, the authors of this book introduced to the practice of Hispanic Marketing the idea that acculturation is not likely linear but at a minimum bi-dimensional, if not multidimensional.[35] It did not make intuitive sense that Hispanics would have to abandon their original culture to become increasingly acculturated. Hispanics could keep their original culture, add elements of the second culture to their repertoire, abandon their original culture in favor of the second culture, or claim a new identity, as we have discussed earlier.

In addition, acculturation should happen in a continuous and not a discrete fashion. There can be literally infinite gradations of culture acquisition. This means that individuals can vary quite a bit along acculturation dimensions even in relatively homogeneous subgroups.

Figure 5.3 illustrates this bi-dimensional approach to acculturation segmentation.

This empirical classification generally is built through the creation of indexes that incorporate measures that reflect one or the other cultural orientation. In other words, the *X* axis represents language and behaviors that are strongly associated with Latino culture, and the axis itself is built by means of a mathematical function, like a simple sum, of these variables. Similarly the *Y* axis represents English-language dominance and behaviors typically associated with an Anglo orientation. It can be observed that individuals can vary in their degree of belongingness to each of the quadrants. That is possible because their endorsement of cultural behaviors is variable. Thus an acculturated person can lean more toward the Hispanic end,

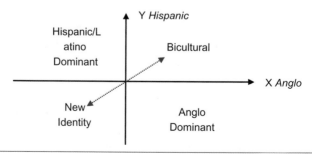

Figure 5.3 Bi-dimensional approach to acculturation segmentation.

be equally Hispanic/Anglo oriented, or be highly Anglo and relatively low in their Hispanic orientation. Each quadrant allows for different degrees of the cultural orientation represented by the quadrant.

This Cartesian coordinate system shows that individuals falling in the upper left-hand quadrant are Hispanic Dominant. Clearly this label is a simplification, but it is intended to refer to those Hispanics who are culturally and linguistically defined by their Hispanic origin. These are individuals who depend on the Spanish language for communication. Their attitudes are strongly aligned with the values of their countries of origin. They tend to be heavily dependent on Spanish-language didactic information to make consumer decisions. These are individuals who tend to be quite open to commercial messages because they depend on them for learning about products and services. They have not adopted the cynicism that characterizes their "assimilated" counterparts.

Bicultural individuals combine their cultural repertoires to different degrees. These are people who can navigate between the Hispanic and Anglo cultures. They tend to make consumer decisions based on the relevance of the cultural cues of the situation and their reference group when making choices. They have a more ample repertoire of behaviors available to them. In many ways this quadrant represents the position in which most Latinos are likely to find themselves eventually. That is, individuals who do not give up their Hispanic culture but who learn how to navigate the mainstream culture, thus becoming bicultural.

The McDonald's–d expósito & Partners Case Study provides an example of a campaign targeted to Spanish-preferred and bilingual and bicultural New York Hispanics based on cultural similarities versus those of language and acculturation levels. The Hispanic Tangustoso campaign for the McDonald's Angus Third-Pounders emphasized the benefits of the taste of the Angus burger and the overall feeling of satisfaction after consuming it, commonalities which they confirmed through focus groups. This orientation to the senses for Hispanics differed culturally from the main benefit of price for the non-Hispanic general market advertising.

The word "Tangustoso" was created specifically for this campaign by combining two Spanish words meaning "so" and "tasty." d expósito & Partners developed a prelaunch "teaser" around "what is Tangustoso" using radio, event activation, and outdoor channels for leading Latino consumers totangustoso.com. The agency followed with a hard launch using bilingual TV, print, nontraditional outdoor media, and various other buzz-generation means. They extended the campaign with an online media plan to keep interest and motivation alive. The focus which drove the success of the entire campaign was the combination of the culturally shared benefits of taste and satisfaction common to these Hispanic acculturation segments. It demonstrates the power of shared heritage across various stages of Latinos' integration into the larger US culture, and the persistence of Latin roots in shaping the cultural landscape.

Biculturals will become a dominant group if US society continues to value Hispanic culture and allows for plurality to flourish. Otherwise, other quadrants will become more dominant in the future. At this time in history the US seems to have learned to appreciate Hispanic culture, and Hispanics are led to believe that their culture and language are valued. That is why Hispanic music, food, fashion, and other cultural manifestations are increasingly popular. It has to be acknowledged, nevertheless, that sociopolitical attitudes have been in flux.

Anglo-dominant individuals are those who have largely adopted Anglo behaviors and orientations. These are individuals who may still have some emotional relationship with Hispanic cultural manifestations but who generally identify themselves as "Americans" as opposed to "Hispanic Americans," "Mexican Americans," or another combination. They are likely to speak English almost exclusively, and they resemble non-Hispanics in their cynicism toward commercial messages. Individuals in this quadrant, however, seem to be living through a period or "root" searching as they realize that their Hispanic background is now desirable and valuable. Many are prompting their children to learn Spanish and they, themselves, are increasingly attempting to learn the Spanish that either they have forgotten or never learned. A process of retro-acculturation is likely to take increasing importance among these individuals.

New identity individuals are, in concept, those who have not allied themselves with the US Anglo-dominant culture, and have not preserved to any large extent the culture of their parents because they do not identify with it. They are "not from here and not from there." They are those third-culture individuals discussed earlier. They can be those who have identified themselves as Chicanos, Nuyoricans, Raza, or some other unique label. These are individuals who feel pride in their unique identity and either reject or are unable to identify with their culture of origin or the dominant culture of the US. In terms of consumer behavior, these are individuals who like to experiment and innovate because they have little to lose. Thus, they wear unusual clothing like baggy pants, or drive extravagant cars (low riders). Many of their innovations set trends that other groups pursue later. These individuals build a cultural identity out of the need for one.

The bi-directional arrow in Figure 5.3 from "New Identity" individuals to "Biculturals" is intended to represent the complex conceptual relationships between these two types of people. It seems as if a large part of those who are "Bicultural" can also be "New Identity" Hispanics. Almost as if it were a matter of degree the extent to which a new identity is being explored and enacted, going from the extreme lower left corner to the extreme upper right corner. That is, a scale from a very unique new identity to a more blended cultural mix.

A bi-dimensional segmentation like this has been helpful to marketers in identifying acculturation subtleties that will impact interest in and purchase of products and services. The relatively large segments it provides have been useful to differentiate Latino targets by cultural and language attachment and preference.

This bi-dimensional acculturation segmentation, however, can be further enhanced by including product usage and other attitudes and behaviors among the variables utilized in the statistical analysis. This approach can be very useful in guiding the marketer in identifying those more likely to purchase a product and also what beliefs and values are associated with specific subsegments. Clearly, the planning of the questionnaire used for any segmentation will heavily influence its usefulness.

Cultural Segmentation in Multiple Dimensions

The reader may be interested in considering what would happen if cultural variables were measured in the overall population, including all the emerging minorities that are literally changing the color palette of the US. The variables would include cultural practices, preferences, attitudes, beliefs, and other behaviors. In such a scenario it would be possible to plot the cultural attachment or cultural affinity of every individual in a Hispanic, Anglo, African-American, Asian, American Indian, etc., multidimensional space.

This approach would make sense because individuals living in the US are likely influenced not just by Anglo culture but also by all other cultures that share the life of the nation. An effort like this would represent an important exploration and a contribution to our understanding of cultural behavior for marketing purposes.

Crossing Acculturation with Other Variables

To enhance the usefulness of acculturation segmentation approaches it is suggested that other variables or dimensions be crossed by acculturation types. Some marketers have experimented with this idea.

Life Stage

Crossing acculturation with life stage can be quite useful when attempting to refine the types of people that are more likely to be more or less acculturated. Table 5.3 exemplifies how one such approach would look.

TABLE 5.3 Crossing Acculturation with Life Stage

	Young with No Children	Young with Children	Mature with Grown Children	Senior
Hispanic Dominant				
Bicultural				
New Identity				
Assimilated				

This approach refines the segmentation based solely on acculturation by adding the nuance of typical life stages. As the marketer understands what characterizes the consumer behaviors of each of the cells in the 4 × 4 classification, he or she can make decisions about what products would be most relevant to each subsegment, and also what communications and media would be most appropriate for each. Based on knowledge from past research, data reported elsewhere in this book, and past experience one could hypothesize that young people without children are more likely to be concentrated in the lower left-hand cells. These Latinos would most likely be relevant to the marketers of MP3 players, for example, to be reached via social media online, and communicated to with the symbolism prevalent in multicultural youth culture and in English with perhaps some code-switching. In all cases, specific messaging should be developed based on insights derived from in-depth qualitative investigation.

Shopping Style

Another approach with which some marketers have experimented is to cross acculturation by shopping styles. This can be useful when trying to assess what characterizes the shopping style of Hispanics in different stages of acculturation. Table 5.4 exemplifies this type of segmentation.

In this example, and also based on experience, we could hypothesize that the entertainment seekers and bargain hunters would be concentrated in the upper right-hand area of the table, while the explorers and planners would be more likely to be found in the lower left-hand area. It should be emphasized again that only in-depth research can enable the marketer to understand how to approach each of the cells in the table. Clearly, the virtue of the granularity added by looking at other dimensions in addition to acculturation alone can make the work of the marketer more productive.

Other Combinations

An attempt that also includes additional dimensions is the recently publicized "Hispanic Lifestyles" segmentation by research company Millward Brown.[36] They also created a two-dimensional space in which one dimension goes from Spanish/Latin culture to

TABLE 5.4 Crossing Acculturation with Shopping Styles

	Explorer	Planner	Entertainment Seeker	Bargain Hunter
Hispanic Dominant				
Bicultural				
New Identity				
Assimilated				

Anglo/US culture, and the other dimension is a Liberal to Conservative dimension. Within this space they located clusters of Hispanic consumers characterized by their attitudes and perspectives on life:

- The Social cluster who are group oriented, for whom image is important, and enjoy living the moment.
- The Go-getter "Yuppie" cluster who are image oriented, risk taker, and liberal.
- The Virtuous who tend to be religious, family oriented, and conservative.
- The Progressive who are entrepreneurial, independent, and open minded.
- The Pragmatic who tend to be fatalistic, resentful, and conservative.

In their investigation, Millward Brown found that those who are more pragmatic tend to be likely to be oriented toward the Latin culture and be more conservative, while those who are "go-getters" tend to be more oriented to US culture and be more attitudinally liberal.

The approach that this effort represents is interesting because it attempts to characterize Latino consumers with greater precision. While some of the labels used in this approach may be controversial, the effort is innovative. In this example one can see a movement toward a more complex view of Hispanic consumer behavior as it relates to values and life orientations.

Taking Cultural Identification into Account

There are market research and consulting companies that in their data explorations have realized that those Latinos that can be categorized as Hispanic or Spanish dominant can many times be subsegmented further based on their identification with their culture of origin. Thus, companies like Synovate have created concepts such as Cultural Tension to describe Hispanics that may be similar to each other in most demographics and language use but who experience the relationship with the receiving culture differently. Thus, there are Latinos who feel discriminated, and have a strong attachment to the traditions of their country of origin and long for those who are still there. Conversely, there are those Hispanics who do not feel that discrimination in the US is something that affects them, have strong links to family and friends in the US, and are very willing to learn and adapt to their new cultural environment.

The Multicultural Marketing Study of the Yankelovich Monitor uncovered that there are Hispanics or Spanish-dominant Hispanics who have strong cultural affinity with the folkways of their country of origin, but that others do not. Those Latinos who do not experience cultural affinity with their origins are more eager to learn and adapt to the mores of the US.

These two sets of discoveries are important for marketers. First, because they refine the understanding of those who are generally categorized as Hispanic or Spanish dominant, and second because they provide insights as to how to approach these consumers. Those who feel a strong connection with their culture of origin can be targeted with appeals that emphasize their cultural roots. In the case of those who feel less cultural identification, appeals to change and become a member of the new society ought to be more motivational.

A Note About "Unacculturated" Hispanics

There have been segmentation efforts that have labeled Latinos who are Spanish or Hispanic dominant as being "unacculturated." That label is problematic. If a human being lives in any society he or she has have gone through the process of learning their own culture or enculturation, and possibly also the process of learning another culture or acculturation. Being unacculturated suggests that there are Latinos in the US that have not been acculturated at all. That seems rare and unlikely as acculturation is a process, not a fixed state. The description of someone being more or less acculturated seems more accurate than labeling all those who are Hispanic or Spanish dominant as unacculturated.

How to Make Segmentation More Productive

As contemporary marketing strives to establish relationships with individual consumers, consumer segments will become smaller and more finely tuned. Although language and cultural data will continue to make the work of the marketer easier in product design and messaging, many other behavioral consumer variables will be incorporated in future segmentations. The more actionable the segmentation is the more productive the results of using it. A combination of finely tuned cultural, attitudinal, behavioral, geographic, and demographic factors will make the marketer increasingly powerful. But marketers have generally grown savvy in their understanding of consumer behavior. They increasingly realize that consumers have a lot more choice and control and that marketing efforts need to be geared to the creation of long-lasting relationships based on trust.

More Complexity

As more Hispanic consumers are born in the US and as more of those born abroad become bicultural or assimilate, the less useful are segmentations based on acculturation alone. It is not enough to know if you can target Latinos in Spanish or English, or both languages. It is important now to understand how individuals and households may be different even if their stage in the acculturation process is the same.

Consider the example of two families in Table 5.5.[37]

While both families would normally be classified as Hispanic or Spanish dominant in most current segmentations, these two families have greatly different perspectives on life. They see the world in different ways beyond their current acculturation stage. Consequently, the marketer that limits him- herself to aggregating Hispanics according to number of years in the US and/or their language ability would be ignoring much of the lifestyle that may benefit his or her plans.

TABLE 5.5 Differences Between Latino Families in Same Stage of the Acculturation Process

The Ulibarri Family	The Galeano Family
10 years in the US	10 years in the US
More fluent in Spanish	More fluent in Spanish
5 children	1 child
Mr. Ulibarri has two jobs	Mr. Galeano has one job
Mrs. Ulibarri is a homemaker	Mrs. Galeano has a job
Both are rushed making ends meet	Both continue their education in the evenings
Go to parks on weekends	Go to the movies and malls on weekends
Feel somewhat left behind and the subject of prejudice	Look forward to the future with optimism

Segmenting by Brand Engagement

To illustrate the need to go beyond acculturation we will use some of the data from the 2009 Multicultural Marketing Study of the Florida State University Center for Hispanic Marketing Communication and DMS Research, with the collaboration of Captura Group. The data was collected online from multiple cultural groups but this analysis focuses on Hispanics who either preferred to answer the questionnaire in Spanish or in English. In this national sample 541 respondents answered in English and 351 answered in Spanish. Part of the questionnaire was about the concept of brand engagement.[38] The eight original items of the Brand Engagement Scale[39] were included in an index. The eight items were:

- I have a special bond with the brands that I like.
- I consider my favorite brands to be a part of myself.
- I often feel a personal connection between my brands and me.
- Part of me is defined by important brands in my life.
- I feel as if I have a close personal connection with the brands I most prefer.
- I can identify with important brands in my life.
- There are links between the brands that I prefer and how I view myself.
- My favorite brands are an important indication of who I am.

The resulting index was then submitted to a cluster analysis routine (*K* Means) to see if different types of Hispanics could be categorized using this scale. Two clear clusters of types of Latinos emerged, those that are strongly brand engaged and those who are weakly brand engaged. To check that an indicator of acculturation was not redundant with these two types of consumers, we cross-tabulated the high and low brand engaged with those who answer the questionnaire in English or in Spanish. Table 5.6 shows the results.

TABLE 5.6 Language Used to Answer Survey Spanish by Cluster of Brand Engagement

Language Used to Answer by Cluster of Brand Engagement

| | | | Clusters | |
			Low	High
Answered	English	Count	243	298
		%	53.5	68.0
	Spanish	Count	211	140
		%	46.5	32.0
Total		Count	454	438
		%	100.0	100.0

While there was a statistically significant tendency for those who answered in English to be more brand engaged, and those who answered in Spanish to be less brand engaged, the association is far from perfect. It can be seen that about half of the low brand-engaged Latinos answered in English, and that almost a third of those highly engaged answered the questionnaire in Spanish. Thus, if we had limited ourselves to segment on acculturation only we would have missed much nuance in these types of Hispanics. The reader may be surprised by these findings because less-acculturated Latinos have been usually characterized as being more brand loyal. Brand loyalty and brand engagement are different concepts. Brand loyalty is brand specific while brand engagement is about an overall relationship with brands in a general sense.

In further examining the data we compared low and high brand-engaged Latinos with respect to their media behaviors. We found that those low brand engaged are more likely to be exposed to Spanish-language TV and the Internet than their highly brand-engaged counterparts (5.8 hours per week versus 4.4 for TV, and 4.1 and 2.7 hours for the Internet). No such differences were found for weekly Spanish-language exposure to radio, newspapers, magazines, or books. Also, there were no differences in brand engagement by age or number of people living in the household. Income did differentiate between low and high brand-engaged Hispanics with those with higher income being more brand engaged.

If we had ignored an important concept like brand engagement in segmenting Hispanics we would have missed much of the differences among them. This is why future segmentations ought to go farther than segmenting by acculturation alone. While acculturation has a relationship with brand engagement it is not redundant with it. Brand engagement helps explain further Latino consumer behavior. The finding that those with somewhat higher incomes are more brand engaged is not surprising as more affluent Hispanics have more opportunities to develop affinities with brands.

We further examined some other differences between Hispanics who are low and high in brand engagement. Those who are low brand engaged were found to be less likely to use social networking sites online to express themselves or to stay connected with their culture than those more highly brand engaged. These findings are of importance to marketers because they can capitalize on these insights to connect with Latino consumers. Those Hispanics more likely to use social networking sites for self-expression and for cultural connection will have a tendency to engage with the brands in those sites. We also found that those more brand engaged are more likely to indicate that "if an athlete of my same culture/ethnicity endorses a product I am more likely to buy it" than those less brand engaged.

The variables utilized for specific segmentation needs will vary depending on the needs and goals of marketers. The point we have demonstrated here, however, is that acculturation alone does not account for much of the variability that modern Hispanics exhibit in this more complex social and marketing environment.

General Segmentations That Include Ethnic/Cultural Segments

What makes Hispanics Hispanic, again, is their culture, both objective and subjective. While language is part of the culture it is not the only element that differentiates Latinos, particularly not so at a time when Hispanic youth is mostly US born.

General consumer segmentation approaches that include attitudes, brands, category usage, values, and perhaps use of leisure time, should now start including cultural variables that can help highlight cultural elements in segments. Thus, consciously including cultural values, beliefs, and other culture bound elements, including some acculturation variables into general segmentations is becoming a necessity. That is true particularly now that the growth of the US consumer market is being more strongly fueled by emerging minorities.

Thus future segments should identify cultural affinities and other cultural elements that will help understand that, for example, a "cosmopolite" segment has a strong Asian and Latino component. That would be very useful for travel and leisure industries so they can strategize accordingly. Knowing the cultural/ethnic composition of segments can also highlight the way in which these particular segments can be approached and communicated to.

It is unlikely that having separate Latino or African-American segmentations, for example, can be sustainable in the long run. What marketers need to understand is that they can have general segmentations but that these segmentations need to measure cultural variables so that specific cultural targets can be addressed properly and profitably. What the marketer should not conclude is that we have come to the end of ethnic or cultural marketing. That is not the case at all. We are arriving at the stage where diverse cultures in the US are driving marketing efforts and that the non-Hispanic White segment is not anymore the denominator of marketing efforts.

A culturally based general segmentation can be very useful in delineating the groups of people that will be important targets for a brand. The cultural element should be used to emphasize how to communicate those brands to different segments. After all, all marketing is cultural.

All Marketing Is Cultural

Many marketers still ask the question: What is different about marketing to Hispanics, Asians, African-Americans, etc.? Is not marketing just marketing?

Marketing is marketing but few marketers consciously realize that what they do is cultural marketing. So when they target women with children, they are really addressing a subculture in the US. When they address young people they are addressing another culture within a culture. When they target middle-class homeowners they are not just addressing a so called "demographic," they are addressing a culture.

There is little awareness of what a culture is. A culture is a set of designs for living that are shared by many people, and sometimes those designs for living are passed on from generation to generation.

Most advertising would not work if it were not cultural. The marketer attempts to connect with consumers who share something in common, but the "demographic" is not what they share in common, it is the way of being, thinking, doing, valuing, and feeling.

Thus, it should not be surprising that to reach out to Latinos, for example, the marketer needs to understand their culture. And that is profound because it goes to the core of who people are. That is what ethnic marketing consists of. It is the understanding of the culture and the contextual issues surrounding it. It is different because the culture is different, but also because it is a lot harder to market to a different culture than to the one you are part of. See, culture is like water for the fish, we are seldom aware of it. We think a joke is funny just because it is funny. Not so, a joke is funny because it is culturally bound. A joke is funny to a group of people who share a culture, and not to others. An emotional appeal is emotional to those who share a common reaction to that appeal.

When the marketer crosses cultures he or she needs to make many assumptions explicit. There is no more obviousness of water to the fish. The fish needs to become aware of the water in order to succeed. That is what has to happen with marketers. They need to step out of the comfort of their own culture to be effective in another. That is why it is so difficult to do cross-cultural marketing.

But, all marketing is cultural, and it is hard for many to realize that. So, now, why do we need to make special efforts to market to Hispanics, African-Americans, Asians, etc.? Because they swim in different waters. This is why segmentations need to be culturally informed, but not segregated. That is because cultural mores and tendencies are not isolated to those who come from that culture alone. Others have learned about the culture of diverse groups in the US and identify with their ways of life. This is an argument for more complex and more aware culturally based general segmentation.

Conclusions

The US has historically been a nation built on and influenced by immigration from various parts of the world. The resulting dynamic of cultural contacts continues to alter the identities of those who arrive and the nation as a whole ... we are always in flux. Currently the largest waves of immigrants swelling the population are from Latin America and Asia. Latinos make up the largest emerging minority segment, and now they continue to expand their numbers with that growth rate driven more by births than by immigration. At this same time that Hispanics are growing in their presence in the wider population, particularly among those who are younger, the predominantly non-Hispanic White population is both shrinking and aging. It is therefore critical for marketers to understand—what are the emerging cultural trends among these Hispanics who are becoming part of the broader US population as well as how are non-Hispanics being changed by their influence.

The process of cultural change implied by immigration and acculturation into a new cultural environment presents important opportunities to marketers. Acculturating individuals are open to new inputs and influences. They need to understand and participate in their new environment in order to succeed and reach an integration comfort level emotionally. However, they also want to maintain their own identity, formed in the early years of enculturation in their countries of origin or passed on by their parents if born in this country.

Early generations of immigrants to the US, mainly from Europe, became part of what was referred to as "the melting pot," generally taking on an American/Anglo identity and shedding their prior heritage. However, Latino immigrants, particularly the largest segment from Mexico, have been found to treasure their countries of origin, with many intending to return. Therefore, acculturation has become the more realistic term for their integration into this country, meaning the assumption of aspects of a new cultural identity while maintaining one's own.

The complex dynamics of acculturation, thought of as a continuous process rather than a one-dimensional progression, can be clarified for marketers through cultural segmentation. A bi-dimensional cultural approach which looks at degree of Hispanic and Anglo cultural affinities results in an empirical classification of Latinos. This segmentation approach yields four main segments—Bicultural, Hispanic/Latino Dominant, Anglo Dominant, and New Identity—and provides a useful starting point for understanding Latino acculturation.

What is particularly important for marketers to take into consideration is that the largest acculturation segment of the US Hispanic population is now bicultural, indicating that they are not only accepting of their own cultural roots, but the culture of the broader US society as well. This suggests a new Hispanic segment created through acculturation with a multidimensional capacity for seeing the world from two different perspectives and behaving according to those perceptions.

There is also another acculturation segment which appears to be leading in the definition of a new US Latino identity. This is the New Identity segment which is forged by the influence of being a Latino in the US rather than by being traditionally Latino or Anglo oriented. In some cases those sharing this emerging identity are close to being bicultural as well. It seems that there is a new Latino essence being created by the commonalities of being "neither from here nor from there."

The US non-Hispanic population is also being changed by the dynamic of Hispanic population expansion. More non-Hispanics in the US are being daily impacted by Latinos who live in their cities and neighborhoods, go to school with their children, become part of their families, or work with them. Evidence of Latino-objective culture is evident everywhere we turn in music, food, fashion, and everyday life. Non-Hispanics vary from welcoming these new Latino cultures to rejecting them and wanting Hispanics to leave the country. Yet, even those who reject these cultures are likely to eat Mexican food or dance to salsa music. Many non-Hispanics also realize that the younger Latino population will indeed be those who power the workforce of the future and support them in their older ages.

How the broader population is changing in attitudes and behavior as a result of the emerging Latino and other ethnic/cultural segments also needs to enter into the segmentation studies of the wider population. It is important for marketers to understand and tap into culturally related values, tastes, and behaviors stemming from emerging cultural influences affecting the nation.

IMPLICATIONS FOR MARKETERS

- Refine your understanding of your Hispanic target according to acculturation segmentation making sure to include relevant social and behavioral elements in the segmentation as well. This will provide breadth to your appeal across the market as well as guidance on appropriate communication.
- Remember that success in the US culture is critical for Hispanic consumers, and your marketing communications which acknowledge and support Latino achievements can contribute to their acculturation.
- Give attention to the fact that Hispanics generally maintain pride and fond remembrances for their own heritage, and that the non-Hispanic market also displays interest in Hispanic culture and its manifestations.

- Recognize that bicultural Hispanics are by far the largest segment of the US Latino population. This consumer target is complex and merits meticulous research to identify its potential relationship to your product or service.
- Keep up with the ongoing changes among Hispanic consumers. Hispanics creating a New Identity—neither predominantly from their culture of origin nor from the mainstream US culture—are influencing others on what it means to be Latino. The combination of Latinos who are bicultural with those who focus more on their evolving "third culture" is creating a wave of excitement in this country about all things Latino.
- Latinos are the largest minority in the US and are growing not only by immigration but even more so by births. They are a young market and in many respects represent the future of the country. Review your marketing strategy with this in mind. Your Hispanic initiatives may be central to the future of your company.
- Remember that all marketing is cultural, and that understanding the ways of being, thinking, acting, and feeling shared by a group is central to your success as a marketer, whether investigating the Latino population in the US or any other segment.

CASE STUDY: CONILL–TOYOTA MOTOR SALES

Company/Organization
Toyota Motor Sales

Advertising Agency
Conill Advertising

Campaign/Advertising Title
"Tundrazo"

Intended Hispanic Consumers
Working class, blue-collar Mexican men living in the Southwest who used their pickup trucks as work gear

Background
Ford and Chevy dominated the full-size pickup (FSPU) segment. Toyota's Tundra lingered in fifth place, because of its smaller size and lower payload compared to domestic models. Although the new Tundra was a bigger, tougher, and more powerful vehicle, it would be a challenge to change existing perceptions and show customers that the new Tundra had more "cojones" than any truck in the FSPU market.

Discovery Process/Research
Truck sales data from R.L. Polk, which measures Hispanic Registrations for the automotive industry, showed that conquering the Heartland would be critical to the new Tundra's success. Purchase funnel and imagery data indicated that FSPU intenders were predominantly Mexican and foreign born. Most held blue-collar jobs and had strong emotional ties to their Mexican heritage. FSPU owners in Texas told Conill that owning

(Continued)

a Ford or Chevy truck was their lifetime dream because back in Mexico these two brands symbolized strength and authenticity.

In order to track evolution of vehicle perception throughout the campaign, attributes such as "popular truck" and "looks tough" were added to the Toyota Ad Hoc Model Imagery Tracking Study. This research tool measured attributes, benefits, brand projections, and purchase funnel for each of the automotive segments in the Hispanic market.

Conill and Toyota had a difficult task ahead. Having an incredibly capable truck would not be enough to change these Latinos' perceptions. Tundra had to prove that it was worthy of their respect.

Cultural Insights

The audience viewed Tundra as a leisure vehicle, driven by white-collar professionals who avoid getting their hands dirty, not a truck for hardworking Mexicans. Latino intenders (people who identify themselves as Hispanic/Latino and are planning to buy a new FSPU within the next 2 years) looked up to an idealized psychological profile that they described as "*El Jefe*" (The Boss). They are "real men," highly respected by family, friends, and neighbors. To earn the title of El Jefe, Mexican men must live by the following unspoken code of values:

- Not afraid to work
- Never fear pain
- Never give up
- Live by example
- Never forget where you came from

Tundra had to earn El Jefe's respect and show it understood his lifestyle by demonstrating its capabilities and sharing his cultural pride.

Jefes were very proud of their music and the sport of charreadas (Mexican rodeo). While Regional Mexican music concerts were gaining unprecedented popularity, charreadas needed a push to be taken to the next level in the US. Tundra would join the target in their quest to give charreadas more notoriety by developing Tundrazo Charreadas.

Tundra would also support their music by developing the Tundrazo Music Tour. It is important to note that we chose the word "Tundrazo" instead of "Tundra" because adding the ending "azo" to any word in Spanish infuses it with a large dose of power.

Expression of Insights in the Campaign

Cultural insights permeated the entire engagement effort. The Communications Idea the agency developed, "Tundra, as strong as the man who drives it," welded the target's self-perception to the tough personality that Toyota needed to infuse into the Tundra. Used as a tagline, it connected all the pieces of the campaign.

Tundrazo Charreadas

These events paid homage to our target's Mexican rodeo tradition in the most respectful manner. We incorporated the Tundra's message of strength in the following ways:

- Elements of the sport were compared to a particular feature or benefit of the new Tundra, drawing powerful parallels between the two.
- A Charro Museum, developed by Conill and Toyota Motor Sales, served as a tribute to the sport's rich history and culture. Unobtrusive yet impressive images of the new Tundra were placed alongside the images of strong, valiant Charros.

Toyota Motor Sales "Tundrazo" campaign.

- Outside the museum, games related to the art of charreria were placed for Jefes and their families to enjoy while interacting with the Tundra. In one of the games, participants had to lasso Tundra's towing hitch to win.
- A personalized coffee-table book was awarded to men who successfully completed the charreria games. In it, winners were named Charro Completo, the highest level in charreria. The book featured striking color photos of charreadas alongside the new Tundra. On the back cover of each book was a photo of each proud Charro Completo (taken against a green screen) with text reading, "A truck should be as strong as [participant's name]."
- Attendees also received giveaways. These premiums would act as reminders of Tundrazo Charreadas and the strength the new Tundra stood for. They included branded Tundrazo Charreadas iPod covers, hats, belt buckles, and key chains.

The Tundrazo Music Tour
The Tundrazo Music Tour was a series of concerts that touched another of our target's emotional triggers: Regional Mexican music. It featured leading Mexican musicians, including Conjunto Primavera and Los Tigres del Norte. Conill chose bands that struck a chord in the target, known for the moving corridos (ballads) that are revered in Mexican truck culture. The event reminded our Jefes of their Mexican heritage once again, and showed them that Tundra has not forgotten where they came from.

Each concert kicked off with a Tundra video that played before the bands came onto the stage. Before an audience filled with anticipation and excitement, the video depicted the musicians' trailer breaking down on their way to the show. Luckily, the new Tundra

(Continued)

arrives to give them a lift and they make it to the show just in time. As the video ended, the musicians appeared and the concert began, all thanks to Tundra.

Integrated Media
Traditional elements of the campaign propelled the message that drivers of the new Tundra possess all the qualities of a Jefe. The tagline was reiterated in each piece: "Tundra, as strong as the man who drives it."

- TV spots showed drivers who are not afraid to work, never give up, lead by example, and do not fear pain. A national broadcast campaign was supported by a spot market buy in key Heartland markets.
- Print and out-of-home bolstered the theme.
- A soccer integrationz[40] tapped into this additional source of strength for our Mexican male target. It featured the new Tundra's impressive towing capabilities, as it appeared to drag the soccer game onto the TV screen.
- The campaign's interactive portion included banners that, once again, paid homage to the shared strength of the new Tundra and El Jefe. Then the mini-site featured the new Tundra's imposing capabilities, as well as elements of Tundrazo Charreadas and the Tundrazo Music Tour, reminding the target of Tundra's commitment to their heritage. Together, these pieces created a campaign that worked to make Tundra the unwavering Badge of Respect.
- Micro-documentaries honoring the beloved charreadas rodeos were produced and aired on Discovery En Español. They also ran inside of the Charro museums.

Effect of the Campaign
- Tundra was at 9% market share right before campaign launch and achieved its market share goal of 13% before the target date, enjoying a 42% growth in registrations year-over-year.
- A 7-point jump nationally in the "Looks Tough" attribute.
- A 21-point leap in the Heartland for the "Makes Me Look Tough" attribute. The Toyota Ad Hoc Model Imagery Study was used to measure Tundra's campaign performance.
- Consideration, Purchase Intent, and Popularity all increased.

What makes these results even more remarkable is that Tundra achieved them in a segment that declined in registrations 4% year-over-year between 2006 and 2007. Meanwhile, arch-rivals Ford and Chevrolet suffered, with Ford F-Series' registrations dropping 18% and Chevy Silverado's decreasing 6% in the same time period.

CASE STUDY: ALMA DDB–STATE FARM

Company/Organization Name
State Farm

Advertising Agency
Alma DDB with FiRe Advertainment

Campaign/Advertising Title
La Banda del Pueblo Reality Show

Intended Hispanic Consumers

The target for this advertising was US Hispanics with high cultural affinity toward their Hispanic culture, 18–49 years old. Even though language was a consideration when developing the idea for the show, which was developed in Spanish, cultural affinity was an even greater factor to consider. Young bicultural, bilingual Hispanics were not dismissed from the picture since we were aiming to create a cultural connection with our target—not just one based solely on language.

Background

In 2008 Alma DDB worked with its long-time client State Farm in creating a campaign that would strengthen the bond between the brand and its Hispanic consumers. The campaign, called Intersections, played out the natural tension that exists between what one wants and what one needs to achieve their dreams, and how State Farm was there to help consumers achieve their goals.

One of the TV spots, featuring a struggling group of musicians looking to make it in the US, turned into something much bigger. Sponsored by State Farm, the Band "Los Felinos" became the center of a multimedia advertisement campaign that included TV appearances, CD, videos, Internet presence, and a series of concerts, transforming a simple TV spot into a complete brand experience.

In 2009 Alma DDB and State Farm decided to leverage this award-winning campaign into a reality TV show on the Telemundo and Mun2 networks.

Thus was born La Banda del Pueblo, an 8-week reality series about the struggles of an up and coming regional Mexican band. The show, which aired from August through November 2009, brought State Farm inside Hispanic homes each week for a full hour through the gripping story of the members of the band and their road trip across the US riding in their well known blue van from the original TV commercial.

Additionally to the TV episodes we extended the on-air presence with a social media strategy. We had our very own paparazzi following the band and providing consumers with all the behind the scenes happenings.

Discovery Process/Research

Since "La Banda del Pueblo" show was an attempt to blur the boundaries between advertising, entertainment, and real life, a good amount of consumer research was involved in the developing of the band *per se* and of the reality show project.

Almost 2 years of findings and insights went into the developing of a format and a show that would ring true with Hispanics.

In 2008 Alma DDB planners and creatives attended grassroots events, like Fiesta Broadway in Los Angeles, conducted ethnographies, and one-on-ones. In as many ways as possible, the questions "What do you care about?" and, more importantly, "How do you know when someone cares about you?" were asked. The Alma DDB researchers immersed themselves in the lives and dreams of US Hispanics of all walks of life; they opened their homes to the Alma researchers and welcomed them to their families: the Alma DDB researchers ate, watched TV, went out, drove around town, and attended family events. They got to know the Hispanic target in real life, not in a lab setting.

Then, throughout 2009, the agency conducted specific research around the band and the relationship the target had with it. The goal was to understand the level of connection and relevancy, and the impact the band (and State Farm's sponsorship of it) had on the

(Continued)

brand's perceptions, especially those around "This is a company for people like me" and "This is a company that understands Hispanics." We found out that not only the perceptions had grown more positive; the sponsorship of the band even impacted consideration of State Farm and gave current customers more reasons to stay.

Finally, given the way consumers now integrate digital and traditional media when looking for entertainment and information, a series of focus groups were conducted to understand this relationship and the way Hispanics approach the Internet and the social networking tools it provides.

Cultural Insights

Several cultural insights came into play in the design of "La Banda del Pueblo." Each component of the show and its media strategy was supported by a strong cultural insight.

Why Will They Relate to the Band?

We know Hispanics come to the US in search of opportunities. It is a quest for a better way of life often impossible to attain in their countries of origin. Even for those born in the US, life achievements come in a less-predictable order with the road ahead not always clearly defined. As tough as the journey may be, hope is the engine that drives them toward the big prize at the end of the road, making it all worthwhile. They, therefore, celebrate every achievement, major or minor, knowing that accepting the accompanying responsibilities is just part of the price they pay to live in a great land of opportunity.

State Farm: "La Banda del Pueblo" Reality Show campaign.

Why Will They Believe State Farm as a Suitable Partner?
During the past couple of years US Hispanics had been feeling like the dream they had been working so hard to achieve was moving further away from them. Job losses, foreclosures, a weakened economy; everything they thought they left behind was again part of their lives. Hispanics always turn to each other to overcome difficulties like these, but in a foreign system there are things they cannot always help each other with, so they turn to companies they can trust. And, for Hispanics, a trustworthy company is more than a service provider, they want a friend, a partner, an extended family member who will take the time to get to know them and help them tackle the problems in becoming more established, while respecting where they are at right now.

That is why State Farm's promise—"Like a good neighbor, State Farm is there"— had the potential to resonate with this target and become extremely relevant.

Why a Reality Show Supported by a Strong Social Media Presence?
Hispanics have a natural ability to empathize with human stories, even more so with those that are real and that showcase the whole range of human emotions. They cry, laugh, get angry, and excited with and for the characters and they love to get involved in the story by voicing their opinions and sharing them with others. They have done it with novelas for a long time and now that Reality TV has become mainstream, and digital social networks give them the perfect platform to take their involvement one step further. Alma DDB wanted to create a real experience that went beyond the TV, a story they could live and share however they decided to.

Expression of Insights in the Campaign
From the beginning the idea was to personify the Hispanic consumer's quest for a better life, in a very tangible way, through the story of a Regional Mexican band struggling to achieve their dream of fame and glory in the US. And it was not a hard thing to do since the agency was dealing with real Hispanics, really trying to achieve their dreams. The way they related to each other, the love they felt for their families, the hard work they put into their endeavor, and the way they never stopped enjoying their journey, there's nothing more Hispanic than that.

Brand and consumer were integrated into the story organically: the brand was there to support and enable the band through 10 challenges they had to overcome in order to show they had the drive to be full-fledged musicians, including choosing a new name. The audience had the opportunity to participate in the action; thanks to the backstage access, our paparazzi provided with live feeds and posts in Twitter and Facebook; they were always connected to the story, even when the show was not on air.

Effect of the Campaign
Almost 2 million viewers watched the show over the 8-week period, mostly men of Mexican origin and young adults, ages 18–34. Three-fourths of the audience lived in Spanish-dominant households.

The series did so well in the ratings (up 73% from first to last episodes) that it aired again in prime time on Mun2. Positive perceptions of State Farm increased from 23% at the beginning of 2009 to 42% after the reality show was aired. The show also affected the likelihood to switch for noncustomers: from 24% at the beginning of the year to 37% after being exposed to the show.

CASE STUDY: MCDONALD'S–D EXPÓSITO & PARTNERS

Company/Organization Name
McDonald's

Advertising Agency
d expósito & Partners

Campaign Title
McDonald's Angus Third-Pounders—Tangustoso

Intended Hispanic Consumers
Spanish-preferred and bilingual/bicultural adults, ages 18–49, living in the New York Tri-state area

Background
When McDonald's launched support for the new, premium Angus Third-Pounders, the advertising strategy focused on the size of the burger. General market consumer research showed that consumers knew the premium quality of Angus beef, and the general market agency determined size was the key differentiator for the McDonald's product. However, d expósito & Partners suspected the word Angus had very little meaning with Spanish-dominant Hispanics, and although bilingual and English-speaking Hispanics might be a bit more familiar, the agency questioned whether they were fully aware of the benefits of Angus beef.

d expósito & Partners suspected that most Hispanic consumers were unclear on *why* Angus beef was of higher quality and deserving of a premium price. Knowing that Hispanics are value oriented, the agency could have accepted the general market strategy as the right approach for the Hispanic market since a larger size would mean more burger for the buck. However, their intuition suggested that consumers might have other motivations, like the better flavor of the beef, the seasoned patty, and the fresh, quality ingredients.

Research
To identify the strongest consumer-purchase motivator, d expósito & Partners conducted extensive qualitative research in the form of focus groups. As part of their research objectives, they conducted a general exploratory to gauge the Hispanic consumer awareness and knowledge specific to Angus beef, as well as key benefits inherent to the McDonald's Angus Third-Pounder. The agency discussed benefits, including size, taste, and other product attributes (seasoned patty, quality ingredients, and freshness), to understand and confirm our hypotheses and unearth further insights to create greater product appeal in our communications. Additionally, they concluded the research with product trial to gain consumer reaction.

Cultural Insights
While all product attributes discussed earlier were found to be of importance, ultimately, the superior taste of the Angus beef was paramount to the Hispanic consumer and a key motivator when making a final purchase decision. Additionally, consumers in the research found the combination of the burger's taste and size really satisfied their hunger and yielded an overall feeling of being content. The agency leveraged this consumer feedback when determining how to express the "taste" insight within the creative platform.

Expression of Insights in the Campaign

d expósito & Partners determined the strategy had to lead with the superior flavor of the Angus beef but also include the sense of total satisfaction yielded by the size of the burger. As a result, the agency leveraged two product attributes to advertise to New York Hispanics: the superior flavor of the beef and the Angus name itself. They formed a marriage out of the taste and the type of beef to give birth to an ownable expression, which proved to be a strategically sound big idea, "Tangustoso."

This fusion of two Spanish words, *tan* and *gustoso* (literally meaning "so tasty"), was used to capture the essence of the Angus burger and why it is so tasty and satisfying. By merging the words, the agency created a term used to educate New York Latinos on the product and its benefits in a way that was intended to be tangible, intriguing and easily understood. The agency felt that the name had a ring, and they discovered that it was appealing to both Spanish and non-Spanish speakers.

To create initial interest and buzz, d expósito & Partners developed and executed a teaser campaign to spark the question, "What is Tangustoso?" They utilized extensive radio, event activation, and outdoor channels to create curiosity and drive consumers to tangustoso.com, a bilingual website originally designed to serve as the Angus campaign anchor. During the teaser portion of the campaign, consumers could go to tangustoso. com to find video content created to entertain and contribute to increased anticipation for the "big reveal."

For the campaign's hard launch, the agency used traditional contact channels such as bilingual TV, geo-targeted cable, radio and print, and more nontraditional outdoor media formats, like wild postings and mobile billboards, in high-density ethnic and foot traffic areas. They also used buzz-generating tactics such as DJ chatter, product integration, and public relations.

As the campaign evolved, the agency needed to ensure consumer interest remained high so as to sustain sales beyond the initial campaign launch. As such, they developed a TV spot called "¿Probaste?", which essentially tells consumers that if they have not

McDonald's Angus Third-Pounder "Tangustoso" campaign.

(Continued)

tried the Angus burger that they should due to its quality ingredients and great flavor. They also evolved tangustoso.com to include product descriptors, webisodes with inter-active endings, and downloadable coupons. Finally, to ensure continued traffic to the site, the agency included banner ads and search-engine marketing as part of the online media plan.

Effect of the Campaign
Our campaign achieved demonstrable results. d expósito & Partners met and/or exceeded all key hurdles on awareness, trial, and repeat purchase, and now the Angus burger continues to perform well according to brand statistics, even while in *hiatus* from market-wide advertising. As a result, this effort received McDonald's Corporation rec-ognition, as it was awarded the 2008 Best Bets Award in the multicultural category.

End Notes

[1] US Department of Homeland Security, *Yearbook of Immigration Statistics, 2002*. Washington, DC: US Government Printing Office, 2003, p. 6.

[2] US Department of Homeland Security. *Yearbook of Immigration Statistics: 2008*. Washington, DC: US Department of Homeland Security, Office of Immigration Statistics, 2009, p. 12. http://www.dhs.gov/xlibrary/assets/statistics/yearbook/2008/ois_yb_2008.pdf

[3] Please note that immigration from Canada is minimal compared with other countries. In 2008 there were only about 15,000 legal admissions from Canada.

[4] Margaret J. Wheatley, *Leadership and the New Science*, 2nd ed. San Francisco, CA: Berrett-Koehler Publishers, 1999, p. 78.

[5] Paul Pedersen, *The Five Stages of Culture Shock: Critical Incidents Around the World*. Westport, CT: Greenwood Press, 1995.

[6] A colloquial way of referring to the US, that is, "the other side."

[7] See the interesting article on Hispanic immigrant entrepreneurship: Tyce Palmaffy, "El millonario next door: the untold story of Hispanic entrepreneurship." *Policy Review* 90, 1998. http://www.hoover.org/publications/policyreview/3564007.html

[8] http://blogs.wsj.com/numbersguy/ketchup-vs-salsa-by-the-numbers-191/tab/article/

[9] David A. Sylvester, "Best thing since sliced bread—Tortilla sales are rolling in the US, could surpass white bread by 2010." *San Jose Mercury News* December 2, 2003.

[10] http://www.hispanicprwire.com/news.php?l=in&id=954&cha=7

[11] http://www.doubletongued.org/index.php/dictionary/guey/

[12] http://www.pbs.org/wgbh/latinmusicusa/#/en/exp/cat/welcome

[13] John S. Roberts, *The Latin Tinge: The Impact of Latin American Music on the United States*. New York: Oxford US, 1999, p. ix.

[14] http://www.brandweek.com/bw/magazine/article_display.jsp?vnu_content_id=1003674384

[15] Yueh-Ting Lee, Clark R. McCauley, and Juris G. Draguns (eds), *Personality and Person Perception Across Cultures*. Mahwah, NJ: Lawrence Erlbaum Associates, 1999, p. 5.

[16] Ibid.

[17] Harry C. Triandis, *Individualism & Collectivism*. Boulder, CO: Westview Press, 1995.

[18] John W. Berry, "Acculturative stress." In *Readings in Ethnic Psychology*, Pamela B. Organista, Kevin M. Chun, and Gerardo Marín (eds). New York: Routledge, 1998, pp. 117–122.

[19] Roger Waldinger, *Between Here and There: How Attached Are Latino Immigrants to Their Native Country?* Washington, DC: Pew Hispanic Center, 2007. http://pewhispanic.org/files/reports/80.pdf

[20] John W. Berry, Ype H. Poortinga, Marshall H. Segall, and Pierre R. Dasen, *Cross-Cultural Psychology: Research and Applications.* Cambridge, England: Cambridge University Press, 2002, p. 354.

[21] Ibid, p. 345.

[22] This is similar to the concept of interaction in statistics. In a statistical interaction the actual interaction effect is the joint effect of two or more variables and cannot be attributed to any one of the original variables. Thus, what we generally call biculturalism contains a certain degree of syncretism that constitutes the uniqueness of a new identity.

[23] Roger Waldinger, *Between Here and There: How Attached Are Latino Immigrants to Their Native Country?* Washington, DC: Pew Hispanic Center, 2007. http://pewhispanic.org/files/reports/80.pdf

[24] Peter Homel, Michael Palij, and Doris Aaronson (eds), *Childhood Bilingualism: Aspects of Linguistic, Cognitive, and Social Development.* Hillsdale, NJ: Lawrence Erlbaum Associates, 1987.

[25] Ibid.

[26] Samuel P. Huntington, *Who Are We: The Challenges to America's National Identity.* New York: Simon and Schuster, 2004.

[27] Robert A. Wicklund and Jack W. Brehm, *Perspectives on Cognitive Dissonance.* Hillsdale, NJ: Lawrence Erlbaum Associates, 1976, p. 290.

[28] David C. Pollock and Ruth E. Van Reken, *Third Culture Kids: The Experience of Growing up Among Worlds.* London: Nicolas Brealey Publishing, 2001.

[29] Marginal here is not necessarily a negative condition but simply a condition of not belonging.

[30] Susan E. Keefe and Amado M. Padilla. *Chicano Ethnicity*, 1st ed. Albuquerque, NM: University of New Mexico, 1987.

[31] Juan Flores, *From Bomba to Hip-Hop: Puerto Rican Culture and Latino Identity.* New York: Columbia University Press, 2000, p. 55.

[32] Ibid, p. 142.

[33] Don E. Schultz and Heidi F. Schultz, *IMC, the Next Generation: Five Steps for Delivering Value and Measuring Financial Returns.* New York: McGraw-Hill, 2004.

[34] Malcolm McDonald and Ian Dunbar, *Market Segmentation: How to Do It, How to Profit From It.* Burlington, MA: Elsevier Butterworth Heinemann, 2004.

[35] Kevin M. Chun, Pamela B. Organista, and Gerardo Marín (eds), "Acculturation: advances in theory, measurement, and applied research." In *Decade of Behavior*, 1st ed. Washington, DC: American Psychological Association, 2003.

[36] http://www.thecab.tv/main/bm~doc/hispanic-men.pdf

[37] Both Ulibarri and Galeano are names found in Latin America. We wanted to make the point with these names that there is ample variety of surnames among Hispanics.

[38] David Sprott, Sandor Czellar, and Eric Spangenberg, "The importance of a general measure of brand engagement on market behavior: development and validation of a scale." *Journal of Marketing Research* 46, 2009, 92–104.

[39] Ibid.

[40] An integration is the appearance of a product or service in a broadcast program or movie, paid for by the manufacturer to gain exposure for the product or service.

LATINO SUBJECTIVE CULTURE: INSIGHTS FOR POSITIONING

▌ The Core of Cross-Cultural Marketing

In prior chapters you have studied the Hispanic market in many of its defining characteristics; this chapter's goal is to provide stimulating ideas for insightful and effective marketing and communication strategies. This chapter concentrates on the subjective aspects of culture that can help marketers connect at deeper levels with Latino consumers. This is an exploration into the cultural beliefs, values, perceptions, and behaviors shared by Hispanic consumers with the aim to establish successful relationships. These are the elements that lie under the surface, as in the submerged part of an iceberg. They are difficult to ascertain because they are difficult to articulate but when understood can provide for powerful connections between brands and humans.

Subjectivity is at the center of marketing, and cultural subjectivity is at the core of cross-cultural marketing. Hispanic cultural subjectivity influences much of what is important to us in life. It influences how we feel about life, death, children, relationships, gender, time, space, spirituality, among other concepts. Subjectivity is shaped by the culture that ancestors have passed on, by common experiences in countries of origin and communities, and by the synergistic relationship among original and adoptive cultures. Cultural archetypes and their dimensionality will be addressed here to provide inspiration and a way of thinking that can

195

Hispanic Marketing: Connecting with the New Latino Consumer.

radically change how marketers think about establishing relationships with Latino consumers.

As we indicated earlier all marketing is cultural but marketers that operate within their non-Hispanic culture seldom realize that what they are capitalizing on are cultural patterns that are important to consumers. "Just do it" is as cultural as the values of competing, winning, reacting quickly, and being determined.[1] "Have it your way" is rich in meaning and talks about the value of being able to be different, to be special. Some of these values are shared cross-culturally but even then they may be attributed to different meanings. Understanding how Latinos feel about important aspects of life may reveal if an approach is cross-cultural or if it is culture specific. Even cross-cultural elements are subject to different interpretations. Many powerful insights that connect with non-Hispanic Whites may be understandable but somewhat irrelevant to Hispanics. Conversely, many ideas and concepts that have strong meanings and associations for Hispanics may be meaningless to non-Hispanic Whites. The American ideal of equality among humans many times impedes the discovery of cultural differences. Human equality in terms of opportunities and rights is a laudable ideal, but that has little to do with the reality of differences in the cultures we come from. These days, cultural differences are increasingly praised for bringing diverse points of view to societal conversations. Differences can be of great value if properly understood.

Positioning for Brand Success Among Hispanics

Insightfully positioning a good product can make the difference between success and failure.[2] Insights, however, are not what many people usually associate with this concept. Insights in marketing demonstrate that the marketer is psychologically close to the consumer far beyond the use of stereotypes. Insights demonstrate a sense of empathy, almost complicity, in sharing with consumers something exclusive to them.[3] And what is more shared exclusivity than culture.

True insights are a key element of differentiation that everyone in the marketing and advertising industry wants to arrive at. Winners and losers are differentiated by how a product, service, or idea connects with consumers. Yet, comprehending the subjective cultural domain where the key to successful positioning lies is one of the most elusive, most challenging, and most often missed arenas of the US Hispanic market. There are articles in the advertising and marketing trade that talk about Hispanic cultural insights as knowing that Hispanics love family, or that many love soccer. While these are generally known cultural patterns they are not insights, because there is no exclusivity of knowledge in them. This chapter offers a way to understand Latino cultural insights and present some applied examples.

SUCCESSFUL POSITIONING

Positioning is a concept or idea that elicits desired responses about a brand or product from customers when communicated. It is the communication of brand messages that uniquely resonate with certain types of consumers.

You can determine your position in the marketplace on the basis of what business or category you use to define your position, your primary short-term benefit, and how you are better than your competitors. These elaborations on the brand principle are used as the basis for current communications until elements in the marketplace cause you to revise your position.[4]

An interesting angle on cross-cultural positioning is that a cultural insight can be a powerful differentiator or product emotional benefit. Positioning is the communication garment that dresses the product or service to appeal to the consumer. Over the years multiple companies and authors have described positioning in different ways. Most of them seem to converge on the idea that positioning in advertising is a symbolic attempt at characterizing a product or service in a way that it connects with potential users and sets it apart from the competition. The most basic form of positioning consists of specifying a benefit and reasons that support that benefit. Currently in an environment in which multiple products within a category are almost identical the benefit is usually an emotional benefit to assist in differentiating the product.

Knowing about the subjective culture the consumer comes from allows the marketer to establish an emotional connection with the consumer in regard to a specific brand. In elaborating a cross-cultural communication strategy the marketer should go beyond psychological and sociological considerations to uncover cultural values, beliefs, ways of thinking and feeling. We addressed this earlier in the book, the need to escalate consumer understanding beyond individual and social commonalities to understand aspects of their culture that are not obvious to competitors. Thus, this is not a trivial exercise and it requires consulting cultural experts and conducting in-depth research to learn about opportunities to link your brand to a cultural trait that has deep meaning. As it is well said these days, market research is more about listening than about asking questions.[5]

MARKETPLACE DIFFERENTIATION: INSIGHTS, ARCHETYPES, AND DIMENSIONS

Many ways of thinking, feeling, valuing, and believing are transmitted from generation to generation within cultures. The reason these are passed on is because they have value in facilitating social life. These important patterns of inner and overt cultural behavior can be used as points of engagement in the communication strategy with consumers that come from a different cultural perspective, Latino in this particular case. As in any effort to engage human beings, be it courtship or sales, we look for aspects in the prospect's life that will help us make a better connection. In the cross-cultural case the parallel is encountering cultural patterns that will allow the marketer to demonstrate that his or her product has deep affinity with the Hispanic consumer.

Marketing and Courtship

We think that marketing is a special case of courtship. We tend to identify with those with whom we are trying to connect emotionally. That identification promotes understanding. In marketing, when the marketer is motivated enough to identify with the Latino consumer, he or she communicates in ways that will tell the prospect that he or she is genuinely interested and actually understands the target. In a basic sense we want consumers to fall in love with our brand. If we make sincere efforts and actually reflect our understanding of the consumer, we are more likely to succeed, "Nike, for example, has just five values: performance, authenticity, commitment, innovation, and teamwork."[6] These are values that one commonly expects to find in personal relationships, and in the case of Nike, they are found in the company's core values. And these are values of importance to the culture Nike appeals to.

The Alma DDB–McDonald's Case Study at the end of this chapter illustrates how a well-known brand strives to maintain authenticity in their relationship with young Hispanic adults by showing a deep understanding of their culture and relevancy in the ways in which they communicate. Understanding that music is a key passion of Hispanics, the brand and agency made a decision to use it as the vehicle for expressing cultural connection with young Latinos. Alma DDB used two phases of ethnographic research to culturally ground their campaign. First, they created a multimedia research initiative using blog diaries with digital pictures and music tracks to gain insight into the key influences in the lives of "influential" young Latinos. Then, they dug into their music scene by having young Latinos develop audio/video diaries of their daily lives and the music that was a part of them.

Through their research, Alma DDB developed insights into relevant issues in the lives of young Latinos, particularly their strong involvement in community, the need for multifaceted content for broad appeal, and the attraction of newer bands for the younger elements in their target. They developed their 360° "Sabemos lo que te mueve" campaign which featured undiscovered as well as known musical artists and made use of local and national TV, online, nontraditional media, and community outreach. The diversity of this campaign included such innovative elements as a traveling music exhibit, sweepstakes combined with street parties and cultural events, and school visits by music-industry experts and musicians. The sum total of this outreach was numerous connections for the brand with young Hispanics and a strong statement by McDonald's that they understand what these consumers love and are committed to their relationship with them.

Dimensions Are Continua

A typical and overused cultural dimension employed to market to US Hispanics is that of individualism versus collectivism. For a long time most ads directed to Hispanic consumers showed or communicated in different forms that Hispanics are family and friends oriented. In its most basic form this is one of the most primitive dimensions in which Hispanics rate very high on the collectivism end of the continuum. And it makes definite sense that Hispanic audiences will react more favorably to portrayals of family and friends than to more individualistic portrayals. Clearly, overusing a cultural dimension can lead to its wearing out and becoming a commonplace rather than an insight. Here we will explore other dimensions that form the bases for cultural kernels or archetypes.

We ask the reader to ponder that apparent continua may not be so. At first glance individualism and collectivism are ends of one continuum. It can also be said, however, that they represent two different dimensions. Although this may seem counterintuitive, it is possible to think of cultures that can be both individualistic and collectivistic to different degrees, as masculinity and femininity are not extremes of one dimension but separate dimensions on which individuals can vary. There will be further elaboration on these issues later.

In many cases archetypes represent ranges within dimensions that characterize a culture. Thus, for example, on the individualism and collectivism dimensions, the high end on one and the low end on the other continua could be characterized as an orientation to friends and families. Figure 6.1 illustrates the quadrant in which the family and friends orientation can be characterized.

A strong orientation to friends and family represents a cultural archetype because this tendency acts as a mold for behaving, thinking, and feeling within a culture. We call these molds which shape the way in which members of a culture look at the world—archetypes. Archetypes can be said to represent syndromes of cultural inner and overt behavior. These archetypes can be general and universal. They can also vary depending on cultural manifestations. So, for example, the universal archetype of the hero becomes modified as a partial expression of *machismo* among Latinos.[7] Even further, and more radically, it has been said that "every human culture, therefore, is a variant expression of the genome we all inherit."[8] This is a very interesting perspective because instead of denying the basic commonality of our humanity it reaffirms it and then explains that cultural variation has to

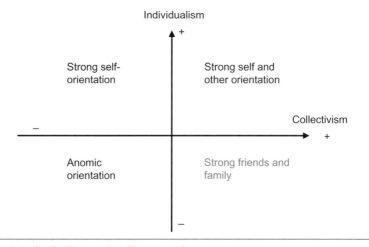

Figure 6.1 Individualism and collectivism dimensions.

do with differences in expression. But make no mistake in interpreting this important line of thinking. Cultural variation is not accidental and it is not superficial, it is constituent part of how our humanity is manifested in our social milieu.

From Universal to Particular Manifestations

This is why marketers who are able to identify important cultural dimensions and archetypes may claim important positions in the minds of members of a target culture. This is particularly true if these dimensions and archetypes have not been overused. That is, if they represent novel and unique cultural ways of dressing the character of a brand.

Historically Latinos have been taught that loyalty to others in power positions has survival and advancement value. The assertion of power in Hispanic cultures traditionally has been a strong determinant of the social order. This is why it is important for marketers to understand that Hispanic loyalty to persons in powerful positions is influential and that their sales representatives and agents need to claim authority and credibility first. Once authority is established then Latino customers are likely to be loyal to the brand. In the cases of insurance, real estate, loans, automotive, and other categories where personal sales are important, the brand is closely linked to the authority and credibility of the representative agent. That representative can then be influential in selling and cross-selling multiple product categories and complementary brands.

The case of authority illustrates the fundamental link between a general archetype use and its particular application to Hispanic consumers. This process will become clearer as more examples are presented. As a result of establishing a strong relationship with the consumer, the marketer should aim at having it continue over time.[9] This chapter is particularly important because it touches on what makes Latino consumers unique. Not just their language use, but much more. It is the way in which their humanity is manifested in daily interaction and survival. By the way, language is also an archetype. The basic ability for language is universal,[10] but the specific language used, based on the experience of groups of people in different geographies and conditions, is the actual code or manifestation used, that is, Spanish, English, German, Hebrew, and Cantonese. So there is the cultural universal and the particular, and the code itself influences further how we look at phenomena. What a profound difference derives from a universal ability.

A Place to Find Archetypes: The Dimensions of Culture

Many archetypes can be found when examining different dimensions of culture. Some important dimensions deal with use of time, perceptions of leadership, salience of groups, gender, attribution of causality, and spirituality, among others. Earlier we discussed how the intersection of dimensions can provide a nesting place for some archetypes. Other archetypes may constitute ranges of values on a dimension. Thus, a high level of gregariousness would characterize Latinos, for example.

TIME AND CULTURE

The late Edward T. Hall, the well-known anthropologist, in his multiple works dealing with time and cross-cultural communication, identified two dimensions that characterize how members of different cultures handle time. These two dimensions are polychronism and monochronism.[11] In his view these two dimensions are powerful cultural differentiators. Monochronic and polychronic are different in the ways in which they conceptualize, perceive, and handle time. People in polychronic cultures tend to handle multiple tasks at one time, and those in monochronic cultures are more likely to manage tasks linearly, one thing at a time. Also polychronic individuals are less likely to concentrate on being on time, as they try to tend to multiple events. Monochronic individuals emphasize punctuality in their quest to organize their obligations in a sequence.

When we hear that someone is on Latin Time, Mexican Time, etc., they are describing a different way of handling events and tasks. In many regions of Latin America it is impolite to abruptly terminate a conversation, thus one may be late for an appointment. Or a person may try to fit one more task in an already crowded schedule because he or she believes they can be handled simultaneously. A Latino may multitask to handle multiple important obligations: work, children, spouse, friends, entertainment, etc. In contrast, those who handle time more linearly try to limit their obligations and attempt to stay on schedule. These are not just curiosities but actual lifestyle differentiators that marketers need to understand to better serve Latino consumers.

Varying Experiences of Time

We tend to take for granted our use of space and time. Nevertheless space and time are the most basic dimensions of knowledge.[12] Our knowledge is framed in them in an almost imperceptible way. We order things chronologically and spatially to compare, contrast, and order our worldly experience. Culture, as a template of emotion, thought, and action, influences how we handle space and time.

If you have ever experienced travel in Latin-American countries, you may recall seeing that clerks in stores talk to several customers at the same time. Similarly, hotel receptionists talk to different guests simultaneously and it seems natural. They seem to multitask quite seamlessly. In Western countries, particularly the US and Northern Europe, people handle time more linearly; they do one thing at a time. Doing multiple activities simultaneously is confusing to monochronic people, and often considered impolite.

Imagine a situation in which a monochronic and a polychronic person are trying to establish common ground. You could anticipate that the monochronic person will become increasingly impatient with the polychronic individual, and conversely that the polychronic person will become bored with the interaction.

Values of polychronic individuals tend to differ from monochronic ones but not just on the use of time but in how they experience relationships. Polychronic people generally place more value on the relationship than on accomplishing a goal. That is why businesspersons from monochronic cultures become irritated when dealing with polychronic individuals. The Latin-American businessperson is trying to build a relationship by getting to know his or her counterpart, while the American is trying to close the deal quickly.

Time Affects Customer Relations and Product Use

In the area of customer service, many marketers have encountered that interactions with Hispanics take longer and that these customers tend to enjoy longer and more reassuring interactions. That is considered undesirable because it raises the cost of handling the specific incident. Still, the Latino customer is more likely to remain loyal to the company if he or she finds an attentive and gracious listening ear on the other side. Further, the customer service representative needs to be trained to handle the interaction with this type of customer. The representative needs to know how to listen, react, and engage the consumer. They need to understand the mental frame of reference the customer is coming from.

From a different perspective, when considering product-usage polychronic consumers are more likely to use products with less attachment to schedules and timeframes. Thus, product consumption occasions may need to be addressed differently when dealing with Hispanic consumers. Thus coffee and orange juice many not just be for the morning, and salty snacks not just for later in the day. When the marketer becomes better informed regarding the perspective of Latino consumers, he or she will better match products to life rhythms, work habits, occasions, celebrations, and other markers. When one understands product-usage opportunities one can expand how our products are used and thus increase revenue and customer loyalty to our brand.

Time and Media Planning

Media planning has become increasingly complex as touchpoints proliferate and diversify. Simultaneous use of media channels has become more prevalent. For example, the use of three screens (computer, cell phone, and TV) is more likely to overlap. If Hispanics are more polymorphic then one can reasonably hypothesize that they would be more likely to use these three screens simultaneously, and this is a hypothesis worth testing. Overlapping use of other combinations of media is also likely to be more prevalent among Hispanics.

The programming and planning of media for commercial messages should now happen at times that a few years ago would have been considered atypical. A token example is the use of radio (in several of its forms) at the same time as Hispanics eat, work, and enjoy family time among other activities. Radio messages for Latinos are not necessarily more likely to reach them only during commute times.

The use of social media as other computer-oriented tasks are being conducted is another form of overlap. Latinos have been found to be some of the most aggressive users of social media.[13] Since social media can serve messages depending on time of day and increasingly with additional information about the user, media planning can be more targeted and specifically geared to the intersection of different types of multitasking.

One important guideline to capitalize on the polychronism of Hispanics is to understand how their matrix of time and touchpoints behaves in their daily lives. Understanding product usage in different time parts along with media use can enrich the marketer's ability to be present when the right occasion arises.

The Dimensions of Social Influence

Cultures are characterized by the type of influence they respond to. Different types of leadership function more effectively in specific societies. Cultures that hold on to more traditional values have been found to have a higher prevalence of leaders that exert leadership in multiple areas.[14] So called "modern" cultures exhibit a higher concentration of specialized leadership. Thus in a more traditional society, a car salesman can be considered an expert on homes, children's schooling, and societal issues. In a more "modern"[15] society, a car salesman is just a car salesman. It is the perception of specialization that varies with the degree to which a society is traditionally oriented. The literature on diffusion of innovations has labeled leaders that are perceived to be influential in several realms as polymorphic, and those who are very specialized in one area as monomorphic.

Latinos tend to be oriented to a more polymorphic type of leadership and the phenomenon manifests itself in a variety of ways:

- The Hispanic man that purchases an automotive insurance policy from an agent who happens to be particularly attentive and personable starts depending on this agent for advice in other areas. This customer is likely to approach the insurance agent for many other types of insurance, and even immigration information, or for help in identifying a school for his children. In this case the agent has great influence and can cross-sell products and ideas with relatively little difficulty.
- Similarly, the Hispanic woman who purchases a home from a competent realtor eventually depends on the realtor for advice on marriage issues, health concerns, and even on what life insurance to purchase for her husband. This type of dependence, if ethically understood, can facilitate multiple sales and strong customer relationships.
- Consider also the Latino worker who admires his or her boss and will not only go to him or her for job-related advice but for many areas of interest from entertainment to high-involvement purchases. This example is particularly interesting because the use of influence networks among Hispanics can be much more influential than among others. That is because someone's credibility extends to many areas of opinion leadership.

Clearly, these behaviors are not unique to Hispanics, but they are more prevalent among Hispanics than they are among non-Hispanics in the US. Also, as with most cultural traits, the perception of leadership may change over time because culture evolves and changes to satisfy life demands.

The phenomenon of polymorphic leadership shapes the ways in which brands diffuse and grow through Hispanic interpersonal networks. Once these polymorphic leaders start believing in a particular product, brand, or idea, they spread the word through their wide spectrum of influence. As Hispanics immigrate to the US they depend on these types of leaders to learn about, for example, Sony, Folgers, Pepto-Bismol, Charmin, Ipod, Kix, Huggies, American Airlines, and other brands that are popular in the community.

Reaching out to Hispanic leaders can be extremely fruitful, but remember that natural leadership is not necessarily by ascription or position. A priest, teacher, or salesperson may or may not be a leader. It will depend on whether the people enacting those roles have actual leadership attributes and command respect from their followers. Most community leaders do not have a formal position in their communities but have much influence on others who respect their opinions. In investigating leadership sociometric research can be very useful. Understanding who talks to whom about what can be very important in knowing who to influence in the first place. The dimensions of polychronism and monomorphism provide conceptual guidance in characterizing Latino consumer behavior. These dimensions, however, are not a substitute for specific research designed to answer targeted strategic questions.

Orientation Toward Others and Oneself

Individualism and collectivism are the two dimensions most commonly discussed when addressing the US Hispanic market. Most marketers these days have heard that Hispanics are group, family, or collectivity oriented.

As with most aspects of culture these are not inherent characteristics. Hispanics are not collectivistic by nature, and non-Hispanics are not individualistic intrinsically. Societal evolution and the institutionalization of human life can largely explain these orientations. In most Hispanic societies, the interdependence of group or family members is basic for survival. In societies where there are few reliable institutions for its members' security one would expect that a system of social obligations and mutual dependence would thrive.

Many Hispanic parents still expect that their children and grandchildren will help support them in their old age. This is why planning for retirement is not as relevant to many Latinos. In addition, particularly in less-affluent segments, group interdependence helps achieve economic goals. For example, there are Hispanics who purchase homes and cars with a pool of friends and/or relatives. Different families put their resources together and purchase a home; then, when they have enough additional money they buy the second home, and so on, until all families have one. Similar approaches are used in the purchases of cars and other expensive items. These are strategies many learned while living in their countries of origin. These ways of acquiring expensive items have even been institutionalized in Latin America where large companies organize the pooling of money and then raffle the high ticket items until everyone contributing has their item. Clearly, satisfying everyone doing this can take a long time. Perhaps this has not taken root in the US because of legal considerations, but savvy US marketers may take note and attempt to capitalize on this accepted Latin way of buying.

In the US social institutions like Social Security, Medicaid, Medicare, and financial credit substitute for group interdependence among non-Latinos. These functions in US society did not originate with an individualistic orientation. They evolved as US culture created institutions on which people could rely as opposed to relying on others like themselves. Many Hispanics are starting to realize that dependence on social institutions in the US is possible. This will happen over time as they are exposed to and come to trust social service type institutions. Still, there are economic events that send Latinos figuratively back to their collectivistic roots. The two major economic disasters of the 2000s have shown many that it is difficult to rely on institutions and that after all, all one has at the end is one's social capital. It is likely that many non-Hispanics have in the 2000s best understood Latinos and their attitudes toward social reliance. After all, many non-Hispanics have also felt betrayed by the institutions they relied upon.

At this point marketers must reassure consumers in general and specifically Hispanics that they are in fact in good hands and provide some evidence of that. It is not easy to reclaim trust once it has been betrayed. Clearly, there are many advantages to lessen dependence on one's family and friends as they themselves may be lacking the resources needed. Thus, marketers who have reliable financial and health-related products that the Latino consumer can trust, and who also understand the motivations and view of the world of these consumers, can argue for the importance of building a legacy and a more independent path for the future.

Having a higher value for collectivism and a lower appreciation for individualism has implications for many efforts targeted to Hispanics. The simplistic notion of having groups enjoying products and services can be many times much more effective than presenting products that are enjoyed individually. Ads that do not show human elements or that do not show social enjoyment have been shown repeatedly to be of less interest and appeal to Hispanic consumers.[16] There are more subtle ways in which to represent the value of collectivism. For example, the suggestion that a product is for group consumption is likely to be more effective than emphasizing individual enjoyment. Suggesting that a product, a truck, for example, is for helping friends and relatives do things can be very powerful as the owner of the truck becomes the hero of the social situation. Achievement of social goals can be the context of much advertising. Helping others feel good by our use of a product can be an important motivator. Ultimately, Latinos are less likely to think of themselves as atoms but more as part of complex molecules that travel together through time.

Gender

Androgyny is the degree to which humans manifest some degree of masculinity and femininity at the same time. A higher score on the dimensions of femininity and masculinity characterize androgyny.[17] While many people many not have thought about this, femininity and masculinity can be conceptualized as separate dimensions and someone can be high on both, low on one and high on the other, or low on both. After all, masculinity and femininity are a product of our socialization. Being gentle and well mannered are not characteristics of women only, and being assertive and hard driving are not men's traits alone either. The cultural archetype here is androgyny and it represents an area in the space created by the dimensions of masculinity and femininity.

The hypothesis of these authors is that androgyny is more prevalent among Hispanics than among non-Hispanics. This is based on many observations of Latino behavior particularly in qualitative research. Non-Hispanics seem to adhere to more sex-typed behaviors. Hispanics, perhaps because of the syndromes of *machismo* and *marianismo*, tend to exhibit higher levels of both masculine- and feminine-type behaviors.

A stereotypical macho states that he does not cry, does not care about things that women care about, and so on. Nevertheless, his music is heavily loaded with laments and crying for the lost love. He falls in despair due to emotional disenchantment and resorts to crying and drinking to drown his disillusionment.[18] The macho becomes highly emotional at the smallest provocation. Thus, this individual is highly masculine, but also highly feminine at the same time. The macho, however, would never admit to having feminine traits. This is an apparent contradiction. The explanation may reside in the display rules associated with different emotions.[19] This means that under specific circumstances males to be macho can display emotions usually associated with femininity like crying and displaying tenderness. Latin-American music, including mariachi music, tango, and boleros, provide excellent examples of males that display traditionally masculine and feminine emotions in their singing.

Marianismo is considered the woman's behavioral syndrome that complements *machismo*. The stereotypical Hispanic woman suffers, cries, lives for her children and marriage,[20] and laments her unfortunate existence. Contradictorily, the same woman is the manager of the household and aggressively conducts the affairs of her home and family. This woman fights to preserve the integrity of her family, and can be very aggressive when needed. She changes from being the virginal figure to a fierce fighter.[21] In a way she can be seen as being contradictorily strong and defiant. Thus androgyny applies to Latino women as well. Clearly, this androgyny is also circumstantial and dependent on display rules. It is almost as if extreme behavioral demands from society push through to create their own opposites. A man who has been pressured to be macho and a woman who has been coerced to be subservient both seem to compensate by exhibiting contrary behaviors under specific conditions.

Androgyny makes the behaviors of marketing targets less obvious in the Latino market. As the discipline of marketing evolves to more finely define prospective product purchasers and brand loyalists, Hispanic targets need to be more clearly understood in their complexity. For many home products the woman head of household may not be the main decider or the only decider. Both men and women, and children, are likely to contribute to decision making for the home. We have found that consumer decisions among Latinos are more likely to be influenced by the

TABLE 6.1 Importance of Family Influencers on Product Purchase

	How Important Are Each of the Following in Influencing the Products You Buy?				
	Hispanics-Spanish	Hispanics-English	Asians	African-Americans	Non-Hispanic Whites
Spouse	3.74	3.42	3.44	3.09	3.33
Children	3.79	2.79	2.38	2.91	2.22
Other family	3.37	3.06	3.17	3.11	2.64

Scale: Five points from "not at all important" to "extremely important."

spouse, children, or other family members than among non-Hispanic Whites. In particular, Hispanics who prefer Spanish appear to be more likely to say that these "significant others" are important in influencing the products they buy as shown in Table 6.1.

These data were collected in 2008 as part of the ongoing Multicultural Marketing Study conducted by the Center for Hispanic Marketing Communication at Florida State University and DMS Insights. The national sample had approximately 500 respondents in each segment. The study was done online. Tests of statistical significance were conducted but omitted from the table to make it more readable. Overall, Hispanics who responded in Spanish to the survey were more likely than most other segments to report being influenced by family members in general. Hispanics who responded in English were also more likely than most other segments to report being similarly influenced. Non-Hispanic Whites were found to be less likely than Hispanics in general to be influenced by their family members. Asians and African-Americans were generally in between or not statistically different from Hispanics who answered in English, or not different from non-Hispanic Whites.

These revealing tendencies seem to provide evidence that androgyny is more prevalent among Hispanics. This constitutes an interesting reason for targeting Hispanic consumers in ways in which they had not been before. It is not only the woman head of household that should be targeted. Interestingly, when Latino culture is more prevalent in Hispanic consumers' minds, like in the case of Hispanics who prefer Spanish, the influence of others in the family is larger. Part of the reason for this phenomenon is that among newer immigrants Latino men are more likely to immigrate first to the US and then bring their wives or female companions after a period of time. Because of this men have to learn about brands and products in the absence of women, thus forcing them to enact behaviors that could have been considered feminine where they came from. Many of these men influence the brand purchased for the home in many product categories. Moreover, these categories may be somewhat unexpected because they include detergents, toothpaste, food, beverages, shampoo, and even home cleaners. This phenomenon should be further studied as traditional marketing practices may have many times missed the mark by failing to reach important decision makers.

Explaining the Causes of Behavior

We all learn to attribute the causes of behavior to different types of people or agents depending on our socialization within a culture. There are cultures that emphasize that the individual is responsible for his or her destiny, and that in fact one is the "architect" of it. There are also cultures that emphasize that the group and society are responsible for the behavior of the individual. Attribution theory is an area of research that attempts to explain why in some circumstances people attribute the causes of their behavior to internal causes and sometimes to external ones.[22] This is how one can think about two attribution dimensions: internal and external. Thus a culture may be high in internally attributing and low in externally attributing the causes of behavior, for example. If members of one highly internally attributing culture and a highly externally attributing culture interact they are likely to encounter that they disagree on many issues and ways of doing things. For example, the person from a highly internally attributing culture may argue that accomplishing a task is very much an individual effort and one is ultimately responsible for success or failure. The person from the more externally attributing culture may point out to the obstacles that the circumstances, or others, have placed on his or her way of achieving something. This can be a very conflict-ridden relationship.

Thinking about US Latinos, cultural differences in attribution exist in the US between them and non-Hispanic Whites. Hispanics are more likely to point to others as the causes of behavior. The reason someone succeeds or fails is because someone helped or someone placed obstacles in the way, or the circumstances were simply not favorable. Non-Hispanic Whites are more likely to attribute their successes and failures to their own doing and sense of responsibility. Being self-reliant is highly valued in non-Hispanic White society. This attribution tendency should not be evaluated as good or bad, but a tendency to look at our position in the world. Latino culture values being in harmony with nature, while non-Hispanic White culture values dominating nature. Consequently Hispanic attributions to external causes are consistent with accepting that nature, or the external world, is likely to strongly influence our behavior. On the other hand, non-Hispanic White attributions to internal determination and disposition are compatible with the notion of controlling and shaping nature.

The Casanova Pendrill–General Mills Case Study at the end of this chapter demonstrates insights into how Hispanics look at nature as a part of their surroundings whether they are visiting a nearby park, admiring a tree, nurturing a plant, or eating something natural. In contrast non-Hispanics find nature by going away to climb high mountains or raft river rapids. Based on this cultural insight Casanova Pendrill established their Hispanic conceptual target for General Mills' Nature Valley brand to be "Urban Naturals." To develop Nature Valley's campaign for Latinos, Casanova Pendrill conducted ethnographies to discover what nature meant to their target and how it was connected to their environment. To their Latino target, Nature was omnipotent and omnipresent, indeed an emotional ideal. The agency also discovered another cultural insight—that Hispanics believe what is natural is good for you.

Casanova initiated the Nature Valley campaign in the outdoor natural setting most commonly used by Hispanics—their local parks. They placed outdoor advertising in or close to the parks depicting a natural landscape image in the shape of a bar with the campaign's headline "take a little bit of nature in your pocket" and the tagline "natural ingredients for a natural life." They also chose radio advertising instead of TV so their target could imagine their own natural images linked to the sounds of nature. By understanding the underlying cultural relationship of Hispanics to nature, Casanova Pendrill and General Mills were able to create an emotional connection to Nature Valley for their Latino target which in turn resulted in considerable growth for their brand.

A Latino tendency to make external attributions has implications for marketing in different ways. A Hispanic is expected to be more likely to look at cues in the environment for making purchase decisions. If someone important to the Latino consumer uses or recommends a product that should help justify the purchase and use of that product. That would be in contrast to being individually unique or different from others.

Word-of-mouth and grassroots marketing has been shown to work well among Hispanics because their reasons for using products or endorsing ideas originate from the outside, from the social group. What others say or do is more influential among Hispanics, a product used by many is more appealing than a product used by a select few. When asking consumers about their use of a product, let us say Pepto-Bismol, one of their most important reasons for using it is that others they trust also use it. Non-Hispanic Whites are more likely to refer to the functional benefits of the product and less so to the endorsement or use by significant others. Latinos have shown to be more externally or group oriented in their decision making than their non-Hispanic White counterparts.

An orientation to others in contrast to an inner orientation has been eloquently discussed in the classic book *The Lonely Crowd* by David Riesman.[23] He postulates that societies can be differentiated by the orientation of people. Hispanics are more "other oriented" and non-Hispanic Anglo-Saxons are more "inner oriented." Marketers who understand this differentiation will emphasize an external locus of influence when communicating with Hispanic consumers. For Latinos it is acceptable and desirable to conform and be like others. The reader may have made the connection between collectivism, as discussed earlier, and an "other orientation." Latinos are more likely to behave as a colony of coral, or as other organisms that strongly depend on each other, even though they may have specialized roles. It is as if the value of the social system goes far beyond the value of the simple addition of individualities.

Based on this logic marketers may conclude that an emphasis on social pressure in marketing communications is likely to influence Latinos more than others. That is a plausible conclusion. For example, an ad that emphasizes a mother's disappointment at some of her kids' behavior is more likely to influence Hispanics than pointing out to internalized motivations. Further, the happiness of a child or spouse as the result of a purchase for the home can be more powerful than emphasizing the benefit to the end user alone. Having shiny teeth and minty breath is for the admiration and approval of others. Ultimately, how the consumer explains his or her behavior to him- or herself can be one of the most important motivations for purchasing products and services. In this case the Latino cultural archetype is the emphasis on external attributions to motivate behavior.

MARKETING INSIGHTS, CULTURAL TENDENCIES, AND ARCHETYPES

At the deepest level, insights derived from archetypes should be considered to be most powerful in connecting with consumers. There are many ways in which the term archetype is used in available literature. Generally it is considered to be a model or example within a culture that is aspired to or emulated by members of the culture. It is a pattern of behavior or ways of thinking. Archetypes can be conceptualized as cultural instantiations of more universal principles or molds that can be archetypes themselves.[24] Archetypes have been described as templates "clothed in symbolic forms that arise in interaction with a real-world experience."[25] Archetypes are manifestations of how a culture evolves its ways of life in a particular manner. Thus the macho is an instance of the hero. Mestizo is an instance of the duality of the Universe; the unique emergence of the mixture of Indian and European has been seen as the emergence of a new race "la raza de bronze."[26]

Archetypes can also be conceptualized as portions or intersections of dimensions that characterize a culture as the above discussion exemplifies. The archetype of femininity in Latino culture is the syndrome of behaviors associated with the Virgin Mary or *Marianismo*. This is at the high end of femininity and the low extreme of masculinity. It is also, in a way, the *anima* or the image of the woman in the man's psyche.[27]

Archetypes are driving forces that come from inside the culture. Stereotypes, however, are generalizations based on insufficient data that outsiders impose on a group of people to characterize them. It is critical for marketers to distinguish between the two, to develop powerful positioning and advertising based on arche-types, and to avoid grave mistakes based on stereotypes.

Insights derived from deep understandings of a culture can be powerful because they go beyond the surface. They touch the consumer in primitive ways by making a product, package, or communication uniquely emotionally relevant. Cultural archetypes can many times be inferred from knowing how the members of the culture think and feel. Still, there is usually the need to uncover archetypes as they emerge from consumer language and interaction. And many times one needs to test assumptions about archetypes that are taken for granted. Those who are familiar with the cultural patterns of Mexico, for example, likely know that death is a mixture of sorrow and celebration at the same time. For life insurance, for example, this way of thinking about death makes the sale of this product complicated since the consumer may not feel the pressure to prepare for death that other consumers feel. Thus understanding how people of Mexican origin think about death in more depth can help clarify what would be conceptual openings for life insurance to become relevant. As an example of a potential positioning for life insurance, knowing the archetype of death, it may be best to cast it as "the celebration of your life."

Ways to Obtain Cultural Insights and Archetype Ideas

There are several sources of inspiration and information leading to insights that are cultural in nature and that may include relevant archetypes as well. Popular culture and literature can provide a great number of insights into the folkways of Hispanics that can allow for better communication and marketing. Latin-American, US Hispanic, and Spanish literature, music, TV, movies, dance, paintings, sculpture, rituals, and other cultural expressions can help the marketer understand themes that are deeply imbedded in the culture. For example, understanding the celebratory meaning of death in some pre-Hispanic cultures can be gleaned from looking at what happens in a cemetery on the day of the dead.[28] Seeing people around graves consuming food and drinking alcoholic and nonalcoholic beverages in celebration of the deceased provides a deep perspective on the meaning of death for Mexicans. It is a good habit for the marketer to routinely read the literature and be exposed to other cultural manifestations of Latinos to be inspired and to think about ways in which he or she can connect his or her products, brands, and ideas with the cultural ways of Hispanics.

Ways to obtain deep insights and archetypes can also come from carefully designed in-depth interviewing and ethnographic research as illustrated in many of the case studies in this book. The marketer should become in spirit, if not in practice, an anthropologist curious about how Latinos use symbols, think about occasions, and socially determine the meaning of objects, products, and brands.

Reading Garcia Marquez, Carlos Fuentes, and Octavio Paz for Insights That Connect

Holly McGavock, a former student of the authors, and now a prestigious advertising account planner, took the initiative to put in a paper the insights she found through studying Latin-American and US Hispanic popular literature after being exposed to the first version of this book.[29] In illustrating the concepts of destiny and fatalism, Ms. McGavock used the following three quotes:

> *Marin, under the streetlight, dancing by herself, is singing the same song somewhere. Is waiting for a car to stop, a star to fall, someone to change her life.[30]*

> *Death followed him everywhere, sniffing at the cuffs of his pants, but never deciding to give him the final clutch of its claws.[31]*

> *Think of the most unbelievable thing that could happen, and believe me, Destiny will outdo you and come up with something even more unbelievable. Life's like that. My God! What a telenovela our lives are![32]*

The analysis and implications for marketers follow:

> *As evidenced in the quotes above and in numerous other occasions in the literature, Hispanics believe that their lives are guided by destiny. This means that they feel that some kind of outside source is responsible for their fates. This orientation also leads to feeling a lack of control over one's own life or fatalism. People don't take control of situations, rather they wait patiently for something to happen to them. Octavio Paz asserts this same idea in The Labyrinth of Solitude. Speaking of the Aztecs, he explains that "everything was examined to determine, from birth, the life and death of each man, his social class, the year, the place, the day, the hour. The Aztec was as little responsible for his actions as for his death" (p. 55). It seems as though over hundreds of years very little has changed. This belief in destiny also has serious implications for health, as seen in the "Health" section of the paper, and is closely related to religion, as seen in the "Religion and Spirituality" section of the paper.*

> *In One Hundred Years of Solitude, destiny manifests itself in the names of the characters. When a child in the Buendía family is given a name, he or she always has the same character and ultimately the same fate as the others of the same name. The power of destiny can also be evidenced in the second quote above, where Death has the ultimate power to choose when someone lives and when they die. Destiny exists, and Hispanics resign themselves to their destiny, allowing it to take control of their lives. This resignation is an acceptance that "I can't control my own life" and is seen throughout*

the novels. In Anglos, however, this belief is notably absent. In <u>Caramelo</u>, Celaya notices this because Americans never add "if God wills it" to their plans, "as if they were in audacious control of their own destiny" (p. 208).

Destiny also plays an important role in <u>Caramelo</u>. It is talked about frankly by the members of the Reyes family, as though it were something obvious and unquestionable. When the family maid disappears, the only response to her disappearance is "El destino es el destino" (p. 69). In fact, when destiny is mentioned in the novel, it always appears with a capital "D," the same way most people write "God" with a capital "G." Destiny is the reason the maid disappeared, the reason that Uncle Old and his sons look pitiful (p. 137) and the reason Celaya is still alive after getting beat up by schoolgirls (p. 357).

Implications for Marketers

- *This is a difficult situation to tackle, because marketers need to work to show Hispanics that they don't have to be resigned to destiny. The aim of marketers here needs to be showing Hispanics how to make smart decisions which can affect their future and give them some control over their lives.*

- *That Hispanics are more likely to be fatalistic is important because, for one thing, that says that living for today is important and that means spending today as well. Also, the reader should consider that fatalism, though an important part of the culture, may not necessarily be the ideal. The reason so many Hispanics have immigrated and continue to immigrate to the United States is to achieve control over their lives. Marketers can provide solutions to feelings of lack of control.*

- *In the health field, special emphasis needs to be placed on educating Hispanics about preventive care. Again, it is necessary to show Hispanics that small changes in their behavior can give them more control over their health.*

- *The same kind of education would also be effective for the insurance and financial services industries. For the insurance industry, it is important to show how having insurance can change a huge unforeseen tragedy into something more bearable. For the financial services industry, educating Hispanics about how to build credit and invest their money will allow them to buy homes, save for retirement, and pay for their children's education.[33]*

The reader can envision that there can be other implications for marketers as well. For example, the marketer may emphasize something along the lines that "your destiny has changed and it is now a healthy future with …." This approach would show the consumer that the brand understands how he or she feels but that things have evolved. Also, regarding insurance, the marketer may play on the idea that destiny is now to have a good future for the family even if one is not there to help anymore. Attempting to change belief systems is very difficult but due to self-selection, as Holly McGavock indicates, those who have immigrated to the US are likely to have done so because they long for a sense of control.

The above should serve as an example of how popular representations of culture in literature can guide the marketer in his or her quest for positioning and better communication with Hispanic consumers. While literature may be idiosyncratic, much of the literature that becomes publicly acclaimed generally represents elements of culture that touch consumers much in the way in which marketing and advertising should.

Mariachi, Boleros, and Baladas: More Than Just Music

Popular music is also an interesting source of insights and archetypes. The emotions expressed in music can be very highly revealing of cultural patterns and can provide ideas on how to communicate with Latino consumers.

Three students at the Florida State University Center for Hispanic Marketing Communication, Natalie Kates, Antonieta Reyes, and Celeste Eberhardt, conducted a study analyzing 166 top songs listed on the US Hot Latin Track of Billboard Magazine from 1997 to 2008. They rated 34 cultural categories in each of the songs. Their inter-coder reliability was 84%. Some of their main findings included:

■ Over 40% of the songs that made reference to partying and celebrating also emphasized the importance of appearance and the impressions people make on others. This trend substantiates the high importance that social occasions have for Hispanics. Having a good time is associated with feeling good about how one looks and behaves. This is a more traditional perspective that manufacturers and retailers can benefit from understanding in depth.

■ Cosmetics, clothing, and other elements of one's presentation of self are salient in social situations. Latinos are likely to trade up in these categories. Marker events, such as birthdays, coming-of-age "quinceañera" parties, graduations, weddings, religious confirmations, baptisms, and simple get-togethers are important events in which one's appearance counts and marketers can help.

■ Of 73 songs that contained sensuality and sexuality, over 20% also emphasized religion or spirituality. As Hispanics grow up with a more conservative perspective on sex they also link it to a sense of mysticism and spirituality: "Que un beso nos lleve al cielo volando en tus sentimientos …" (That a kiss take us to heaven flying on your feelings) as stated in the song by Carlos Vives "Luna Nueva."

- Interestingly, and also representing a more conservative perspective on sex, over 90% of the songs with sexual references included euphemisms and metaphors: "Voy a desnudar tu alma beso a beso hasta sentir que tu cuerpo se derrama como lluvia sobre mi" (I will bare your soul kiss by kiss until I feel that your body pours like rain over me) from the song "Son" by Four. This example illustrates the tendency of elevating sexually charged lyrics to something poetic and romantic. That is in sharp contrast with non-Hispanic songs in the top popular songs in 2005 Billboard list in which researchers found that 65% of 103 songs with references to sexual activity were degrading.[34] In the Latino study there were no degrading references at all. Thus, marketers should be careful in their use of sexual innuendos or references to sex. Explicit portrayals of sex as recreation or as instrumental can cause embarrassment and be offensive to Hispanics. Tasteful and more "romantic" references to sex are more likely to be acceptable. Those working on sex education and other sex-related programs should understand how Latinos perceive these issues.

The tendencies uncovered by this content analysis of popular Latin songs is inspirational and goes beyond what one can discover by asking consumers directly how they feel and think about something. This approach to understanding culture goes deep to the root of subjective cultural manifestations. The reader can find a presentation that summarizes the findings at http://hmc.comm.fsu.edu.

The reader and students of marketing concentrating on the Hispanic market or other culturally distinct markets are encouraged to explore these multiple forms of cultural manifestations. These can be fruitful and in some ways more illuminating than other types of research. Still, these types of efforts require informed hypotheses and well-designed studies that systematically go to the depth of cultural expression.

Qualitative Consumer Insight Generation

Consumer research can be conducted to yield important insights and many times uncover or confirm the existence of cultural archetypes that can help connect with Latino consumers. In the opinion of these authors there is no one approach that works best. There are authors like Clotaire Rapaille who claim to have a unique way of unlocking cultural codes. In his book *The Culture Code: An Ingenious Way to Understand Why People Around the World Live and Buy as They Do*[35] he describes how he has dug into consumers' minds to obtain kernels of knowledge that give clues as to why consumers purchase specific products. The systematic replicability of his approach, however, can be questioned. Still, this is a provocative approach.

Other recent approaches include that of Gerald Zaltman. In his book *How Customers Think: Essential Insights into the Mind of the Market* he talks about his approach to eliciting metaphors in in-depth one-on-one interviews with consumers.[36] Gerald Zaltman and Lindsay Zaltman further elaborate the approach in the more recent book: *Marketing Metaphoria: What Deep Metaphors Reveal About the Minds of Consumers*.[37] They claim that there are 16 basic metaphors that humans use to talk about their experience, and that these metaphors go beyond culture and segment differences. The authors of this book indicate their approach is proprietary and that it works much better than other qualitative research approaches. The elicitation of metaphors in qualitative research has been in use for many years, and it can be very helpful in understanding how consumers relate to aspects of their life and also their culture.

Other authors and researchers have recently been using biometric approaches in trying to uncover deep emotions in people's reactions to stimuli. An example of the latter is Martin Lindstrom's book *Buyology: Truths and Lies About Why We Buy*[38] in which he documents how by means of MRI studies he has been able to obtain in-depth data from consumers. All these are useful approaches, and also simpler and more modest ways of understanding people can work very well. What seems to matter most is understanding consumers and knowing how to frame questions and issues. Traditional focus groups and other group or individual interviewing techniques can be quite fruitful as well as the more in vogue use of ethnography in consumer research.[39]

To illustrate how conventional focus groups can lead to an important insight, we provide the case study of Hispanic mothers' motivations for using disposable diapers. The objective was to understand how to position disposable diapers among Hispanic mothers. The following laddering exercise took the form of repeated "why" questions to attempt to reach an emotional element that could differentiate a brand of diapers from another. Latino mothers reacted to the notion of disposable diapers in this approximate sequence:

Disposable diapers keep my child dry and without rashes
(Why is that important?)
Because as a mother I want them to be comfortable
(Why is it important to you that they are comfortable? (even if this question sounds strange and with an obvious answer))
Well, because my children are the most important things in my life
(Why are they the most important things in your life?)
Mhm ... because they represent my future ... a continuation of me
(Why is that important?)
Because I see myself as a line of people coming from my ancestors and extending to my children
(Why, then, is it important to keep them dry and without rashes, when thinking about their being your extension to the future?)
By keeping them dry and without rashes I am giving them the right start in taking the first steps toward their future.

Culturally, the archetypal way of thinking in this example was a belief Latinos express regarding generations as temporal extensions and continuity, not as discrete entities. The insight was that life is not only one's life but the life of our lineage, and that every little thing we do to enhance the chances of success of that lineage is an important effort. The marketing finding was that helping the mother give the right start to the child would be highly motivational because that would contribute to continuity into the future. The campaign based on this finding was very successful.

Key Pointers in Insight Generation and Identification of Cultural Archetypes

Obtaining subjective cultural insights and archetypes consists in understanding behaviors related to the product or service, not how consumers perceive the product itself in most instances. Thus, generating insights about driving is not about how the car feels or looks but about mobility, lifestyle, dreams, and aspirations, among other issues surrounding the importance of a car. Asking "what do you think about the Toyota Camry?" may only result in relatively obvious answers like "great design," "great driving experience," "a car for the family." But asking for "what are your dreams these days?" can result in important discoveries like "breaking up with a life without hope," "moving ahead, beyond what others think I can do," "being like an eagle, soaring near the clouds," for example. These answers, if consistent across Latino consumers, could hint to the possibility of positioning Toyota Camry as "the car that takes you beyond the ordinary because the sky is the limit."

The context of product and service usage can many times be much more important than how consumers perceive the product itself. Clearly, the product must have credible desirable properties because if the product does not deliver no positioning will help. But beyond delivering value the positioning insight ought to be about the important subjective perspectives on life that can enhance the relationship with the brand.

The remainder of this chapter will highlight several areas of archetypes that can be important when marketing to US Hispanics. The following are offered as thought-provoking areas of investigation that can be pursued with different product categories.

MEANINGFUL AREAS OF LATINO SUBJECTIVE CULTURE

Whether your area of work is in food, beverages, insurance, transportation, communications, technology, retail, or any other, you can benefit from obtaining a deep understanding of Latino cultural aspects relevant to your category. If your area of work is in life insurance, for example, understanding how Hispanics think about wealth, death, and posterity can help in better designing products and how to communicate them. Keep in mind that knowing how the consumer feels about life insurance may not be as important for your purposes as how they feel about the issues affected by life insurance. That is where the power of insights and archetypes resides.

Wealth and Material Well-Being

Material well-being is important to members of most cultures, but how it is perceived can vary in important ways. In many ways wealth is surrounded by a "sour grapes" type of attitude. The vast majority of Latin Americans have endured several hundred years of poverty and abuse by wealthy elites. Wealth has been traditionally associated with a privileged few that have also tended to be corrupt and unconcerned with the well-being of the larger segments of the population. The experience of wealth and materialism as unattainable has created a sense of cynicism in many Latinos. In some ways the Catholic religion has also praised the virtue of being poor and sacrifice. Both of these forces create a syndrome of alienation from wealth and worldly attainment.

A life of poverty is seen as a better alternative to being wealthy but corrupt,[40] as if both were natural opposites. One accepts suffering and deprivation as one's lot in life. Thus, money has less of a positive connotation. Enjoying life, on the other hand, has a very strong positive tone. Multiple manifestations in literature, music, drama, and film have idealized this paradox. Enjoy the moment because the future is elusive, and money does not matter as long as you are happy. Telenovelas, the well-known genre of Spanish-language soap operas, many times exploit the virtue of poverty and the corrupt evilness of wealth. Movies like *Nosotros los pobres* that "make idilious and romantic the cruel question of poverty"[41] is a fine example of how many of Latin-American origin conceptualize being poor.

Making more money, while attractive, needs to be addressed as being related to generosity and happiness. The marketer of financial services needs to understand that greed alone may not be enough with those who come from a background of poverty.

The concepts of debt and mortgage are related to wealth. Few of us stop to think that eight centuries of Arab domination of Spain may have left a profound mark in Latin-American consciousness.[42] Lending with interest has left a subtle stain in the culture so that those who lend for profit are seen as unethical. We believe this explains why borrowing money in most of Latin America is something you do when there is no other choice. In contrast, in the US, borrowing money is a way of life. Marketers of loan-related products need to be aware that Latino consumer reeducation can be very important if borrowing money is to acquire a positive meaning. It does not help, of course, that many Hispanic consumers have had serious problems with credit card issuers because many of these borrowers have not understood the implications of using these credit cards.

Some lenders advertise in Spanish that they have low-interest mortgages without realizing that they are committing a double mistake. First, emphasizing the interest part has a negative connotation. Second, the term mortgage in Spanish is *hipoteca*. In Latin America, you rely on a *hipoteca* only when you are in real trouble.

For Hispanics placing a *hipoteca* on your home means you are endangering the future of your family. In contrast, a mortgage in the non-Hispanic US is a common and accepted thing; that is, having a mortgage is simply enjoying the opportunity to have a home. However, when lenders use the term *hipoteca* to Hispanics, they are referring to an unpleasant association. Things would be so much easier if translations were just so simple. Using the term *prestamo* or loan is likely to be more acceptable. This category, as well, is likely to experience difficulties for some time to come because of the recession created in the late 2000s by mortgage products that put consumers in jeopardy. Many Hispanics lost their homes because they had not understood that their interest rates would jump dramatically after a period of time. Further increased unemployment exacerbated the home-loss trend. Still the dream of owning a home is likely to survive in the struggle for happiness of US Latinos.

Life Markers, Transitions, and Happiness

Latinos literally rejoice in being alive—a well-grounded generalization in our experience. In qualitative research we have found that every day is seen as a gift that should be enjoyed. That is why celebrating every day is important, and that is also why delay of gratification is weak versus immediate pleasure. This archetype comes from lessons learned over the many years of subjugation first in the Native American kingdoms that dominated Latin America, and later with the foreign dominance, destruction, and enslavement of the peoples of the continent. Nothing can be taken for granted. Mothers tell their kids to pray before going to bed so they can be given the gift of another day. That is why waking up and celebrating the morning is a joyous experience.

That the morning is a time for celebration helped a coffee brand succeed among US Hispanics. We probed the meaning of the morning among Hispanics of multiple countries of origin. We found that invariably Latinos associated waking up in the morning with the celebration of being alive. The brand paired the celebration of the morning with the consumption of its product and in a subtle way created a strong link with the consumer. The religious and mystical origin of this way of perceiving the morning was never made explicit but Hispanic consumers seemed to have made the connection. That is a connection which is deeply emotional and has very little to do with logic.

Que Será, Será—Whatever Will Be, Will Be

The perception that life is ephemeral and unpredictable nurses a deep sense of fatalism that is strongly rooted in many of the Native American and Mestizo groups of Latin America. Although immigration to the US is paired with the ambition to leave behind the uncertainty that leads to fatalism, this philosophy of life persists for a long time in the US as well. It is linked with a worldview pervaded by the unpredictability of life and the events surrounding it. Saving for tomorrow is less important than throwing a great *quinceañera*[43] party today because tomorrow is uncertain.

Why Mañana?

As the famous song states "tomorrow never comes," Latinos, despite their ambition to excel and triumph in the US, still have in the back of their mind their ancestors lessons that tomorrow cannot be counted on. Saving and many other "preventive" types of products and behaviors fall in this category. If activities do not provide some type of immediate gratification then the behavior is less appealing. This is normal among humans but it is pronounced among those who come from contexts where only the present can be counted on.

Thus, the joy of saving for one's kids and one's retirement needs to be paired with assurances of trust and accountability. It also requires for the marketer to help the consumer envision an attainable and happy future. The reason why many Hispanics talk about postponing things to tomorrow is because tomorrow is out of sight and out of mind. It is something not to be worried about because it may never come. Changing that sense of fatalism to *no dejes para mañana lo que puedes hacer hoy* (do not live for tomorrow what you can do today)[44] is a challenge to the marketer consisting in putting together the traditional logic of the consumer with the demands of modern life in a credible context.

Suffering Is My Destiny

Subjugating oneself to the circumstances and becoming a victim is another theme in Latino cultural heritage. A history of general submission to power in ancient pre-Columbian times to becoming dependent on Spanish colonialists, and a religious tradition of "being happy with one's lot in life," all contribute to a fatalistic submission to misery.

This perspective presents life on earth as being less valuable than the next life. Life in this world is many times referred to as a valley of tears—*un valle de lágrimas*. This contributes to living for today as opposed to tomorrow and explains why death is celebrated. In the collective mind of the culture death has the redeeming qualities of being the end of suffering. In addition, death has the promise of a better life.

It may seem contradictory that many Hispanics prefer to enjoy the present moment and also look to the peace of death and the afterlife. It is not a contradiction but an artifact of the same logic. One ought to enjoy the present as much as possible because the future is uncertain. The only other certainty beyond the present is death and the promise of a better life thereafter. It is the gap between the present and the thereafter that makes life on earth difficult and many times painful.

As a marketer you can see the challenge of persuading Latino consumers to plan ahead as if they could count on a predictable future. The economic recession of the late 2000s, the irrational immigration xenophobia, and the catastrophic BP oil spill in the Gulf of Mexico can only contribute to reinforce a perception of lack of predictability and uncertainty. Marketers can rely on truthful and honest relationships with Hispanic consumers in which the marketer recognizes fears and concerns and addresses them sincerely. The glamour of hyped creativity needs to be tempered by a deep understanding of consumer perspectives.

Individual or Group Responsibility?

The notions of guilt and shame are parallel but have a different locus of control. The first resides in the person and the other in the social group. The first is a transgression due to a weakness, the second is not living up to the expectations of the social group. Catholicism has imparted a sense of guilt to Latin Americans. From the original sin to the notion that there is something wrong with the individual who transgresses, Hispanics live with a constant need to atone. Statements like *me remuerde la conciencia* (my conscience bothers me) and continual references to *culpa* (guilt) are the staple of popular culture in Telenovelas (Spanish-language soap operas). Ruth Benedict[45] in her differentiation between Western and Eastern civilization argues that the West is more characterized by guilt, an internal driver that attributes responsibility to the individual. She states that Eastern cultures like the Japanese are shame cultures where the individual is expected to live up to the expectations of the group.

Latinos talk about their guilt feelings and experience them in a variety of circumstances. Our research with mothers, in particular, has shown that many Hispanic mothers suffer much guilt because they cannot do all they believe they should do for their children and spouses. Products and services can be positioned to reduce guilt feelings. Helping the consumer alleviate guilt can be beneficial to both the consumer and the marketer by establishing a complementary relationship. If mothers feel guilt for not providing the best nutrition to their children, a product offering can emphasize how good a mother feels by providing the nutrition the children require while at the same time pleasing them. That is a double avenue for guilt reduction as she can not only help the kids' health but also make them happy.

A Child-Centric Society

Children are highly prized in Latino families and considered to be a blessing from God. Hispanics tend to have large families, which are a matter of pride to parents, and a great deal of attention is provided to their care, upbringing, education, and well-being. Children are an integral part of the family as a group, thus all the family spends much of their time together: they shop together, play together on Sundays in the park, eat together, and have strong bonds with larger groups of family and friends. Extended family members often contribute to child-rearing, particularly grandmothers and aunts who actively help mothers caring for their large numbers of children.

There are specific roles in the family that guide these interrelationships. The mother has primary responsibilities for tending to the children making sure that they are healthy, nicely dressed in clean and as attractive clothes as the family can afford, and that they eat healthy and tasty foods. Mothers are very affectionate with their children and want to please them. They find reconfirmation in their identity as a mother when their children love the things they provide for them. Conversely, mothers tend to feel enormous guilt when they cannot give their children the things they want.

The father is also dedicated to his children but his role tends to be more along the traditional male norm of working for their economic well-being. However, he is seen as the head of the family so that he has the final say in major decisions regarding his children. He may also become involved when there are more serious discipline problems with children because fathers generally insist on respect, although the mother is almost always a part of these matters. In cases where fathers may be more strict and authoritarian, "The mother often acts as mediator between an authoritarian father and the children."[46]

Hispanic fathers are generally very loving and affectionate with their children. They revere their daughters, hug and caress them, and are typically very vulnerable to their wishes. They also tend to be somewhat protective of their daughters, particularly as they enter adolescence and attract young men. Fathers also highly value their sons, who are seen as providing for the future of the family. Hispanic *papas* share their love of sports with their sons, and can be seen playing soccer in the park or watching sports on TV with them. As the key disciplinarians they demand that their children show respect to them as the head of the family and to their elders. As the sons grow older, they may be expected to work, to help pay for the expenses of the family.

Children are very close to their mothers and admire their devotion and sacrifice for the happiness of their sons and daughters. The children are influential in choices their mothers make, a fact that can be observed in supermarkets where Hispanic children are present on family shopping expeditions. This is an important fact for Hispanic marketers to realize. It is also important for marketers to recognize that mothers often get caught in dilemmas; they want to satisfy both the demands of their children as well as provide food and services that are good for their health.

Even though children have the love and attention of their mothers and the dedication of their fathers to provide for their needs, they also have their own responsibilities and behavioral norms. They are socialized to be loving, sociable, and respectful of others in the family. Older siblings are expected to help out with younger family members. Often, in terms of the household, girls are asked to help their mothers with cooking, taking care of younger children, and carrying out other household chores. However, these chores, fulfilled in the company of mothers or grandmothers, are often remembered as happy times in the lives of these young women. This image portrays the relationship between women in the family—mothers, grandmothers in traditional household chores.[47]

Boys, in contrast, tend to be catered to more in the family than girls, continuing in some ways the patriarchal structure and *machismo* of their Hispanic heritage. They may work with their father on weekends in gardening or construction or have responsibilities consistent with those of other male family members.

There are some aspects of child-rearing that receive less emphasis in Hispanic versus non-Hispanic families such as toilet training and weaning from nursing from the breast or the bottle milk. These behaviors are seen as part of nature and being a child, which will end according to nature's own timing. Indeed, it is not unusual to see Hispanic children drinking from their bottles or sucking on pacifiers at 3 or 4 years of age.

Hispanic parents pay strong attention to symbolic religious and coming-of-age ceremonies for their children. Even for Hispanics who may struggle economically, it is considered extremely important to have celebrations for baptisms, first communions, coming-of-age *quinceañeras*, the 15-year-old coming-of-age parties for their daughters, and weddings. After the religious rites in the church, large parties are organized for relatives and friends, elaborate clothing is purchased for the children honored, and food and drink are served in abundance. These occasions are used to reconfirm the bond that their children have with the extended family and community, and to solidify the place of each child and the family in the eyes of others. Families will spend lavishly on these celebrations, even though they may have to sacrifice in other areas to afford them. The connectedness of generations of Hispanic families is a deeply emotional element of the culture.

Gender Relationships

We have previously touched upon the concepts of *machismo* and *marianismo* as extreme expressions of the masculine and feminine dimensions. We addressed the issue of androgyny and the complexity that it adds to our understanding of male–female relationships in Latino culture. Here we will discuss in more detail how Latino women and men interact.

Machismo and *marianismo* have traditional historical roots for US Hispanics. They have European seeds that were spread through Latin America via colonization and cultural synergies. The European concepts associated with *machismo* developed from male-dominated religions, male divinities, male leaders of the church, and male heads of state. *Machismo* emphasized the strong, indomitable male who ruled others with an unswerving iron will. The concept of *marianismo* was the flip side of the coin defining the female as the powerless, compliant, and suffering counterpart of the male, circumscribed by religion, law, and social norms, and associated with the purity of divinity of the Virgin Mary. The conquerors of Spain brought their sense of dominance and male–female relationships to the new world. Alan Riding sees this as deeply rooted in the Mexican history of male–female dominance: "Mexico's *mestizaje* began with the mating of Spanish men and Indian women, thus immediately injecting into the male–female relationship the concepts of women's betrayal of their culture and associated with conquest, domination, force, and female's suffering and degradation through rape. Just as the conqueror could never fully trust the conquered, today's macho must therefore brace himself against betrayal."[48]

Although these early explanations of *machismo* and *marianismo* are heavily laden with negative connotations, they also historically have had their positive dimensions. The macho male image has been associated with leaders who were victorious in battle and in life, who always showed a confident face and dared not show emotions lest their enemies take advantage; who were valiant and benevolent with those less powerful, particularly women and children (perceived as lesser beings); and who were among equals only with males of their society with whom they could celebrate their manhood. The woman according to *marianismo*, modeled after the purity of the Virgin, comes from "the cult of feminine spiritual superiority, which teaches that women are semidivine, morally superior to and spiritually stronger than men."[49]

Coming to conclusions about what is the current balance between *machismo* and *marianismo* of US Hispanics is not within the scope of this book. Suffice it to say that this is an element of culture going through change, a trend that can also be said of the male–female relationships in the wider US culture. Knowing the history of these interlocking concepts—*machismo* and *marianismo*, as well as the more paternalistic tendency of the Hispanic culture—suggests that marketers need to be sensitive to research questions around gender, raise issues particularly around decision making in Hispanic families, and construct strategic directions in tune with cultural and emotional realities of men and women.

Though there are weaknesses that can be encouraged in the extremes of *machismo* and *marianismo* from male boorishness to female vulnerability, there are important strengths inherent in them. These strengths may include male responsibility and pride in providing leadership for his wife and family; and female strength, tenderness, and devotion in caring for her husband and children. Marketers need to understand these terms and their implications for male–female relationships from within the Hispanic culture, and be careful not to develop campaigns based on the potent and often judgment-laden gender perceptions within their own cultures.

Recent research findings from the 2005 Yankelovich Multicultural Marketing Study indicate that "91 percent of Hispanic women, versus 83 percent of non-Hispanic white women, agree women have as much financial responsibility to support a family as men do."[50] Also "68 percent of Hispanic women, versus 34 percent of non-Hispanic white women, say they really would like to start their own business."[51] These are counterintuitive findings and indicative that there is movement in the Latino community toward more female entrepreneurship and an increasing role of women in home finances. As more Hispanic women enter the labor force and as more Latinos in general attain higher degrees of academic achievement, it is likely that traditional roles will evolve to incorporate a new perspective on gender roles and expectations. Marketers, however, need to be cautious in concluding that these roles will be the same as those in the non-Hispanic White world. Most likely there will be a complex integration of traditions and emergent identities. That is, an interplay which is likely to result in new gender role relationships characteristic of an evolving Latino identity in the US.

Medicine, Remedios, and Health

Latinos have been lagging in their access to health care for a long time. Partly because of the types of occupations many hold and partly because many of their employers have not provided health insurance. Another important set of obstacles are cultural in nature. Hispanics often go without the care they need for themselves and their children, or, if they succeed in getting treatment, they are often dissatisfied with their care. Access to health care in the US is very different for most Hispanics than in their countries of origin. In many Latin-American countries health care is an overall benefit for workers and their dependents, and healers are available with traditional remedies to deal with everyday illnesses and types of health problems that doctors or nurses do not treat. In the US, many Hispanics are without health insurance and even those with it feel uncomfortable in the predominantly English-speaking health institution environments. They complain that there are impersonal administrators or health professionals with whom they have difficulty communicating their problems even if they do speak English, and whose remedies they may not trust.

However, it is also important to note that experts, particularly doctors, are highly respected in the more hierarchical Hispanic culture so that Hispanics in the US also feel it is important to take their opinions into consideration. In addition, Latinos appreciate many aspects of their life in the US and have been incorporating many health-related practices. Still many experience stress in reconciling their traditions with the new practices they encounter. This is particularly critical because they need their health so they can work and take care of their families economically and physically, and they are devoted to keeping their children, who are the center of their lives, healthy.

Physicians, nurses, and other health-care providers express frustration in trying to understand what the real health problems of Hispanic patients are and why these patients frequently do not comply with recommendations and prescriptions. In addition, many Latinos who are sick often do not go for health treatment until they are extremely ill and need to go to the emergency room. Clearly, this has been the result of lack of health-care coverage as well as some distrust of the system. With the new health-care law passed in 2010 many of these issues will change. Some problems will be exacerbated and others addressed. Questions still not addressed at the time of this writing include the problem of undocumented migrants and their need for health care.

Beyond structural and legal issues, there are Latino beliefs that often appear to the medical profession as superstitious and irrational. Traditional remedies related to cultural theories about disease have been divorced from modern medicine instead of being incorporated. In addition many Hispanics are used to obtaining prescription medicines from pharmacists without having to go to a physician first. Beyond what the pharmacists offer, Hispanics often prepare their own home remedies—frequently herb teas, brews, and pomades—made from recipes handed down over generations from their mothers and grandmothers. These are many times called "remedios."

In the Grupo Gallegos–California Milk Processor Board Case Study at the end of this chapter, Grupo Gallegos peals back layers of Hispanic culture to discover a benefit of milk which had not previously been addressed in their California advertising to Hispanic women. After 2 years of successful advertising to Hispanics, 98% of individuals reported they had drunk milk in the past week. The agency decided to conduct qualitative research with their target to check out benefits that might have been missed in order to achieve even greater penetration.

As a new approach they decided to investigate the benefits served by other beverages which milk might also provide for Hispanics. Herbal teas are well-known to be used in Latino households for a wide variety of maladies. Through their qualitative research the agency learned that these teas were used to reduce premenstrual symptoms. The agency recognized that this was also a benefit of milk. They also learned that traditionally Hispanic women had been told by their mothers they should stay away from milk during their period.

The challenge for the agency became how to bring this unrecognized benefit of milk to Latino women on a topic which they found to be culturally taboo. The brand chose to do this in the humorous way typical of the Got Milk and Toma Leche overall campaign, and to make use of a supernatural element of traditional Hispanic culture. In their creative they used a fairy tale about a mean witch in a mystical town who came once a month to haunt it, but was suddenly no longer a witch. At the end of the TV spot only the message that milk helps reduce symptoms of PMS was given. This combination of cultural factors discovered mainly through qualitative research led to the increase of milk consumption in California, a challenge previously considered next to impossible.

There are differences in the way many Hispanics traditionally understand the causes of illness. Modern medicine in the US attributes illness to more scientifically described origins, whereas Hispanic culture tends to assign the routes of an illness to many different levels of experience.

Many Hispanics believe that illness can be caused by:

1. *Psychological states such as embarrassment, envy, anger, fear, fright, excessive worry, turmoil in the family, or improper behavior or violations of moral or ethical codes;*
2. *Environmental or natural conditions such as bad air, germs, dust, excess cold or heat, bad food, or poverty; and*
3. *Supernatural causes such as malevolent spirits, bad luck, or the witchcraft of living enemies (who are believed to cause harm out of vengeance or envy).*[52]

Felipe Castro, Pauline Furth, and Herbert Karlow conducted a study of Mexican, Mexican-American, and Anglo-American women to understand the relationship between cultural beliefs about health and their reactions to Western health-care directives. They found that even though Mexican women tend to maintain their traditional cultural beliefs, they also take directives of modern health givers into account. "These results suggest that Mexican-origin women have a dual system of belief which tends to weaken but not disappear with increasing acculturation. The dual system however would not appear to interfere with their ability to accept and comply with prescribed biomedical health regimens."[53]

Traditional Healers

Contributing to how Latinos experience US health-care institutions is Curanderismo. *Curanderos* or healers have been a traditional part of Mexican and other Latin-American cultures. They treat illnesses with various types of aids, such as herbal remedies, handed down to them through from past generations. They handle the physical and emotional manifestations of illnesses in the context of the family and the community.

Robert Trotter II and Juan Antonio Chavira conducted ethnographic research on *curanderismo* in the Lower Rio Grande Valley of Texas:

The simplest and most common gift of healing among curanderos is the ability to work on the material level ... The objects (healers use) include herbs, patent medicines, common household items (eggs, lemons, garlic, and ribbon, for example), and religious or mystical symbols (water, oils, incense, perfumes, and so forth). The ceremonies include prayers, ritual, sweeping or cleansings (barridas or limpias), and other complex rituals using all or some of the special objects.[54]

Trotter and Chavira found that it was not uncommon that those they studied would use both *curanderos* and institutional health care for the same illness. *Curanderos* also work on the spiritual and mental levels, bringing special powers to bear that involve the supernatural. *Curanderos*, as polymorphic leaders, cover treatment areas that would ordinarily include family doctors, psychiatrists or psychologists, and priests in the US cultural context.

This tendency to be able to hold both an appreciation for traditional cures as well as for the expertise of the doctor in US culture can be important for marketers involved in the US health-care industry to understand. Marketers should investigate cultural patterns regarding the emotional or traditional remedies to increase the appeal of health-related products and services. In many ways, linking the past to the present and the present to the past can create synergies. That is not farfetched as we witness how the US medical establishment is slowly realizing the power of traditional cures and understanding how the old and the new can have a role in healing.

Also, marketers should pay attention to how certain over-the-counter medications acquire the powers of traditional remedies as they become part of the culture. Pepto-Bismol®, for example, has become a "traditional" multisymptom remedy among Hispanics. Like chamomile and coriander seed teas, Pepto-Bismol® and Vicks® VapoRub® are also part of a tradition that marketers and health-care providers need to understand.

Temperature

One of the most elaborate frameworks for the conceptualization of disease in Latin America is the "Hot and Cold" approach to understanding illness. As David Hays-Bautista found:

> *We also have heard variations on an age-old Mexican hot-cold theory as a source of arthritis: a too-rapid change from warm to cold—throwing ice water on someone perspiring in the Mojave Desert or moving too quickly from the summer warmth into a cold meat locker—is believed to bring on the disease.*[55]

Although this has come down through generations in Latin America as folk remedy, it had its origin in early scientific medical thinking brought to the Americas from Spain and Portugal in the 16th and 17th centuries. There were originally four dimensions to the Hippocratic theory: dry, cold, hot, wet, or a combination of these:

> *Illness ... is believed to result from a humoral imbalance which causes the body to become excessively dry, cold, hot, wet, or a combination of these states. Food herbs, and other medications, which are also classified as wet or dry, hot or cold, are used therapeutically to restore the body to its supposed natural balance.*[56]

It can be of therapeutic and also marketing importance to understand that remedies fall into either hot or cold categories; wet and dry were dropped over time, depending on how the diseases are described. The prescription is that "cold" remedies are given for "hot" ailments and vice versa, in order to restore the balance of health to the sufferer. For generations, Hispanics have received treatment according to these categories, and have continued to treat their children under the same philosophy. Since this theory is alien to most US health-care providers they are mystified when they suggest, for instance, that their patients drink cold fruit juices as treatment for a cold, but their patients end up not following this advice. They miss out on the understanding that a cold drink is not considered an appropriate cold remedy for a cold disease in the hot–cold classification system. More typically, a hot ginger or sunflower tea can be more acceptable for treating a cold.

Health-care professionals who understand this system can work within it so that they do not have to disrupt deeply held beliefs that can hinder their own credibility. Since the classification of remedies changes with the different forms in which they are given—for instance vitamins are considered hot remedies and can be taken for colds or other cold diseases such as menstruation—doctors can prescribe them instead of insisting on cool drinks and formulas. Thus, marketing communication strategies should incorporate knowledge of traditional beliefs in order to achieve acceptance and viability with Hispanic consumers. Marketers need to deploy in-depth qualitative research to gain a competitive advantage when it comes to archetypes that are central to Latino culture, and potentially the difference between a failed or successful marketing strategy.

Conclusions

Successful Hispanic marketing efforts are those that develop a close connection between their brand and Latino consumers at the emotional level by tapping into their cultural roots. To make that emotional link it is important to discover the cultural dimensions that impel these Hispanic target consumers to laugh, cry, love, grieve, decide, and ultimately commit to a particular product or service. Subjective culture of US Hispanics has been shaped by the synergistic relationship between their ancestors and early socialization in their countries of origin and their adoptive culture in the US.

This chapter suggests that through understanding dimensions of culture and cultural archetypes marketers can discover the emotional fit needed for successfully positioning their products or services for Latinos. With an initial awareness of the cultural dimensions of Hispanic consumers, marketers working with experienced Hispanic researchers, can use in-depth interviewing and ethnographic research methodologies to reach deep emotional levels related to their brand. They can also discover related archetypes through literature, music, sculpture, painting, TV, movies, and other forms of art and popular culture both traditional and contemporary.

By understanding the unique subjective culture of Hispanics in contrast to the norms of US non-Hispanics, marketers can grasp why conceptual development of marketing communication must be done from a within culture basis. Examples of key cultural dimensions on which Hispanics differ from non-Hispanics are:

- The polychronic nature of the Hispanics, who are comfortable with many things happening simultaneously in the media or in customer service versus the monochronic preferences of non-Hispanics for one subject treatment and orderly processes.
- Hispanic preferences for polymorphic leadership styles, in which one trusted expert can provide guidance in a wide variety of areas versus the monomorphic preferences for non-Hispanics who trust experts with deep knowledge and experience in one field.
- The strong inclination of Hispanics to collectivism, believing that the family and the groups to which they belong are essential to the functioning and enjoyment of their lives versus the pride of non-Hispanics in achieving on one's own merits and competing with others for success.
- The Hispanic tendency to attribute causality to sources outside of themselves— to other people or other forces versus the non-Hispanic belief in the power of self-reliance to create one's own path to success.

Marketers also discovered cultural archetypes in this chapter, which can be powerful tools for deep cultural understanding of Hispanic consumers. Each of these archetypes forms a cultural mold with the potential to shape Hispanic reactions to a marketer's product or service. Archetypes for Hispanics may come from their Spanish heritage in their countries of origin as well as from their experience as immigrants living in the US. For instance, their history of oppression from Spanish domination may motivate them to enjoy today for tomorrow may never come while their experience in the US may influence them to strive for a better future. It is vital that marketers discover the relevant cultural dimensions and archetypes which influence Latino motivation for their brand and to build this into their positioning and strategy.

IMPLICATIONS FOR MARKETERS

- Go to the core of Latino subjective culture and grasp its meaning relative to your marketing objectives. To successfully position brands in the US Hispanic market, you must tap into the emotional benefits which can make your brand complicit in communicating with this target. While overt differences in cultural behavior and artifacts are easier to observe, it is critical to move beyond these and understand subjective differences.
- Understand the cultural dimensions and archetypes that affect the attitudes, feelings, and behaviors of US Hispanics. You can learn about the dimensions and

archetypes which relate to your brand through exposure to Hispanic literature, art, cinema, and music as well as through in-depth qualitative research.

■ Recognize that the Latino market is complex and that the influence of Hispanic cultural roots permeates the new identity being created in the adoptive country of these consumers. The US Hispanic culture is a unique amalgam of the influences of home country heritage and those of their new culture in the US. Without an understanding of the shared cultural roots of Latinos you have little chance to grasp the current mindset of your Latino target.

■ Suspend the comfort level of your own invisible subjective culture and make a personal and professional decision to move into the unknown, yet fascinating, space of another culture, in this case the US Hispanic culture. This is *the* way to latch onto the emotions of the Hispanic market for the positioning of your brand. Make sure to have a culturally trained research and marketing companion with the expertise to act as a guide for your journey. Well-crafted campaigns, based on solid cultural understanding, should be the result, and your increasing sophistication will continue to lead to future Hispanic marketing successes for your brand.

CASE STUDY: ALMA DDB–MCDONALD'S

Company/Organization
McDonald's

Advertising agency
Alma DDB

Campaign/Advertising Title
"Sabemos lo que te mueve" (We know what moves you)

Intended Hispanic Consumers
Hispanics 18–49 with a bull's-eye of young Hispanic adults 18–34

Background
In a marketing landscape where everyone is appealing to Hispanics' "passion points," particularly music, McDonald's was looking for a way to stand out despite a limited budget. They needed a way to compete with brands that were outspending them in the music area many times over.

Discovery Process/Research
Alma DDB felt they did not need research to confirm Hispanics' top passion points; what they needed to learn was how to be more relevant when playing in those areas. As part of the agency's Cultural Curators' work they developed a multimedia ethnographic research initiative to unearth insights among their core target consumers. They recruited peer-identified influential teens and young adults and asked them to create online blog diaries complete with digital pictures and music tracks identifying what they felt were places, people, companies that influenced them and those that they influenced. These

blog diaries were followed up with online video and web chats to dig deeper into their initial reports. The methodology proved especially useful since it allowed the agency to uncover the reasons why some elements of these Hispanics' lives were considered more influential to them than others and it gave clear direction into why certain brands were considered authentic participants in their lives.

This first phase helped identify *how* Alma DDB should engage with the consumer, but they still were missing the component of achieving *relevancy* in regard to the music passion area. To that end, the agency undertook a second research initiative. This time, they asked recruits to report on a "day in their life." But this was not a diary exercise; because they were dealing with young adults, they identified another way to seamlessly fit the research into their targets' lives. They asked the Hispanic recruits to record their "day" as the music they listened to and the digital photos that accompanied those moments. The resulting submissions were uploaded mobile photos with song title captions. Because the required reporting action was a very normal one for them, we found that the daily snapshot was not only more truthful than a diary, but also came in an up to the minute stream. These day-in-the-life audio/video diaries helped the agency identify not only some of the off-radar musicians that these teens and young adults were listening to, but also helped them see how these Hispanics found them (online, through friends, on blogs, and social networks) which in turn gave a comfort level to the agency with recommending an unknown yet high potential band to headline the advertising efforts.

Cultural Insights

Alma DDB believes that Hispanics overall, and young adults particularly, respond when a brand makes a genuine cultural connection. But achieving authenticity goes beyond a logo next to a band's name while on tour. It requires a genuine interest not only in their passions but also in their community in order to demonstrate that the brand involvement goes deeper than their commercial interests. This was a key finding from the agency's research: Hispanic young adults are more involved in their communities than ever and brands hoping to make a connection need to be involved as well. This finding influenced our decision-making process heavily as we developed elements of the 360° efforts.

Expression of Insights in the Campaign

To begin with, the brand recognized that to be impactful they needed to interact with consumers one on one (a logo would not suffice). They also understood that in today's hyper-connected world, it is easy to overlook one-off marketing efforts. And finally, they were conscious that the obvious big-name band would not be enough to demonstrate a genuine understanding and interest in their consumer.

So what was the solution? Demonstrate that McDonald's was "in-the-know." Develop an approach that not only generated reach by having multifaceted content that appealed to the broader consumer target, but also drove frequency among the bull's-eye consumer by aligning the brand with meaningfully relevant bands.

The solution: "Sabemos lo que te mueve", a 360° campaign that featured undiscovered artists that appealed to cutting edge music lovers as well as well-known acts that were of interest to a broad consumer base. The campaign involved local activations, national TV spots, online promotions, nontraditional media, and most importantly community outreach .

(Continued)

McDonald's "Sabemos lo que te mueve" (We know what moves you) campaign.

Effect of the Campaign

Advertising

TV campaign featuring three up and coming bands. The first band featured experienced a 54% increase in traffic for its YouTube video the first month. The band has since been nominated for an MTV award and numerous articles and blog posts have been published about them. Credit has gone to McDonald's for helping them gain mass reach.

FiestaTour McDonald's a traveling music exhibit featured memorabilia from more than 50 Latino artists who have contributed to the advancement of music, culture, and education.

The exhibit visited 31 Hispanic events in 13 markets from March to November 2009, reaching 5.2 million consumers.

Multiplatform Sweepstakes

Latin Grammy Sponsorship of street parties and cultural events: connected customers to the Latin Grammy telecast and sent lucky winners to the live show: over 34,000 unique entries.

Community Outreach

A panel of music-industry experts and musicians visited schools in New York, Chicago, Miami, Los Angeles, and Dallas, which generated thousands of impressions and positive media coverage. Students had the opportunity to speak face to face with music-industry experts and also learned about RMHC/HACER®, the McDonald's Hispanic scholarship program.

Public Relations

The sum of the campaign efforts generated over 43 million unpaid media impressions with positive coverage of McDonald's efforts to reach out to Hispanics communities, specifically Hispanic youth.

CASE STUDY: CASANOVA PENDRILL–GENERAL MILLS

Company/Organization Name
General Mills

Advertising Agency
Casanova Pendrill

Product
Nature Valley

Campaign
Nature

Intended Hispanic Consumers
Urban Naturals (see Section "Research" later)

Background
Nature Valley was an underdeveloped brand with Hispanic consumers despite this segment's affinity toward natural products. Both consumption and awareness levels of Nature Valley were lower with Hispanic consumers than the general market. The brand had never directly addressed this consumer segment.

The brand's question was: How does the Nature Valley Brand tell the Nature Valley story to Latinos?

In the general market, when the brand asked "Where's your Nature Valley?" the answer was: hiking to the top of the mountain, leaving muddy footprints on hundred-year-old ruts, kayaking a wild rapid, and other great stories about how nature in all its majesty was conquered.

So, when the brand asked "Where's your Nature Valley, for Latinos"? the Agency said, "yeah … not really out in nature."

While Casanova Pendrill was not likely to find ski lifts in Boyle Heights, or trails with ruts near the downtown area, the agency was similarly going to use the target's living environment to tell the brand's story. The agency uncovered that Latinos do not have ski lifts, but they have city parks. These parks served as the nature nucleus from which the agency built the story out. The city park was the local link to a much-needed connection to open space, in other words nature can live in the city. All the Nature Valley brand needed was to make a relevant connection with Latinos.

Research
The agency and brand's strategic research process had a formal path, and a philosophy. The plan was to start a broad conversation about nature with the consumer and learn every important dimension of nature that impacted their life. The philosophy was simple, learning comes first, timelines were second.

The process started with traditional focus groups and ethnographies across key US Hispanic markets. The goal was to understand what nature meant to our target, as well as how this meaning connected to their living environment. Through a figurative

(Continued)

process the agency used diverse nature-related visuals to understand the symbolic meaning of nature beyond the literal interpretation. To the target nature was both omnipotent and omnipresent. The target saw nature in deserts and in the oceans as well. However when the agency showed photos of forests and greenery, there was an emotional response. This was of key importance to the brand because Nature Valley's imagery is represented by majestic forests. As the conversation moved closer to the images that represent the brand, the target's emotional connection to nature was highlighted. Some of the research respondents had stories about hugging beautiful and ancient trees. A few respondents talked about their love of the lonely plant that lives in their apartment. The agency learned that nature is an ideal, an emotion that is not limited to the physical. Nature can live anywhere even in the city. This inspired the conceptual target name of *Urban Naturals*. The agency used this learning to develop several creative territories for testing and continued to learn from the target's reactions.

The campaign's initial market test execution was set with a pre–post sales analysis through the use of sales data from a retail partner. The test market selected was Los Angeles. Uniquely, the test was designed around two principles, impact sales at selected stores and impact at the area's nature. This meant that the areas around the local parks were surrounded by Nature Valley billboards and sampling at the parks occurred during the weekends. The execution was concentrated in one geographic area of Los Angeles, not the entire market. This approach allowed the brand to test in the biggest Hispanic market without a big-size budget and obtain the appropriate learning for expansion.

Cultural Insights

Urban Naturals believe that all good things come from nature. After all, they never felt guilty for eating a bowl of fruit, not only that but they believe that every piece has a purpose. To them, that is just the way it is: things from nature are natural and good for you. It is like that feeling they get when they step out onto the grass, listen to the sway of the trees, see the flowers in bloom—and take a deep breath: a moment of tranquility, serenity, and connection. Their minds need this moment, but their soul yearns for it.

Urban Naturals are different from the non-Latino consumers, they are not outdoor enthusiasts. They do not go skiing, or trekking, however they too have a deep connection to nature.

Expression of Insights in the Campaign

The agency's approach to the campaign started with one key principle: brands do not change, it is the consumer situations that are different. Nature Valley's iconography and brand would not be altered. What this meant was that while the general market had used the "nature lifestyle" to get to the product's natural ingredients, the Latino Market will use the natural ingredients to get to the nature lifestyle.

It all started with Natural Ingredients: Nature Valley crunchy bars originally started as natural ingredients bars, they still are. Making the connection to nature the brand leveraged the outdoor enthusiast's natural lifestyle to sell the bar's natural ingredients.

For the Latino market the agency planned to come at the story from the other way around: ingredients to lifestyle. A cultural insight discovered by the agency is that for many Latinos the word, insinuation or belief that something is natural or of nature, is taken as an indication that it must be good for you.

On some competitor energy bars that are made with mostly nonnatural ingredients, there are things that are visually obvious as not being natural; on the Nature Valley crunchy bars the natural ingredients are visible with nothing else added. With Nature Valley crunchy bars the target *knew* they were getting a natural product and all the benefits of nature.

Build out from the park: The Agency approached the communications plan as if it was telling a story. The agency started with the city parks. Casanova Pendrill used billboards, bus-shelter wraps, and bulletins to surround the parks with a very simple image: a natural landscape in the shape of a bar, with the campaign's line "natural ingredients for a natural life."

Then the agency targeted events that were held in parks to hand out coupons. The brand was sampled at parks and coupons were offered where people walked.

The agency chose radio over TV. They felt that a radio message allows people to imagine nature in its most perfect state—as they see it. The radio title was "It's Natural." The announcer asks the listener to imagine beautiful and powerful aspects of nature—wind, stream, birds, rain, and thunder accompanied by their sounds. Then, the announcer wraps up with the message, "It's amazing what nature can create with all natural ingredients. In Nature Valley, we only followed in her footsteps (nature); our granola bars are made with natural ingredients to give you all the "delicious"/great taste of nature and all its energy too."

Throughout the campaign, Casanova Pendrill used the headline, *Take a little bit of nature in your pocket* and the tagline, *Nature Valley, natural ingredients for a natural life*. They leveraged the ingredients to tell the Nature Valley lifestyle so the target may savor nature, not conquer it.

Effect of the Campaign

The following results confirmed the Nature campaign for Latinos as a success for the brand: The brand's activity grew from one market to eight in 2009. Hispanic sales showed strong growth rising 27% and continuously outperformed general market results.

TV produced for the Hispanic market in 2009 was then adapted to use in the general market in early 2010.

General Mills Nature Valley Brand, Nature campaign.

CASE STUDY: GRUPO GALLEGOS–CALIFORNIA MILK PROCESSOR BOARD

Company/Organization
California Milk Processor Board

Hispanic Agency
Grupo Gallegos

Campaign/Advertising Title
Fighting Crankiness One Glass of Milk at a Time

Intended Hispanic Consumers
California Hispanic Moms

Background
For approximately 2 years prior to this campaign, the California Milk Processor Board, better known as the "Got Milk?" or "Toma Leche" people, had been advertising to the Hispanic market quite successfully. Grupo Gallegos had helped them increase both consumption and perception ratings of milk among Hispanics in California with memorable and effective advertising that consumers loved, according to the agency's extensive consumer qualitative research.

And because of this success, the agency ran into a seemingly insurmountable and quite unexpected roadblock: most California Hispanics were not only drinking milk, but they were drinking it multiple times a day.

At 94%, milk had achieved almost universal household penetration among Hispanics. At the individual level, 98% of Hispanics had consumed milk within the past week. Finally, the majority of Hispanics were drinking milk often: close to three quarters (71%) of Hispanics in California were drinking it either multiple times a day or at least once a day. In a nutshell, Hispanics were having milk in the morning, as a snack, before going to bed. There were simply no more milk-drinking occasions left. Or so it seemed.

Grupo Gallegos' strategic challenge was to get the core target of Hispanic moms to drink an extra glass of milk.

The Agency's objectives were to:
1. Raise awareness of lesser-known benefits and
2. Increase frequency of consumption.

This meant provide consumers with new reasons that would lead to new drinking occasions and, ultimately, would drive frequency up among Hispanics across California.

Discovery Process/Research
By the time Grupo Gallegos started the planning process for 2008, they already knew Hispanics were big fans of milk and that they were drinking it often. What they did not know at the time was what would make them drink even more. That is where their research story began. To start identifying an answer, the agency decided to gather every shred of research done on the benefits of milk.

Grupo Gallegos was determined to find more reasons for Hispanics to drink even more milk than they already were. Once the research review was completed, the list of benefits was impressive: milk helps with stronger nails, it helps build strong teeth and reduce the risk of cavities, it also helps promote a better sleep, build stronger bones and hair, have radiant skin, rebuild muscle after a workout and so on. According to the agency, this stuff appeared to be a wonder tonic. But alas, Hispanics knew this already. Grupo Gallegos had been telling them these sorts of benefits for a couple of years now. And they had listened and were drinking more milk already.

Grupo Gallegos needed to uncover new opportunities. With that objective in mind, the second chapter in their research story unfolded. The agency set up group discussions among the core target: Learner and Straddler (low and mid-acculturated) Hispanic women around the state of California. Grupo Gallegos had identified these two segments as the most critical ones through their proprietary LSN® Segmentation Model—a model that segments the Hispanic market through the lens of acculturation. These Learner and Straddler women are the purveyors of milk for their family, and how much everyone drinks is pretty much up to them.

But instead of talking to these groups about milk and what it was good for, the agency decided to talk to them about sodas, orange juice, teas, and water. They decided the only way to increase milk frequency of consumption would be to steal share from these unrelated drinks. So Grupo Gallegos wanted to understand what the Hispanic women used them for.

The logic was simple: figure out why and when these Hispanic women use orange juice, for instance, and then refer to our list of milk benefits to see if milk would actually be a better drink choice for the moment. And within a few groups, the agency hit pay dirt: tea. Learner and Straddler women in California were drinking a ton of herbal teas.

One particular tea-drinking occasion outshone the rest: herbal teas to help reduce the premenstrual symptoms. Benefit #14 on the list of milk benefits described earlier was also just that: the calcium in milk may reduce the symptoms of PMS. Susan Thys-Jacobs and her colleagues had conducted a medical trial that demonstrated calcium is a simple and effective treatment in PMS[57].

Grupo Gallegos brought this up in their focus groups and women were frankly quite surprised. The agency knew through one of their ongoing studies (Hispanic Perception Tracking Study), that only a fraction of the target (29%) associated this benefit at least somewhat with milk. What they did not know through this quantitative data was why. That answer came from the group discussions. These women had been told by their mothers that they should avoid drinking milk right before and during their period, as it would make their premenstrual symptoms worse. Instead, they had been advised to drink more teas.

The agency quickly did the numbers and was completely shocked. If a majority of low and mid-acculturation Hispanic women in California were avoiding milk for 3–5 days a month, that translated into almost 1/3 gallon per woman, per month, times the number of Hispanic women in California.

There was however a potential glitch that the agency discovered during the third chapter in their research story. As they further explored through additional qualitative research the opportunity of convincing Learner and Straddler women to drink more milk during their periods as a way to cope with PMS, they uncovered a latent issue.

These women were a bit uncomfortable talking about their periods. It just was not an easy topic, topics like the weather or the latest family news. Most advertising

(Continued)

California Milk Processor Board's "Fighting Crankiness One Glass of Milk at a Time" campaign: "Bruja" TV spot.

that touched on this issue tended to be endearing, sweet and kind, or informational. It seemed to be all about feminine hygiene. The agency did not want to go there. They felt that if they created informational advertising it would simply be boring and off-brand character. If they did something sweet and kind and understanding it would get lost in the style of the maxi-pad universe. And, if they did something that was clearly about menstruation, it would likely turn these women off.

The learning was clear: the agency felt they needed something unexpected in tone. And they needed something that would not even talk about the period upfront and run the risk of turning these women off. They had to deliver the message somehow without tipping their hats to the fact that the agency was talking about this somewhat "taboo" topic until the message was actually delivered.

Expression of Insights in the Campaign
The new campaign aimed to raise awareness of this promising benefit as a way to encourage women to drink more milk during their periods. It did it in a way they believed, that not only differentiated the California Milk Processor Board's efforts from those of feminine-hygiene products, but that was true to the brand's DNA and humorous tone of voice.

The creative consisted of an engaging fairy tale story of a mystical town where a witch haunts once a month. The town knew this witch and was afraid. And she was mean. But one day she discovered milk, the story goes, and suddenly she was no longer a witch. The town rejoiced and everyone lived happily ever after. Only at the very end of the spot is the point revealed: "Milk," the announcer says, "helps reduce the symptoms of PMS".

The message was delivered in a Got-Milk-&-Toma-Leche-like funny tone. The intention was that it should be—outrageous enough to cause some controversy, funny enough to be laughed at, cute enough to not be insulting to women, and not at all like other maxi-pad ads.

The campaign used TV to build awareness; leveraged the buzz through PR efforts and directed consumers hungry for more to the website TomaLeche.com, where they could find additional information on this benefit.

Effect of the Campaign

The campaign met the goals Grupo Gallegos set up, driving the growth of key metrics as follows:

Objective 1: Raise Awareness of Lesser-Known Benefits

After the launch of "Bruja," more consumers recognized the attributes of milk the agency aimed to popularize. The fact that milk reduced PMS symptoms went from 29% recognition and association with milk in 2007 to 49% just 2 months after the launch of the campaign. That is a 69% growth in attribute association.

Objective 2: Increase Frequency of Consumption

As far as consumption goes, tracking data from the CMPB's ongoing Consumption Tracking Study revealed that 87% of California Hispanics report having drunk white milk in the past 7 days, up from 82% from the previous year.

End Notes

[1] http://www.pittmag.pitt.edu/jan97/sportsh.html

[2] It should be emphasized that if a product does not live up to the expectations of consumers, no communication will make it succeed.

[3] For an interesting presentation on the subject see "Using consumer insight in advertising: From classic advertising to social network" by Giulio Bonini. http://www.slideshare.net/giuliopsy/eng-the-use-of-consumer-insight-in-advertising

[4] F. Joseph LePla and Lynn M. Parker, *Integrated Branding: Becoming Brand-Driven Through Companywide Action*. Westport, CT: Quorum Books, 1999, pp. 77–78.

[5] See for example the 2010 Advertising Research Foundation Book, *The Listening Playbook* by Stephen Rappaport.

[6] F. Joseph LePla and Lynn M. Parker, *Integrated Branding: Becoming Brand-Driven Through Companywide Action*. Westport, CT: Quorum Books, 1999, p. 48.

[7] For an interesting discussion see *Evolution and Archetype: The Biology of Jung* by John Ryan Haule, specifically the chapter on "Cultural archetypes." http://www.jrhaule.net/evol-atp/index.html

[8] Ibid.

[9] Regis McKenna, *Relationship Marketing: Successful Strategies for the Age of the Customer*. Reading, MA: Perseus Books, 1991.

[10] Noam Chomsky, *Nature and Language, with an Essay on "The Secular Priesthood and the Perils of Democracy"*, Adriana Belletti and Luigi Rizzi (eds). Cambridge, England: Cambridge University Press, 2002.

[11] Edward T. Hall. *Beyond Culture*. New York: Anchor Books/Doubleday, 1976.

[12] Immanuel Kant, Paul Guyer, and Allen W. Wood, *Critique of Pure Reason*. Cambridge: Cambridge University Press, 1998.

[13] See the article by Felipe Korzenny and Lee Vann, "The multicultural world of social media marketing." *Quirk's Marketing Research Review* June, 2009.

[14] Everett Rogers, *Diffusion of Innovations*. New York: The Free Press, 1986.

[15] The reason for enclosing the word modern in quotation marks is because modernism is a relative term that we consider does not necessarily imply superiority.

[16] The authors have conducted multiple pieces of qualitative and quantitative research for specific companies and organizations that have demonstrated the appeal of group enjoyment and the superiority of executions that feature human elements.

[17] Carolyn Dean, *Andean Androgyny and the Making of Men*. In *Gender in Prehispanic America*, Cecelia F. Klein (ed.). Washington, DC: Dumbarton Oaks Research Library and Collection, 2001.

[18] David T. Abalos, *The Latino Male: A Radical Redefinition*. (Boulder, CO: Lynne Rienner, 2002, p. 118.

[19] Peter Salovey and David J. Sluyter (eds), *Emotional Development and Emotional Intelligence: Educational Implications*, 1st ed. New York: Basic Books, 1997, p. 145.

[20] Myriam Y. Jehenson, *Latin-American Women Writers: Class, Race, and Gender*. Albany, NY: State University of New York Press, 1995, p. 4.

[21] Interestingly the origin of the word *marianismo* comes from "Virgin Mary" because that women are supposed to be like her: immaculate, sacrificial, motherly, suffering, and very kind.

[22] John H. Harvey, William J. Ickes, and Robert F. Kidd (eds), *New Directions in Attribution Research*. Hillsdale, NJ: L. Erlbaum Associates, 1976.

[23] David Riesman, *The Lonely Crowd*. Studies in national policy, 3. New Haven, CT: Yale University Press, 1950.

[24] Bina Gupta (ed.), *Sexual Archetypes, East and West*. New York: Paragon Press, 1987, p. 3.

[25] Richard M. Gray, *Archetypal Explorations: An Integrative Approach to Human Behavior*. New York: Routledge, 1996, p. 6.

[26] This is translated as the race of bronze, which represents strength and moral fortitude at the same time that it represents skin color and a new identity.

[27] Richard Payne, "4: Circles of love: In search of a spirituality of sexuality and marriage." In *Sexual Archetypes, East and West*, Bina Gupta (ed.). New York: Paragon Press, 1987, p. 61.

[28] The day of all Saints, also the occasion for the US Halloween.

[29] Find the report at http://hmc.comm.fsu.edu/Publications/Reports.

[30] Sandra Cisneros, *The House on Mango Street*. New York: Vintage Books/Random House, 1991, p. 27.

[31] Octavio Paz, *The Labyrinth of Solitude*. New York: Grove Press, 1961, p. 6.

[32] Sandra Cisneros, *Caramelo*. New York: Vintage Books, 2002, p. 428.

[33] Holly McGavock and Felipe Korzenny. *Hispanic Marketing Insights Inspired by Latin American and US Popular Literature*. Tallahassee, FL: Center for Hispanic Marketing Communication, Florida State University, 2007, pp. 14–16.

[34] Brian A. Primack, Melanie A. Gold, Eleanor B. Schwarz, and Madeline A. Dalton, "Degrading and non-degrading sex in popular music: A content analysis." US National Library of Medicine, National Institutes of Health, Washington, DC: *Public Health Reports*, 2008, 593–600.

[35] Published by Broadway Books, 2006.

[36] Published by Harvard University Press, 2003.

[37] Published by Harvard University Press, 2008.

[38] Published by Broadway Books, 2008.

[39] See for example the book by Patricia L. Sunderland and Rita M. Denny, *Doing Anthropology in Consumer Research*, Walnut Creek, CA: Left Coast Press, 2007.

[40] See for example the lyrics of the song "Soy Mexicano" at http://www.musica.com/letras.asp?letra=1169196.

[41] http://www.imdb.com/title/tt0039668/

[42] Ar-Riba is the Arabic concept indicating that lenders are unethical if they charge interest.

[43] *Quinceañera* parties are celebrations of coming-of-age of young women at age 15. It is traditional to spend large amounts of money on these celebrations that can last several days. See interesting marketing efforts around this important event at http://www.quinceanerasmagazine.com/

[44] This is a well-known Latin-American proverb that is interestingly a challenge to cultural traditions.

[45] Ruth Bennedict, *The Chrysanthemum and the Sword*. New York: World Publishing, 1967.

[46] Maureen B. Slonin, *Children, Culture, and Ethnicity: Evaluating and Understanding the Impact*. New York and London: Garland Publishing Company, Inc., 1991, p. 166.

[47] Roberta Maso-Fleischman, "Archetypal research for advertising: a Spanish-language example." *Journal of Advertising Research* 37(5), 1997, 81(4).

[48] Alan Riding, *Distant Neighbors*. New York: Vintage Books, 1985, p. 10.

[49] Evelyn Stevens, *Marianismo: "The other face of machismo in Latin America," Female and Male in Latin America Essays*, Ann Pescatello (ed.). Pittsburgh, PA: University of Pittsburgh Press, 1973, p. 91.

[50] From "The New Cachet of Being Hispanic" in the January/February 2006 issue of *Hispanic Business Magazine*. http://michaelsaray.com/%20News%20Articles/Hispanic%20Cachet.htm

[51] Ibid.

[52] C. Molina, R.E. Zambrana, and M. Aguirre-Molina, *Latino Health in the US: A Growing Challenge*. C. Molina and M. Aguirre-Molina (eds). Washington, DC: American Public Health Association, 1994.

[53] Felipe Castro, Pauline Furth, and Herbert Karlow, "The health beliefs of Mexican, Mexican American and Anglo American women." *Hispanic Journal of Behavioral Sciences* 6(4), 1984, 365–366.

[54] Robert T. Trotter and Juan A. Chavira, *Curanderismo, Mexican American Folk Healing*. Athens, GA: The University of Georgia Press, 1981, 62–63.

[55] David E. Hayes-Bautista, *La Nueva California: Latinos in the Golden State*. Berkeley, CA: University of California Press, 2004, p. 186.

[56] Alan Harwood, "The hot-cold theory of disease: implications for treatment of Puerto Rican patients." *JAMA* 216(7), 1971, 1153.

[57] S. Thys-Jacobs, P. Starkey, D. Bernstein, and J. Tian, "Calcium carbonate and the premenstrual syndrome: effects on premenstrual and menstrual symptoms. Premenstrual Syndrome Study Group." *American Journal of Obstetrics and Gynecology* 179(2), 1998, 444–452. Also online: http://www.ncbi.nlm.nih.gov/pubmed/9731851?dopt=Abstract.

Chapter 7

CULTURALLY INFORMED RESEARCH AMONG LATINOS

What makes members of your culture think differently? Is it their belief in an after-life? Is it a sense of social responsibility? Is it a belief that after all one is in this world alone? If you are an astute and informed observer you may be able to come up with some answers to this question. These are not easy answers to obtain? Most people do not think about these issues during their daily lives. Subjective culture is not obvious and it is not top-of-mind for most people.

Savvy marketers need to make extra efforts to uncover the internal reality of the consumer. Marketing across cultures is particularly vulnerable to overlooking aspects in consumers' lives that can make the difference between making connections or alienating consumers. What the marketer intends to communicate and what the Latino consumer perceives can be quite different. And in modern marketing thinking, mak-ing connections is a matter of how well the marketer listens to the consumer. It is a lot about listening.

Digging Deeper but Not Finding

Diligent marketers attempt to measure as much as they can when they endeavor to understand Hispanic consumers. They try to figure out all of the different angles that **245**

Hispanic Marketing: Connecting with the New Latino Consumer.

can potentially deliver the consumer insights needed. The typical mindset is to cover "all the bases" to make sure the Hispanic consumer is truly understood.

Paradoxically, the more the marketer keeps digging the less he or she finds the needed cultural insight and understanding. This happens because conducting cross-cultural marketing research requires a considerable amount of cultural information to start with. Without enough cultural information the marketer would not be able to figure out even how or where to start asking questions that can lead to constructive cultural understanding. This paradox is reminiscent of what Marieke K. de Mooij states in the book *Cultural Marketing and Advertising: Understanding Cultural Paradoxes*: "Value and lifestyle studies developed in the United States are used in Europe; and within Europe, studies developed in one country are sold to other countries as if equally valid."[1] This is largely because many marketers still take culture for granted.

Cross-cultural marketing can strongly benefit from a psycho-socio-cultural perspective so that culture is taken into consideration. Those who design the research and/or the strategy need to be conversant in Latino culture in more than a casual way. These culturally competent individuals can inform the research that otherwise could be useless. If one understands how Hispanics feel about their everyday activities the researcher can ask relevant questions.

Naïve questions generally produce naïve answers. In a very simple case, asking about use and attitude regarding a particular item may result in finding that Latinos do not like or use a brand. The marketer is likely to conclude that the answer is in and that the brand has no potential among Latinos. That may not be true at all. We conducted research on refrigerated dough products among relatively less-acculturated Hispanic consumers. When asked about them consumers assumed they would not like that type of product as refrigerated dough sounded alien, and they had not tried and consequently did not use that type of product. After probing many recalled having seen specialty refrigerators in grocery stores with these products but had not understood what they were for. Thus, when a product or ingredient is not part of a culture the inquiry must follow a different course. It should not start from the assumption that "after all everyone knows what refrigerated dough is all about."

A culturally informed marketing team member is likely to be aware of the shopping environments many Latinos come from originally. A typical A&U (Attitudes and Usage) study can be useless for some categories and products. A culturally informed marketer/researcher would be more likely first to understand how Hispanics consume bread, cookies, and so on. Then he or she would conduct taste tests and actual demonstrations of the product to assess potential. Another productive practice in cases like these would be to place the new product in the homes of consumers with instructions on how to use it. That would produce a much more realistic view of a product's potential.

Once the consumer bakes the product at home and the kids and spouse try it and enjoy it or dislike it, then the consumer would be likely to provide more realistic answers. Replicating this in the real world would take the shape of store demonstrations and sampling. It could also take the shape of baking demonstrations at consumers' homes. If the marketer understands the background of the consumer to begin with, he or she is likely to go about asking questions in different ways, and interpreting the data in alternative ways as well.

There are cases that call for more attention to the process of inquiry. For example, the product could be a product that contains baking soda. Baking soda is known to be of high value to many Latinos as it is used as an aid in cleaning, cleansing, cooking, and even as a remedy. Having consumers talk about their perceptions of baking soda would likely be more productive than directly asking about "how do you feel about toothpaste that contains baking soda?" This is because understanding first the general cultural aura of the ingredient is more likely to guide the thinking of the marketer. The associations and memories related to baking soda would be a stronger indicator of appeal and potential purchase than direct questioning.

Direct questioning could actually lead to answers that could discourage further inquiry. If the consumer imagines that the product would taste bad because of the baking soda, then that could lead to the erroneous conclusion that baking soda is of no interest to Hispanics. Also, the consumer may be imagining a product that does not correspond to the reality of the product concept. This pattern could be misleading and lead to incorrect conclusions. Hispanics use baking soda to clean their teeth and believe that it has great cleaning and health attributes. Thus, the moral of the story is to incorporate a culturally savvy marketer in the team, and try to go from general to specific in the questioning sequence.

Translator, Traitor

Umberto Eco in the article Rose by Any Other Name articulates the difficulties of translation and refers to the ancient Latin statement "traduttore, traditore" to indicate the frustration experienced by authors when seeing their intended meanings lost in translation. Basically that translation cannot but betray the original. He states:

> *The job of translation is a trial and error process, very similar to what happens in an Oriental bazaar when you are buying a carpet. The merchant asks 100, you offer 10 and after an hour of bargaining you agree on 50 ... Naturally, in order to believe that the negotiation has been a success you must have fairly precise ideas about this basically imprecise phenomenon called translation.[2]*

Market research and marketing in general are not free from the perils of translation vagaries. Instruments, or questionnaires as they are commonly known, require translations when conducting research with members of different cultures.

A request that appears reasonable to most people is for the marketer to request a translation of a questionnaire into Spanish for administration to Hispanics who prefer to answer in Spanish. It seemed to work well with non-Hispanic Whites, so why should not it work with Latinos. But language is not a simple code that can just be put into another neutral code. Translation is a lot more complex than most intelligent marketers know. That is because cultural and linguistic literacy is not a priority in business school or most schools for that matter.

The reader, by now, is aware that language is a living entity that serves the purpose of the experience of a particular set of people. Languages change over time and if you are not part of the linguistic group the reader may be quite surprised about the difficulties encountered in translation. Translators typically look for close word equivalents. Equivalence, however, is also subjective. Translation is likely to result in messages that resemble the original but the margin of variation is quite ample depending on the person doing the translation. While many translators would argue that their work is excellent, the most seasoned ones would recognize that perfection is quite elusive.

The simple item, "how much do you agree or disagree with the following statement: I try to be agreeable when dealing with other people" can be complex. The term agreeable, which in Spanish should be something like "estar de acuerdo," is generally rather translated as "agradable" which actually means "pleasant" in Spanish.[3] As the reader can tell being agreeable is not necessarily being pleasant at all. There is no direct equivalent of "agreeable" in Spanish with the exception of elaborating on the term and indicating something like "estar de acuerdo con otros," which can be awkward in Spanish, particularly in the context of a marketing questionnaire. A simple term in a statement that is supposed to elicit agreement or disagreement can actually be translated in a way that the original version and the translated version evoke dissimilar meanings. This, as you can imagine, severely hinders the interpretation of the findings.

Conceptual Adaptation from Scratch

Among professionals in this area of work the notion of cultural adaptation has become a viable alternative to translation. Cultural adaptation requires that the person doing the adaptation understands the idea in English and then recasts it in Spanish "from scratch"—that is, without having the limitations of vocabulary obfuscating the process. Here the concept of understanding is crucial because if the person doing the work does not understand the idea very well, the resulting product is likely to be incorrect.

Another term used in ways similar to cultural adaptation is transculturation. Transculturation, however, is generally used incorrectly as it was originally intended to refer to the process of cultural change that happens when people acquire a second culture and create a new one, similar to the idea of the creation of a new cultural identity that we have discussed in this book.[4] The marketer should take into consideration that the term transculturation has deeper and more precise historical meanings. Nevertheless, the important issue here is to have a bilingual individual understand an idea originally cast in one language and then recast it in the second language to try to obtain the desired meaning beyond translation.

TRANSLATING BACK TO THE ORIGINAL LANGUAGE

In attempting to obtain conceptual equivalence researchers and others use a technique called back translation. In back translation:

One or more translators adapt a test from the source language to the target language. Different translators take the adapted test (in the target language) and adapt it back to the source language. Then, the original and the back-translated versions of the test are compared.[5]

The comparison of the source language and target language can then be judged for conceptual equivalence. Back translation is logically appealing but has important drawbacks. Since language use is highly subjective and dependent on the experience of its users, the translators involved in the original and back translations have to be quite familiar with the cultures and topics involved. Then, even if the original and the back-translated version look equivalent, it is not necessarily proof that the translation into the second language actually conforms to the spirit of the original. In particular, what is difficult to achieve is that the gist of the communication be conveyed in a way that sounds as if it had been originally encoded in the target language.

Carefully crafted cultural adaptations are more likely to convey the intended meanings than back-translation approaches. Checking the meaningfulness of a culturally adapted communication resides in what the users of the communication or questionnaire understand. That is why we advocate that marketers behave conservatively in this regard and test any culturally adapted questionnaires or materials with the target audiences to assess whether or not the intended meanings have been conveyed.

THE LOGICAL PROBLEM OF LINGUISTIC EQUIVALENCE

There is a paradox of linguistic equivalence involved in every translation and cultural adaptation effort. The key problem presented by this paradox is that the more conceptually equivalent a translation of an instrument is to its original, the less likely it is for the researcher to find differences between the populations that use those languages. The converse is that the less conceptual, but more literal a translation is, the more likely it is for the researcher to find differences between two linguistic populations.[6]

Cross-cultural research is complicated and that is put in evidence by this paradox. Marketers many times hypothesize cultural differences, and other times hypothesize cultural homogeneity. It highlights that equivalence across languages is more than changing from one to another. It makes salient the cultural nature of language and the difficulties involved in attempting to convey meanings across cultures. This phenomenon dramatizes that the more we strive for language equivalence the more likely we are to find no cross-cultural differences. That is because the cultural differences can be washed out by manipulating the language. The more we strive for conceptual equivalence, the more likely we are to use terms that have more universal relevance, as opposed to culturally unique meaning. The marketer should then ask whether or not the similarities found will help him or her better understand the cultures in question or actually further add error to the strategy.

Uncertainty is part of life when comparing cultures. Marketers who are aware of these issues will be better off since they will be more adept at interpreting findings and more discerning regarding how to approach diverse cultures.

Localization for Better Globalization

Here we address the use of culture-general approaches for overall marketing themes and culture-specific approaches for specific implementation. Globalization and localization have become increasingly salient in international marketing. The dictum "think global, act local" has become part of marketing wisdom. Many marketers talk about globalization as parallel to strategy and localization as parallel to tactical implementations.

There are multiple fundamental expressions of emotions and behaviors that are universal to all human beings. The expressions of fear, surprise, awe, surrender, and others are quite general.[7] We take for granted that most humans love their children, for example. Interestingly, with the discoveries associated with the human genome, all humans seem to be related genetically, at least as second cousins of each other.[8]

Anthropologists have adopted the terms "emic" and "etic" to describe two types of logical systems for observing cultures. An emic perspective on human consumer behavior would be to examine each culture individually without attempting to establish a mold for comparison across cultures. An etic perspective on consumer behavior would establish metrics to apply to several cultures so that they can be compared and contrasted. In 1954, Kenneth Pike published definitions and a discussion of the two terms.[9] An analogy of the emic and etic approaches to language and culture can be exemplified with objects. In the case of housing, the emic approach could consist of examining a home as a complex set of structural interrelations and character. The etic perspective would look at many homes in a comparative chart of homes by their traits. Thus, homes could be compared with respect to their number of bathrooms, bedrooms, and so on. The emic approach would look at how the home feels, its feng shui, and its Gestalt. The etic approach would look for a comparative examination of elements that exist across homes.

Most marketers we have come across would generally feel much better if he or she could conclude how diverse cultures are similar or different across dimensions. There are others, however, who claim that it is more productive to understand a culture on its own, independent of other cultures, making no comparisons. There are good reasons for both lines of thinking. Overall we believe that is more productive to try to understand the Latino culture on its own. That is because we understand the perils of comparisons in which one tries to force preconceived molds so that cultural comparisons can make sense.

Most likely the etic and emic approaches need to coexist. This is because to get to know anything, we need to start from what is known, perhaps by comparing visible elements of culture. Then, once particular inconsistencies or discontinuities emerge, we need to delve deeper into a culture without further comparison to other cultures.[10] While it is a generally accepted observation that Hispanics are more collectivistic than non-Hispanic Whites, one needs to understand how these dimensions play out within the context of the culture itself. Many times Hispanics also exhibit individualism, and many times non-Hispanic Whites behave as a collective. It is the observation within the culture itself that would facilitate the explanation of when one behavior is likely to be displayed than the other.

It is understandable that marketers prefer to make comparisons across cultures because in their attempt to create overarching strategies they prefer to capitalize on similarities. Nevertheless, it is more likely that the connection with the consumer will be stronger with an approach that has particular resonance to the individual in the context of his or her culture. With this in mind, the idea of "think global, act local," may need to be reconsidered. Marketing efficacy can come from thinking globally and also locally, with strategic approaches at both levels. Perhaps the question that may lead to a more productive answer is "how can my local strategy contribute to the global approach?"

Marketers should be better off understanding a culture on its own right because that gives them power over their competition. While all humans share much in common, what makes marketers effective is the understanding of subtle differences that have a strong impact on how consumers think. Since culture is one of the important common denominators of US Latinos, then understanding how they feel and think as cultural beings can make a brand more relevant to them.

Latino Scale Use

The assumptions that numeric skills are universal and that people can accurately quantify their view and options are just that, assumptions. While in some cultures numeric and mathematical skills are very high, in others they are not. Further, the measurement of attitudes, opinions, beliefs, and values requires being educated in the logic of scale usage. It is not intuitive to assign numbers to our feelings and thoughts, it is something we learn. Many Hispanics who have not had sufficient amounts of formal education can be mystified when asked to use scales in questionnaires. Many have difficulties understanding the logic of scale usage. In addition, it has been found that Latinos have the tendency to use the extremes of scales, particularly the upper part measurement scales.

This tendency to use extreme values in scales may reflect an actual way of feeling and thinking. Hispanics may just be more passionate. Thus, Latinos really love or hate "things." This seems to be a good cultural explanation as Hispanics are more emotional, in general, about the products and services they use than their non-Hispanic White counterparts.

Generally, the tendency to use the extremes of scales results in lower variability within Hispanic samples. That is a problem because without variability the possibility of finding associations among attitudes and other behaviors is reduced.

There are some who think that the tendency to use the extreme of scales is a bias or a systematic error.[11] There are some who have engaged in sophisticated experiments to see how this bias can be removed. For example, Martin Cerda and Ilgin Basar of the company Encuesta, Inc. published the results of an experiment they conducted among US Hispanics and non-Hispanics and found that there seem to be some scales on which Hispanics are more likely to exhibit extreme response style.[12]

Clearly, the wording of the items in a questionnaire is likely to influence whether responses provided are more extreme in some cases. Piloting these instruments with relevant consumers is likely to be one of the most important steps in assessing whether a scale is behaving as expected or not. The report of Cerda and Basar concluded that the use of scales with less points and more anchors show less of an extreme response style phenomenon. This conclusion is somewhat counterintuitive as classical scaling theory suggests that scales that allow for more variability and contain less anchors provide the respondent with a better opportunity to represent their opinion.[13] This makes intuitive sense, if you are asked to respond on a scale of "Like a lot," "Like a little," and "Do not like at all," your range of choices are very limited compared with responding on a scale where "0" means "do not like at all" and "10" means "like a lot." In the latter scale the respondent can use finer differences to express his or her opinion. So, we think that using less points in a scale is not a logical solution. There have been researchers that recommend alternative approaches and most of them use some type of distribution modification to remove the variability attributable to the specific cultures and leave only the variability due to individuals.[14]

The so called "cultural bias" phenomenon has been more strongly observed in situations in which Latinos respond positively to certain items. Some have argued that the demand characteristic called "social desirability" is more prevalent among Hispanics. Many argue that Latinos are naturally disposed to behave in ways that please others, or that make them feel good. In this way, strongly agreeing with an item like "Education is of great importance to me" would be the socially desirable thing to do. The problem in resolving this difficulty is that Latinos are likely to both think that education is of great importance and at the same time experience a sense of social obligation in agreeing with the statement. In this case we believe it is better to err on the side of believing that Latinos mean what they say and that if their responses are extreme and with relatively low variability it is because that is the way they actually feel.

A less numerically judgmental and "etic" way of understanding if a culture is more prone to use extremes consistently may be the inclusion of control items in the questionnaire. A question like "how much did you enjoy answering this questionnaire?" followed by a scale from "0" to "10," "not at all" to "enjoy a lot," could provide a measure of relative propensity to rate items highly or not across cultural groups. This variable can be used as a statistical control across the cultural groups. The reader can envision that other items can also be included in the questionnaire to assess cultural tendencies to answer questions. For example, "In general, how happy a person do you consider yourself to be?" could also be used as a cultural control for if the answers are systematically different across cultures then one can control for it if deemed desirable.

Statistical control removes the variability due to the perception of phenomena on the scale and makes "etic" comparisons more plausible. Still, observed differences are what they are. It is the duty and responsibility of the researcher and the marketer to be informed as to what cultural issues may be at play depending on wording, order, place of administration, and other factors. The fact that one can control for cross-cultural variability does not mean that the marketer must do so. In fact, cross-cultural variability is the element that can provide the marketer with specific insights for his or her brand's advantage. When understanding the culture, one can better resonate with its members and one's brand can become more genuine and appealing. Answering with extreme values may simply suggest that the marketers' expression of emotion should be parallel so that the consumer can identify with the communication.

Answering Survey Questions Is Not Intuitive

We cannot take for granted that when doing research across cultures people can use the scales we are accustomed to administer. Many of us have been taught about the tradition of attitude and opinion measurement in the US. An issue is that people from many other cultures have not been taught how to answer those scales. That is part of the problem in interpreting cross-cultural research. Do members of other cultures understand the questions and scales the same way as intended by the US researcher? Things would be a lot easier if everyone were just the same, but we are not. Part of the paradox explained earlier is that if we teach everyone how to answer questions the "American way" then we may just find no differences. But if we do not instruct people then we may never know what they were responding to. Here we can illustrate some of the issues in using scales to make the marketers aware of some of the potential problems.

AGREEING AND DISAGREEING WITH STATEMENTS

Rensis Likert was an educator and organizational psychologist who developed a well-known scale named after his name. Likert-type scales that rate a respondent's agreement or disagreement with an item seem simple enough. So, for example, "How much do you agree or disagree with the following statement: I try to preserve my privacy every time I can—READ: STRONGLY AGREE, AGREE, NEITHER AGREE NOR DISAGREE, DISAGREE, AND DISAGREE STRONGLY," can produce problematic responses just due to the scale, above and beyond the problems with the cultural issues involved in the statement. We have observed the following types of problems that Latinos experience with these scales:

- A likely response is, "Yes, I try to preserve my privacy." The interviewer, as all good interviewers are instructed, restates: "Thank you, but would you say that you STRONGLY ...." At which point the disoriented consumer starts doubting the intelligence of the interviewer and responds, "Didn't I tell you I try to preserve my privacy?" Clearly, this exercise can become very complicated because the respondent believes he or she has complied with the interviewer's request but the interviewer must get the response as demanded by his or her trainers and supervisors. The interviewer is supposed to obtain a response in the strongly agree to strongly disagree Likert-type scale. In practice the interviewer would likely try a roundabout approach, restating the response scale by saying "would you say you strongly try or just try" until he or she gets an answer. This exercise forces the consumer to answer using a scale he or she is not familiar with. Beyond not being familiar, the respondent expects a question not something to agree or disagree with. When the respondent states that he or she tries to preserve his or her privacy, this is his or her answer, without gradations on a strongly agree to strongly disagree scale. Also the respondent is answering a question, not responding on an agreement scale.
- We have also heard "I agree" to this question using the scale provided. Due to the pattern discussed earlier, the interviewer is usually uncertain as to whether

or not the answer is "agree" or "strongly agree." In practice we have found that this happens often. The Latino respondent confronted with an unusual questioning situation responds with agreement, but he or she is reluctant to elaborate by adding the adjective "strongly" because it seems unnecessary to represent his position. A solution that has been used to address this problem is to probe and ask "do you just agree, or strongly agree?" This additional probe brings about further issues. From the research designer perspective the clarification is very useful after having found that many respondents economize words and state either agree or disagree without qualification even when they actually meant to. Nevertheless, Hispanics seem to have a cultural tendency to be pleasant to others, including interviewers. At the probe of whether the agreement is simply or strongly, the Hispanic respondent may feel that he or she is being asked for something else because he or she did not provide the "right" answer, and thus may answer "strongly agree." This "strongly agree" may be somewhat false because the respondent just meant "agree." Also, the "strongly agree" may be inherently invalid because the respondent may not differentiate between levels of agreement. For many Latinos degrees of agreement are unusual as in their lives they either agree or disagree.

■ And, as suggested earlier "agree–disagree" Likert-type scales may be unfamiliar or illogical to the respondent. The logic of such scales is highly idiosyncratic to Western social science. Many Latinos in the US, we have found, appear to be more comfortable with questions that ask for a reply. After all, that is what questions are for. Many respondents have answered this type of Likert-type scale with a "yes" or "no," with the consequence of a tedious and uncertain dialog with the interviewer. Thus, the respondent needs to be familiarized with the logic of many scales conventionally used in Western social sciences. The researcher should not assume that the respondent will understand how to use these scales. That is why in many surveys researchers find that the high end of the scale is used much more than any other point. The respondent is using the scale as a dichotomous bipolar scale as opposed to using it as gradations of agreement. Training the respondent is not impossible, but it does take survey time. As the US Hispanic population grows in the US and as more surveys are administered, more respondents are becoming used to the utilization of Likert-type scales, and other measurement schemes. Still, the cross-cultural marketer should not take for granted that a measurement scheme is universal.

In marketing the consumer is the measure of all things. Hispanic consumers not only differ in many ways regarding their consumption habits, values, and beliefs, they also differ in how they react to questions, items, and scales. This is something that the marketer and the market researcher need to keep in mind as they attempt to better connect with Latinos.

ANSWER OPTIONS THAT MORE CLOSELY REFLECT CONSUMER THINKING

There are different ways in which respondents can be provided with options to respond to questions. There are different types of scales and different classifications of scales.[15] There are some known as nominal because they label groups or sets of items. These labels do not have a quantitative relationship to each other. Examples include items such as nationality, religion, race, football team preference and so on. Generally speaking being a fan of the FSU football team does not mean it is less or more than being a fan of the Clemson football team, even though some may think so.

Ordinal scales, as their name indicates, are types of scales that suggest that one item has more of an attribute than another. An ordinal scale can be used for items such as acculturation to denote, for example—high, medium, and low acculturation.

Relatively speaking, and for a higher level of precision, there are interval scales. These allow for the measurement of the difference between any two adjacent points on a scale and these differences are supposed to be the same as the differences between any other two adjacent points in the same scale. So, for example, the difference between the points 1 and 2 on the scale is supposed to be the same as the difference between points 3 and 4 on the scale. An important attribute of these scales is that their numbers can be subjected to addition and subtraction and the numbers preserve their meaning.

A ratio scale is generally considered to be more powerful than an interval scale because it possesses an absolute zero. When a scale has an absolute zero it can be used for multiplication and division, beyond addition and subtraction. This is an important attribute because this type of scale can be very powerful for statistical manipulation. The presence of an absolute zero is important because of interesting properties that this number has. Anything multiplied by zero remains zero, and anything added to zero leaves the original number as it was. Nevertheless, the reader should keep in mind that these descriptions of types of scales have been debated and that their appropriateness or lack of it for specific analysis is not a dogma.[16]

This discussion hopefully triggers in the reader's mind the idea that if we can use ratio scales, or scales that approximate ratio scales in our measurement, we may be able to better detect trends and uncover new relationships in the data. Also, a ratio (or ratio like) scale allows for finer discrimination in measurement. That is that one can better differentiate one consumer from another.

A simple type of scale that approximates a ratio scale, even though many would argue it is not a true ratio scale is a 0–10 scale.[17] In this case, zero is true in the sense that if someone has zero of something he or she has none of it. Also, the intervals can be assumed to be equal in the scale. In our research practice we have found that this type of scale is understood by most Hispanic respondents we have worked with. Also it seems to discriminate much better than alternative counterparts.

The finding that Latinos can use this type of scale quite well was somewhat seren-dipitous. The explanation for this phenomenon is that in many school systems in Latin America, and particularly Mexico, teachers use a 0–10 scale to grade students. This type of scale then has become part of the culture and its use has become intuitive.

A way of stating this type of scale would be "On a scale from 0 to 10, where zero means no preference at all and 10 means absolute preference, how much do you prefer well-known brands over store brands?" In our experience it is important to specify both anchors (0 and 10) and their "meaning," for the first few question-naire items; then respondents learn the logic and continue without much difficulty. Findings using this scale tend to render more discrimination between behaviors and preferences than almost any other scale. After conducting many Hispanic market research studies, it has been found that the face validity of this measurement scale appears to be as good as can be achieved.

MULTIPLE WAYS OF MEASURING

There are many ways of measuring consumer feelings, opinions, values, perceptions, thoughts, attitudes, intentions, and behaviors. While one can ask many questions of many types that does not mean that we can obtain valid responses just by asking. The marketer/researcher needs to understand that there are many factors that affect how consumers respond to questions and how they rate items. Among Hispanics there are some cultural tendencies, some of which we have outlined above, that impact how people respond. So, for example, if the culture has a strong value for maintaining har-mony, then helping the questioner save face becomes important. Similarly, a culture that is highly empathic, as Latinos tend to be, may produce a consumer tendency to try to please the questioner. The ratio-type scale highlighted above helps mitigate some of these issues. Still, the mode of administration will also have an impact. The interviewer can impact the responses as well as most modes of administration.

Being cognizant of these issues can help to think of ways of obtaining data that are more likely to be useful and that actually reflect consumers' perspectives. The use of different scales is highly dependent on whether the consumer is used to using the scales in question. As Latinos have become increasingly socialized to the ways of the US, they are more likely to use and understand more types of scales. That does not mean, however, that Latino culture does not have an influence on how they respond. We feel that when it is the culture that influences responses no further cor-rections or modifications are needed as it is precisely cultural influences that are important to the marketer.

Explore Using Intuitive Alternatives

The reader is encouraged to consider the use of scales such as the Osgood Semantic Differential Scale.[18] It is a simple and elegant way of assessing perceptions, which

Figure 7.1 Little faces scale.

Osgood originally used in an attempt to uncover universal or cross-cultural dimensions of meaning. By means of the use of this scale in different countries he found that most cultures judge objects in three main dimensions: evaluation, strength, and activity. This has been a particularly important finding in the social sciences because it documents underlying ways in which humans perceive elements of knowledge. These are dimensions as fundamental as time and space.

In our current effort of marketing to Latinos these scales can be very useful for specific measurement problems. The Osgood Semantic Differential Scale is bipolar, with opposite adjectives on each end such as:

Weak _ _ _ _ _ _ _ _ Strong
Slow _ _ _ _ _ _ _ _ Fast
Passive _ _ _ _ _ _ _ _ Active

Respondents are asked to place an X on the line that is closer to the meaning that a particular word has. In this way the respondent can evaluate many objects, subjects, and brands: Nike, family, home, shopping, and Best Buy, for example. This type of scale is pretty intuitive and seems to be understood with minimal instruction.

With populations that are less literate and less familiar with market research procedures the "little faces" or *las caritas* can be very useful. This type of scale is even more intuitive and has a very direct denotation to emotional states. The limitation is, of course, that the little faces only show affect and no other dimension; that is, from liking a lot to not at all (Figure 7.1).

The number of faces can be five or three. We recommend the use of five to allow for more variability in responses. Their major limitation is that the administration does not work on the phone but works well in almost all contexts: online, in-person, mail, and self-administered.

What Type of Data Is Needed?

Determining the type of data the marketer or researcher needs strongly influences the data-collection method. We recall with some amusement conversations with marketers in which the question was: What would be more economical qualitative or quantitative research? Clearly, finances should not determine this type of decision since qualitative and quantitative market research have fundamentally different objectives.

Qualitative research, in the form of ethnographies, focus groups, in-depth interviewing, observation, both online and off-line, is generally geared to obtaining a sense of understanding of a phenomenon. These approaches are aimed at finding out the symbols, language, elaborations, and explanations of human phenomena. In conducting qualitative research the researcher may be in search of insights that then become hypotheses for further exploration. Also, the researcher may be in search of red flags pointing to problems with a particular stimulus, package, product, or advertising. This is because if only a few people point to a problem, the problem may be a real problem. If an ad does not clearly communicate a message, that should be uncovered qualitatively. If Latinos have a strong attachment for milk and milk products, it is enough to hear a few of them explain why. This latter example also contains a quantitative statement. That is, "a strong attachment." To determine the degree of the attachment one needs quantitative research. But the explanation of why can be answered qualitatively.

Quantitative research can take the form of surveys in multiple modes of administration. They can be online, in-person, self-administered in a church or school, sent by mail, etc. Quantitative studies can also be done by measuring certain behaviors of a large sample of people. For example, measuring traffic in certain supermarket aisles. The primary purpose for conducting quantitative research is to obtain magnitudes, prevalence, and quantities of items. Thus, a survey is best used to find out what brands of coffee Latino consumers purchase most often, or how many Hispanics go to mom-and-pop stores to purchase products from their country of origin. One restriction that applies to quantitative research is that the data needs to be collected in specific ways in order to trust the answers. So, for example, quantitative data needs to be collected from a random sample of the population of interest, and the sample size needs to be large enough so that the results can be generalizable to the population of interest.

From the above discussion the reader may infer that many marketing projects actually benefit from having both a qualitative and quantitative component. The quantitative part finds general facts, and the qualitative research explains them.

FINDING THE WHY

Qualitative research is geared to answering the question "why?" There are different types of qualitative research that can be more productive for one purpose than for another. For example, if you want to have an in-depth discussion of how women feel about being mothers, then a conventional focus group can be quite useful. If, however, you are trying to figure out whether an ad you intend to produce has a good chance of communicating and convincing the target audience, then you may conduct mini-groups so that each respondent has ample opportunity to react but also discuss the ad just seen.

If on the other hand you need to understand how women with families go about organizing their morning and the products they use, then an ethnographic interview could be very efficient. Now, if you want to have exchanges during the day regarding the different activities that Latinos engage in, then text messaging can be very useful. You can send a text message to the respondent every hour and ask them to tell you what they are doing at that time and if they are using any products to tell which ones. Over a few days you can have a very interesting composite qualitative picture of how Hispanics spend their days and the products that are part of their lives. Generally, the limit to the design of qualitative research is the imagination of the researcher, the ethics of the situation, and the validity of the data that can be obtained.

Almost all types of inquiries can benefit from a qualitative exploration. One of the most common types of qualitative research objectives is to obtain insights about consumers that will help position a brand. Thus, if you have a cleaning product, and you know that Hispanics are obsessive about cleanliness, you may want to find out how Latinos conceptualize "clean," or what does it mean to them. If you understand the meaning of "clean" you can then associate the attributes of its meaningfulness with your brand for a winning proposition.

The market researcher may design a qualitative study to test a communications concept or a product prototype. In many cases almost any idea can be submitted to qualitative consumer reactions. In general, qualitative findings can be very useful to bring the marketer closer to the world of Latino consumers and to serve as feedback in the overall marketing process.

Two case studies follow which illustrate the use of research to develop cultural understanding of the deeply held attitudes that influence purchase decisions for two diverse types of business—automotive and communications (Full case studies are included at the end of this chapter). In each case, qualitative research is used to bring the brand closer to the broader reality of Latino consumer experience related to their products as well as the emotional aspects of their usage. The first case study combines several qualitative research methodologies. The second allies qualitative ethnography with quantitative attitudinal segmentation.

The CreativeOndemanD–Volkswagen of America Case Study describes the challenge of convincing Hispanics with children that a German brand generally associated with smaller vehicles now offers a minivan which is strongly relevant to their needs. Volkswagen of America understood from US Census statistics that Hispanics tended to have larger families than other non-Hispanic groups, and could provide an excellent sales opportunity for their minivan, the Routan. The agency, CreativeOndemanD, chose to use a mix of qualitative research methodologies to grasp the cultural nuances of Hispanic family travel and vehicle experience. This included focus groups with a clinical trial of the Routan, street interviews, and an online consumer panel.

Through this qualitative research the agency tapped into the complexity of emotions elicited in Hispanic family vehicle travel. They discovered that the mixed feelings of both family love and need for control came into play for parents. They developed a humorous TV, radio, and billboard advertising campaign and also partnered with Univision for a multimedia contest. All the advertising focused on the Routan with its German engineering coming to the rescue of family vehicle travel mayhem. The highly successful campaign was based on the insights uncovered through culturally attuned qualitative research.

The Dieste–AT&T Case Study provides an example of extensive research to make decisions on strategy for promoting AT&T's new bundling of communication technology options for Hispanic customers. In order to understand what drives Hispanic motivation for deciding on which company can provide them with the best options, Dieste first conducted ethnographies nationally with consumers in their homes, places of business, and while shopping. Their intent was to get close to the consumer experience related to their products in diverse types of Hispanic markets across the country. The agency learned that it is attitudes that drive Latino choice differences, and therefore decided to make use of attitudinal segmentation for their quantitative research. The brand used a process of overlaying attitudinal segments on their customer database for defining product features, messaging, and communication strategy.

Through their research AT&T and Dieste learned that the use of technology for supporting and enhancing relationships provides the most important benefits for Hispanic consumers. AT&T's Hispanic advertising is focused on lifestyle benefits that their products support compared to the general market advertising centered on product features and competitive advantage. Dieste made use of direct response TV and Direct Mail in the advertising campaign to emphasize the life experience and benefits of bundling with AT&T. For example, in one TV ad a professional Latina makes use of various AT&T products to handle her many life roles and have fun at the same time. The overall campaign developed by Dieste resulted in strong gains for AT&T with Latino consumers.

Qualitative Research Modalities

Here we discuss some of the most common qualitative research modalities. It is important to realize, however, that the ways of conducting qualitative research are changing rapidly as online tools become increasingly available and more sophisticated.

THE FOCUSED GROUP DISCUSSION

Robert Merton[19] in the 1940s conducted the first focus groups then called "focused interviews," in which a group of respondents were given a topic to think about before attending a group discussion. The discussion was guided with semi-structured questions. The main reason behind the focused interview was to have the synergy of the interaction among participants evolve into information that would not have been obtained by interviewing individuals. A focus group is only justifiable if the discussion and synergy of the group enhance the outcome. A focus group should not be a substitute for 8–10 individual interviews. A focus group is for debate and give and take, not for finding answers from individuals. The questions one needs to ask is "Does my research question benefit from having consumers discuss and debate an issue?" If the answer is yes, then focus groups are a good choice. We believe that essentially conceptualizing a focus group as an interview can be misleading because generally we associate an interview with questions and answers. A focus group is the process of stimulation by the moderator and discussion by the group, in a sequence that generally goes from more abstract topics to more concrete ideas.

Many have debated whether or not Hispanics like to debate topics in a focus-group environment. Some marketers and others have type-casted Latinos by national origin. They have argued that those of Mexican origin are much less likely to discuss and tend to be quiet in focus-group sessions. They have also said that Cubans and Puerto Ricans are great in focus groups because they are opinionated and animated.[20] There is a tendency for some Mexicans to be more deliberate in expressing their opinions and for Cubans and Puerto Ricans to be more extemporaneous. Nevertheless, social class and other factors interact with country of origin to create a particular way of communicating. Generally, Hispanics as most other humans we have worked with over the years will produce valuable insights if the conditions of the focus group are conducive to a relaxed and engaged conversation.

Making a Latino Focus Group Work Better

There is much mythology among research providers and users about what makes for a productive focus group with Hispanics. There are some that are obsessive about respondent qualifications so that at the end they wind up doing research with people that represent very few actual Latino consumers. There are others that believe in certain rules like only females can do research with females, etc. Most of these dogmatic approaches are generally not very useful. Generally, there are elements of the chemistry of a focus group that need to be kept in mind but the main goal is always to obtain the needed insights in the right social environment.

The Moderator/Facilitator/Cultural Interpreter

An essential element for the success or failure of a focus group is the facilitator or moderator. The right moderator must be a social scientist, a great group facilitator, a marketing consultant, and be someone who has fun talking with people. The moderator, as a social scientist, needs to be versed in the logic of the scientific method so he or she can judge the quality of the data. This person must understand how causality can be inferred and be versed in the rules of evidence. As a group facilitator, the moderator allows the group to flourish and produce rich insights and information.

We believe that a facilitative style is generally more productive than a directive style of conducting a group discussion. This seems to be particularly true with Hispanics because Hispanics tend to acquiesce when directed and to feel free to express themselves when facilitated. A facilitative moderator is almost invisible and lets the consumers shine in their discussion. This facilitator becomes a cultural interpreter between the back and the front rooms in a typical focus-group facility[21] or in any other arrangement, physical or virtual.

In addition the facilitator needs to have an understanding of marketing theory and practice. Without this he or she is not likely to provide the clients with actionable recommendations based on the research. The facilitator must know how to derive implications from the data he or she obtains. The facilitator cannot just narrate the results. The facilitator's most important role is to figure out what to do with the findings and feel free to make sensible and practical recommendations.

The facilitators must be sociable and truly enjoy people. Someone who does not enjoy socializing may produce a group that freezes and/or that just does whatever is necessary to get out of there and get their incentive. As with any other cultural event, understanding Latino culture is fundamental for a moderator to encourage the genuine participation of respondents. Knowing how to use cultural cues is crucial so respondents get in the rhythm of the conversation and enjoy the interaction. The interesting angle of this is that cultural cues cannot be readily faked. That is because the cultural expressions and references are usually associated with a cultural context that makes particular behaviors relevant and appropriate. It is not likely you can teach someone to given an "abrazo" (hug) to demonstrate affect without that person understanding how, when, and under what circumstances that would be welcomed and appropriate.

There are still some who believe that the facilitator should be of the same national origin as the group. That is not necessary at all. The above skills are quite a bit more important than nationality. We have several times emphasized that the Spanish language is quite homogeneous across national groups assuming one avoids localisms and dialectical variations. Spanish-language commonalities are much more prevalent than the differences. Even when differences arise, a moderator can simply ask for clarification and this becomes a finding in the research as opposed to a problem. If one were to be concerned about dialectical variations it would be a never-ending story because even in small regions of countries one can find them. What matters is that the moderator be a native Spanish speaker if the participants in the groups are native Spanish speakers, or the facilitator must be a fluent English speaker if the group participants prefer to communicate in English. Just make sure not to mix people that prefer to communicate in English with those that prefer to communicate in Spanish because the communication will be difficult and confusing.

The facilitator of groups conducted in Spanish needs to also have sophisticated skills so the intended meaning of the respondents is understood by observers. Respondents may utter expressions that may be translated by the interpreter in the back room in ways that may not be either accurate or in context. Thus the moderator has to sometimes paraphrase or explain what he or she has understood so that the clients in the back room obtain a more accurate idea of what is transpiring in the group discussion. Sometimes the facilitator may punctuate changes in the discussion by "summarizing" what he or she has heard and request confirmation from participants. This summary also serves to orient those in the back room regarding the direction of the conversation.

The moderator also has a role to play at the end of the focus group. Debriefing in the back room is a very important element of any focus group, and fundamental when the focus-group project is cross-cultural. After a series of focus groups the moderator and clients must get together to debrief what they have learned and to clarify any cultural nuances and ideas that emerged during the groups. It is a good practice to audio-record this debriefing session so the moderator and/or clients can have a record of the ideas produced in that session. These can then be used in the elaboration of the research report.

Language Considerations

Recruiting "bilingual" respondents so that the observers can understand what they are saying is illogical, but we have come across marketers that ask for that. Since bilingualism comes in gradations, from very little English much Spanish to much English very little Spanish it is very difficult to get a homogeneous groups just by specifying they should be "bilingual." People in that continuum are not likely to be equivalent in their attitudes, beliefs, or even communication skills and preferences. Two individuals who claim to be bilingual may not understand each other just because one is more dominant in Spanish and the other in English even though they may both claim to be bilingual. English or Spanish proficiency should be important considerations but they should be relevant to the marketing problem not to the convenience of the observers.

The marketer may be interested in the potential of a strategy that spans English- and Spanish-language touchpoints. That, however, should not be a reason for mixing levels of language proficiency as the lack of homogeneity may hinder communication and may be counterproductive. The Latino market is increasingly complex and we are likely to continue to see more sophisticated approaches that cross languages, media, and use of many other touchpoints. Still the virtue of having a group discussion to provide insights assumes that the respondents have many things in common, including their language ability and preference.

Mixing Countries of Origin

Clearly not all Latinos have the same backgrounds, not just in terms of country of origin but in terms of many other factors. As a rule, the groups should remain as homogeneous as possible to obtain clearer observations. For specific purposes the groups can contain mixed countries of origin. For example, for translation verification, mixing nationalities can be an asset because the individuals in the group will debate the acceptability of the terminology that varies across countries. For food that represents regional preferences, mixing nationalities is likely to be unproductive. For cars and TV sets, however, mixing nationalities may be acceptable, depending on the level of affluence of the consumers. As a rule, the more affluent and formally educated the consumers the more they can be mixed. Less affluent and the less formally educated consumers tend to be more idiosyncratic about their preferences and cultural orientations.

Mixing Men and Women

There is no firm rule regarding mixing men and women in the same groups. Nevertheless, for gender-specific issues, the groups ought to be divided by gender, for example, when the group deals with venereal disease. Men and women are likely to feel more comfortable talking about these issues in gender-segregated groups. Regarding other issues, segregating men and women is also dependent on affluence and education. More formally educated and affluent respondents have little difficulty debating issues in gender-mixed groups. In lower socioeconomic segments, it generally works better to segregate genders just because men may be more dominant than women. Still, the key consideration in deciding whether Hispanic men and women should be mixed in the same group is the purpose of the research. If the purpose of the research is to investigate decision making about food consumed by the family, then it may be relevant to have at least some mixed groups to better understand the dynamic of the decision-making process between men and women. It may even be productive having family discussions for this type of topic. Having the parents and kids talk about food preferences can be highly revealing to marketers. Clearly this type of conversation should happen with one family at a time.

As we have documented earlier in this book it would be inaccurate to assume that many purchase decisions among Latinos are made individually. The assumption of individual decision making is very common in the marketing arena. In the case of Hispanics, however, who are characterized by their collectivistic attitudes and behaviors the assumption of individual decision making needs to be reconsidered. Just think, by interviewing men and women individually regarding a process that is likely to be collective, the marketer may be excluding the interaction itself. Understanding the interaction between men and women in some decision-making processes can be more important than the fears of male domination, and so forth. That is why it is crucial to understand the culture in order to even start asking the appropriate questions in a research situation. And since kids have an important role in the decision-making process in the Latino household they should many times be considered and consulted in the research process.

Where to Conduct Focus Groups

Originally focus groups were conducted in the homes of consumers who in turn invited their friends to the sessions. As the industry became more professionalized, a series of facilities sprouted throughout the US. These are meeting rooms with a one-way mirror behind the moderator so that observers can unobtrusively watch the discussion. These facilities tend to be located in modern office buildings in most major metropolitan areas. There are very few facilities that resemble the original home environments these days.

Clearly, Hispanics would have no problem attending a get-together in the home of someone they know. These days, however, respondents are recruited to attend sessions in modern facilities by means of lists of people who have shown an interest in participating in such sessions. Sometimes respondents get invited to participate as a referral from someone else. But inviting Latinos who are not familiar with these procedures can be very difficult.

Many Hispanics these days are already familiar with focus groups because they themselves have participated or because they know someone who has. Still, many Latinos are suspicious of invitations to attend such meetings at a formal office location. We have had the experience of facilities having a very difficult time recruiting Latinos with no prior focus-group participation experience. In one particularly difficult case none of the women respondents showed up. When we called the women at home and asked why they had not attended they said that their husbands were suspicious about such an invitation. We told them they could bring their husbands along if they wished and that seemed to alleviate the fears of several of them who actually came to the session with their spouses.

In order to make respondents feel more comfortable we have sometimes held focus-group sessions in church halls, community centers, and other known public locations. The location can make a major difference if the respondents are unfamiliar with these research approaches.

Clearly, undocumented individuals have additional reasons for being suspicious about being invited to focus-group sessions. The research and the recruiter have no way of knowing who is undocumented but among recent immigrants many of Latinos lack legal residency. In these populations it is important to pre-recruit and recruit via friendship networks so potential respondents can feel comfortable attending. An example of a failure of this type of respondents to show was when in Houston, Texas, the recruiter chose a facility that was located across the street from an office of the US Citizenship & Immigration Services of the Department of Homeland Security. Respondents did not show up at all at that facility to the dismay of the clients and moderator.

Further, the internal environment of the facility should be considered. When the respondents prefer to communicate in Spanish there should be a host at the facility who is a native speaker of Spanish. This person should be very welcoming and warm to create the right environment. Clearly, respondents of any background will appreciate a warm reception and hosting. In the case of Latinos this is more important because the respondents are less likely to be cynical about the research situation, and may feel vulnerable in the strange environment. Anything that can be done to make the respondents feel at home will result in a better research experience.

Recruiting Sensitivity

It is now more common for facilities and recruiters in the US to have become aware of some of the issues surrounding the recruitment of Latinos. In particular the recruitment of Spanish-dominant Hispanics is more sensitive and requires more expertise. In general, recruiting, as most research activities, is subject to cultural understanding of the research participants. Establishing good rapport and trust is fundamental to a successful project.

The issue of cultural competence is aggravated by the fact that most facilities and recruiting services are owned and managed by non-Hispanics. This affects the appropriate staffing of recruitment teams and facilities. When recruiting Hispanics who prefer to communicate in Spanish the recruiter should have native fluidity in the Spanish language, and should understand the culturally based objections that respondents may pose when being recruited. If the supervisor is also a fluent Spanish speaker he or she will contribute to a better recruitment. If the needed respondents are fluent in English they can be recruited by English speakers but they should have a sense of Latino culture to be relevant. A Hispanic recruiter can usually be more effective in recruiting, assuming they have similar qualifications and skills.

The screener or questionnaire used for recruiting is another aspect of the recruitment effort that should be carefully considered. If respondents are going to be recruited in Spanish it is highly recommended that the screener contains a Spanish and English version side by side. This is important because having the Spanish version available ensures that the recruitment is done in a homogeneous and consistent way, instead of relying on idiosyncratic interpretations by the recruiter. Further, if the supervisors do not understand Spanish, having the English version helps the management of the recruitment process.

Interpreting for Observers

Backroom translators or interpreters are a very important element of focus groups conducted in Spanish. We prefer to call them interpreters because they do not simply translate words but interpret what respondents utter in Spanish to cast their expression into English. These interpreters sometimes use wired or wireless headsets so that those in need of interpretation can listen to the English-language version. There are many ways in which arrangements are made but for those preferring to listen to the original Spanish they can simply listen to the speakers or have dedicated headsets with the original language.

An interpreter may have multiple official certifications and still their ability to simultaneously interpret Hispanic focus groups cannot be taken for granted. We already discussed that translation and interpretation, in general, can be fraught with problems. Interpreters in the back room should be formally educated in both languages and ideally should have native fluency in both languages. As a minimum, the native fluency should be in English besides a very good ability in Spanish. The reason why native fluency in English is so important is because this is the version that the clients will be listening to in the back room. Discriminating clients should not accept mediocre fluency in English because then they miss much of the nuances of the original conversation in Spanish.

An effective simultaneous interpreter does not just speak words as they are uttered in the room but produces gestures to convey the connotation of the expressions. He or she uses the inflection of the voice to enrich the observers' understanding of the group dynamic. A poor interpretation experience brings about misunderstandings between the clients and the facilitator because each is listening to a different version of the same event. Even if the simultaneous interpreter is very good, he or she should still be briefed about the project and the vocabulary that will be used. This is to enhance the chances that the language used by the facilitator, interpreter, and observers will be similar and that will minimize misunderstandings.

Key Principle on Focus Groups Variations

The reader has been exposed to the various issues that conducting focus groups with Latinos need consideration. The facilitator, the facility, the recruiting, and the interpreter are just some of the issues that need careful consideration. There are others who have written on these issues. For example, Peter Roslow, Martha Bethart, and Cristina Bain-Borrego published online in 2005 a booklet on how to set up and conduct Hispanic focus groups.[22]

There are multiple variations on focus groups. They can be shorter or longer, mini-groups or maxi-groups. They can be conducted with fewer or with more respondents. They can even happen over time. We have done focus groups that meet twice or thrice over a period of several weeks to investigate how the experience with certain products evolves in the household and in the opinion of consumers.

Sometimes we give assignments to respondents in one session and they come to another session to discuss their assignment. The key principle here is that qualitative research sessions can be customized to meet objectives. A dyad can be conducted with a woman and her best friend to discuss intimate issues that would be difficult to address in a group but that the dynamic of the dyad can help bring out. A mini-group can be very appropriate for copy testing because it provides a better context for in-depth discussion among three or four respondents.

When Group Synergy Does Not Add Value

In-depth one-on-one interviews can be very productive when the conversation and discussion among respondents does not add value to the objectives of the research. These are still qualitative sessions, but they focus on uncovering regularities regarding values, ways of thinking, and perceptions among consumers by making multiple individual observations. In-depth interviews are best for understanding deep emotions and ideas that take a long time to express and understand. During this type of interview it is common to use projective stimuli that will encourage the respondent to express emotions that would otherwise be difficult to elicit. The conversation with respondents can turn very productive by means of the elicitation of metaphors and narratives,[23] such as "what is it like to ..." or "tell me the story of what it is like to grow up ...."

One-on-one in-depth interviews can be conducted in people's homes, facilities like those for focus groups, work places, and sometimes even public places and events. The choice of location depends on the adequacy of the location to the goal of the study and the logistics involved. There are marketers and researchers that have a strong preference for one-on-one in-depth interviews because they argue this type of research has the best chance of being valid. Others have a predilection for focus groups because they feel the group dynamic allows for ideas to flourish. In our opinion, the choice of research design should be made on the bases of what is needed as an outcome. If group dynamics are important then some type of group activity works best. If on the other hand one wishes to dig deep into people's fears, dreams, and hopes as individuals then interviews are best.

Understanding How People Live

Ethnographic research has become increasingly popular in marketing.[24] Ethnographic methodology is a qualitative approach used by anthropologists.[25] It consists of observing and recording aspects of everyday life as they occur; including the symbolic interaction that takes place among humans, and between humans and other species and also with objects. It is generally an in-depth exploration of the symbolic world different types of humans inhabit.

In marketing ethnographic interviews are of short duration compared with the length of time that an anthropologist may spend studying a community. A marketing ethnography may take between two and six hours, whereas an anthropologist doing field work could spend months observing the symbolism and behaviors of a group of people.

Ethnography is useful because by observing and interviewing individuals in their own space and surroundings the researcher can observe much more than a person can describe in a less naturalistic research setting. People remember more aspects of their own behavior when they are in their own environment. In this type of context respondents can point to items and artifacts that contribute to their lifestyle and that have special meaning to them. This is something that cannot be achieved in other research environments. Ethnographies can also be conducted while driving a car, while shopping, while at work, school, and any other naturalistic environment.

Cross-cultural market research benefits from ethnographies in particular because the discovery process presents a stronger cultural contrast. The researcher typically videotapes and/or photographs the home environment or the shopping situation at the same time that a respondent addresses questions and issues. Marketers and researchers become more sensitized to the culture of the respondent as they participate in a different cultural environment.

We have found that this type of research is particularly enriching in the process of product development and positioning. We have seen marketers observe consumers prepare a type of food in their own home, and immediately start thinking about line extensions or products that could satisfy a need or preference. Further, in the process of communicating the new product the marketer capitalizes on his or her learning regarding the context of consumption. This knowledge is applied to the elaboration of ads and other communication pieces to better reflect the lifestyle of the intended consumers. We encourage the reader to investigate further how he or she can enrich his or her Latino marketing initiatives by means of naturalistic research such as ethnography.

Netnography   Robert V. Kozinets invented the term "netnography" to describe the conduct of ethnographic research online.[26] Kozinets indicates that "netnography examines the individual interactions resulting from Internet connections or through computer-mediated communications as a focal source of data."[27] He sees netnography as a form of participant observation research in which computer-mediated communications in online communities provide the opportunity for observing how social meaning is negotiated.

Latino online interactions and the meanings that are created and negotiated in the ensuing interactions provide a great source of data for marketers to understand at a deep level how Hispanics feel and think not only about brands but also about issues relevant to brands and consumption. The unit of observation and analysis in this case is the social group, not the individual.[28]

This is a new and well-documented set of procedures that allows for the study of Latinos' social behavior as it occurs. It takes market research from asking questions to actively listening. Marketers are strongly encouraged to further investigate this approach and to use it as a new source of valuable data.

Homework, Assignments, and Creative Activities

For identifying cultural insights the marketer can use diverse type of activities and assignments to elicit the production of metaphors and storytelling. Scrapbooks, diaries, photo albums, videos, as well as looking at the social networking sites of respondents can be excellent stimuli to get consumers to elaborate on what is important to them.

What can be more valid than the symbolic production of the consumer? When they talk about their own creations they externalize what is important and valuable to them. This can be done in diverse qualitative research settings, from focus groups to ethnographies, depending on the appropriateness of the stimuli for the type of research design. We have asked Hispanic consumers to create collages of images as homework to be completed at home before coming to a focus group. We provide them with a topic relevant to the marketing project we are working on. Then they bring their assignment to the group and narrate to others how their collage represents the topic in question. This stimulates conversation and at the same time helps uncover the commonalities and differences among Latinos regarding a particular topic. Here the unit of observation and analysis is the individual not the group.

In a one-on-one in-depth interview situation the researcher may ask the respondent for permission to jointly look at their Facebook, Myspace, or Hi5[29] page. This can be an excellent stimulus for discussion of what is socially important to Latino consumers. Clearly, the evolution of social media has created a vast new set of opportunities for studying consumer behavior.

Quantifying Latino Consumer Opinions and Behaviors

When one decides to "measure" Latino consumer behavior it is because one needs to know, among other possible items:

- The extent of a phenomenon, like use of a brand, importance of an issue, etc.
- The prevalence of a trait, idea, opinion, value, belief, etc.
- The description of aspects of a population.

The answers produced by quantitative research can be used to ask qualitative questions, or may be used to quantify ideas and insights found while conducting qualitative research. Both approaches are complementary. Some researchers lean toward the use of quantitative research and others prefer qualitative research. But preference for these approaches should not be due to taste or liking, but based on the type of question being asked. How many? How much? These are the types of questions that should be answered quantitatively.

In the prior version of our book *Hispanic Marketing* we analyzed different approaches to collecting data. We looked at mail, door-to-door, telephone, online, intercepts, etc. In this book we are skipping this analysis as there are methods books[30] that do a good job in orienting researchers to the advantages and disadvantages of different data-collection approaches. Also, data collection has experienced much turbulence due to major changes in the technological, legal, and attitudinal landscape in the US. Because of these changes much of the comparison of methods may not be as useful as a discussion of trends. Here we will present some of the Latino-specific tendencies that the marketer may want to keep in mind when thinking about research. Then we will address some of the new ways in which research and modes of data collection seem to be shaping the future of marketing to Hispanics.

DATA-COLLECTION TENDENCIES

- Mail seems to work relatively well particularly with less-acculturated respondents as they seem to be less cynical about "junk mail" than their more-acculturated counterparts. Still, mail overall appears to be in decline as the US Postal Service sees its role diminished due to new technologies. In our opinion, an error in using this approach was that the 2010 US Census placed on the envelope the legend "Your response is required by law." We consider that an error because if someone is undocumented, he or she would be intimidated by such a command and would likely ignore the mailing. And it appears contrary to the goal of the Census which is to get all people living in the US to participate regardless of immigration status. So, while less-acculturated consumers may be somewhat more inclined to respond to mail requests for information, the way the request is framed can be crucial to the success or failure of the study.
- Doing door-to-door research these days is less likely to be productive as the costs and risks associated with collecting data this way have increased dramatically. While some companies still conduct surveys this way, the representativeness of this approach becomes increasingly questionable.
- Telephone interviewing is still a common way of interviewing Latinos. Many Hispanics have replaced their land lines for cell phones and that adds some complexity to sampling. Further, while the "do not call" for commercial solicitations list does not apply to market research, many consumers believe it does and get mad at market research callers stating that they are included in the "do not call" registry. Also, because of the difficulty of ensuring equal probability of selection to individuals based on phone numbers, the representativeness of telephone surveys is also increasingly in question.

■ Intercepts and central location interviewing are valuable tools but should not be considered representative approaches to data collection. These approaches are more likely to be productive when used for qualitative research and/or to obtain ideas about trends, however claims of generalizability to populations are questionable.

■ Online research has grown fast and has become increasingly powerful. Companies that specialize in this research modality create large panels of respondents that obtain rewards for participating in surveys. Also there are companies that use what is called a "river" methodology in which Hispanic respondents are intercepted when they are online and invited to a survey. Clearly, these are people who have been identified as willing to participate in this type of surveys. Many of the samples derived from these panels are increasingly likely to be representative. But because there are certain segments of the population that are not online or are not frequently online, some of these samples have to be complemented with telephone interviews to obtain higher levels of representativeness. Latinos who are recent immigrants are still underrepresented online. According to recent estimates 51% of foreign-born Hispanics use the Internet compared with 85% of US-born Latinos.[31]

It seems to us that now a combination of online and phone and/or mail data collection is likely to approximate a representative sample of Latinos. Clearly, when trying to represent foreign-born Hispanics the phone and/or mail are likely supplements in a data-collection effort.

EXAMPLES OF APPROACHES

Data Mining

Data mining is the new and controversial approach of appending to Census data information known about specific consumers. That appended data comes from loyalty programs from supermarkets, or from credit card companies, or even from Internet companies that collect consumer behavior data like Google. These data are many times also entered into Geographic Information Systems (GIS) programs to map and create geographic representations where current or potential customers are. Below are some examples of services that add value and make Latino data useful and accessible.

Claritas

There are many companies that do this type of work these days. Claritas, a Nielsen company, is one of these providers. They have a proprietary segmentation by the name PRIZM which provides 66 geodemographic clusters.

Geoscape

Geoscape is a company that deserves special mention because it has concentrated its efforts on cultural groups in the US, particularly emphasizing Latinos. In the Geoscape GIS program we requested a map by county highlighting counts of foreign-born people of Mexican origin projected to 2015. The results are given in Figure 7.2.

This map highlights the centers of immigrant population prevalence from Mexico by 2015. This level of detail allows marketers and planners to look into the future and design informed strategies.

Another interesting output provided by Geoscape includes projections of population by race. Even though the US Bureau of the Census provides the data, the formatting and processing become more expeditious with their application. Table 7.1 tabulates the projection of population by race for the year 2015.

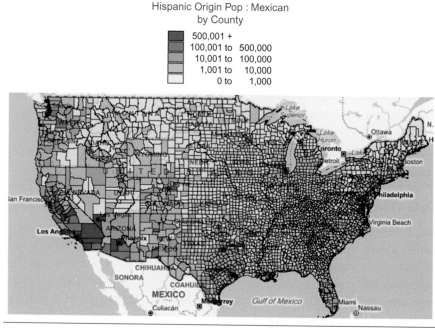

Figure 7.2 Hispanic origin population: Mexican by county by 2015.

TABLE 7.1 Projection of Population by Race for Year 2015

Total	White	Black	American Indian	Asian	Pacific Islander	Hispanic	Other Race
323,335,919	256,318,299	42,208,747	3,285,217	15,973,162	616,344	55,874,883	4,934,150

At the time of this writing there were in the US, according to the US Census Bureau, approximately 310 million people.[32] This number, by the way, coincided with the projections of Geoscape for 2010. This means that in 2015 it is expected the US will have grown by about 13 million people if you look at Table 7.1. The US Census Bureau projection for 2009 for US Hispanics was of 48.4 million,[33] and the Geoscape projection for 2010 was of almost 50 million people. The 2015 projection is of almost 56 million people, that means that it is expected that the Hispanic population will grow by about 6 million people in the next 5 years. If these numbers are close to accurate, almost half of the population growth of the US is expected to come from Hispanics alone. This is just an illustration of how having ready access to population characteristics projections can have powerful implications for marketing. Can marketers ignore a cultural group that is likely to contribute almost half of the total population growth in 5 years?

Geoscape also offers products that allow for appending data to databases the reader may already have, and is able to generate lists of names, addresses, phone numbers, expenses, and many other variables by household in a wide variety of geographic locations. What makes this service particularly relevant is that it highlights ethnicity, race, Hispanic origin, and culture as important variables among its resources.

US Census Bureau

American Community Survey The US Census Bureau (American Community Survey) also offers important tools that the user can access at no cost. One important resource is the American Community Survey data access portal at http://factfinder.census.gov/servlet/DatasetMainPageServlet?_program=ACS&_submenuId=datasets_1&_lang=en&_ts=. Here the user can request data or more easily and efficiently obtain 1- or 3-year estimates of the American Community Survey. The difference between these two types of estimates is that the 3-year estimates are based on 3 years and some users may find them more reliable even if not more up-to-date. The American Community Survey is conducted every year from January to December and it encompasses 3 million housing and group-living units. It replaces the old "long form" of the decennial US Census. In the products page referenced above you can go to the American FactFinder and there obtain actual tables of estimates in a simple and usable form. As shown in Table 7.2 we reproduce a fraction of a table comparing the overall US population with Hispanics, for the years 2006–2008, that is a sample of 9 million people.

The original table, that you can easily obtain, contains also data on relationship, type of household, school enrollment, educational attainment, fertility, disability status, place of birth, language spoken at home and ability to speak English, employment status, and many other variables. Just in the portion reproduced earlier you can observe that in the overall population those in ages 5–17 account for 17.6%, while among Hispanics the figure is 23.1%. Further the table shows that the median age for non-Hispanics is almost 37, while the median for Latinos is 27.

TABLE 7.2 Comparison of Overall US Population with Hispanics for 2006–2008

Subject	Total Population	Margin of Error	Hispanic or Latino (of Any Race)	Margin of Error
Total Number of Races Reported				
Total population	301,237,703	—	45,432,158	±5,828
One race	97.8%	±0.1	96.1%	±0.1
Two races	2.0%	±0.1	3.6%	±0.1
Three races	0.1%	±0.1	0.3%	±0.1
Four or more races	0.0%	±0.1	0.0%	±0.1
Sex and Age				
Total population	301,237,703	—	45,432,158	±5,828
Male	49.3%	±0.1	51.6%	±0.1
Female	50.7%	±0.1	48.4%	±0.1
Under 5 years	6.9%	±0.1	11.2%	±0.1
5–17 years	17.6%	±0.1	23.1%	±0.1
18–24 years	9.8%	±0.1	11.3%	±0.1
25–34 years	13.3%	±0.1	17.6%	±0.1
35–44 years	14.3%	±0.1	15.0%	±0.1
45–54 years	14.6%	±0.1	10.4%	±0.1
55–64 years	10.8%	±0.1	5.9%	±0.1
65–74 years	6.5%	±0.1	3.2%	±0.1
75 years and over	6.1%	±0.1	2.3%	±0.1
Median age (years)	36.7	±0.1	27.4	±0.1
18 years and over	75.5%	±0.1	65.7%	±0.1
21 years and over	71.1%	±0.1	60.8%	±0.1
62 years and over	15.3%	±0.1	6.9%	±0.1
65 years and over	12.6%	±0.1	5.5%	±0.1

These are revealing and important comparisons that anyone can have available by going to the American Community Survey site.

Current Population Survey The Current Population Survey is a yearly survey of about 78,000 people, which collects data regarding employment, wages, and other work-related subjects. It has an excellent resource called the Current Population

TABLE 7.3 Educational Attainment of Non-Hispanics and Hispanics

	Non-Hispanic PCT	Hispanic PCT
Totals	100.00%	100.00%
Educational Attainment		
Children under 15	18.80%	29.20%
No high school diploma	12.60%	29.70%
High school or equivalent	24.10%	19.70%
Some college, less than 4-year degree	22.10%	13.90%
Bachelor's degree or higher	22.40%	7.60%

Survey table creator at http://www.census.gov/hhes/www/cpstc/cps_table_creator. html. Or, you can simply type Current Population Survey table creator in a search engine. An example of the table created with the Current Population Survey table creator is given in Table 7.3.

Table 7.3 shows the striking differences between non-Hispanics and Hispanics in terms of educational attainment. While almost 30% of Hispanics have no high school diploma, less than 13% of non-Hispanics are in the same situation. Further, having a bachelors degree according to these data is still a very scarce commodity among Latinos, even though the percentage is also surprisingly low among non-Hispanics. This example is just a small token of what any marketer can find in the resources of the US Census Bureau website. The US Census Bureau also offers the service of a "Data Ferret" at http://dataferrett.census.gov that allows for the examination of multiple US Government datasets. Readers are encouraged to experiment with this productive tool as well.

A Changing Way of Collecting Consumer Data

Cookies

The Wall Street Journal published an interesting special report on "The Web's New Gold Mine: Your Secrets."[34] The reporters detail how much information is usually contained in what is called a "cookie" that identifies the user of a particular computer. A single code has information about age, interests, entertainment preferences, and many other aspects of people's life. One of the potential identifiers is ethnicity and culture based on patterns of browsing and other demographic information that can be extrapolated from specific behavioral patterns. In this way the "cookie" can notify websites that are being visited that the specific visitor is likely to be Latino and has specific preferences.

What this means is that tracking technology may allow the marketer to customize its offerings to a very unique individual. In addition, knowing what aggregates of consumers like this enjoy, the marketer can make some generalizations about cultural preferences that are likely to be of interest to the visitor and thus complete a sell that is profitable and satisfactory to the consumer.

A consumer that browses the Web in Spanish can be identified and then the website can provide him or her with ads in Spanish. That is even before offering a product that is likely to be of interest. Companies like BlueKai.com auction consumer data to portals and websites interested in targeting specific consumers. This company in particular claims that the data they sell does not have personally identifiable information.

While privacy concerns should be paramount to marketers, the availability of this type of data makes segmentation, extrapolation, and identifying of consumer profiles an important new reality. Companies like Google use the browsing data of consumers to selectively place relevant ads in the same page where the browsing happens. So if you are looking for "tamales" you may get an ad from the Texas Tamale Company who places bids to show its ads when people search for the key word "tamales." You can see that the possibilities are infinite and that targeting Latino consumers will become more precise, and also more individualized.

Aggregate Browsing Data

There are other types of data that are aggregated but that help understand trends and what people are looking for. Google.com/insights/search is a great tool for understanding trends. For example, if you search for the word "tamales" in Google search insights in the US you find that interest in tamales peaks every year in December and then declines substantially, making it clear that tamales are a seasonal food for Hispanics. Further the consumers that most search for this item are in Texas followed by New Mexico, Colorado, and Arizona, and then California. A new manufacturer of tamales would definitely welcome this information. These data are aggregated and reported only as percentages with 100 being the largest number of searches in a specific time period. And by the way, searching for tamales has been going up in the past few years.

Another interesting example is that searching for "telenovelas" has also increased over the past few years and has reached the highest point in 2010. To us that means that as more Hispanics who prefer Spanish go online, the more they are likely to search for items like telenovelas. Interestingly, at the time of this writing, searches for the term "Hispanic" were declining and searches for "Latino" were increasing. This finding alone provides some idea of current trends in the use of nomenclature.

Panel and River Methodology Data

DMS Insights[35] is a company founded by AOL. They specialize in providing samples for the market research and marketing industries. They offer panels as many companies do these days. Panels are formed by people recruited for their willingness to participate in surveys. Panelists also provide some basic information on the basis of which they are recruited for specific relevant studies. DMS has a Latino panel called "Tu Opinión Latina" and participants are classified by levels of acculturation among other demographics. This Hispanic panel is a very useful resource for marketers interested in reaching Hispanics, particularly those who prefer to communicate in Spanish.

DMS has been an innovator in what is known as the "river methodology." This "river" approach is compared to random-digit dialing for the Web. DMS intercepts US consumers who visit specific sites and offers them rewards for participating in surveys. These sites are visited by almost 80% of household Internet users. We at the Center for Hispanic Marketing Communication at Florida State University have benefited from this methodology by drawing national samples of Hispanics, African-Americans, Asians, and non-Hispanic Whites. Many of our studies have been graciously supported by DMS Insights, not only by use of their "river methodology" but also by access to their respondents in "Tu Opinión Latina."

E-Rewards is a company that offers panels of Hispanics in the US. These panels are created by invitation only, thus reducing the problem of professional survey takers that contaminate online research. E-Rewards provides incentives for participation on a system of points that can be traded for rewards of different types.

As with all populations, Latinos are not completely represented online. That is why, depending on the type of study, online river or panel data is supplemented with phone interviews and/or intercepts to account for people who are not online. While these approaches to supplementing data help to account for online and offline consumers in the same study, there are issues that the researcher needs to consider in interpreting the data. For example, are the samples used to supplement adequately drawn to account for those not online or are they just convenience sample supplements? While perfection is very difficult to attain, experimenting with these diverse approaches is currently an ongoing pursuit.

Why Should Survey Research with Latinos Be Different?

It is the culture and experience of the consumer that the marketer needs to understand. We discussed earlier that while all human beings are essentially very similar to each other in their potential for performance culture, and experience make a major difference in how to approach different populations. Many times it is assumed that any data-collection company can do a good job with Hispanics. That may not necessarily be true because the cultural competence, and many times the language competence, of the supplier may not allow it to do as good a job as a company that has the appropriate personnel and the experience with Latino consumers.

By now the reader has seen that there are multiple issues in translation and cultural adaptation. In addition there are complexities in supervision, and even word order that need to be understood ahead of time. Many times the cultural input that should be included in the formulation of the questionnaire is nonexistent to the detriment of the marketing effort.

Most researchers know that word order makes a difference, but the difference varies with culture. Also, where items are located in the flow of the questionnaire can entice respondents to cooperate in a sincere way. One simple example, in which wording and the order of possible choices made a difference, illustrates this point. Interviewers were having a difficult time with a beer study. They could not find very many beer drinkers to interview. Their suspicion was that among Hispanics, particularly Mexicans, to admit that one drinks alcohol can be a strong taboo. When in the screener for the interview a question read, "do you drink beer," respondents generally said no, and thus they did not qualify for the study. The researchers reasoned that the question should be placed in a context. The question was reformulated as follows:

"Please tell us whether or not you eat or drink each of the following:
READ

a. Soft drinks
b. Coffee
c. Mexican food
d. Beer"

Having placed "beer" after "Mexican food" dramatically increased the number of people who said they drink beer. The cultural reasoning behind this reformulation was that Mexican food and beer are strongly associated in the culture, thus after admitting they eat Mexican food, respondents would not have difficulties admitting they drink beer. After this relatively simple example, you can see that any study may produce different results just by the researchers' knowing some of the issues associated with the intended questions and products.

Getting respondents to cooperate with interviewers on the phone, or via other administration methods, is difficult. With Hispanics, one key to getting their cooperation is knowing what is important to them and talking with them in a way that they feel the interviewer is empathic and *amable*. The concept of *amabilidad* is not directly translatable. It is related to the concept of kindness, but saying someone is *amable* means the person has a good disposition and treats the consumer with warmth. Just to show the complexity of this concept, the following terms were considered English equivalents in a Google translation inquiry:

1. kind
2. nice
3. lovable
4. pleasant
5. gentle

6. darling
7. bland
8. sympathetic
9. friendly
10. comradely
11. amiable
12. neighbourly
13. neighborly
14. helpful
15. thankful
16. decent
17. good
18. gentle
19. agreeable

All these potential equivalents for "amable" do not add up to the cultural concept. In understanding concepts like this resides the concept of culturally competent research.

Interviewing Latinos in a machinelike fashion and just reading the interview protocol is likely to result in a rejection. The interviewer has to engage the consumer. We have witnessed the differences between interviewers that for the same study could interview more than six respondents in one evening compared with others who could barely get one or two completed interviews. The key difference was not the Spanish language, nor the professionalism; it was the *amabilidad* in engaging the interviewee from the very beginning.

Although interviewers cannot deviate from the way the questions are worded, when conducting surveys with Hispanics, particularly Spanish-preferred Hispanics, some latitude needs to be provided. This latitude should be homogeneous and rehearsed before the actual interviewing takes place, however. This means that if the interviewer detects that the interviewee is not understanding a question, or is responding in a rote way, the interviewer should have "ready to go" alternatives right on their computer screen or questionnaire. Clearly, it is better to modify the questions after a problem is detected, but given ample variations in the level of education of Hispanics, some may understand the original question perfectly well, and others may not understand it at all. The provision of alternatives is a way to make the study more valid, as long as all interviewers are trained to do the exact same thing when required.

Understanding what data means is difficult in qualitative and quantitative studies. In quantitative studies the interpretation is particularly difficult when the analyst is not part of the culture. For example, finding out that Hispanics spend over $100 a month in long-distance calls compared with a much smaller figure for non-Hispanics is interesting but not terribly illuminating. Digging further into the data with hypotheses in mind can highlight issues that clarify the phenomenon, but for that the researcher analyzing the data needs to know more to begin with. For example, someone who understands the market would ask for an analysis by years of residence in the US. Also, the researcher could think of other factors such as number of relatives and friends living abroad or in distant locations can make a major difference.

Even when doing research online, the selection of colors in the survey instrument, the way in which questions are framed, and the way in which questionnaire sections are introduced can make a cultural difference. Giving the respondent culturally relevant reasons for answering questions and placing these questions in a context that motivates the respondent to answer honestly and with care is important. There is no such thing as a culturally neutral questionnaire.

How Relevant Research Guides Effective Campaigns

Three case studies at the end of this chapter and the case studies in other chapters of this book are useful for marketers in understanding how research guides effective marketing communication with Latinos. The Lopez Negrete Communications–Walmart Case Study at the end of this chapter provides an illustration of the extensive use of both qualitative and quantitative research modalities to inform the development and evaluation of a communication campaign centered around Hispanic Heritage Month (HHM). In order to communicate the message that Walmart truly cares for and understands Hispanic customers, Walmart supported by their agency Lopez Negrete Communications (LNC) shifted their strategy in this campaign from product-centric to consumer-centric initiatives.

To make sure the HHM campaign spoke to both the emotional as well as rational needs of Hispanic female customers, the agency made use of multiphase campaign development and campaign measurement research processes. Qualitative research clarified the values of Hispanic mothers regarding their children and their heritage which lead to the campaign's focus on education. Quantitative testing in pre-campaign development clarified that both English and Spanish languages should be used in advertising.

The strategy which framed Walmart's initiatives was to reinforce their commitment through support of higher education opportunities for Hispanic youth, and to address the emotional needs of Hispanic mothers by recognizing their devotion to their children's success and their Latino heritage. The core initiatives of the integrated Hispanic consumer campaign included Hispanic scholarships and the launch of a dedicated Hispanic website. The results of HHM campaign measurement indicated successful achievement of all of Walmart's objectives including improvement of overall brand perception.

Planning Latino Insights

Ultimately, it is the role of someone in the research or creative entity that will have the responsibility to extract insights from what respondents said or marked in a questionnaire. This responsibility in an advertising agency falls in the hands of the role of Account Planner.[36] It goes beyond research and goes beyond intuition. The account planner has the responsibility to have a deep understanding of the consumer as it relates to the brand under consideration.

The account planner is not only a researcher, but also a creative individual that knows how to communicate to the rest of the advertising agency the core of the consumer insight. It is this planner that will make the marketing effort a success or failure as the ambassador of the consumer in the advertising enterprise. This account planner condenses the lessons learned from qualitative and quantitative research, and also from secondary data, to come up with a hypothesis of what positioning will make a difference in establishing a brand–consumer relationship.

We believe that this is the type of role that needs to grow further and develop in the marketing industry so that it is culturally oriented and sensitive. This is particularly true in the case of marketing to Hispanics.

Conclusions

Throughout this book there has been an emphasis on the importance of understanding culture as key to developing successful Hispanic marketing strategy. Again and again, research has been highlighted as an essential avenue for listening to the "close to the heart" subjective levels of Latino consumers. Now, this chapter emphasizes that everything that is a part of the research process itself must be conceived, constructed, implemented, and analyzed based on firm cultural grounding. Otherwise, the marketer can be lulled to a false sense of security through research initiatives that do not reflect the subjective reality of the Latino market and may actually distort it. After a great deal of effort on costly research initiatives, both qualitative and quantitative, the well-intentioned marketer could emerge with positioning that fails to attract this major growth target.

While this chapter is full of specific suggestions for keeping productive Latino and cross-cultural research on track there are some general guidelines that act as underpinnings for the whole process. There need to be culturally competent professionals involved including the research professionals as well as others on the marketing team who will move the process forward from conceptualization through the analysis of the findings in a culturally relevant way. An account planner can play a special role representing the voice of the consumer as revealed in the research by translating it into insights to guide brand strategy and communications. In the research process, marketers should move from investigating general perceptions of Latino consumers related to the category to their more specific relationships to the brand and product. Moving from the general culturally steeped background to the more specific opinions and behaviors in research allows for the emergence of a rich culturally based knowledge of Latino consumers—which is, of course, the core of competitive advantage for the brand.

This chapter has provided guidance and the cultural rationale for specific aspects of the research process with Latino consumers where our experience has informed us there's ample opportunity to lose cultural focus and relevance. For example, literal translations of questionnaires conceived in English or word-for-word style simultaneous interpretation from Spanish to English for observers at focus groups are apt to distort the intent of the research or the meaning of what is being said respectively. Cultural adaptation in translations and an emic within culture approach, for both quantitative and qualitative research, yield findings which are more closely attuned to the emotions and backgrounds of Hispanic consumers.

There is often pressure in multicultural research projects to adapt a global strategy and to "think local." Our opinion is that it is more effective culturally to consider how local strategy can contribute to a global approach. Only in this way can the emotional connection inspired by common cultural background of Latinos and other cultural groups be forged. This is true not only when considering similarity between research instruments, but also in all elements of research projects.

Cultural guidelines for both qualitative and quantitative research abound in this chapter. Qualitative research provides rich avenues of interaction and observation for uncovering subjective culture. This is critical for insights to guide the development of strategy and inform deep levels of understanding for why and how Latinos relate to a brand. Depending on the research objectives there is a whole range of techniques for eliciting insights to use such as focus groups conducted in facilities, in-home ethnographies, and direct observations of the brand being purchased or used in an environment close to its reality. How choices are made for conducting qualitative research all need to be geared to the most culturally relevant environments and methods possible for these consumers. Cultural relevance from conceptualization of the qualitative research initiative throughout its implementation is detailed in this chapter and can make or break the success of the research.

There are many new and changing options for conducting quantitative research with Latinos which can become fascinating and effective avenues for marketers to explore. Quantitative research is needed for understanding the questions of how many and how much related to Hispanics. We all know that the numbers are changing fast in the Latino market, and that only informed brands will effectively target these consumers. Latinos are culturally connected as we discussed in early chapters of this book, yet they are a complex and evolving market. Foremost, understanding how to target this market requires a culturally competent professional quantitative researcher. Questions on whether to use door-to-door, telephone, online or a combination of both for surveys are discussed in this chapter with indications of trends and the rationale underlying them.

There are also a range of new online methodologies for gathering quantitative information on these consumers including data mining possibilities to inform marketers on market potential and specific targeting options. The U.S. Bureau of the Census provides a rich source of data accessible through tools for using their American Community Survey and Current Population Survey data. There are organizations that provide their clients with mapping tools to understand current Latino population characteristics and to project future numbers across broad areas of the country. Other companies have online panels of Latino consumers ready to respond to marketer's questions including the possibility of online interceptions.

Research is central to understanding Latino consumers, and critically important for discovering the underlying subjective culture where emotions are touched and connections with the brand are made. The good news in this chapter is that there are numerous options for consideration for the culturally competent researcher. The bad news is that without the involvement of culturally trained professionals in all aspects of the research process, the marketer can dig and dig and end up nowhere with Latino consumers. The message of this chapter is: Marketers take heart, there is truly a Hispanic market out there which may be the growth opportunity you have been seeking for your brand. Yet, proceed only with cultural guidance, informed professionals, and an emic in-culture approach in all aspects of your research for connecting your brand to the dynamic US Hispanic market.

IMPLICATIONS FOR MARKETERS

- Collaborate with a researcher trained in marketing to the Hispanic culture and an account planner competent to represent these consumers in order to think through what approaches will be best suited to answer your research questions.
- Decide whether you need to conduct qualitative or quantitative research, or both to gather knowledge and insights on the Hispanic market based on your research questions.
  - Use qualitative research to develop insights into how Hispanics within your target group think, feel, and make decisions about your product or service.
  - Use quantitative research to get at the numbers on the size and location of your target and awareness, attitudes, and usage patterns generalizable to them, as well as to track these over time.
- *For qualitative research:*
  - Work with an experienced Hispanic qualitative research company whose references and prior work you investigate thoroughly.

- Maintain cultural sensitivity at every step of the research process in order not to derail the relevance of your research.
- Refer to the many suggestions in this chapter such as: the development of bilingual screeners, recruitment by a well-supervised bilingual team, moderation by an "amable" (warm or kind) professional Hispanic qualitative researcher, and simultaneous interpretation by a qualitative research interpreter experienced with Hispanic focus groups, and with native fluency in both languages.

■ *For quantitative research:*

- Select a firm that is experienced working in the Hispanic market, has excellent references, and has a Hispanic research team which will lead and implement the project.
- Consult the specific guidance in this chapter on the numerous aspects of quantitative research that require your cultural consideration from the development of the instrument, through data collection and interpretation.
- Be aware that there are pitfalls at every step should the marketer ask questions irrelevant to Hispanic consumers, ask questions in a way that biases their answers, speak to the wrong respondents, and/or use data-collection procedures that are not appropriate for reaching the target.

■ Make sure to take advantage of the numerous research options that new technologies have contributed to the marketing research field for both qualitative and quantitative research. They afford access to Hispanic consumers and information about them that open up the scope of what has been possible to learn in the past.

- Explore options such as online focus groups, netnography, data mining, and panel methodology, making sure that they are culturally relevant to your Latino target.
- Consider a combination of new and old data-collection methodologies if appropriate to research objectives and culture. For example, consider using online data collection to cover the growing number of Hispanics who now use the Internet. Then, supplement the sample by telephone interviews to include those less-acculturated Hispanics who may not yet be reachable electronically.

■ Use research to enhance your knowledge of the Hispanic market, develop positioning and strategy that speaks to them in culturally relevant ways, and cultivate a relationship which will connect your brand to these consumers over time.

CASE STUDY: CREATIVEONDEMAND–VOLKSWAGEN OF AMERICA

Company/Organization
Volkswagen of America, Inc.

Advertising Agency
CreativeOndemanD

Intended Hispanic Consumers

The intended target was minivan switchers and "minivan drivers in training." The demographics were 25- to 39-year-old mothers with two or more children or at least a second baby on the way. And because the car was not your typical Volkswagen (VW) model, communications would have to reach current VW drivers as well as non-VW drivers.

Background

VW, the brand that had spent nearly 60 years in the states building a fun, young, quirky personality, was now going to launch a minivan! The plan, considered unconventional at best and sacrilegious at worst, presented quite the challenge for VW and its agency. The launch was set for June 2008.

Looking at the brand's goals in the US to greatly increase sales volume and become a major player in the automotive market, and accepting a notable broadening of their vehicle portfolio became a reality for VW and CreativeOndemanD. With US Census data showing Hispanic demographics support larger family sizes and number of children, it was expected that Hispanics would over-index in terms of their contribution to achieving the brand's lofty sales goals for this vehicle, the Routan. But the agency felt that a VW minivan was going to be no easy feat. Clearly it was not a natural fit, especially to current VW drivers, so the goal was to find the intersection of (1) VW, (2) minivan drivers, and (3) Hispanic drivers.

Research

Research began by speaking with Hispanic minivan drivers and to-be minivan drivers in New York, Miami, Houston, Los Angeles, and San Diego. Focus groups were conducted, including a clinical trial where consumers had the chance to interact with the Routan. Additionally, to get the best insights, street interviews and an online proprietary consumer panel were all used in the research mix.

Cultural Insights

While very different opinions were voiced about VW, the brand, offering a minivan, the most interesting findings came from how people described the family dynamic on car trips. The conventions in the category of "family togetherness" and "the family unit" were framed incorrectly by other automotive manufacturers. Time in the car/van/SUV was nothing even close to calm, peaceful, and orderly. Yes, love is always in the air, but placing a family in an enclosed 6' × 10' space is more likely a recipe for chaos.

The insight came from Hector, a loving father of four from Houston who seemed a cross between a typical 33-year-old Mexican father and MacGyver. Like any other father he worked his hardest to provide for the family and taught his kids about their Mexican culture, good values, and dedication. But he also knew a trip in the minivan with his wife and four children was the definition of entropy: total disorder. But, doing his best to keep things in check, Hector took things into his own hands. He installed 2-way wiring around the interior perimeter of the car, just above the top of the windows, along with microphones. Even better (/worse?) was that Hector drove with headphones on and a microphone attached. The idea was he could pick up on any misbehaving, shenanigans, or picking on by the children and quickly take care of matters without missing the turn to Matagorda Bay to catch that trout he wants to catch.

(Continued)

The agency questioned: "A little extreme was Hector?" and responded "Maybe". But a valuable lesson was learned: a ride in a minivan was not only family magic, but rather *family mayhem*.

Expression of Insights in the Campaign

Creatives operated off the action idea of "You can't stop family mayhem. You can only hope to contain it." The Routan included available features like power outlets, 3 TV screens, a 30gb hard drive, individual headphone connection points, multiple "hidden" storage spaces and pocket seating as its RTB's (Reasons To Believe) or better said MM's (Mayhem Mitigators). Agency creatives were tasked with creating two TV spots, one radio commercial, several OOH (out-of-home) executions, online banners, and an undefined Web component.

The anchors of the campaign were the two TV spots, "Frog" and "Spill." The two spots focused on the juxtaposition between all the luxury the VW Routan offers and the inevitable mayhem that will ensue inside a minivan. The idea was brought to life using a deep, dramatic voice to deliver a cool, calm, and collected voice-over of all the elegance within the Routan, while the spot showed physical mayhem brewing and manifesting itself quickly over 30 seconds. The message was "Not to worry—the Routan can handle it all." Both ads landed on the tagline: Ingeniería Alemana al Rescate (German engineering to the rescue). The radio spot "Road Trip" followed a similar routine, focusing on the sounds of mayhem on a road trip. Billboards also captured the typical family mayhem in a snapshot with the Routan coming to the rescue as the hero, and the online banners showed the development of mayhem and how the Routan squelches it.

But in order to get the word out to a group of consumers that had never been spoken to in the past by the brand, consumers who did not have the VW brand within their consideration set, the campaign needed to truly be 360. The online component did just that. First is the website, www.routanalrescate.com, which allowed consumers to interact with the family members in the minivan, including the parents, abuela (grandmother), two kids, dog and frog (a tie-in from the TV spot). It also allowed consumers to check out photos, take a 360° tour of the vehicle, and see all its characteristics, learn about games to play in the Routan to help avoid pandemonium while on a trip, create your own family stickers, watch the TV commercials, and download screensavers.

Last but certainly not considered least by the agency was the partnership with Univision to create a multimedia contest that was featured in Sabado Gigante and the SG website. The contest asked consumers to submit entries by uploading two-minute videos

Volkswagen of America Routan campaign.

Routan. Ingeniería alemana al rescate.

showing how the VW Routan and its German engineering could help their family contain the mayhem of their day-to-day life. The top three videos were selected by a panel of judges based on originality and creativity. Those three videos were then posted on Univision's webpage for the public to vote and select the top video. The winning family traveled to Miami to receive their prize in front of a live Sabado Gigante audience.

Effect of the Campaign
The results were undeniable according to Routan's statistics. After only 2 months of sales data, 11% of all Routan registrations were coming from Hispanic consumers, higher than VW's overall Hispanic registration share of 9.8% and higher than industry average for the minivan segment (6.6%). Over the 4-week entry period, the Routan contest was Univision's highest and most successful upload program to date.

CASE STUDY: DIESTE–AT&T

Company/Organization name
AT&T

Advertising Agency
Dieste

Campaign/Advertising Title
AT&T

Intended Hispanic Consumers
Connected Progressives and Ernest Climbers
   Because of the ubiquity of AT&T product relevance and usage across the US Hispanic population, Dieste shifted away from demographic and socioeconomic targeting and instead they have created an attitudinal target. Their primary attitudinal targets are the *Connected Progressives* and *Ernest Climbers*.
   Connected Progressives are hyper-social connectors who use technology to strengthen and enhance connections to friends and family, to make new connections, and to creatively engage in communication and sharing (designing their own greeting cards, creating customized digital photo albums, social networking). Connected Progressives are fairly evenly split between foreign and US born and tend to be bicultural in their language use and media consumption.
   Ernest Climbers fit a more classic Hispanic target profile. They are a bit more likely to be foreign born (60%) and often prefer to speak Spanish at home, but not necessarily at work. They are dynamic users of technology and are very optimistic and aspirational about the role it plays in their life. They see technology as a potential equalizer that can be a catalyst for getting ahead. They also see it as a very important source for entertainment and a status symbol telling their community that they are on the right track.

Background
In the increasingly competitive world of consumer technology, AT&T is focused on staking out their territory as the emerging leader. While AT&T has been generally

(Continued)

known as a telecom leader for years and firmly established themselves as a wireless leader with the acquisition of Cingular in 2006, they face a serious challenge in establishing and maintaining "total home" bundled technology leadership.

As landline penetration declines, and will continue to do so, TV seems to be increasingly the anchor for all of the technology in a home. Now, consumers mostly make decisions about Internet based on their TV provider (satellite, cable), whereas in the past they would bundle with their landline. As such, AT&T faced both a branding challenge—awareness of AT&T as a TV provider has hovered around 10% since they entered the market, and a conversion challenge: how does the agency establish a clear benefit that will motivate consumers to bundle with AT&T, how do they make this relationship truly worthwhile?

The year 2009 was an interesting one for AT&T because it was the first year in which they launched a truly integrated bundle offer: a "choice"-centric bundle that lets consumers choose three out of four products to bundle; wireless phone, TV, DSL, and home phone. This offer emphasizes the company's competitive advantage through the use of the full range of the product portfolio and with an emphasis on literally "untethering" the consumer from their homes.

Research

Over the course of 2 years, Dieste engaged consumers in a longitudinal conversation about technology utilizing both qualitative and quantitative methodologies. The agency started broad and fielded a nationwide ethnography by spending time with consumers in their homes, in their places of business, while shopping, and exploring. The agency wanted to frame the technology conversation in the real world of US Hispanics and not accept any preconceived or syndicated frameworks as the full story. In order to get a full picture of the dynamic Hispanic market, they not only fielded to get a national snapshot, but also carefully chose different kinds of markets—urban, suburban, rural, established, and emerging.

Coming out of this initial research, the agency made the decision to move toward developing an attitudinal segmentation approach, versus demographic or behavioral, because they had surmised that it is really attitude that drives meaningful distinctions in behavior in the category. As such they followed the qualitative with a national quantitative survey with the intent of identifying key attitudinal segments and bringing specificity and depth to the key drivers and attitudes that define each segment. In January of 2008, Dieste started the process of overlaying the attitudinal segments on the AT&T customer database and since that time they have been refining and testing the segmentation approach as it defines product and feature emphasis, messaging, and communications strategy.

Cultural Insights

Dieste's big headline finding coming out of the research was that technology is valued most by Hispanic consumers when it supports and enhances their community of relationships: the rhythm, the energy, the social relationships that they value most. According to the research, the educational role, the status, the features, and functions are important, but are secondary to the role of technology can play as an organic extension of their social and communal lives. The agency found that the aspirational experience of connecting anywhere through wifi, of programming their TV content remotely through their mobile phones and of connecting to the fastest 3G network were the features that laddered up to the spontaneous, hyper-social lifestyle these Hispanic consumers are cultivating and value most.

Interestingly, the agency uncovered a technology practice common in Latin America that they believe is part of the driver of technology practices in the US. Internet cafes are to be found on many corners all over Latin America—in cities and small towns alike. As such, going online and using the Internet is frequently associated with being in a public, social place, of mixing activities—going online and computing while having a cafecito, hanging out with friends, etc.

Expression of Insights in the Campaign: Executional Elements

Dieste's creative strategy was to bring to life the real-world benefits of bundling with AT&T by contextualizing the benefits in the world of our consumers. As such, the agency's work always originates with the consumer's life and cascades down through the mobility-centric category and product benefits. In this regard, their Hispanic executions are distinct from the general market in that they focused on the lifestyle benefits that the products support, whereas the general market focuses on product features and competitive advantages.

In order to achieve the goal of increasing brand awareness and excitement while at the same time driving conversion (calls, visits, and sales) the agency focused on Direct Response TV and a phased Direct Mail campaign that included a calling card promotion, and a drive to retail strategy.

The mix of Direct Response TV and Direct Mail allows the agency to connect at the mass media level to generate excitement and interest while zooming in on the most qualified potential new customers and current customers with upgrade potential. Additionally, because the entire campaign was direct response, they can measure and evaluate every tactic and were able to optimize throughout the campaign to drive campaign efficacy and ROI.

Dieste developed two Direct Response TV spots that bring to life the experience and benefits of bundling with AT&T.

In "Bruja" the spot depicts the fanciful story of a man who falls in love with a woman he sees on TV—a beautiful witch. He uses his AT&T products to find out more about her, searching online, and using his GPS to find her house on "Bella Bruja" lane.

In "Arquitecta" our heroine is living a rich and busy life where her personal and professional worlds intersect and she needs all of her AT&T products to juggle her many roles and responsibilities, all while having fun.

With Direct Mail the agency brought the same energy and excitement to three Direct Mail phases:

1. Phone card promotion: This piece depicts our consumers in the middle of their busy lives supported by AT&T and emphasizes the benefits of being able to choose from the complete portfolio of AT&T products. This piece featured a free phone card to motivate consumers to call in and learn more about the offer and benefits of bundling from our representatives at the call center.
2. Drive to retail: This piece, while utilizing the same creative execution as the phone card promo, featured a customized message that let consumers know about the

(Continued)

AT&T Direct Response TV spot, *Arquitecta*.

AT&T retail store closest to them so that they can "test drive" the AT&T bundle for themselves.

3. The final piece focuses on a very strong savings message—the more you choose the more you save to continue to distinguish the brand's products and offer within the context of consumer's lives.

Effect of the Campaign

Brand awareness and recognition of AT&T as leading provider of bundles increased by 35 percentage points pushing AT&T into the leadership position. Both TV spots exceed normative levels of unaided awareness and consideration. Cost per call and calls per spot objectives were surpassed by 40%. Posted bundles sales were highest in recorded history and ROI measures point to most effective integrated campaign since AT&T entered bundles market.

CASE STUDY: LOPEZ NEGRETE COMMUNICATIONS–WALMART

Company/Organization
Walmart

Advertising Agency
Lopez Negrete Communications (LNC)

Campaign/Advertising Title
HHM 2008 and 2009

Intended Hispanic Consumers
Spanish-dominant Hispanic moms, between the ages of 18 and 49, with children under 18, living at home and a household income of $20,000–$45,000.

Background
HHM was instituted by President Ronald Reagan in 1988 in recognition of Hispanics' contribution to the country. It extends from September 15 to October 15, and was timed to coincide with the celebrations of independence of seven Latin-American countries (Costa Rica, El Salvador, Guatemala, Honduras, Nicaragua, Mexico, and Chile); as well as, the discovery of America. Yet, among Hispanics, this celebration lacked due to the vast differences among the history and culture of diverse Hispanic nationalities. Consequently, every year during this month, Hispanics were bombarded by irrelevant, product-centric campaigns designed to stimulate additional consumption of products Hispanic consumers were already purchasing, such as consumer packaged goods, beer, and soft drinks among others.

Walmart understood how crucial the Hispanic consumer segment was to the marketplace, representing the fastest growing population group in the US (US Census, American Community Survey, 2008). Hispanics shop at Walmart more than to any other retail store (OmniTel Retail Study, March, 2005). Walmart also employs more than 170,000 Hispanics, making it the largest employer of Hispanics in the country (http://walmartstores.com/pressroom/news/9376.aspx). Although it has not been widely publicized, Walmart has been supportive and continuously committed to the Hispanic community for many years (http://walmartstores.com/CommunityGiving/236.aspx).

The LNCs' 2008 HHM campaign represented an ideal opportunity to develop a uniquely focused program that would communicate to Hispanics how Walmart truly cares and truly understands them.

The business objectives for this campaign were as follows:
- To improve overall brand perception by positively impacting social reputation measures.
- To increase overall sales.

The overall campaign objectives were to:
- Acknowledge the importance of Hispanics to Walmart as a customer, employee, and as a vital component in the future of the US.
- Increase awareness of Walmart's long-term commitment to the Hispanic community.
- Deliver a relevant program by shifting the focus from previous product-centric initiatives to truly consumer-centric initiatives.
- Identify a unifying theme that would

(Continued)

- communicate Walmart's commitment to the Hispanic community by showing its understanding of key drivers of success for the Hispanic target, and
- be intrinsically entwined to the meaning of heritage for Hispanics in order to generate a strong association with HHM.
- Develop an initiative that will comprise a comprehensive multiplatform, multidepartmental effort within Walmart.
- Improve consideration, favorability, shopping intent, increase visitation, and loyalty.

Research

Research was commissioned to gather key consumer insights to substantiate the strategic development of the campaign. Following LNC and Walmart's proprietary methodology, five pieces of research were used to create the campaign.
- Campaign Development (5)
  - i. GRA's Nationwide Hispanic Omnibus Study
  - ii. LNC's exploratory
  - iii. LNC's concept development
  - iv. ARS concept testing
  - v. AcuPOLL concept testing

I. GRA's Nationwide Hispanic Omnibus Study

In March 2008, Walmart submitted several questions to be included in Garcia Research Associates' quantitative, quarterly nationwide omnibus study.

Objective: To gather insights for Walmart's seasonal programs.

Findings: Several initiatives were considered relevant by the target for retailers to support during HHM; however donating and contributing to the education of Hispanics dominated over all.

Main Implications: The findings led Walmart to commission LNC to conduct further research to determine the central initiative for the development of the HHM campaign.

II. LNC Proprietary Qualitative Exploratory Research

In April 2008, LNC conducted exploratory focus groups in three Hispanic markets.

Objective: To understand the meaning of HHM, and potentially identify a single theme linked to this month that all Hispanics could relate to.

Findings:
- After motherhood, cultural pride is the second key element in Hispanic's self-description.
- Education is considered the most essential goal to improve their children's future, and a key measure of their own success in the US.
- Higher education for Hispanics is considered the most relevant cause for corporate support, but not "owned" by any company.
- Low awareness of Walmart's community involvement and prior support for education.
- Low awareness, inconsistent meaning, and lack of relevance of HHM.
- No identifiable category purchase pattern or impact on product consumption during HHM.

Main Implications: Higher education was a cause not previously owned by any company in the mind of the consumer. Walmart needed to be further involved with the Hispanic community through a unifying initiative, and education was the most engaging. Linking Hispanic education opportunities to HHM seemed like a natural fit. Along with the academic implications, education also aligns with knowledge of language, food, traditions, manners, and values. Thus, a combination of cultural cues led to the campaign's central idea.

III. Qualitative Concept Development
In May 2008, LNC conducted concept development focus groups in two top Hispanic markets.
   Objective: To gather understanding of consumer interpretations/reactions to the different creative concepts for the HHM campaign, in order to incorporate key findings into the final executions.
   Findings: Previous insights from the exploratory groups were validated and led to a strong new insight. Participants were not familiar with and were intimidated by scholarship/loans/college application processes, especially online. In order to help their kids, they needed access to detailed guidance and simplified information.
   Main Implications: Due to the universal appeal for education, and its relevance for HHM, the proposed initiative should focus on encouraging Hispanics' higher education. Further testing was conducted to determine if the concept was relevant to English-speaking Hispanic women. The campaign should include the strategic development of a consumer-centric 360° media touchpoint including a refined AMVM (Ahorra Más, Vive Mejor) website offering college-related guidance—college preparation, planning, and budgeting.

IV and V. ARS and Acupoll Quantitative Pre-Testing
In June–August 2008, the ad was tested through quantitative research by ARS among English-speaking Hispanic mothers, and AcuPoll among Spanish-dominant Hispanic mothers.
   Objective: To gather consumer feedback on perception and interpretation of HHM ad.
   Findings: The studies led to the recommendation of airing the HHM ad in both languages. The ad positively affected and reinforced most participants' perceptions of Walmart across both English- and Spanish-speaking Hispanic targets. Through the ad, Hispanic mothers were persuaded that Walmart offers real opportunity for Hispanic communities to get a better education and advance in life. This perception translated into positive goodwill and purchase intent.

Cultural Insights
The key cultural insights, derived from the research conducted for this campaign, were:
- After motherhood, cultural pride is the second key element in participant's self-identification.
- Education is considered the most essential goal to improve their children's future, and a key measure of their own success in the US.
- Broader meaning of education: academic development as well as cultural heritage.
- Higher education for Hispanics is considered the most relevant cause for corporate support, but not yet "owned" by any company.
- Low awareness of Walmart's community involvement and prior support for education.

(Continued)

- Low awareness, inconsistent meaning, and lack of relevance of HHM.
- No identifiable category purchase pattern or impact on product consumption during HHM.
- HHM was a cause not previously "owned" by any company in the mind of the consumer.
- HHM initiative should focus on encouraging Hispanics' higher education.
- Through both Spanish and English ads, Hispanic moms understood Walmart's commitment in the community, which in turn led to positive goodwill and purchase intent.

Based on an analysis of insights, it was concluded that supporting higher education opportunities for Hispanics was the most powerful cause to add true meaning to HHM. Furthermore, this was a cause that Walmart truly believed in, that they could "own" and that would more than likely have a positive impact on both sales and brand image. Education served as a rallying theme among Hispanics that brings true, concrete, and universal meaning to HHM.

Expression of Insights in the Campaign

Strategy

Following the campaign objectives, the strategy was designed to positively impact Hispanic mothers' overall brand perceptions by addressing their rational and emotional needs. Rationally, Walmart was going to reinforce its commitment to Hispanics by offering tangible resources to help them achieve higher education opportunities and overcome significant barriers to their development and success. Simultaneously, Walmart would further reinforce Hispanic mothers' identification and emotional connection with the company by relating to two of the most significant elements of their self-identities: *good mothers* who want to help their kids succeed, and *proud Hispanics* who want to pass their culture to their kids.

Core Initiatives: Two core initiatives were developed as the heart of an integrated consumer-centric 360° campaign.

- During HHM, Walmart donated to the Hispanic Scholarship Fund (HSF).
- Concurrently, Walmart launched the first dedicated Spanish-language website, www.Ahorra MasViveMejor.com (AMVM), to address their Hispanic online audience. The website was launched as the backbone to the overall campaign message.

Tagline

The tagline for the campaign came from a popular Hispanic saying that was spotted during the focus groups: "La mejor herencia es una buena educación[SM]" (The greatest heritage is a good education[SM]). In Spanish, "herencia" means heritage and inheritance. This wording firmly communicated the idea and importance of "passing down" an education and connected with HHM; hence, the message territory that gave meaning to the celebration for all Hispanics was born.

Effect of the Campaign

Further research was conducted to measure the campaign success. Following LNC and Walmart's proprietary methodology, six pieces of research were used to create and evaluate the campaign.

- Campaign Measurement (6)
    - i. Global Research Partner
    - ii. Social Quest Brand Anthem

Walmart HHM 2008 and 2009 campaign.

 Cada año, más y más hispanos pueden asistir a la universidad gracias a los aportes millonarios que Walmart hace a organizaciones como el Hispanic Scholarship Fund (HSF). Por eso, durante el Mes de la Herencia Hispana, tan importante es recordar de dónde venimos, como es pensar hasta dónde podemos llegar.

Para más información visita: **AhorraMasViveMejor.com**

iii. Big Research
iv. PR Track
 v. Walmart's Online Track
vi. Walmart's Sales Data

(Continued)

I. Global Research Partners Study

In October 2008, Global Research Partners interviewed Hispanic consumers on the Internet across the US (Dallas/Ft. Worth, TX; Miami, FL; Houston, TX; Los Angeles, CA, and Phoenix, AZ) and at central interviewing locations. Respondents were given the choice of completing the interview in Spanish or English.

Objective: (1) To gauge awareness of Walmart's HHM advertising, (2) to determine its impact on people's perceptions of Walmart, (3) to gain an understanding of the importance of HHM, and (4) to gain an understanding of how Hispanics feel about the way this celebration is observed and what they would like companies to do to recognize it.

Findings: The relevance of the education focus for HHM across segments was validated. Thus, Walmart became Hispanic consumers' top-of-mind brand when thinking of companies that contribute to Hispanics' education, positively impacting brand perception in addition to the highest levels of HHM ad awareness.

II. Social Quest Brand Anthem Research

A brand anthem qualitative messaging testing research was conducted for Walmart by Social Quest, in December 2008, among Spanish-dominant, bilingual, and English-dominant Hispanic segments in three top Hispanic markets.

Objective: To understand the positive impact that Walmart's HHM campaign had on the brand image.

Findings: Participating Hispanic mothers have developed a deep, rational, and emotional relationship with Walmart. They feel as if Walmart is a company that shares their values, is a company that Hispanics can count on and truly cares of about the advancements of the Hispanic community.

III. Big Research

In November 2009, a national survey was conducted by BIG Research among Spanish-dominant, bilingual, and English-dominant Hispanic mothers.

Objective: To measure the overall impact of the campaign on participants' perception of Walmart.

Findings: Affirmed that the campaign positively affected consumers' perception of Walmart.

- *Social Responsibility:* Most consumers exposed to the campaign agreed that Walmart supports higher education and cares about Hispanics.
- *Emotional Appeal:* Consumers aware of the campaign tend to further admire, respect, and trust the company and feel smarter when shopping at Walmart; in addition to the perception of Walmart's quality and innovative products and services, low pricing, and one-stop shopping.
- *Products and Services:* Consumers who were aware of the campaign also had a better perception of Walmart's quality and innovative products and services, low pricing, and one-stop shopping.

Additional tracking of the effects of the campaign is given in the following paragraphs:

IV. PR Track

Objective: The effectiveness of the PR efforts was measured through a standardized tracking and valuation tool for PR (PRTrack).

Findings: There was a 78% increase (vs. 2007) in media impressions and an 836% increase (vs. 2007) in publicity value.

V. Online (AMVM Webpage) Track
Objective: Measure traffic on the AMVM website traffic through Walmart's Omniture Tracking.
Findings: The HHM initiative significantly drove website traffic (113 index vs. goal).

VI. Walmart's Sales Data
Based on Walmart's proprietary sales data study, the HHM campaign led to a +2.89% sales lift. This is significant in light of Walmart's already high sales volume and according to industry standards.

Summary of Effects of Campaign

The HHM campaign represents a very successful story for Walmart. All objectives were achieved and exceeded, since the meaningful positive impact of the 360° initiatives on the Hispanic community reinforced Hispanic mothers' emotional and rational connection to the brand.

Results show notable improvement in the overall brand perception, due to a positive impact on social reputation measures, as well as a significant sales lift. The successful outcome led to the extension of the campaign during 2009 and 2010. Walmart's executives were so pleased with the campaign results that the company's government relations representatives presented the education initiative to the US Congress. Consequently, the HHM campaign positioned Walmart as an industry leader that empowers Hispanics by providing funds for education and a future for Hispanic youth and for the country as a whole. In 2010 this campaign was recognized by the Advertising Research Foundation with the Gold David Ogilvy award in the Multicultural category.

End Notes

[1] Marieke K. de Mooij, *Global Marketing and Advertising: Understanding Cultural Paradoxes.* Thousand Oaks, CA: Sage Publications, 1998, p. 9.

[2] Umberto Eco, A Rose by Any Other Name, William Weaver (trans.). *Guardian Weekly* January 16, 1994. http://www.themodernword.com/eco/eco_guardian94.html

[3] Examine the output of the excellent translation website of Google when looking for the translation into Spanish of "agreeable," at http://translate.google.com/#.

[4] Edna M. Rodriguez-Mangual, *Lydia Cabrera and the Construction of an Afro-Cuban Cultural Identity.* Chapel Hill, NC: University of North Carolina Press, 2004.

[5] Ronald K. Hambleton, Peter F. Merenda, and Charles D. Spielberger (eds), *Adapting Educational and Psychological Tests for Cross-Cultural Assessment.* Mahwah, NJ: Lawrence Erlbaum Associates, 2005, p. 12.

[6] Lee Sechrest, Todd L. Fay, and S.M. Hafeez Zaidi, "Problems of translation in cross-cultural research." *Journal of Cross-Cultural Psychology* 3(1), 1972, 41–56.

[7] Paul Ekman and Richard J. Davidson (eds), *The Nature of Emotion: Fundamental Questions.* New York: Oxford University Press, 1994.

[8] Richard Dawkins, *The Greatest Show on Earth: The Evidence for Evolution.* New York: Free Press, 2010.

[9] Kenneth L. Pike, *Language in Relation to a Unified Theory of the Structure of Human Behavior*, 1st ed. Vol. 1. Glendale, CA: Summer Institute of Linguistics, 1954.

[10] Geert Hofstede, "A case for comparing apples with oranges: international differences in values." *International Journal of Comparative Sociology* 39(1), 1998, 16+.

[11] Dianne A. Van Hemert, Chris Baerveldt, and Marjolijn Vermande, "Assessing cross-cultural item bias in questionnaires: acculturation and the measurement of social support and family cohesion for adolescents." *Journal of Cross-Cultural Psychology* 32(4), 2001, 381–396.

[12] Martin Cerda and Ilgin Basar, *Extreme Response Style (ERS) Among US Hispanics vs. Non-Hispanics: An Experiment of Rating Scale Usage and Implications for Survey Design and Analysis.* Miami, FL: Encuesta, Inc., 2010. http://americanospoll.com/prsummary/AAPOR_ERS.pdf

[13] Bernd Wegener (ed.), *Social Attitudes and Psychophysical Measurement.* Hillsdale, NJ: Lawrence Erlbaum Associates, 1982.

[14] Ronald K. Hambleton, Peter F. Merenda, and Charles D. Spielberger (eds), *Adapting Educational and Psychological Tests for Cross-Cultural Assessment.* Mahwah, NJ: Lawrence Erlbaum Associates, 2005.

[15] Paul F. Velleman and Leland Wilkinson, "Nominal, ordinal, interval, and ratio typologies are misleading." *The American Statistician* 47(1), 1993, 65–72.

[16] Ibid.

[17] Some would say it is not a true ratio scale because it has two anchors, one at "0" and one at "10." A true ratio scale, according to some, would only be anchored at one point in the scale. See for example the book: Joseph Woelfel and Edward L. Fink, *The Measurement of Communication Processes: Galileo Theory and Method.* New York: Academic Press, 1980.

[18] Charles E. Osgood and Oliver C.S. Tzeng (eds), *Language, Meaning, and Culture: The Selected Papers of C.E. Osgood.* New York: Praeger Publishers, 1990.

[19] Michael Argyle, *The Scientific Study of Social Behaviour*, London: Methuen, 1957.

[20] Louis E.V. Nevaer, *The Rise of the Hispanic Market in the United States: Challenges, Dilemmas, and Opportunities for Corporate Management.* Armonk, NY: M.E. Sharpe, 2004.

[21] The typical focus-group facility has an observation room and a room where the discussion takes place. Usually the two rooms are divided by a one-way mirror.

[22] http://www.roslowresearch.com/studies/97.pdf

[23] Gerald Zaltman and Lindsay H. Zaltman, *Marketing Metaphoria: What Deep Metaphors Reveal About the Minds of Consumers.* Boston, MA: Harvard Business School Press, 2008.

[24] Patricia L. Sunderland and Rita M. Denny, *Doing Anthropology in Consumer Research.* Walnut Creek, CA: Left Coast Press, 2007.

[25] Isadore Newman and Carolyn R. Benz, *Qualitative–Quantitative Research Methodology: Exploring the Interactive Continuum.* Carbondale, IL: Southern Illinois University Press, 1998.

[26] Robert V. Kozinets, *Netnography: Doing Ethnographic Research Online.* Los Angeles, CA: Sage Publications, 2010.

[27] Ibid, p. 8.

[28] It is important for the reader to understand that in some cases one observes and analyzes collectivities and sometimes one observes and analyzes individuals. Sometimes, the researcher may observe individuals but analyzes aggregations of individuals. When studying social interactions the group is a more meaningful unit of study.

[29] Or any other social media location where the respondent creates content.

[30] The reader is encouraged to go to "Listmania!" in Amazon.com and search for "Survey Research Books" to find a great list of survey research methods books.

[31] Gretchen Livingston, *The Latino Digital Divide: The Native Born Versus the Foreign Born.* Washington, DC: Pew Hispanic Center, 2010. http://pewhispanic.org/files/reports/123.pdf

[32] According to the US Population clock at http://www.census.gov.

[33] From Facts for Features, Hispanic Heritage Month 2010: September 15–October 15, by the US Census Bureau. http://www.census.gov/newsroom/releases/archives/facts_for_features_special_editions/cb10-ff17.html

[34] Published in the *Weekend Journal* section of the Saturday/Sunday edition of July 31, 2010, pages W1 and W2.

[35] http://www.DMS-Research.com

[36] Jon Steele, *Truth, Lies, and Advertising: The Art of Account Planning.* New York: John Wiley & Sons, 1998.

Chapter 8

THE US HISPANIC MARKETING INDUSTRY

The US Hispanic marketing industry has its origin in entrepreneurs who came with waves of Latin-American immigrants and recognized their opportunities in this small, fast-growing market that shared a common culture. It also has its roots in journalism that attempted to bring to light political and social issues affecting Latinos in the US since early on.

While elements related to Latino marketing, journalism, and advertising were present in what now is the US since before the Mexican-American War, the fermentation and growth of these elements happened relatively recently. In 1950s the industry was rather known as Spanish-language advertising and media. The language characterized the work that was done at that time. Some emerging advertising agencies were practically translation services. That was a time when marketers did not realize that marketing to Latinos was more than translating advertising and placing it in the nascent Spanish-language media.

Many advertising pioneers were immigrants from Cuba at the time when Fidel Castro created a diaspora of the intellectual and economic elite of the island. Clearly there were players from many other countries but Cubans were characteristically some of the first to establish advertising agencies. Mexicans constituted an important wave of advertising entrepreneurs in the late 1970s and 1980s, as the Mexican advertising industry grew and crossed borders, literally. Cubans tended to concentrate in the East and Mexicans in the West.

Hispanic Marketing: Connecting with the New Latino Consumer.

The media had diverse impetus. Spanish-language print had deep roots in the US since the mid-1800s with the establishment of "El Misisipi" in New Orleans.[1] Another notable achievement was the establishment of the first full-time Spanish-language radio in the US, KCOR-AM, originating in San Antonio, Texas.[2] Full-time Spanish-language TV started in 1955 with the establishment of what eventually became KWEX-TV in San Antonio, Texas. Emilio Nicolas Sr. along with Rene Anselmo, Emilio Azcarraga of Mexico's Televisa, and other investors seeded the station group that became Spanish International Network, which eventually became Univision after being sold to Hallmark and then bought back by a group of investors.[3]

The proliferation of Spanish-language media and the players in the industry have grown dramatically. The realization that US Latinos were becoming increasingly bilingual or dominant in English also brought about the creation of companies like SiTV and Mun2 to better connect with a fast-growing Hispanic constituency. That segment had strong roots in Latino culture but their language ability had been shifting to the English language.

The growth of the Internet promoted the creation of companies that have had varied degrees of success. StarMedia was a pioneer as an online portal but others have been more successful in their approach to keep the attention of US Hispanics. Univision. com following the synergy of its parent TV company has been very successful in attracting Spanish-dominant Latinos. Terra has slowly carved a substantive niche in the online world with offerings that appeal to younger constituencies. AOL Latino has also become a symbol of Hispanic online dedicated efforts. Latinos online, however, have diversified interests and tastes as many other cultural groups do and they do flock to Google, and the very popular social media sites such as Facebook, MySpace, and Hi5.

Overall, this growing and important aggregate of components of a prosperous cultural sector finds itself now in the process of assessing strategies for the future. The US Hispanic population passed the 50 million mark in 2010 and has become more complex and segmented. The one-size-fits-all of the initial stages of the industry is now becoming obsolete. Still, the recognition that cultural insights that pertain to a differentiated cultural group makes this industry vibrant and viable for the future. It will not be a Spanish-language play only but it will be a cultural play in a more general sense. The new identity that Latinos are claiming will be the center of growth of the different elements that serve US Hispanic consumers.

Here we will attempt to provide a perspective on trends that affect major elements of the industry. The following sections focus on media, marketing support, and intra-company organizations.

Media or Touchpoints?

In the relatively placid environment of broadcast radio, broadcast TV, and print, speaking of media was relatively straightforward. While the Hispanic marketing industry has always struggled for recognition, the battle was confined to a few channels that carried the messages intended for US Latinos. As technology, Hispanics, and the industry experience turbulent changes, speaking of touchpoints is more relevant. We do not anymore use a channel of mass communication to reach out to Latino consumers. Communicators and consumers interact and mutually create meaning. Brands leave their mark in different places, channels, and contexts. These constitute the points of touch or contact.

The US Hispanic marketing industry has grown and evolved in ways that were not anticipated just a few years ago. The industry has several interrelated components. The following Latino touchpoint clusters will be elaborated to highlight areas of opportunity and growth.

BROADCAST, CABLE, AND SATELLITE

While it is important to emphasize that TV and radio are not what they were 20 years ago or even 5 years ago, their essence continues to be recognized but the forms of delivery are changing rapidly. Soon watching TV will be so similar to browsing the Internet that our way of thinking about the medium will be forced to evolve. That evolution has been even faster in the realm of what we have known as radio. In the meantime, while TV and radio morph in a more complete way, we can still talk about them as relatively discrete entities. Further adding to the complexity of the touchpoint landscape of relevance to Latinos is that Spanish-language touchpoints are not the only game in town anymore, if they have ever been.

SRDS Hispanic Media & Market Source is a publication that lists media and organizations that reach Hispanic consumers. In its June 2010 edition, for example, it listed over 560 radio stations dedicated to the US Hispanic market. The number of TV stations listed in that same issue was almost 200. In addition the following cable and satellite networks were listed: Bandamax, De Película, De Película Clásico, Discovery en Español, Discovery Kids en Español, Fox Sports En Español, Galavisión, mun2, Ritmoson Latino, SíTV, ¡Sorpresa!, and Telehit. These listings are not a complete representation of the universe as there are obvious omissions like ESPN Deportes, among others.

Exposure to TV

In this chapter we will present some of the data obtained from the Multicultural Marketing Study of the Center for Hispanic Marketing Communication at Florida State University in collaboration with DMS Insights.[4] The samples varied for different years but in most cases we had an online US national sample of approximately 2500 people divided about equally into non-Hispanic Whites (NHW), African-Americans (AA), Asians (A), Hispanics who answered in Spanish (HS), and Hispanics who answered in English (HE). Figure 8.1 visually summarizes the

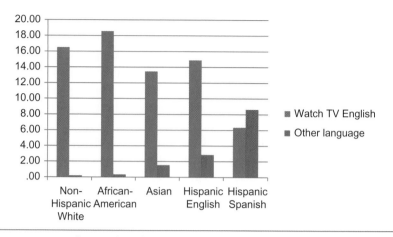

Figure 8.1 Average hours of weekly TV exposure.

average exposure of each of the subsamples to hours of TV during an average week in 2009.

The fact that these data come from an online sample represents a limitation to the generalizability of the study. Nevertheless, we believe that this data provides a good approximation to the reality of the US, particularly as the Internet becomes ubiquitous and increasingly available.

When looking at Figure 8.1 we can safely assume that the "other" language of TV programming that Latinos report watching is largely in Spanish. It can be clearly seen that those Hispanics who answered the questionnaire in Spanish have more exposure to Spanish-language TV but that they also spend a substantive amount of time with English programming. The opposite is observed with those Latinos who chose to answer in English. For them, most of their exposure is in English but they still watch a few hours of Spanish-language TV per week. The other groups are included for comparison and it makes sense that US Asians, in general, would also use TV in other languages to some extent. TV in Asian languages is not as available in the US as it is in the Spanish language. It is also important to notice that the TV viewing reported may have been watched in a combination of broadcast, cable, satellite, and online. As the medium crosses platforms that will become an interesting and challenging measurement puzzle.

Figure 8.2 shows the striking difference in patterns of adoption of satellite TV among the different cultural groups in the US.

Hispanics who preferred to respond in Spanish are most likely to currently have satellite TV and are also most likely to state that if they do not have it now they are most likely to plan to have it next year. Hispanics who responded in English were generally found to parallel their Spanish-preferring counterparts but to a lesser degree of adoption and plans for it. Other cultural groups were somewhat

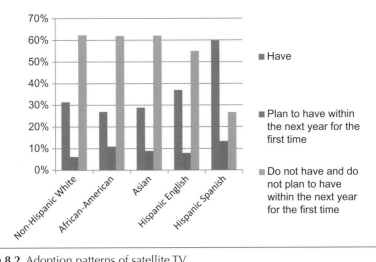

Figure 8.2 Adoption patterns of satellite TV.

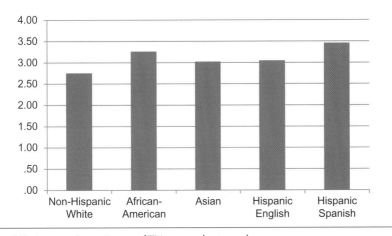

Figure 8.3 Average importance of TV on product purchase.

more homogeneous and less likely to state they have or plan to have satellite TV. The Latino preference for this medium is likely to be related to the familiarity of Hispanics with satellite TV as it is common in Latin America.

In terms of the importance of TV in "influencing the products you buy" Latinos who prefer Spanish are more likely than others to say that this medium is important[5] as indicated by the means on a of zero to five scale of importance in Figure 8.3.

The least likely group to find this medium to be an important influence are non-Hispanic Whites. Perhaps because they have been saturated with commercial messages for so long that they have become relatively more cynical about messages in this medium. Spanish-speaking Latinos, on the other hand, still appear receptive to this form of influence. This is an interesting corroboration of the industry claim that Hispanics are more welcoming of commercial messages. Nevertheless, it is not all Hispanics that are more likely to be influenced by the medium but those who are relatively less acculturated.

The top 10 Hispanic local TV markets according to the Advertising Age Hispanic Fact Pack 2010 (Nielsen Co's Hispanic Station Index January 2010) in descending order are:

- Los Angeles
- New York
- Miami—Ft. Lauderdale
- Houston
- Dallas—Fort Worth
- Chicago
- Phoenix
- San Antonio
- San Francisco—Oakland
- Harlingen, Texas

The Spanish-language broadcast networks with highly rated programming in 2010 were Univision, Telemundo, and Telefutura according to Nielsen. The programming most watched included the culturally unique "Telenovelas," as well as musical, variety, and dance shows along with some sports offerings. English-language broadcasting also claimed important ratings and share with CBS, NBC, Fox, and ABC, with diverse sports, serials, contest, and reality shows.

Regarding cable and satellite TV, these two delivery forms basically share the same types of offerings. There are some exceptions, however, as these outlets seek to differentiate their packages in the eyes of Latino consumers. The cable/satellite channels directed to Hispanics that enjoyed the highest ratings in 2010 were Galavision, Discovery en Español, Fox Sports en Español, ESPN Deportes, and Mun2. Cable/satellite English-language offerings most popular among Latinos were on MTV, E!, USA, BRAVO, ESPN, TNT, OXYGEN, TLC, TBS, COMEDY CENTRAL, A&E, LIFE, and TRUTV.[6] These were the networks with top-rated shows on cable/satellite outlets. Clearly, there are many more networks that compete for the attention of Latino viewers, and the diversity of tastes and interests of Hispanic consumers are divided among the multiplicity of offerings. It is important to note how Spanish-language outlets increasingly compete with their English-language counterparts for segments of this important audience. Further, as we will see later there are online outlets that consolidate TV outlets for online viewing.

Exposure to Radio

Figure 8.4 with 2009 data shows weekly exposure to radio by the US national sample online described earlier.

The pattern of exposure is similar to that of TV but the average weekly exposure is lower than that to TV. Clearly, there are complexities in explaining these findings. For one thing the nature of the online sample may account for somewhat lower than expected average number of hours of exposure to radio per week. In fact, Arbitron[7] reports larger numbers for weekly exposure for Latinos in hours and minutes as can be seen in Figure 8.5.

Now, the measurement of radio exposure and other media is controversial, particularly in the Hispanic Market. Arbitron indicates in their 2009 "Hispanic Radio Today" report that "PPM ratings are based on audience estimates and are the

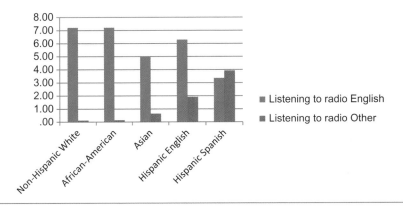

Figure 8.4 Average hours of weekly radio exposure.

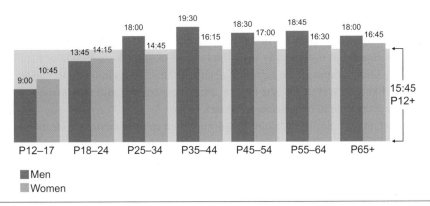

Figure 8.5 Average time spent weekly listening to radio by Hispanics—Arbitron.

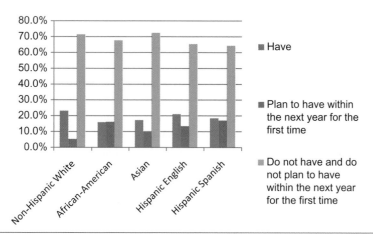

Figure 8.6 Access to satellite radio.

opinion of Arbitron and should not be relied on for precise accuracy or precise representativeness of a demographic or radio market." As some readers may be aware the PPM or Portable People Meter has been the subject of much controversy and that is likely reason for the warning. Still, the actual numbers are hard to come by. The above estimates from our own studies and Arbitron provide a guidance in terms of relative listening by different cultural and age groups. Further, as radio becomes more available in different formats and contexts, respondents may not have included their hours of radio exposure via online, mobile, or satellite access.

Figure 8.6 shows the details of access to satellite radio.

Here one can see that in 2009, among those online, having satellite radio was somewhat more prevalent among non-Hispanic Whites and Hispanics who responded in English. What is perhaps more notable is that all Latinos and African-Americans are more likely to aspire to have access to this medium within the next year.

In general, the popularity of radio can be traced to its strong roots in Latin America. Radio has traditionally been the town crier and the disseminator of information to communities in the region. No surprise that the tradition continues in the US. It is likely, however, that the cost of access to satellite radio may make it more currently accessible to non-Hispanic Whites.

But when it comes to the radio being important in influencing the decisions on what products to buy, radio seems to be most influencial among Latinos who prefer Spanish as detailed in the graph (Figure 8.7).

The importance that Latinos assign to radio as a source of influence in their decision making is parallel to the importance they assign to TV as shown in Figure 8.7 (importance scale is 0–5). Over the years marketers have become aware that less-acculturated Hispanic consumers are less likely to be cynical of commercial

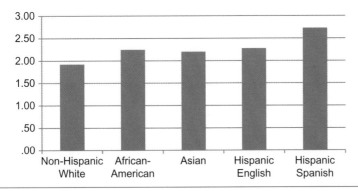

Figure 8.7 Average importance of radio on product purchase.

messages, and are more likely to find them useful. This is an important confirmation in favor of the effectiveness of traditional media for those who are newer to the saturated advertising landscape of the US. This also serves as an interesting warning to advertisers in avoiding saturation that creates a sense of satiation and cynicism on the part of consumers.

The Health Care Education Pilot Case Study at the end of this chapter illustrates how the largest health-care insurer in the state of Florida made use of radio as the main communication media for introducing its Vida Sana health information campaign. From its secondary research sources the health-care insurer understood that Hispanics in Florida had reached over 20% of the state's population and that 30% of them did not have insurance for affordable health care. They learned from their own research that lack of information on how the health-care system works in the US and worries about costs were key barriers. They chose radio for their Vida Sana information campaign to address these issues because of its importance as an influence on less-acculturated Spanish-dominant immigrants. To support Vida Sana, the health-care insurer held health-care events and developed a custom website. Partnerships with supermarkets, local media, and insurance agencies also added to the reach of the Vida Sana campaign. This case study underscores the positive role that radio plays in increasing access of Hispanics to important elements of the overall US culture.

PRINT IN THE FORM OF NEWSPAPERS, MAGAZINES, AND BOOKS

Print directed to Latinos has changed quite dramatically over the past decade. It has had an ascent to popularity after distribution, content, and readership increased in the late 1990s, and some bumps along the road as the distribution of content has been more easily available online, and other bumps due to the "lost decade" of the 2000s in which so much wealth was lost and so many industries were transformed. The economic crisis of 2008–2010 brought about the closure of many print outlets and the modification and mergers of others. Further, the so-called "immigration debate" that has scared many Hispanics back to their countries of origin, combined with the lack of economic opportunity, has contributed to some decline in the audience for print, particularly in Spanish. Still, this seems to be an industry posed for growth as it learns how to combine the tangible paper medium with the online world.

Newspapers

The Latino Print Network (www.latinoprintnetwork.com) claims that it represents 625 newspapers directed to Latinos with a combined circulation of more than 19 million. Then, there is Impremedia, a relatively new company, derived from established newspapers including La Opinion from Los Angeles. They argue that 31% of US Hispanic adults use at least one of their products. Impremedia is on and off-line and has its presence in the largest Latino markets in the US. These are examples of the growing footprint and entrepreneurship of Latino-directed print.

According to the Advertising Age Hispanic Fact Pack 2010, the top 10 Hispanic newspapers in the US measured by advertising dollars (based on data from kantarmedia.com 2008) were as follows in descending order:

El Nuevo Herald	Miami
El Diario La Prensa	New York
La Opinion	Los Angeles
El Diario	Juárez, México
Hoy	Chicago
El Norte	El Paso, Texas/Juárez, México
La Raza	Chicago
El Sentinel	Miami—Ft. Lauderdale
Washington Hispanic	Washington
Al Dia	Dallas

Reading newspapers according to the FSU/DMS Insights data of online consumers shows the distribution of average hours spent with newspapers in the past week in Figure 8.8.

Interestingly all the cultural groups spend more than 2.5 hours to slightly more than three hours per week reading newspapers, when considering the addition of English- and other-language publications. Amount of time reading newspapers per week among Latinos has traditionally been considered to be lower than among non-Hispanic Whites but in the case of these consumers, when both languages are considered, exposure to newspapers seems to be relatively homogeneous. This also

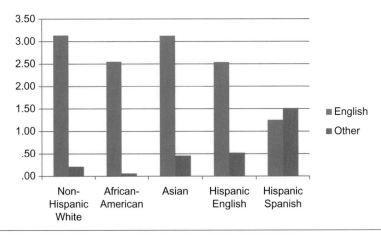

Figure 8.8 Average hours spent with newspapers in the past week.

contradicts stereotypes that have been perpetuated over time about the print orientation of Hispanics. Latinos demonstrate being print oriented at least in the case of those who are already online.

Magazines

Magazines, as most media, experienced difficulties during the recession of 2008–2010. Nevertheless there were magazines that distinguished themselves by attracting important advertising revenue. The top 10 magazines by advertising revenue according to the Advertising Age Hispanic Fact Pack 2010 (Media Economics Group 2009 data) were:

- People en Español
- Latina
- TV y Novelas
- Ser Padres
- Siempre Mujer
- Vanidades
- TV Notas
- Selecciones
- Hispanic Business
- Ser Padres Espera

Figure 8.9, based on the 2009 online FSU/DMS study, indicates that all cultural groups spend some more time than non-Hispanic Whites reading magazines per week. Surprisingly, those who prefer Spanish spend substantially more time reading magazines in a week when adding their Spanish- and English-magazine exposure.

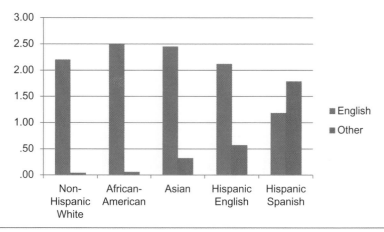

Figure 8.9 Average hours reading magazines per week.

According to the Magazine Publishers of America (MPA), Hispanic/Latino Market Report of 2007,[8] more than 75% of Latinos 18 years of age and older read magazines, and they read them at the rate of more than 12 issues per month. That compares with about 84% of the overall market, which reads about 11 issues per month. Younger Hispanics read more magazines than their older counterparts. According to the same source 80% of Hispanic teens are readers of magazines. Also, according to the MPA the number of magazines dedicated to Hispanics grew from 132 in 2005 to 215 titles in 2009. There have been many magazine failures and mergers in the past few years as well.

To illustrate the effectiveness of magazine advertising campaigns, the MPA shares in their website[9] the case study of Harley-Davidson. This is a 2009 integrated media campaign that included a print component of almost 50%. Harley-Davidson's objective was to direct more traffic to the Hispanic section of Harley-Davidson.com and to generate social media buzz. The campaign was directed to Latino males aged between 30 and 59 and was designed by the agency Carmichael Lynch. The MPA claims that magazines reached first- and second-generation Hispanic males who share the dream embodied by Harley-Davidson. The campaign, Harlistas, was made up of stories that sought to have readers identify with others who have achieved the dream represented by the brand. The brand claims an 8.2% increase in share of motorcycles with Latinos, and a very large increase in traffic, of over 600% to the Hispanic section of the website www.harley-davidson.com/harlistas. An interesting aspect of the campaign and the website is that the campaign was mostly in English but with a cultural slant that appeals to Latinos from the point of view of affinity and a sense of achievement. The ads were calls to share stories and one of them had an emotional appeal that makes sense in the context of the intersection of Harley and Latino culture: "The true measure of a man, is how many lifetimes he can cram

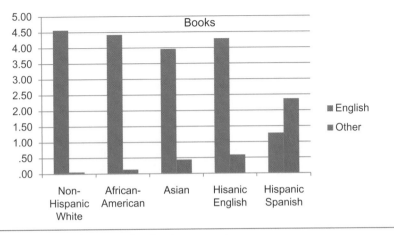

Figure 8.10 Average hours reading books per week.

into one." This is a mixture of Latino machismo with the legendary enjoyment of a Harley but in an English-language context.

The complexity of reaching US Hispanics is demonstrated by the previous example. The choice of media and the choice of message are not independent and the culture of the brand and the culture of the consumer need to be considered.

Books

Literate Latinos have traditionally read books, thus it is not a surprise to see in Figure 8.10 that online Hispanics read as much or more than other culturally unique groups.

What is different, as in the case of other media, in Figure 8.10 is that Hispanics who prefer Spanish spend more time reading books in Spanish. Even Latinos who prefer English spend some of the reading time with Spanish-language books.

Amazon.com, for example, now has a section dedicated to books in Spanish. Barnes & Noble also has a section in their website dedicated to books in Spanish. In our opinion the section of Barnes & Noble is more directly relevant to those who would like to read in Spanish because it takes the searcher first to look at Latin-American titles. The Amazon.com site first takes the searcher to books translated into Spanish on various topics, including dictionaries. Borders also has a section of books in Spanish that resembles the one on Amazon.com. An issue with most of the titles in Spanish that we have looked for is that not many are found in electronic form, thus restricting the access of those who prefer that format.

In general the availability of book titles and related services for readers of the Spanish language in the US are deemed to be deficient.[10] There is a growing number of distributors that specialize in Spanish-language books. According to Teresa

Mlawer,[11] these include Lectorum, Bilingual Publications, Chulain, Mariuccia Iaconi, National Educational Services, Giron, Latin American Book Source, Spanish Book Distributors, and Hispanic Book Distributors.

Many Hispanics read in English, and many read books that are of special appeal not only to their Latino heritage but to many other tastes, preferences, and needs. And interestingly there is an increasing number of authors who have distinguished themselves by reflecting the Latin cultural experience but writing in English. Writers like Sandra Cisneros, Sandra Benítez, Rafael Campo, Richard Rodríguez, Rudolfo Anaya, Cristina García, Julia Álvarez, Luis J. Rodríguez, Celso A. de Casas, Margarita Cota-Cárdenas, Enzo Bravo, and many other authors represent this important trend. These authors are very important because they reflect the new and emerging experience of being Latino in the US. This is of particular importance because the reflection of Hispanic life and experience in literature consolidates a way of being that differs from the Latin-American past and the experience of living in the US. It is part of the emerging trend of identity formation.

MOVIES

Movie consumption is becoming increasingly blurred as more and more avenues exist for watching this type of production. To provide an idea of trends, using data from the 2008 Florida State University DMS Insights online Multicultural Marketing Project, the following chart (Figure 8.11) is presented.

According to this sample of US online consumers, Hispanics who prefer English go to the movie theater more times per year than anyone else. Then African-Americans, Asians, and Hispanics who prefer Spanish follow in descending order, and all go to the movie theater more times per year than non-Hispanic

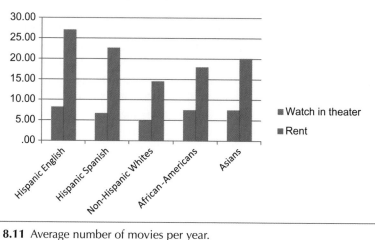

Figure 8.11 Average number of movies per year.

Whites. Interestingly, renting movies to watch at home are most common among Latinos in general and then among Asians and African-Americans. Non-Hispanic Whites, again, are least likely to use this type of entertainment.

Further, the Motion Picture Association of America (MPAA), in their 2009 study of *Theatrical Market Statistics* reports that Hispanics over-index in "tickets sold" compared with the rest of the population. Hispanics account for 21% of tickets sold, while they constitute about 17% of the population. The MPAA study also reports that average annual attendance per moviegoer is highest among Hispanics (8.2). Culturally, films are a strong part of Latino culture and a major form of entertainment that has a deep heritage in Latin America. It is a form of entertainment that is part of family outings and activities.

ONLINE PROVIDERS AND AGGREGATORS

There are multiple companies that operate online that are now offering content to the public in general and some specifically attempt to serve US Hispanics. In this section we will highlight a few of those companies that we think are either making a difference now or will likely be important in the near future.

The portal Maximum.tv aggregates TV from Latin America with the aim of being a one-stop shop for news and entertainment from the continent. It operates almost as a parallel to hulu.com but in the Hispanic domain. They capitalize on relationships with networks and stations in Latin America that do not have a relationship in the US. They are still working out the details of their financing and operation but if successful could present an interesting entry in the competitive TV and information environment.

The one portal related to TV that has been quite successful from early on in the development of the Internet is Univision.com. It serves an important function in complementing the TV offerings of their network and also providing information and service in other areas of relevance to consumers who enjoy Spanish-language content. Univision.com also provides financial, immigration, lifestyle, and many other clusters of information relevant to people who are recent immigrants.

The Lexicon Marketing Spanish-language portal, MundosinBarreras, is described in the Lexicon Marketing–MundosinBarreras Case Study at the end of Chapter 2. This website provides guidance on how to access the resources of the Internet to those Spanish-dominant Hispanics who need support in learning how to access online information. This is an example of how media companies can assist in the acculturation of Latinos in this country.

Terra Networks with their site Terra.com has also been very important among the online sites that US Hispanics visit. They feature many categories of content including sports, lifestyles, music, and other Latino-relevant areas. They also have been one of the most visited sites.

AOL Latino has been a long-term initiative of AOL. It shares similarities with other portals like Univision.com and Terra.com but it has the characteristic look and feel of AOL. Since most Hispanics online tend to have at least some fluency in English, it has been found that many portals that replicate English-language counterparts do generally better with their English-language versions. That may be because these consumers feel they get more ample exposure to the content they are looking for by going to those more general sites. What seems to be largely missing are portals and websites that actually reflect the life of US Hispanics.

The AOL Latino—Tu Voz Case Study at the end of this chapter presents the development of <u>Tu Voz</u>, a website for Spanish-dominant Latino women. Tu Voz is dedicated to the empowerment of Hispanic women in the US who remain close to their Latino roots and face the challenges of the bilingual world in this country as well. Time Inc. Content Solutions identified specific content areas important in the lives of US Spanish-speaking women such as health, career, finance, and relationships, which were not being addressed for them in other websites. AOL Latino, supported by Zubi Advertising, developed Tu Voz, to provide an online resource culturally and linguistically adapted to Latinas. Ford, the unique sponsor of this site, used Tu Voz to connect with Latinas through content devoted to their empowerment rather than direct promotion of their vehicles. Only one separate section of the site was addressed to autos (*Al Volante*) in which female lifestyle and car culture are addressed. Tu Voz is an example of a successful website aimed at the education and acculturation needs of Spanish-dominant Hispanic women.

One of the websites that attempts to serve individuals who are fluent in English but who have strong Latino roots is MyLatinoVoice.com. (See the MyLatinoVoice.com Case Study at the end of Chapter 4.) This is an up-and-coming site that is geared to Latinos that have been in the US for a substantive portion of their lives or who were born here. It is mostly in English but with a definite Latino flavor and features people and events of interest to those who share a Latino heritage. It seems as if the business model of the future is that which reflects the lifestyle of modern Hispanics and that also portrays cultural values at the forefront.

Batanga.com is a music provider that has been persistent in being a specialized Latino music portal. With ups and downs this site continues to survive and appears to be finding a stable business niche. It delivers multiple genres of Spanish language and Latino music that the user can mix and make into a station. It resembles Pandora.com or Last.fm but concentrates exclusively on Latino music. It is a service that delivers unique value not available elsewhere.

Clearly, there are many other established and burgeoning sites that belong to publications, media in general, and others who are realizing the importance of catering to US Hispanics online. Some publications have transformed themselves and now deliver most of their content online like Hispanic Business Magazine. There is ample opportunity for those who pursue specific angles of specialty to serve the Latino market. The cultural opportunity is particularly strong as Latinos who are increasingly becoming proficient in English yearn for their cultural roots.

THE INTERNET AS A CULTURAL FORCE

The Internet has made many important contributions to humankind and in particular it has become a technology of liberation. People who have not been able to be heard since the start of human societies because they were too humble or deprived from power, now can have their own voice without seeking the permission of anyone (almost anyone[12]). The Internet has been embraced by US Hispanics with enthusiasm precisely because it provides avenues of sociability, conversation, and expression. Because of its importance in shaping the future of Latinos in the US we will dedicate the next chapter to this important new medium.

Marketing Support

There are companies that specialize in assisting companies with communication solutions and consumer insights in order to approach the Latino market. This marketing support industry has been going through transformative changes that have brought to the forefront important questions about the role that these specialized shops play. Many larger conglomerates have been purchasing the old pioneers in the industry and few independent organizations of this type remain. Let us examine some of the main categories of marketing support businesses catering to US Latinos.

ADVERTISING AGENCIES

US Hispanic advertising agencies have followed a parallel historical development of that of Spanish-language media. Early on there were small shops that placed Spanish-language ads in newspapers who targeted Spanish speakers in the US. As these shops grew and evolved, as well as newcomers in the marketplace, they expanded to cover the new media of the times including broadcast media, and now the Internet. Nevertheless, there were a few companies that became notable and of substantive importance in the market which started appearing in the early 1980s. These companies strongly contributed to shaping the market into what it is now. Below are some examples of notable entrepreneurs and their agencies.

Siboney was an ad agency that started in Cuba in the 1950s but had to close its doors and move to Puerto Rico and other countries in Latin America after the Cuban revolution. In 1983 it established its presence in the US, in New York, to address the growing US Hispanic market. Its chairman and founder José M. Cubas is one of the living patriarchs of the industry.

In 1976 Tere Zubizarreta founded Zubi advertising in Miami. Ms. Zubizarreta learned the industry starting from scratch as a refugee from the Castro regime in Cuba. Her agency grew to become one of the most prosperous ad agencies in the industry and has been independent to this day. Her son Joe Zubizarreta and her daughter Michelle Zubizarreta run the agency at the time of this writing.

Roberto Orci, a Mexican ad executive, immigrated to the US to start for McCann Erickson La Agencia de McCann in Los Angeles in the early 1980s. He founded La Agencia de Orcí in 1986 and became a counterpart to the Miami Cuban entrepreneurs.

In Texas there were entrepreneurs who also started important agencies in the 1980s. For example, Sosa, Bromley, Aguilar went through several iterations to the present agency, Bromley Communications. The current leader of this agency is Ernest Bromley whose trademark is a strong dedication to consumer insights. In Chicago, Jorge San José, started what is now The San José Group. Jorge San José has expanded his business to Latin America.

An Association Emerged at a Time of Growth

The above are examples of companies that marked the start of an era of Hispanic marketing. There are many others and most are members of the Association of Hispanic Advertising Agencies (AHAA, www.ahaa.org). Hector Orcí was the founding president of AHAA which started in 1996 as an industry association to strengthen the efforts of businesses catering to Hispanic consumers in the US. This organization has now approximately 70 agency members and about an equal number of associate members that tend to be media, research, and other service organizations.

AHAA has been instrumental in promoting the importance of specifically targeting Hispanic consumers because of their substantive buying power and unique cultural identity. This has been somewhat of a struggle as many of the large communication conglomerates and other large advertising and marketing service providers try to bring the business of marketing to Latinos under their own umbrella to get more of the business of their clients.

Acquisitions and Mergers

As the result of the drive by large organizations to become one-stop shopping marketing entities, many of traditionally Latino ad agencies have been acquired and merged with larger entities. That has become an element of friction because those agencies that remain independent resent the competition that comes from groups like WPP, IPG, EURO SCG, MCD, HAVAS, etc., who portray themselves as being providers of most advertising and marketing services to their clients.

The argument that independent shops raise against this devouring trend is that independent shops are able to provide cultural insights and knowledge that those other multifaceted institutions cannot. In theory conglomerates are said to hold these specialty shops as niches and not as true partners in the process of delivering services to their clients. As the leaders of independent shops age many tend to sell their companies and continue this consolidation trend.

Turmoil in Addressing US Latinos

When writing these words, in the later part of 2010, ad agencies and other specialized marketing suppliers are facing strong front winds. One of these obstacles is an immigration reform that has not been defined or enacted. This is a problem because as the economy strives to recover many blame the ills of the US on immigrants, particularly those from Mexico and Latin America. This is a typical problem in that in hard times people tend to find scapegoats that politicians promptly adopt as causes for their political gain.

Some argue that the southern border of the US is a source of danger for the country because terrorists could come through it. That is not a very likely scenario as terrorists usually have better ideas than crossing a desert on foot and suffering thirst, hunger, and exhaustion that few of the readers of this book have experienced.

Many in the US argue that undocumented immigrants take the jobs of Americans and thus should not be allowed in the country, and expelled if found. The reality of the situation seems to be quite different. Most of the jobs in agriculture, construction, and other services that most undocumented workers take tend to be relatively low paying and most importantly backbreaking jobs that few others in the US are interested in doing. Interested readers are referred to consult the arguments that the different farm bureaus and other industry associations raise and the lobbying they have engaged in because they cannot find the workers they need.

Also, as jobs are not as plentiful as they once were, many of those who came to the US without documentation have tended to return to Mexico and other countries, thus leaving in the US those who are more likely to be established and most likely bilingual or English dominant. While cultural insights apply to these Latinos in powerful ways many marketers believe that since they understand English they do not have to make a special effort in marketing to them. As we have explained earlier in this book, that notion is a misconception but a difficult one to address when cultural savvy is not widely available in the marketing industry.

In addition, as many more Hispanics are born in the US, and fewer are coming from abroad, the low-hanging fruit of Spanish-dominant Hispanics has become smaller in size, and the complexity of the market has increased. Now reaching out to Hispanics requires considering many options including:

1. Advertising in English in Spanish-language media.
2. Advertising in Spanish in English-language media.

3. Advertising in English (or code-switching) in English-language media to Latinos by means of cultural insights.

4. Using multiple platforms and media that were not traditionally utilized in reaching Hispanics, including Internet outlets, using Spanish, English, code-switching, but with a focus on cultural ideas that resonate with Latinos.

This complexity many times mystifies marketers who do not know how to address the issues. Added to this is the problem that some agencies are also confronting similar questions. Clearly, the job is not easier now than it was in the 1980s but it is doable. It requires more sophistication and the selection of specific targets among Latinos. It is not possible, particularly now, to address the US Hispanic market as a whole. Segmentation should not be news to marketers. Thinking that the entire US Latino market can be addressed as one is like thinking that all people in Colombia would respond to the same message.

MARKETING SUPPORT PROVIDERS

There are organizations other than advertising agencies that provide market support to reach out to US Latinos. These include specialized PR companies, promotions companies, event organizers, grassroots marketers, web designers, and many others who specialize in aspects of the industry, like print materials, translations, sampling, door hangers, and so on.

Most of these important suppliers do not integrate their offerings but are used either by clients or advertising agencies for specific purposes. Here we provide some examples of these types of providers.

Online

Captura Group, for example, specializes in Hispanic online solutions. They create websites and use other online platforms to reach out to US Latinos. Captura is strategy oriented in the sense that it promotes research in diverse forms in order to better adapt online approaches to the US Hispanic market. (A case study featuring the Captura Group is given at end of Chapter 9.)

MotionPoint deploys multilingual websites by implementing solutions that keep up with changes made on a website so that different languages used are updated to reflect those changes. MotionPoint allows companies to have multilingual solutions for commerce with little infrastructure.

Common Sense Advisory is a consulting company that provides information for globalization. They conduct studies that help marketers to better position themselves in a multilingual environment. Part of their practice specializes in the US Latino market.

There are many other online suppliers that deliver value in multiple ways. Most advertising agencies geared to the US Hispanic market also indicate they offer online solutions, from websites to social media strategies. Clearly, the challenge these days resides in integrating the online and the off-line worlds. It does not seem logical to have separate companies handling discrete media approaches, and when that does happen, the coordination of efforts has to be robust in order to advance the strategic efforts of brands.

Public Relations

While some advertising companies in the Latino marketing space offer PR services, many do not have these services. Some specialized PR specialists are provided here as examples.

The Jeffrey Group that operates in the US and Latin America offers as an expansion of their Latin-American services a specialized practice dedicated to US Latinos. Burson-Marsteller has had a Hispanic PR practice for several years and its efforts are supported by the well-known name of their parent company. Hispania Public Relations is solely dedicated to the US Hispanic market as its name proclaims. Mosaico, a division of Fineman Public Relations, is also a specialty company in the market.

As in the case of advertising agencies targeting the US Hispanic market, many general PR firms are either branching out to target the US Latino market, or are acquiring companies that will enable them to be one-stop shopping PR solutions.

The San Jose Group–US Cellular Case Study at the end of this chapter is illustrative of a PR campaign by a Hispanic-oriented agency which provides both advertising and PR services for their clients. In this case, San Jose Group (SJG) developed an intensive PR campaign which covered a 52-week calendar annually to keep US Cellular in the minds of its Hispanic target. They emphasized the customer service and community-focused orientation of the internal culture at US Cellular in a steady stream of information to the media, attributes important to the Latino market for cellular technology. The SJG PR outreach showed up in human interest stories about US Cellular in local Hispanic media across their 26-state footprint. The PR campaign continuously brought home the warmer personal orientation of US Cellular to its customers in their communities in contrast to the technology-centered messages of the competition, an approach which dovetailed with the group-oriented cultural values of their Latino target.

Market Research

There are multiple market research companies that claim a specialty in the US Latino market. The differentiation is that in order to do relevant market research these companies need to understand the culture. Only with cultural understanding can they ask meaningful questions and interpret the data appropriately. Having Spanish-language proficiency in-house is definitely still an important asset for many of these companies. And it is not just the language ability but the sensitivity to the culture to understand the nuances of language usage.

There are a few companies that remain independent who specialize in the US Hispanic market. They include Garcia Research, New America Dimensions, Encuesta Inc., and Roslow Research. Others with Latino practices that have been acquired by larger conglomerates include Cheskin and Yankelovich. Further, several others were absorbed and their brands obliterated such as Market Development Corporation acquired by TNS, and Strategy Research Corporation acquired by Synovate.

The virtue of specialized market research companies in the Hispanic market has been the offering of culturally relevant and sensitive research to clients and advertising agencies. As clients and advertising agencies acquire research capabilities they tend to look for savings in doing their own research or in integrating it in their overall market research efforts. Those approaches are not necessarily counter-productive but these companies need to keep in mind that separate and specialized suppliers can many times offer the value of impartiality and often cultural research expertise is not available in-house.

Grassroots, Events, and Promotions

While this aggregate may not do justice to each of the rubrics, these companies share a lot in common. The key shared element is that they tend to touch the consumer in a more personal way than most other approaches. Latinos are particularly fond of events in which they and their families can enjoy an outing together, and they appreciate word-of-mouth suggestions and recommendations. Samples in stores and other venues are also strongly favored by Hispanics. A sample in many cases is the best ambassador for a brand. Here are some companies in this category.

- Mercury Mambo
- The RMD Group
- Lazos Latinos
- MASS Hispanic

These companies are examples of those that offer activations to culturally reach Latino consumers. Creativity and strong personal touch tends to characterize their offerings.

Industry Publications

There are several industry publications that have endured over the past several years. These publications serve as information sources for marketers with an interest in the US Latino market. Some of them are free and others require a subscription. Generally they all use advertising as a revenue source.

Perhaps the oldest of these publications is Hispanic Market Weekly (http://www.hispanicmarketweekly.com/) founded by Arturo Villar in 1997. It was started on the bases of faxes, it then evolved into e-mail, and then became an online publication. This is a subscription-based newsletter that includes multiple types of content and reports.

HispanicAd.com (www.hispanicad.com) has also been an enduring publication founded in 1999 by Gene Bryan. It has a widely e-mail distributed newsletter that links to its homepage.

The aggregator Hispanic Trending (www.hispanictrending.net) was founded in 2004 by Juan Guillermo Tornoe. This is a blog style potpourri news and information center which has grown in its information value to many students and industry insiders.

"La Sala de La Tele" (www.lasaladelatele.com) is a blog by Laura Martinez that exemplifies trends in TV advertising to Latinos in the US. Laura Martinez also has a satirical media blog called "Mi blog es tu blog" (http://lauramartinez.wordpress.com/) that provides a special cultural twist to those marketers who are Hispanic cultural insiders.

Produ.com is a media and marketing newsletter and website that serves US Hispanic and also Latin-American marketing professionals. Portada (www.portada-online.com) was conceived mostly as a Hispanic print industry outlet that has expanded to digital and other areas of Hispanic marketing. They claim to be the leading source on Latin marketing and media.

Latino Print Network, published by Western Publication Research and lead by Kirk Whisler, produces a weekly newsletter of topics of importance to US Latinos and also to marketers in general.

Elsewhere in this book we have mentioned SRDS's Hispanic Media and Markets, which is a compilation of media outlets and other organizations serving the US Hispanic market. This is a useful resource for those who plan Latino market campaigns.

Intra-Company Specialty Organizations

There are organizations within organizations that help their companies with Latino-oriented initiatives. Companies like Coca-Cola, General Mills, McDonalds, and others have teams of professionals that tend to Latino-oriented initiatives. Over the years many of these teams have been formed. Some have endured and many have been disbanded. Some, like Procter & Gamble, had a Hispanic marketing team that operated as a unit but now these specialists have been allocated to work in the context of brands instead of being a support organization.

HANDLING CULTURAL DIVERSITY IN THE MARKETPLACE

There does not seem to be a perfect way to handle a new multicultural reality within US companies. Nevertheless, there are several requirements that in our opinion need to be present in organizations.

1. First and foremost there must be members of the cultural groups of interest within the organization at most levels of decision making. These individuals should, at least conceptually, be vigilant about issues that affect their cultural communities. Hispanic in our case.

2. There should be cultural expertise in the organization that goes beyond objective culture to address subjective culture of the groups in question. Ideally these would be cultural anthropologists that also have marketing expertise. As a minimum these should be practitioners that have some in-depth training about the focus culture, even if they are not members of the culture itself. We have explained that being a member of a cultural group does not necessarily imply that the person understands his or her own culture. That is because culture is not evident even to its own members. In-house cultural expertise used in marketing strategies and tactics can help connect effectively with culturally diverse consumers and avoid costly errors. Also, it helps organizations avoid the assumption of similarity that many marketers tend to make because "after all we are all human." We have made the point in this book that using culture as a connecting mechanism becomes a shorthand for better communication with culturally diverse groups.

3. As purposeful marketing claims increased importance in the marketplace, organizations are redefining their mission to become better citizens. Just as the grocery store a hundred years ago had the purpose of serving its community, businesses now are coming back to that enlightened point. Once a sense of purpose guides the organization, the bottom line is also covered. Purposeful marketing requires now that companies act upon the multicultural reality of the US.

4. Integrating decision making in organizations will be an increasingly important endeavor. This is particularly true in marketing. Latinos and other emerging minorities cannot be seen as niches anymore but need to be recognized as driving forces of the entire economy. The Chief Marketing Officer (CMO) can no longer compartmentalize culturally diverse groups as smaller opportunities than the defunct "general market." There is no such thing as a general market, there are segments of cultural groups compounded by subcultures and lifestyles. These need to be understood in a coherent scheme where culture is part of the segmentation scheme, and where culture is part of the strategic thinking of the company.

5. The cultural experience of the company needs to be an ongoing effort. Companies need to keep their radar out in culturally diverse communities to understand trends and changes. Executives need to go on ethnographic interview outings to see where and how their consumers live. They need to experience firsthand consumer practices and ways of behaving. It is not just the research/insights group that needs to be in contact with consumers, it is the decision makers. To do otherwise makes the work of researchers and insight gatherers futile because they will not resonate at the decision-making levels. Marketing needs to go back to the village, larger now but still a village in a psychological sense.

The degree of complexity in marketing thinking and segmentation required by progressive organizations has no parallel in history. As we approach the idealized paradigm of one-on-one marketing we must be ready to address more differences and similarities among people. Marketing organizations that become adept at doing this will not only survive a turbulent economic era but will thrive as their purpose includes recognition for diversity.

Planning as a More Encompassing Effort

The relatively new emergence of account planning in advertising companies and new tendencies in media planning have important implications for thinking about culturally diverse consumers. We believe that account planning and media planning will merge as one discipline because both require a similar way of thinking. Basically they both require in-depth consumer understanding.

The expansion of account planning to manufacturer and service provider organizations seems inevitable. That has started, in a way, by renaming consumer research departments "consumer insights" departments. Account planners inside organizations will have the important role of making the perspective and behaviors of consumers more salient across the organization. This will have the consequence of a stronger sense of purpose in serving communities and consumers.

The "consumer" planner will brief marketers and executives at different levels of trends in specific cultures of interest and how the overall strategy of the company needs to be localized. In-depth localization to specific segments that are heavily weighted by cultural groups will make marketing efforts more relevant and more effective.

Ultimately, the planner should perhaps be the anthropologist we talked about in the prior section. He or she will retool the organization for cultural marketing. And cultural marketing does not have to be exclusive to minority cultures as we know them now but to cultures and subcultures that are part of the overall society. Understanding folkways[13] in our modern society will again illuminate how we think of people, and then how we think of them as consumers of our products.

Conclusions

The evolution of the US Hispanic marketing industry responded to the emergence of the Latino population in the US as Hispanics grew in numbers and changed with the influence of their adopted country. The industry began with nascent signs of activity focused on the Spanish language in the 1950s, took off with an expansion into new media channels and pioneering advertising agencies in the 1980s, and continued to grow in complexity and sophistication to address the largely bilingual Latino market of today. Currently, reaching out to Latinos has never been more complicated given their cultural, linguistic, and lifestyle segmentation as already discussed in previous chapters. Yet, the industry benefits for serving our growing market of Latinos have never been greater, nor the dangers for ignoring their consumer power more real.

HISPANIC MEDIA

It is helpful to look at Hispanic media from the perspective of touchpoints with Latinos that create deep-level connections and attract attention, involvement, and loyalty. There continues to be a two-way influence between the media and Latinos: The Hispanic media serves the unique needs of this cultural group as they acculturate in the US, and Hispanics bring their traditions and their emerging sense of identity in this country to their media preferences.

The history of Hispanic media has a fascinating parallel to the growth of the market. This story begins with early print media in the 1800s and continues to the birth of Spanish-language radio and TV in the 1950s, to the proliferation of programming and channels in the 1980s, to the emersion of bilingual media TV cable, and satellite, and currently to the mix of Spanish- and English-language media, and the Internet. Broadcast, cable, and satellite media provide options to Hispanics which cater to their tastes in TV, radio, and online programming, and allow them to customize their access to language preferences and culturally relevant interests.

Print media including newspapers, magazines, and books, contrary to the stereotyping that Hispanics do not read much, are popular among Latino consumers. When Spanish-language newspaper reading is combined with English-language reading, Hispanics read newspapers as much as other segments of the US population. Latinos have an even higher readership of magazines than other cultural groups, again when hours of Spanish and English reading are combined. In the case of both newspapers and magazines as noted in this chapter, Hispanics who prefer English also read some of their materials in Spanish, and Hispanics who prefer Spanish read some in English.

Latinos are also avid moviegoers and renters. Given that most theaters in the US show movies in English, it makes sense that those who prefer English go to theaters more than those who prefer Spanish. And, it is likely that to accommodate their language orientation, those who prefer Spanish rent more than those who prefer English. The big picture for theaters and Latino marketing in general is that in the US Latinos over-index in ticket purchases and have the highest average cinema attendance per person compared to other groups.

The ability for Latinos to access relevant media for their language needs and culturally unique preferences has been limited in this country since most media availability has been directed to the English-speaking so-called general market. However, media access is currently expanding with a profusion of online providers. Given Latinos' growing sophistication in technology use, they can now individualize their media menus to a greater extent. This permits them to cater to their information interests and needs as they acculturate and express their voices as a key part of the new US mainstream. In a later chapter we will address the Internet as a cultural force.

HISPANIC MARKETING SUPPORT

Marketing support to Hispanics, similar to the media, has been trending with the market through its history in the US. Advertising agencies, PR, market research, promotions, industry-specific associations, and Internet providers are all grappling with the enormous changes in the marketing needs of Latinos in this country. Given the size of the Latino consumer segment, its complexity, and political and historical turmoil, marketing support providers have been undergoing transformations in their structures and services to stay relevant and meet Latino consumer needs.

Advertising agencies have changed from an early concentration on providing Spanish-language communication through newspapers and other emerging radio and TV options, to an emphasis on consumer connections by targeted marketing and strategically defined media touchpoints. Several pioneering advertising agencies in the 1980s shaped advertising to move beyond translation of existing English-language campaigns into Spanish. These specialized agencies developed campaigns with increased sensitivity to the diverse cultural needs of Latinos back in the 1980s. While several of these Hispanic agencies and the professionals who grew them continue to serve the market, there has been considerable reconformation of Hispanic advertising over time with acquisitions, mergers, and the tendency of large agencies to provide marketing to Hispanics from within. This raises the imperative to keep cultural awareness of Latinos as a key element in marketing, and not to have it become subsumed to an Anglo "general market" approach.

In addition to advertising agencies, other marketing support providers have added their particular expertise to the sophistication of the industry. PR companies as well as PR segments within advertising agencies have increased culturally relevant connections with Latinos. Independent market research companies or units within other research companies have specialized in gathering and analyzing Latino consumer data with sensitivity to cultural nuances. Grassroots, events, and promotions companies have provided marketers with personally oriented Latino consumer touchpoints. Marketing support through organizations such as the AHAA as well as intra-company specialty groups have bolstered the professionalism of Latino marketing.

Despite these advancements and adaptations of media and marketing to Latino consumers the industry cannot afford to be complacent. The challenge of handling cultural diversity in this rapidly changing consumer landscape requires new perspectives and continuous growth in marketing capabilities. Managing critical cultural diversity requires the presence of Latinos at all levels of an organization and their expertise in all aspects of the marketing process. The organization must stay close to Latino consumers and monitor the cultural realities of their everyday life. Culturally trained account managers can play a key role by linking all levels of the organization to the realities of Hispanic consumers' lives. These efforts allow organizations to maintain cultural relevance to Latinos from decision making at the highest levels to the cultivation of ongoing relationships in all touchpoints for their brands.

IMPLICATIONS FOR MARKETERS

- Embrace cultural diversity; it is your new general market.
- Proceed with the guidance of an account planner trained in cultural understanding.
- Keep the Latino consumer perspective a part of all of your strategic, advertising, and media planning.
- Maintain all levels of your organization informed of current trends among Latinos and other cultural segments.
- Develop an understanding of the subjective culture of your Latino target relevant to your brand. Here lies your competitive advantage.
- Work with marketing research companies with a specialization in the Hispanic market.
- Realize that the Hispanic market is no longer a relatively homogeneous Spanish-speaking market but a complex segmented component of the US consumer landscape, with a population and spending capacity that rivals most countries in the world.
- Use your account planner to advocate for Latino cultural understanding developed from your research, for all aspects of brand marketing including advertising and other communication touchpoints.
- Merge your account planner and media planner functions into one culturally consumer-oriented effort.
- Consider the broad spectrum of Spanish- and English-language media available to create meaningful touchpoints and build brand relationships with Latino consumers.
- Resist any oversimplification of the changing US Hispanic market by lumping it into the English-speaking general market. The Latino market is defined by cultural similarities stemming from Latin-American roots and the influence of being Hispanic in the US, not simply by language.
- Use your cultural understanding from all of your multicultural projects to become a more relevant and purposeful professional.

CASE STUDY: HEALTH CARE EDUCATION PILOT IN FLORIDA

Company/Organization
Largest health insurer in the state of Florida

Advertising Agency
Wenstrom Communications and Staywell Custom Communications

Campaign/Advertising Title
Vida Sana

Intended Hispanic Consumers
Unacculturated Hispanics

Background
The Vida Sana campaign was created to inform Florida's growing Latino communities about Hispanic health-care issues and familiarize them with the US health-care system. Another goal of the campaign was to enhance Hispanics' understanding of the value of health insurance and how it can be used to protect their family's finances against the high cost of medical emergencies. This understanding is critical, as our research shows that many Hispanics migrate from countries where the health-care system is vastly different than in the US.

Discovery Process/Research
Research shows that by 2012 it is expected that Hispanics will represent 21% of Florida's population.[14] Thirty percent of Hispanic Floridians lack the health insurance needed to give them affordable access to the private health-care delivery system.[15] Besides affordability, one of the reasons often cited by Hispanics for not having health insurance is a poor understanding of how it works.[16] Hispanic marketing experts have stated that Hispanics as well as other minorities "over-index" in their time spent listening to radio.[17] Specifically, 63% of Hispanics are noted as listening to radio/music programming in the course of their daily activities.[18]

Cultural Insights
Given its research, the health insurer recognized that information needs were critical in creating access to a health-care delivery system for the large Hispanic segment in the state of Florida. They realized that the combination of lack of knowledge about how health care in this country works and concerns about affordability were keeping Hispanics away from private health-care systems and specifically from using health insurance to make their health care more affordable. They recognized that Hispanics' affinity for listening to radio and the salience of radio in their lives suggested an excellent, culturally appropriate avenue to gain their interest. The health insurer also built in an introductory face-to-face component to their campaign based on the importance of interpersonal communication for the Hispanic population.

Expression of Insights in the Campaign
In order to maximize target audience reach and message retention, the Vida Sana campaign utilized a multiformat educational approach.
- *Events*—These were held in Florida neighborhoods with high concentrations of Hispanic residents. The events were designed to inform the Hispanic community about

(Continued)

Health Care Education Pilot in Florida: Vida Sana campaign.

the Vida Sana radio shows and provide onsite access to health screenings, healthy eating, and lifestyle advice.

- *Radio*—A series of Spanish radio programs aired where callers could call to ask the health insurer's and local experts about health and insurance.
- *Web*—A custom website was developed (www.vidasanaflorida.com) where people could listen to or read highlights of the radio shows at their convenience as well as view or download a brief "Health Care 101" video created specifically for the Vida Sana campaign.

Effect of the Campaign

Overall, the campaign exceeded all of its goals and created a positive image for the health-insurer's brand. Specific campaign results are:

How many individuals received health care and insurance information?

- 375 event attendees received health screenings and/or health and diet advice.
- 594,600 individuals listened to the shows.
- 7426 hits were tracked in the Vida Sana website.

How many people were exposed to the health-insurer's brand during the pilot's duration?

- Over 2 million brand impressions were generated with TV, radio, and newspaper ads and other promotions.

Campaign Key Learnings

One of the biggest lessons from this campaign was the better-than-expected event attendance and media-purchase savings obtained through partnerships with local media, insurance agencies, and Hispanic supermarkets. With these partnerships, the health insurer was able to significantly increase the number of Hispanics reached by the Vida Sana campaign while remaining within the campaign's established budget.

CASE STUDY: AOL LATINO—TU VOZ

Company/Organization Name
AOL Latino

Advertising Agency
Zubi Advertising

Campaign/Advertising Title
Tu Voz en Tu Vida, http://www.tuvozentuvida.com/

Intended Hispanic Consumers
The target audience for Tu Voz is the Spanish-dominant, Latina woman living in the US. At varied life stages (single, working professional, married, young mother, etc.) she maintains a strong connection to her Latin culture while navigating through life in the US. Regardless of whether she recently immigrated to the US or has lived here for years, she sustains strong ties to her culture and seeks out entertainment, role models, information, and resources that she can specifically identify with as a Latina living in the US.

Background
Via previously conducted research, Ford Motor Company identified Hispanic women as an influential consumer market in the US due to their position as heads of household and decision makers within their families. With that in mind, Ford partnered with Time Inc. Content Solutions to identify the content gaps that existed in current online women's sites. The findings revealed there was a need for quality content that could speak directly to Hispanic women about the themes of empowerment. Furthermore, the best area within Time Warner to speak to Ford's target market was within AOL Latino's women's site, Tu Vida.

Discovery Process/Research
After analyzing the current online women's sites and identifying the content gaps, Time Inc. Content Solutions came up with a series of recommendations as to how we should develop the new destination. This research helped us develop a joint mission statement and revealed the new Ford for Women hub, Tu Voz en Tu Vida, would:

- Be a one-stop shop for Hispanic women who live in the US and are willing to share their experiences about dealing with the realities of their adopted country.
- Focus on empowering women and, in that sense, had a clear, action-oriented, goal in mind; this made the site's mission distinctly different from other women's online sites.
- Provide advice from experts these Hispanic women living in the US admire and have come to trust by reading their books, articles, and seeing them on TV or listening to them on the radio.

Cultural Insights
Tu Voz is a reassuring voice for US Hispanic women who are straddling their strong cultural ties and the lives they are seeking to live in the US.

The site connects with the user through the unique insight that Hispanic women who embrace their Latin culture, regardless of their level of assimilation, are caught in

(Continued)

a bicultural struggle that general market counterparts do not face. Whether due to language barriers, cultural nuances, or taboos, Hispanic women have specific needs and interests in varied life stages and seek information that speaks directly to their concerns.

As a result, Tu Voz's content is developed with the goals to deliberately identify the concerns that are specific to the Hispanic woman and to provide her with the tools and advice she may need to enact a positive change in her life.

Expression of Insights in the Campaign

By understanding that the needs of US Hispanic women are different to their general market counterparts, Tu Voz has developed Spanish-language content in a variety of life-coaching areas: health, career advancement, money management, and lifestyle. In each we have developed content (in the form of articles, blogs, video, and photo), keeping in mind the importance of bridging the gap between their cultural background and their current life here in the US.

The implementation of these cultural expressions has included:

- *Bienestar* (health): Looking at some of the misconceptions Hispanic families have about their health (http://www.tuvozentuvida.com/2009/11/05/las-ideas-equivocadas-de-las-familias-latinas/), diabetes within the Hispanic community in the US (http://www.tuvozentuvida.com/2009/11/11/diabetes-factores-prevencion/), breast cancer precautions (http://www.tuvozentuvida.com/2009/10/01/informacion-cancer-de-seno/).
- *Exito* (career advancement): Examples of successful Latinos living in the US (http://www.tuvozentuvida.com/2009/12/22/los-hispanos-cobran-fuerza-en-el-gobierno-de-obama/), information regarding scholarships for Hispanics (http://www.tuvozentuvida.com/2009/12/10/como-solicitar-una-beca-al-hispanic-scholarship-fund/), how to avoid negative Latino stereotypes in the workplace (http://www.tuvozentuvida.com/2009/10/29/no-permitas-que-te-encasillen-por-ser-mujer-o-latina/).

AOL Latino campaign: "Tu Voz en Tu Vida."

- *Finanzas* (money management): Resources for Hispanic entrepreneurs (http://www.tuvozentuvida.com/2009/11/24/empujon-financiero-accion-prestamos/), tips to effectively plan your retirement in the US (http://www.tuvozentuvida.com/2009/10/28/consejos-para-planear-tu-jubilacion/).
- *Vive Más* (lifestyle): Relationship advice—dealing with a "machista" (http://www.tuvozentuvida.com/2009/07/22/estrategias-de-un-machista/), highlighting the coach's struggles with being Latina in the US (http://www.tuvozentuvida.com/2009/11/26/una-puertorriquena-en-los-ee-uu/).

Sponsorship Integration

As Tu Voz's exclusive sponsor, Ford Motor Company's overriding intent was to connect with Hispanic women via empowerment rather than utilizing Tu Voz as a platform to showcase their products. However, understanding that there was still a need to present a conversation around autos, the Content Team at AOL developed "Al Volante," a unique space highlighting the intersection between female lifestyle and car "culture."

Some examples of content within this section include:

- Al Volante (autos): Tips on keeping your teen drivers safe on the road (http://www.tuvozentuvida.com/2009/11/26/mykey-ford-autos-hijos/), successful Hispanic woman in Ford Motor Company (http://www.tuvozentuvida.com/2009/06/17/ingeniera-mas-importante-nuevo-auto-ford/).

Effect of the Campaign

AOL conducted a survey to gauge the impact Tu Voz has had on our users. From October 29 to November 18, 2009, 1061 users responded to questions regarding their perceptions of the site and its sponsor.

Some of the study's results revealed:

Content is connecting with the users and causing them to return to the site

- 90% of users are likely to return and the majority of first-time users who took the survey (66%) intend to visit again.
- Site's primary target, Hispanic women, award high ratings for the site's content (61% like very much) and 66% like the range of information available.
- 65% of repeat visitors have already recommended the site to others and nearly all others said they would recommend it.

Tu Voz visitors have a positive opinion of Ford sponsorship

- Upon knowing that Ford was a sponsor of the Tu Voz site, 60% of return visitors said they had a more favorable opinion about the brand.
- Unaided recall of Ford as the site's sponsor is strong at 39%.
- Repeat visitors have a higher overall impression of Ford than first-time visitors (42% vs. 27%) compared to last year.
- Repeat visitors that have never driven a Ford are more likely to consider Ford than first-time users (56% vs. 43%).

The site's audience has a higher income, is better educated, and plan to purchase a car in the next 12 months

- 68% of repeat visitors have a household income of $50,000 + .
- 58% of repeat visitors have graduated college or higher.
- 58% of repeat visitors plan to purchase a car in the next 12 months.

CASE STUDY: THE SAN JOSE GROUP–US CELLULAR

Company Name
US Cellular

Advertising Agency
San Jose Group (SJG)

Campaign/Advertising Title
US Cellular: Out-localizing the competition and delivering something better

Intended Hispanic Consumers
Primary target market is Spanish-dominant and bilingual adults 25+, with a secondary target of bilingual Hispanic youth, ages 18–25. These segments tend to drive cell phone usage in the Hispanic market.

Background
Competition in the Hispanic market among wireless carriers is intensely fierce, with telecommunications companies making up the highest spending category in Hispanic media, according to AdAge's 2009 Hispanic Fact Pack. The industry consists of two, national "Goliaths," with US Cellular operating in 26 states and ranking fifth in terms of number of total customers. While the top-four carriers tend to "battle it out" with declarations of the strongest, biggest, or fastest network, US Cellular has opted to win customers over by playing to its own strengths—its award-winning dedication to customer service and strong community presence. In short, US Cellular out-localizes the competition.

While US Cellular has separate advertising programs to focus on branding and promotions across general market and multicultural segments, PR has developed within the company as an important tool to build credibility and show that US Cellular is more than a phone company within a category full of cold, confusing technology. Through meaningful news coverage, US Cellular shows the ways in which it brings people together.

US Cellular Public Affairs leverages local PR agencies for helping the brand stay positioned as a leader in customer satisfaction. Since 2004, SJG has served as US Cellular's PR agency partner exclusively entrusted with Hispanic PR initiatives across the company's 26-state footprint, focusing on priority Hispanic markets.

Discovery Process/Research
SJG utilizes secondary research to uncover Hispanic consumer trends and behaviors related to the wireless category. Research from the client's marketing team also plays a key role in identifying some of the most important factors that Hispanic cell phone users take into account when selecting a wireless carrier. In addition, SJG's constant pulse on US Cellular's corporate culture, operations, and internal developments with the company's people and products, gives the agency access to information that is crucial to being able to express cultural insights inside of the PR campaign in real time.

Lastly, SJG executes competitive PR research to understand who is showing up in editorial coverage in the realm of wireless carriers, and what is being talked about.

Cultural Insights

SJG's research uncovered two main areas of insight that tend to drive annual Hispanic PR programs: the Hispanic consumer's behavior inside of the category, and the intersection between US Cellular's own internal culture and the values of the Hispanic market.

Hispanic consumers are faster adopters of new technology, talk more each month, and over-index on mobile data applications, which are often strong contributors to a carrier's average revenue per user (ARPU). By examining these trends, SJG recognized the high passion point for cellular products and services among Hispanic consumers, and works toward converting this fact into meaningful news for the US Cellular brand.

Client research has also revealed that responsive customer service and helpful bilingual associates are highly valued by Hispanic wireless customers. As such, creating stories around how associates go above and beyond for customers is equally important.

To further help bring this human element to life, SJG focuses on US Cellular's unique corporate culture, which is founded upon numerous customer-centric values that are deeply ingrained into all its associates. By identifying the parallels between US Cellular's values and those of our Hispanic consumers, SJG is able to leverage shared cultural connection points—including pride, diversity, and respect—and help news reporters and producers see these linkages as interesting news items.

Expression of Insights in the Campaign

SJG has built a cohesive 52-week community and media relations program for US Cellular, highlighting the company's community involvement, and serving as an invaluable, year-round information resource for local Hispanic media throughout the US. The agency balances a calendar of preplanned story ideas with more organic media pitching that enables its client to remain responsive to story opportunities week-to-week, quarter-to-quarter.

Through its outreach, SJG has created a constant editorial presence for US Cellular throughout the year. Every month, SJG pitches a steady rotation of story angles to TV, radio, print, and online outlets, taking into account multiple elements including Hispanic holidays or seasonal topics, advertising/promotional programs, local market happenings, and developments with US Cellular's corporate and field associates.

For example, one of US Cellular's call centers, located in Tulsa, OK, has served as the subject of several stories over the past 3 years, with SJG helping to create new dimensions for the pitch and securing full-page articles about the associates working there. This coverage has successfully positioned US Cellular not only as an innovative company dedicated to bilingual customer service, but also a dynamic place to work.

During HHM, possibly the most cluttered time for Hispanic media as any company even remotely interested in targeting the segment launches an initiative, SJG worked with US Cellular to offer free Latin-American flag wallpapers and Latin-themed ringtone downloads to its customers. The program resulted in more than 7000 downloads during the month-long celebration, promoted entirely by nonpaid PR coverage without advertising support.

SJG also packages stories that profile US Cellular's Hispanic associates, putting a face on the people who help Hispanic customers out in the field. This kind of coverage has included full-page articles in some of the country's top publications, including

(Continued)

US Cellular Public Relations campaign: out-localizing the competition and delivering something better.

Chicago's Hoy newspaper, which featured a completely bilingual sales team in a new store location, who are truly a part of that local community.

Effect of the Campaign
SJG's intensive media relations program has resulted in a range of 20–35 hits per month across US Cellular's footprint. In 2008 alone, more than 7 million Hispanics read, saw, or heard US Cellular's stories—an impressive number, considering the total Hispanic population across the company's priority markets is under 3 million. Print coverage frequently consists of cover and full-page stories, and broadcast segments often stretch several minutes long—the longest radio interview to date lasting more than 10 minutes. But most importantly, the tone and content of coverage paints a positive picture of US Cellular as a strong community leader with great people. In all, the net effect of the campaign is that it complements the paid advertising and promotional programs, and in many ways even rivals the paid placements relative to third-party credibility, depth of content, and brand image differentiation in a cluttered category.

End Notes

[1] http://www.enotes.com/american-history-literature/spanish-speakers-early-latino-expression

[2] See the *Handbook of Texas Online* section on Spanish-language radio at http://www.tshaonline.org/handbook/online/articles/SS/ebs1.html.

[3] http://sintv.org/sintv/biography.html

[4] We also thank Captura Group for their support of the 2009 data-collection effort.

[5] The scale used was a six-point scale from "not at all important" to "extremely important."

[6] See *Hispanic Market Weekly's* section on Entertainment at http://www.hispanicmarketweekly.com/.

[7] See Arbitron's *Hispanic Radio Today*, 2009 edition: http://www.arbitron.com/downloads/hisp_radio_today_09.pdf.

[8] See the report by the Magazine Publishers of America, "Hispanic/Latino Market Profile" published in 2007. http://www.magazine.org/content/Files/MPAHispMktPro.pdf

[9] http://www.magazine.org/advertising/case_studies/CaseStudyDetail.aspx?k = 365188D069714269B98BCB15FE1504A6&t = Harlistas + (2010)

[10] Teresa Mlawer, "Distributing Spanish books in the US." *Publishing Research Quarterly* 22(3), 2006, 47–51.

[11] Ibid.

[12] While the Internet does allow free expression there are multiple checks and balances that do temper a total free-for-all.

[13] William G. Sumner, *A Study of the Sociological Importance of Usages, Manners, Customs, Mores, and Morals.* Boston, MA: Ginn, 1906.

[14] *U.S. Population Projections*, US Census Bureau: www.census.gov.

[15] R. Paul Duncan, *A Profile of Uninsured Floridians: Findings from the2004 Florida Health Insurance Study.* Florida Department of Health Services Research, Management and Policy at the University of Florida, February 2005.

[16] *South Florida Signature Program Research*—Primary research conducted by the health-insurer's market research department.

[17] R. Paul Duncan, *A Profile of Uninsured Floridians: Findings from the2004 Florida Health Insurance Study.* Florida Department of Health Services Research, Management and Policy at the University of Florida, February 2005.

[18] Hispanic Radio Today—2007 edition, Arbitron, Inc.

THE DIGITAL WORLD OF US LATINOS

Chapter 9

The online world of US Hispanics deserves special consideration as it has been a major force in altering their lives. The opportunities of both Latino consumers and marketers have been dramatically modified by this truly different paradigm.

A Liberating Technology

There is an inherent problem in trying to separate history and politics when culture evolves. Culture evolves and sometimes makes radical leaps. The changes experienced by cultures are fundamentally affected by the evolution of human institutions and relationships.

The masses of Latin America by being dominated by mostly Spanish and Portuguese conquerors were largely subservient for at least 400 years. The differences in social classes that evolved from the relationships between feudal lordships and the masses of the population have persisted to this day but they are rapidly changing. More democratic institutions and better educational systems started to modify stark class gaps in the 20th century. Only a few decades ago vast numbers of Latin-American populations could not obtain a phone line, or had to wait for years to be able to be assigned one. The postal systems had been generally unreliable and in many cases plagued by corruption. The mass media had been controlled

339

by a few conglomerates that were in turn heavily influenced by governmental forces. The masses were kept "in their place" by these forces as well as other old and well-established institutions. They had little opportunity for upward mobility except perhaps by migrating to the US, Canada, or Europe.

Close to the end of the millennium, in the 1990s the Internet came about as a force that has influenced how the world communicates and relates. Those who could not freely interact became free to express themselves:

- Both Latin Americans and US Latinos increased their communication ability substantially by being able to use e-mail, text, VOIP, and social media. A phone call that not too long ago cost $2 a minute dropped to $0.02 per minute. E-mailing, texting, and social media became virtually free, or very inexpensive. Communicating with others became an on-demand opportunity. Children who had left their parents behind did not have to wait for weeks or months before reestablishing contact. Instead they can reach out anytime. Consumers that had to think twice before calling their friends and relatives can now be with them, virtually, all the time. They can share their views, lifestyles, and perspectives. Freedom to interact and communicate has been fully realized.
- Hispanics that had to consume what the large conglomerates wanted the masses to know or be entertained with became content generators. Hispanics have embraced blogs, websites, and social networking pages as places where they can share content, from pictures to stories. They do not have to ask permission or be privileged to say what they need to express. The generation of content has been embraced with passion after a history of suppression.
- Learning about opportunities had been the privilege of the few. Only those who were connected with power circles knew about ideas and leads that could improve their lifestyle. Entrepreneurship has evolved to include those that could never before expand their horizons. Now Hispanics can consult the Internet to learn what they need, understand, compare, and also become better consumers.

That is why we refer to the Internet as a technology of liberation, and that is why some countries fear it so much. Hispanics in most of Latin America and the US are fortunate that they do not have to live under repressive regimes that attempt to curtail their access to the Internet. The digital world of US Latinos is flourishing.

The names of websites described in this book's case studies reflect the Internet as a liberating force for US Hispanics and as the opportunity for expressing their voices: MundosinBarreras.com translated into English is *WorldwithoutBarriers* (Lexicon Marketing–MundosinBarreras.com Case Study at the end of Chapter 2), TuVozentuVida.com translated into English is *YourVoiceinyourLife* (AOL Latino–Tu Voz Case Study at the end of Chapter 8), and MyLatinoVoice.com (MyLatinoVoice.com Case Study at the end of Chapter 4).

The Internet Redefines Marketing

In 2011 we are in a transitional period in the history of marketing and advertising. While many argue that traditional ways of watching TV or listening to radio are here to stay, and others say that holding a paper book or newspaper is an unreplaceable experience, the trends we observe negate that. Many magazines and newspapers have recently become online editions either exclusively or mostly. As an example in the US Hispanic realm, *Hispanic Business* magazine has encouraged readers to migrate to its online platform, as many others have. Hulu, Google TV, Netflix, Maximum.tv, and others are replacing traditional TV watching. Internet radio is growing with notable examples that include Batanga, Pandora, and Last.fm.

At this point a reasonable prediction is that the mode of distribution of most professionally produced content will evolve into an electronic and Internet-based offering. Clearly, user-originated content will thrive online. Reaching consumers online has become a growing practice. Advertising relevant to the context of the consumer has greatly replaced any disruptive advertising approach.

In the case of marketing to online Latinos there are several issues that will endure for a few years to come:

- What language should be used? Should marketers use Spanish, English, or both languages online?
- Should marketers localize their websites in a Spanish-language version?
- What are elements of websites that make the online experience more culturally relevant? And in general, is online cultural relevance important?

In this chapter we will present data that will likely help the reader address some of these questions.

To begin, here are two case studies in which marketers used the Internet to connect with Hispanic consumers. Both cases, in very different industries, illustrate the careful attention given to the enduring issues mentioned earlier including language needs and cultural relevance.

The San Jose Group–Illinois Bureau of Tourism Case Study at the end of this chapter captures a transition in the use of the Illinois Bureau of Tourism Hispanic website from a support function for more traditional advertising to its centerpiece. The San Jose Group (SJG) introduced this website change because of the double-digit growth of Spanish-dominant and bilingual Hispanic presence on the Internet and their need for more extensive content. To develop the www.disfrutaillinois.com (translation *enjoyillinois*.com) website as the central feature of its advertising communication, the SJG revamped its functionality, expanded relevant information on Illinois tourism, and deepened its emotional connection for potential Latino visitors.

Recognizing the cultural norm of Hispanics to travel with the family, SJG built their online campaign to appeal to the diverse interests of family members and the various personality types likely to be among them. On the new site, visitors could interact with moving Spanish-speaking characters portrayed in a family kitchen and click on whomever they choose to ask questions regarding their vacation trip interests. In order to provide additional culturally relevant support for Latinos who are not as used to online booking they created a mirror page on the site with hoteles. com. The agency used word of mouth and testimonials from famous Chicago Hispanics to drive Latinos to their site. The campaign and the new disfrutaillinois. com website proved successful with Hispanic families resulting in an increased use of the website, visits to the state of Illinois, and length of stay during those visits.

Many of the case studies in this book cited in previous chapters have used websites to support their more traditional communication media such as TV, radio, and print. This generally provides an interactive function which resonates with the social orientation of the Hispanic culture and creates more involvement with their Hispanic consumers over time. Case study examples are: Conill–Toyota Motor Sales and McDonald's–d expósito & Partners both at end of Chapter 5, Grupo Gallegos–California Milk Processor Board at end of Chapter 6, and CreativeOndemanD–Volkswagen of America and Lopez Negrete Communications–Walmart both at end of Chapter 7.

The Allstate Insurance Company–Captura Group Case Study at the end of this chapter provides an overview of the development of a long-term Hispanic online strategy. The objectives were to align a comprehensive culturally attuned educational and informational online initiative for partially acculturated Hispanics with the business objectives of Allstate. Allstate approached this project as a continuation of its years of involvement in the US Hispanic market and with the strong equity that its efforts with the Latino community had yielded. Based on extensive qualitative research with its Latino target, in-person interviews with key Allstate personnel, and competitive analysis of the online insurance market, the Captura Group developed the Spanish-language website MiAllstate.com. This Spanish-language website was created to be culturally relevant to the insurance needs of Spanish-preferred Latinos. It was integrated in a seamless way with the English-language website Allstate.com so that families which included both English and Spanish preferences could easily toggle back and forth between languages in their decision making about insurance.

The case study lays out the numerous ways that MiAllstate.com guided these partially acculturated Hispanics through the complex details involved in insurance decisions in a personal and interactive style. Importantly, MiAllstate.com offered the "quote your way" options on every page of the site providing Spanish-preferring Latino users choice in getting insurance quotes in Spanish online, from a call to a Spanish-speaking agent, or through contact with Allstate's customer service center in Spanish. After the launch of the MiAllstate.com campaign the website became the most-trafficked Spanish-language insurance website and generated strong Latino user engagement.

How Many Latinos Are Online?

While Hispanics have been eager to be online they still lag behind, even though gaps are narrowing. According to a study conducted by the Pew Hispanic Center in 2009,[1] 64% of Hispanics 18 years of age and older used the Internet compared with 78% of non-Hispanics. Clearly young people start using the Internet at much younger ages than 18, but data on younger users were not available at the time of this writing. It is to be expected that the difference between Latinos and non-Latinos in percentages of people 5 years of age and older that use the Internet should be smaller than the reported 14% difference above. This is not a trivial difference as Hispanics tend to be much younger than the rest of the population as we have seen in this book.

When it comes to Internet use based on nativity, the Pew Hispanic Center[2] reports that Hispanics 16 years of age and older born in the US are much more likely to use the Internet than foreign-born Hispanics, 85% versus 51%. Those differences are likely to be due to many factors including residential stability, language use, and disposable income. What this difference appears to make clear is that younger Latinos and those more established in the US are more likely to take advantage of the new technology.

AND THEY ARE MORE LIKELY TO PREFER THE ENGLISH LANGUAGE

And these online Hispanics are more likely to have English as their primary language. According to comScore enumeration data,[3] when Latinos were asked in 2010 "What language do you use most frequently when reading about news and current events, watching videos, and keeping up with friends?" 52% indicated English, 26.1% said both English and Spanish, and 21.9% answered Spanish.

In addition, according to a comScore Custom Study on the US Online Hispanic Market with Latinos 13 years of age and older,[4] when asked "What language do you prefer to use when browsing the Internet?" Latinos prefer English predominantly for browsing the Internet, except for the 21.9% that generally prefers Spanish in the segments described above. These trends are important because marketers ought to be aware that it is a relatively small segment of Hispanics online which prefers Spanish for browsing. That is not surprising, first because most of the content is in English, and second because most Spanish-language sites are generally not up to par with their English-language counterparts. The reader is warned

TABLE 9.1 Hours Using the Internet per Week in English and in Other Language

Hours/Week	Hispanic English Preference	Hispanic Spanish Preference
Other Language	1.52	6.34
English	15.65	6.65
Total	17.16	12.98

not to conclude from this that the online world is homogeneously effective for everyone. Cultural relevance is likely to play an important part in many Internet-related activities. Some of these will be highlighted later.

Once Online What Do Hispanics Do?

The Center for Hispanic Marketing Communication at Florida State University, in partnership with DMS Insights, has conducted a yearly study starting in 2006 comparing online behaviors of Hispanics, Asians, African-Americans, and non-Hispanic Whites. In 2009, this ongoing study also had the collaboration of Captura Group. The data presented here, unless otherwise identified as originating from another source, come from that ongoing Multicultural Marketing Study and specific reports and presentations can be found at http://hmc.comm.fsu.edu.

Use of the Internet

Every year Hispanics were asked about how many hours in an average week they use the Internet in English and in another language. Across the years we obtained very similar results. The findings of 2009 are given in Table 9.1.

What this table shows is that English-preferring Hispanics spend more hours per week online, on the average, than Hispanics who prefer to communicate in Spanish. Even those who prefer the English language spend some of their time online in another language, which we can reasonably assume is Spanish. Those Hispanics who prefer Spanish for communication split their time almost in equal halves between English and Spanish content. It is somewhat surprising that these Latinos who prefer Spanish spend less time online than their English-preferring counterparts. Perhaps more-acculturated Hispanics find more content online that is relevant to them, and/or perhaps they have generally more access. In general we know that less-acculturated Latinos tend to be less present online than those who are more acculturated. Figure 9.1, from 2009, shows that perhaps the main obstacle for

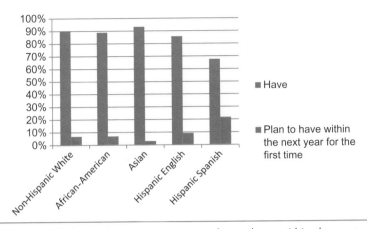

Figure 9.1 Have high-speed Internet access or plan to have within the next year for first time.

Spanish-preferring Hispanics to spend more time online is that they are less likely to have high-speed Internet access.

As can be seen in Figure 9.1, Spanish-preferring Hispanics have less high-speed Internet access, but also are more likely to say they plan to have it soon. As high-speed connections become more prevalent, the amount of time spent online is likely to also increase because of the multiple uses and types of content that can be accessed. Once one can watch movies and TV shows online because of high-speed connections, the Internet becomes more pervasive in the lives of consumers. Why are Spanish-preferring Hispanics less likely to have high-speed access? This is probably due to lower incomes and a higher likelihood to reside in rural or underserved Internet areas.

ONLINE PRESENCE

An interesting indicator of online participation is the degree to which Latinos share information online. Having a blog or a personal website can be seen as benchmarks of online involvement. In 2009 consumers were asked to tell if they have a blog, and if not if they plan to have one next year for the first time Figure 9.2.

The responses were surprising in that Asians and Hispanics who responded in English were more likely than anyone else to have a blog. And also very telling about aspirations is that Latinos who responded in Spanish were more likely than anyone else to state they plan to have one within the next year. The tendencies suggested by these data are evidence of the comparatively strong level of engagement of Latinos with the online world.

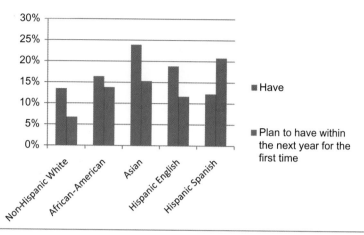

Figure 9.2 Have a blog or plan to have within next year for the first time.

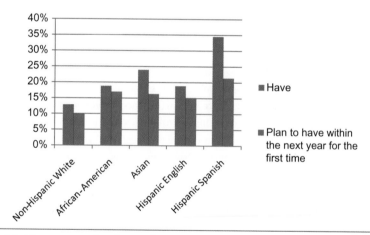

Figure 9.3 Have personal website of my own or plan to have within the next year for the first time.

Respondents were also asked if they have a "personal website of my own." Figure 9.3 contains the findings.

Consistent with the findings of previous years, in 2009 Hispanics who responded to the survey in Spanish were much more likely than any other cultural group to say they have a personal website of their own. It can be speculated that perhaps they interpreted the question to include having their presence on social networking sites that resemble websites. In any case, and taking the data at face value, we can see that these Spanish-preferring Latinos who are online seem eager to share their personal information online. This is why the Internet seems to be a technology of liberation. Precisely because many of the same people that are now

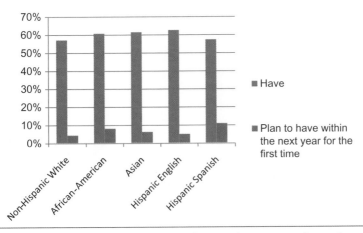

Figure 9.4 Have a personal profile in a social networking site or plan to have within the next year for the first time.

heavily online were deprived of the opportunity to express themselves just a few years ago.

Having a personal profile on a social networking site like MySpace or Facebook is another way of demonstrating online engagement. In 2009 respondents were also asked if they had a profile in a social networking website like MySpace or Facebook Figure 9.4.

These results show that having a profile in a social networking site is relatively homogeneous among cultural groups. Thus, having this type of online presence is not as strong a differentiator as having a blog or a website. It is also notable that Hispanics who answered in Spanish, and to some extent African-Americans, distinguish themselves for having the aspiration to have such a profile within the next year than the other cultural groups.

ECONOMIC ACTIVITY

Shopping, comparing, buying, and being influenced by the Internet are central elements of the online world. Respondents were asked how important is the Internet in influencing the products they buy on a scale of 0–5, 0 being not important at all and 5 being extremely important. Figure 9.5 shows that Asians and Hispanics who answered in Spanish in 2009 were most likely to be influenced in their shopping behavior.

It is also interesting to note that non-Hispanic Whites were less likely to say the Internet is as important to them in their buying behavior. That Latinos who responded to the survey in English were also relatively low in their reported influence of the Internet is surprising, particularly in comparison with their

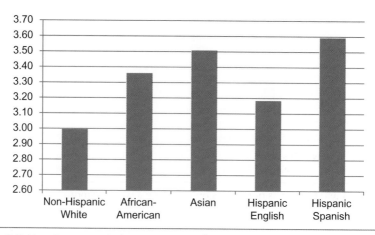

Figure 9.5 How important is the Internet in influencing the products you buy?

TABLE 9.2 Reactions to Advertising

Please Indicate How Strongly You Agree or Disagree with the Following Statements About Advertising (Top-2 Boxes)	Percent of Consumers	
	US Hispanic (%)	Non-Hispanic (%)
Expect advertising to be entertaining	48	39
Remember advertised products when shopping	35	22
Enjoy watching ads	31	19
Advertising helps me to choose products to buy my children	30	15
More inclined to buy from a company that sponsors events	26	14

Spanish-preferred counterparts. Generally, however, the tendency that emerging minorities are being the ones who appear to pay more attention to online information for their purchases suggests that these minorities are driving the online economy. Perhaps that is not yet the case in terms of volume, but definitely in terms of the importance attributed to the medium. Now, in terms of reactions to advertising, the June and October 2010 ComScore studies, cited earlier,[5] found that Hispanics online are more likely to have a more positive relationship with advertising than non-Hispanics (Table 9.2).

These ComScore findings interestingly make evident that online Hispanics, if not the vast majority of Hispanics, are less cynical and more welcoming of commercials messages. What makes this study stand out is that the responses are from Hispanics who are online, thus suggesting that they are more positively disposed to advertising than non-Hispanics. Interestingly, as we will see later, online Hispanics distinguish themselves in many online e-commerce activities.

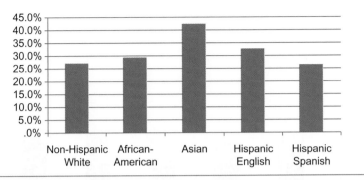

Figure 9.6 Buying products or services online twice a week or more frequent.

Respondents were asked in the 2009 study to tell about the frequency of what they do online. They were asked "approximately how often do you do each of the following online?" and they had the following options for their responses: Every day, Almost every day, A couple of times a week, Two to three times a week, Once a month, Less frequently than once a month, and Never. The following findings in Figure 9.6 are for frequencies of twice a week or more frequent. When it comes to buying products and services it can be observed in Figure 9.6 that Asians and Hispanics who answered in English are more likely than others to make purchases online at least twice a week.

It is surprising that non-Hispanic Whites are relatively low in this measure, very comparable to Hispanics who answered in Spanish. The argument that different cultural groups will eventually become like "everyone else," is contradicted by this data. If that were the case Hispanics who prefer English should exhibit behaviors similar to non-Hispanic Whites and that is not the case. It is to be expected that as Hispanics who still prefer Spanish become more acculturated they will become more similar to their English-preferring counterparts and increasingly dissimilar to non-Hispanic Whites.

Regarding researching products and services online, Asians and Hispanics do so at least twice a week in larger numbers than all other cultural groups, as can be seen in Figure 9.7.

And overall, all Hispanics and Asians are more likely to frequently engage in this activity than others. Another interesting measure that reflects comfort in the use of online services is the conduct of financial activities online. Asians and Hispanics who prefer English are more likely than anyone else to do this at least twice a week, as follows in Figure 9.8.

There appears to be some similarity among Asians and English-preferring Hispanics across several measures. These two groups appear to be more engaged with the online world than anyone else. In general we can see that emerging minorities are driving the online economy. Again, this may not be yet in terms of volume

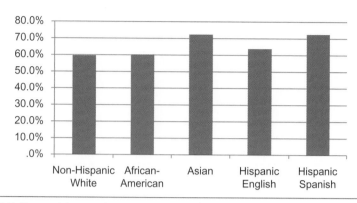

Figure 9.7 Researching products or services online at least twice a week.

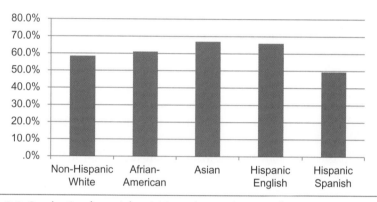

Figure 9.8 Conducting financial activities at least twice a week.

but definitely in terms relative to the size of their online population. Marketers ought to pay attention to the important opportunity they have to better position themselves among these mavens of new technology.

OTHER ONLINE ACTIVITIES

The data contained in this section are also from the 2009 study detailed earlier. The following findings also refer to activities conducted at least twice a week. Visiting social networking sites like MySpace or Facebook at least twice a week was at the time of the study more prevalent among Asians and Hispanics who prefer the English language as seen in Figure 9.9.

While the differences among the groups are not very large, the pattern of online involvement is consistent with the above findings. Respondents were asked to tell about the reasons they have for using social networking sites. Table 9.3 details some of the most popular reasons endorsed.

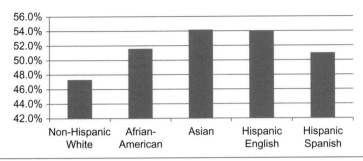

Figure 9.9 Visiting social networking sites like MySpace or Facebook at least twice a week.

TABLE 9.3 Reasons for Using Social Networking Sites

Reasons for Visiting Social Networking Sites	Non-Hispanic White (%)	African-American (%)	Asian (%)	Hispanic English (%)	Hispanic Spanish (%)
Connecting with family	30.7	29.4	30.5	34.9	43.6
Connecting with friends	43.0	46.0	46.0	43.4	42.7
Connecting with people that share my culture	9.3	20.2	17.3	14.0	28.2
Making new friends	15.0	27.0	22.3	22.0	25.9
Sharing my experiences	14.3	17.6	21.5	15.5	18.5
Sending messages	27.9	33.4	34.1	28.8	39.6
Chatting	19.2	24.8	25.1	21.3	30.2

Connecting with family is most common for Hispanics who prefer Spanish, followed by those Latinos who prefer English. While everyone endorses this reason, it is still more prevalent among Hispanics, thus corroborating that online or off-line Latinos are more family oriented. Connecting with friends is not a major differentiator but African-Americans and Asians have the lead on this area. Very interestingly Hispanics who prefer Spanish are most likely to use social networking sites to connect with culturally similar people. This is also a reason for many African-Americans and Asians, and not so much for Hispanics who prefer communicating in English. And this is the least-endorsed reason for non-Hispanic Whites. This tendency speaks of the way in which the Internet is allowing for connections that just a few years ago were impossible. The Internet, in social media in particular, is allowing for the perpetuation and elaboration of culture. Homophily in cultural terms is central to the social networks of people who share a cultural bond. In an interesting twist of historical trends, social media may constitute the first time in which people

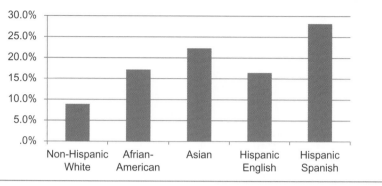

Figure 9.10 Percent indicating interest in online dating-related activities.

can reinforce their culture almost perpetually without having to abandon the culture of their forefathers. This trend is also reflected in the relative importance that emerging minorities place on making new friends online. As the proverb states "birds of a feather flock together." Sharing experiences is salient for Hispanics in general as is messaging and chatting. Social media is used for connecting with others and as we have seen some cultures value this attribute to a larger extent than others.

There are other areas in which Hispanics who prefer Spanish are more interested. For example, dating-related activities as seen in Figure 9.10.

This tendency is particularly interesting as it documents that Spanish-preferring Hispanics are more likely to look for romance online. This cannot be completely attributed to age as in this sample we found that Hispanics who prefer to speak Spanish are older than African-Americans, Asians, and Hispanics who prefer to communicate in English. It is perhaps that dislocation from physical social networks is being replaced by the online world to a larger extent for these less-acculturated consumers than for everyone else.

In an era when mobile phones have become ubiquitous and with the functionality of computers, consumers were asked approximately how many hours in an average week they spend using their cell phone for things other than speaking. We found that Hispanics in general, and African-Americans, spend more time using their mobile phone for other activities, as seen in Figure 9.11.

While the proportions of this type of use of mobile phones for texting, watching videos, or using the Internet are not known, this pattern is provocative and it echoes similar research that has shown that Hispanics are more likely to use their mobile devices for surfing the Web. According to 2010 data from the Pew Hispanic Center continuing a trend first identified in 2009 in research reported by the Center for Hispanic Marketing Communication at Florida State University, "minority Americans lead the way when it comes to mobile access—especially mobile access using handheld devices. Nearly two-thirds of African-Americans (64%) and Latinos (63%) are wireless Internet users."[6]

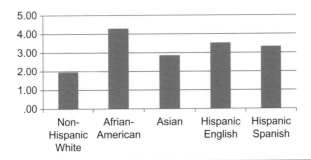

Figure 9.11 Hours per average week using the mobile phone for things other than talking.

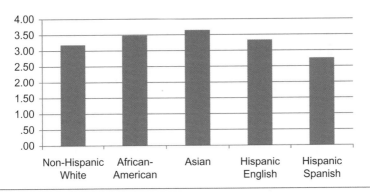

Figure 9.12 I am an expert Internet user.

The Experience of the Online World

Respondents were asked in the 2009 study to report on their online expertise and experience on a 6-point scale from strongly agree (5) to strongly disagree (0). When asked to agree or disagree with the statement "I am an expert Internet user," Hispanics who prefer Spanish were the least likely to agree with the statement as seen in Figure 9.12.

That is not a surprising finding but it corroborates that Spanish-dominant Latinos are relative newcomers to the medium. Lexicon Marketing identified the educational needs for Internet usage of these online Spanish-dominant Latinos. They developed a portal to facilitate their capabilities as described in Lexicon Marketing–MundosinBarreras.com Case Study at the end of Chapter 2. These same Spanish-preferred consumers are more likely to agree with the statement "My favorite websites have cultural elements that resonate with me" (Figure 9.13).

Marketers should take note that Latinos who prefer Spanish do benefit from websites that are more likely to reflect their culture. That trend also applies to other cultural groups to some extent, but definitely not to non-Hispanic Whites.

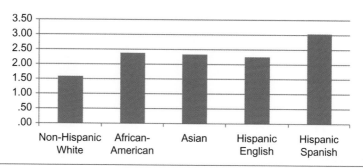

Figure 9.13 My favorite websites have cultural elements that resonate with me.

When asking only Latinos to agree or disagree with "The Spanish language websites I visit have excellent translations," Spanish-preferred Hispanics are more likely to agree with it (mean = 3.4) in comparison with English-preferring Latinos (mean = 2.54). Either English-speaking Latinos are more critical or Spanish-speaking Hispanics are thankful to just have their content in their native language, or both.

Spanish-preferring Latinos, however, do agree more than their English-speaking counterparts with "I would visit more Spanish language sites if they were of the same quality as English language ones" (means of 2.88 vs. 2.39 respectively). Thus indicating that to some extent even Spanish-speaking Hispanics realize that the localization of many Spanish-language websites lacks the quality of English-language versions.

Perhaps more important is that Spanish-speaking Latinos strongly endorse the idea that "A website directed to Hispanics cannot be just a translation but has to be culturally relevant" in comparison with their English-preferring counterparts (means of 3.87 vs. 3.21 respectively). This is a very important finding for marketers because it emphasizes that cultural relevance in websites is important to all Hispanics, but in particular it is more crucial for those who prefer the Spanish language.

Conclusion: Where Do We Go From Here

Latinos are aggressively embracing the virtual world of the Internet. In many areas they lead emerging minorities in their online participation. We have seen that the Internet not only offers opportunities to overcome social disparities, but it allows for the continuation of a culture in ways that were never possible before. Strong interest and participation in Web modalities that allow for interaction, such as blogs, websites, and social media, suggest that the creation and dissemination of thought and knowledge is a primary driver for people who in many cases were not able to manage their communications. Not that the Internet has only been a liberator for Hispanics but that Latinos have particularly benefited from it given their collectivist cultural tendency to share and comingle.

The future of the US is multicultural and Hispanics will have the huge responsibility of being one very large part of the economic engine that propels the country to better levels of existence and quality of life. As Hispanics capitalize on their new online freedoms, they will increasingly close the social and economic gap between themselves and the traditional majority that is now shrinking at a fast rate. All this is to the benefit of the future of the country.

Cross-border commerce and specialized approaches to reaching Latinos online will continue to evolve. Joe Kutchera in his recent book *Latino Link: Building Brands Online with Hispanic Communities and Content*[7] sets an important precedent in further capitalizing on the experience of marketers and researchers to make the Internet a more hospitable world for Hispanics.

The engine of commerce of the US will reside much more centrally on Latinos with their open disposition toward online shopping and their surging purchasing power. Not only will Hispanics be the producers but also the consumers that will drive the economy.

IMPLICATIONS FOR MARKETERS

■ Recognize the strong presence of Hispanics in the digital world as you develop your marketing communication plans. The online accessibility of this younger Latino market and the extent of their online purchasing behavior make them an attractive current and future target for your brand.

■ Realize that Latinos are everywhere online—exploring websites for information and making purchases, communicating on social networks, finding culturally relevant entertainment, and developing websites and blogs. Decide where and how you can best communicate with them digitally and learn about their lifestyles and needs.

■ Do not neglect Spanish-preferred Latinos who currently are online on both Spanish and English sites. They report that the Internet has a stronger influence on their purchases than other US population segments.

■ Be aware that online English-preferred Hispanics may use English sites more often than those in Spanish, but culturally relevant approaches matter to them.

■ Check on whether your website needs to be both in Spanish and English given the diverse language requirements of Latino families. However, remember direct translation pitfalls described in Chapter 4 and make sure that no matter which language you use that the sites are culturally relevant.

■ Take into account that Hispanics and minorities lead in mobile access including their use of cell phones for other than talking, and consider that potential in your communication outreach.

■ Realize that Latinos are finding their voices and forming communities and liaisons online. The extent to which your organization can support this social benefit will build an ongoing relationship with them and gain their loyalty to your brand.

■ Pay attention to acculturation needs of Hispanics as you formulate online strategy. Information, education, and guidance in critical areas such as health, finance, and growth opportunities can establish your brand's presence as a supporter for their successful integration.

CASE STUDY: THE SAN JOSE GROUP–ILLINOIS BUREAU OF TOURISM

Company
Illinois Bureau of Tourism (IBOT)

Advertising Agency
The San Jose Group (SJG)

Campaign/Advertising Title
Illinois. ¡Vive la emoción!

Intended Hispanic Consumers
Chicagoland Hispanics (1.9 million Hispanics, 19% of the Chicagoland DMA). Spanish-preferred 18–49 year olds, unacculturated and semi-acculturated.

Background
The IBOT has been committed to building awareness of the state's many destinations among Hispanic travelers for many years. The SJG has served as its Hispanic advertising agency to fulfill this mission since 2000.

In the early years, SJG had targeted the segment with traditional media, such as TV, radio and print, to raise broad-scale awareness of travel destinations in Illinois beyond the two main attractions with which the Hispanic market was most familiar—Navy Pier and Six Flags Great America. With a foundation of awareness in place, SJG and its client started paying attention to two main trends. First, they sensed that it was time to provide the target with more robust content about the specific destinations available for "staycation" planning. Second, they saw a growing number of Hispanics going online. Faced with conservative, state-funded budgets as a constant challenge, SJG decided to shift its marketing communications approach to the Web to get the most impact out of the marketing dollars.

The original Spanish-language website, www.DisfrutaIllinois.com ("EnjoyIllinois"), which SJG helped build for the first campaigns, provided a baseline source of content, but had truly functioned best as a support tool. While SJG created a culturally relevant site and periodically updated some of the content, it became apparent that the site's look and functionality would require significant planning and resources to serve as the centerpiece to IBOT's new campaigns. SJG would need to attract more robust traffic online and engage the Hispanic traveler in a more meaningful way than ever before.

Research
SJG conducted secondary research in three main areas: (1) Behaviors of the total online segment; (2) Behaviors of the Hispanic online travel market; and (3) Best practices of other state tourism boards targeting the Hispanic segment.

Through secondary research, SJG identified that among its main targets of Spanish-dominant and bilingual Hispanics, Internet use had seen double-digit growth in recent years, and 79% of online Hispanics were using the Internet to do product research to better inform purchase decisions. This supported the notion that more robust content on IBOT's site would potentially pave the way for future travel and transactions.

In SJG's research related to the online market, it found that online customers are typically defined by four dominant online consumer personalities, regardless of ethnic background. These four profiles have been outlined by FutureNow Inc., and derived from Myer-Briggs's personality profiles: amiable (personal, activity oriented), analytical (businesslike, detail oriented), expressive (personal, relationship oriented), and assertive (businesslike, power oriented). These profiles would be integral to SJG's redesign of the website and would allow the agency to align Illinois' hundreds of destinations with the kind of travelers they would most appeal to.

To compile a best practices analysis, SJG looked at 28 Convention and Visitors Bureau (CVB) websites in top US tourist destinations and top Hispanic DMAs to evaluate them based on their ability to connect with the four online personality types as well as features like transculturating content versus straight translation, similarities to the English site, Hispanic imagery, easy navigation, engaging interface, and the ability to make online reservations. This analysis showed that most other CVBs simply translated general market content to create a Spanish microsite, which provided the perfect opportunity for IBOT to differentiate itself in front of Hispanic travelers.

Cultural Insights

SJG found that the common denominator among Hispanic travelers (regardless of online personality profile) was that they are most likely to travel with family, so the content on the IBOT website would need to focus on family-friendly travel ideas. There was also a lack of awareness of Illinois' ties to Latino culture, so SJG wanted to find ways whenever possible to make that connection. Lastly, SJG knew the importance of word-of-mouth endorsements to the Hispanic market, so that drove the agency to find ways to secure endorsements for IBOT.

Expression of Insights in the Campaign

At the newly designed DisfrutaIllinois.com homepage, visitors are greeted by a real, modern home kitchen and two couples portraying the four online consumer personalities talking about travel desires. Each character appeals to one of the four profiles, offering event suggestions, top destinations in Illinois or the opportunity to book right away to help visitors navigate the website. There is also a little girl in the kitchen, who reaches out to kids visiting the site and directs them to a special children's section. The characters remain moving and interacting with visitors, never static, and suggest clicking on objects in the kitchen—a laptop, flowerpot, etc.—to see even more attractions and take one step closer to their destination. All of this engagement is communicated entirely in Spanish.

The new site also bundles Hispanic-relevant travel packages under themes like family getaways, romantic trips, and outdoor activities. Activities that are most appealing to Hispanic travelers are prioritized on the site, for example, water parks—one of the top attractions among Hispanic families in any state. A promotion and online quiz unveils the

(Continued)

Illinois Bureau of Tourism campaign—Illinois. ¡Vive la emoción!

parallels between Abraham Lincoln and Benito Juarez to establish Illinois' cultural ties to Hispanic heritage. The site also establishes word-of-mouth and third-party credibility by featuring famous Chicago Hispanics' testimonials on favorite destinations, including Telemundo anchor Tsi-tsi-ki Felix and Chicago White Sox manager Ozzie Guillen.

Lastly, although SJG recognized that online purchases are not yet prevalent for Hispanic Internet users, the agency wanted to try and stimulate and encourage online booking whenever possible. To that end, it secured a partnership between IBOT and Hoteles.com to build a unique, mirror page on the site so consumers can book overnight stays in Spanish. No other CVB in the US offers this feature.

Now that the site was complete, how would SJG drive traffic to Disfrutaillinois. com? Taking into consideration the budget, aside from radio mentions, a media relations campaign was the main driver of traffic to the website, positioning it as one of the primary resources for Hispanic travelers wanting to explore Illinois. Since Hispanics highly trust the accuracy of news media, SJG secured unpaid editorial coverage that featured top destinations throughout the state the entire family could enjoy and directed audiences back to DisfrutaIllinois.com for more information in-language.

Effect of the Campaign

A new, more interactive, and engaging DisfrutaIllinois.com improved the quality, length, and value of website visits from Hispanics. From 2008 to 2009, average page views per month increased 9%, average length of visit increased 202%, and repeat visitors increased by 61%. Lastly, SJG reached more than 7.8 million Hispanics through PR placements alone, spreading the word about IBOT's new website in a meaningful and credible way.

CASE STUDY: ALLSTATE INSURANCE COMPANY–CAPTURA GROUP

Company
Allstate Insurance Company

Agency
Captura Group

Background
The Hispanic online market represents a compelling opportunity for Allstate as a result of several market forces. First, Hispanics are the largest and fastest growing minority group in the US. The Hispanic online market has reached critical mass with most online Hispanics in their main household formation years, making them an ideal target for insurance products. Coupled with these attractive demographic characteristics, the Internet has become a critical channel in the insurance purchase decision process for many consumers. What is more, Allstate holds a formidable position to capitalize on the Hispanic online market opportunity. With over 10 years committed to Hispanic marketing and outreach, Allstate enjoys strong brand recognition among Hispanics and boasts a powerful network of Hispanic agents across the country.

In an effort to serve the customer how, when, and where they choose to be served, Allstate engaged Captura Group to spearhead a research-based project that led to the development and execution of the company's Hispanic online strategy.

Intended Hispanic Consumers/Campaign Objectives
The overall objective of the campaign was to develop a long-term, comprehensive Hispanic online strategy that balanced Allstate's business objectives with Hispanic consumer needs. Specific campaign objectives included:
1. *Deliver a best-in-class, culturally relevant educational online experience for partially acculturated Hispanics.*
2. *Generate qualified Web traffic, strong user engagement, and top search engine positioning while driving sales.*
In order to guide and inform the Hispanic online strategy, Allstate and Captura Group leveraged a research-based approach consisting of the following research components:
▪   Focus groups with online Hispanics to identify user needs.
▪   In-person interviews with key Allstate personnel across all functional areas to understand objectives and goals.
▪   Quantitative and qualitative Hispanic online insurance market analysis including a competitive analysis to understand the market landscape.

Research
Captura Group's research methodology included focus groups, stakeholder interviews, and a comprehensive market analysis. They conducted focus groups with strategic Hispanic online segments in multiple cities. They ensured that Allstate's target Hispanic online consumer was represented in the groups through segmenting not only by fundamental demographic and acculturation variables, but also by online experience. Captura Group spent several days at Allstate's headquarters interviewing stakeholders to understand the company's business objectives and leveragable assets.

(Continued)

Additionally, to gain an understanding for the competitive Hispanic online insurance market, we analyzed leading insurance websites from both a qualitative and quantitative perspective.

Cultural Insights

The findings of each research component brought a compelling story to life, which was instrumental in developing a Hispanic online strategy for Allstate that has proved to be successful. The research illuminated the following key findings:

1. *There is a general lack of understanding about insurance among online Hispanics and a culturally relevant approach is critical to consumer education.*
   Most people, regardless of background, are not really sure how insurance works or what kind of coverage they need. Our research indicated that for Hispanic consumers, this reality can be even more evident. In addition, we found that to successfully educate Hispanics about insurance, a culturally relevant approach is critical. Hispanics approach insurance with cultural dispositions that are different from the general market and these differences must be addressed. For example, we found that in many Latin-American countries, auto insurance is not as common as it is in the US and, in many, it is not the law. Furthermore, for Hispanics, the main value offered by insurance is the protection of family as opposed to the protection of financial assets.

2. *Agents play a critical role in the insurance purchase process for Hispanics.*
   Culturally, Hispanics tend to value interpersonal relationships and make decisions based on the recommendations of family, friends, and, in the case of insurance, trusted and recommended insurance agents. Additionally, online Hispanics, within Allstate's target segment, tend to be relatively novice Internet users. As a result, they do not consider the Internet as a primary source of information for researching or purchasing insurance. With that being said, Captura's research did indicate that online Hispanics would consider quoting insurance online, and value the option of contacting a Hispanic agent or talking with a Spanish-speaking representative on the phone.

3. *Online Hispanics make purchase decisions collectively and, in many cases, require both English and Spanish to do so.*
   Captura's research confirmed that Hispanics tend to make insurance purchase decisions collectively. In addition, they found that language preferences within Hispanic households may vary with older Hispanics tending to prefer Spanish and younger Hispanics being more bilingual or English preferring. As a result, Captura found that online Hispanics make insurance decisions as a family unit and often require critical sales or marketing information to be available in both English and Spanish.

4. *Allstate held a formidable position in the Hispanic online market.*
   Captura's in-person interviews with Allstate stakeholders revealed that Allstate was well positioned to succeed in the Hispanic online market. First, they found that Allstate had a rich heritage of investing in the Hispanic community and, as a result, holds tremendous brand equity among Hispanics. Also, Allstate had a strong national Hispanic advertising platform with the ability to support Spanish-preferring Hispanics through their customer service centers and national Hispanic agent network. In addition to a strong Hispanic presence, Allstate also boasted a strong

online platform. Allstate.com offered deep content and many advanced features and functionality that could be easily adapted for the Hispanic market.
5. *No insurance company offered a best-in-class Hispanic online program.*
Captura conducted comprehensive research on the Hispanic online insurance market to understand and assess the competitive landscape. We looked at quantitative data to understand Hispanic traffic levels to leading insurance websites. In addition, we performed a qualitative heuristic analysis of Spanish-language insurance websites to measure their quality and depth for Hispanic users. This analysis pointed to the fact that no leading insurance company had a dominant position in the Hispanic online market. Specifically, we concluded that Spanish-language insurance websites were limited in their content, depth, features, and cultural relevance and that no one company dominated from a Hispanic traffic perspective.

Expression of Insights in the Campaign

The research findings were instrumental in the development of a long-term, comprehensive Hispanic online strategy that balances Allstate's business objectives with Hispanic consumer needs. The outcome of the strategy was the development of MiAllstate.com (Allstate's Spanish-language website) with additional enhancements to Allstate.com (Allstate's English-language website), to achieve the objectives set forth above. Specifically, the campaign strategy consisted of the following elements:

1. *Cultural relevance*
   In order to educate and connect emotionally with online Hispanic consumers, MiAllstate.com is culturally relevant. We leveraged the findings from research to develop imagery and content to resonate with the unique cultural identity of Hispanics in the US and address their specific needs as it relates to insurance. The site provides insurance information in a simple and straightforward manner and stresses the importance of insurance for families. In addition, Allstate's involvement with the Hispanic community, including the company's sponsorship of the Mexican national soccer team, is featured prominently on MiAllstate.com.

2. *Quote your way*
   Our findings demonstrated that although Hispanics are open to using the Internet to research and quote insurance, many prefer to do business directly with a Spanish-speaking agent or customer service representative. As a result, we developed a "quote your way" module that provides Spanish-speaking consumers' flexibility and choice when it comes to quoting insurance. Users of MiAllstate.com can quote insurance online in Spanish, easily contact a Spanish-speaking Allstate agent, or call Allstate's customer service center in Spanish. The quote your way module is prominently displayed on the homepage of MiAllstate.com and on all interior pages providing a clear, intuitive call-to-action to purchase insurance from Allstate. Furthermore, a specialized "quote your way" landing page was developed to support marketing campaigns.

3. *Spanish-language educational content and interactive tools*
   To address the need for quality Spanish-language educational insurance information, MiAllstate.com contains comprehensive, culturally relevant educational content about insurance. The content is structured as an easy-to-use insurance guide and walks Hispanic consumers through the insurance process in a friendly and

(Continued)

Allstate Insurance Company—MiAllstate.com (Allstate's Spanish-language website).

approachable manner. The site also includes several interactive Spanish-language features to educate Hispanics about insurance including:

a. CoberTOUR^{SM}—Interactive Video Guide About Insurance
   CoberTOUR^{SM} is a dynamic, culturally relevant interactive video guide about insurance. In a very personal and culturally relevant way, the tool takes users through the complexity of insurance using "real people language" and personal scenarios while providing customized coverage recommendations. The Hispanic video hosts portray realistic personas and give users clear calls-to-action to buy insurance throughout the experience. And at any time, consumers have a "quote your way" choice to contact an Allstate agent in their community who speaks their language, call Allstate directly via a toll-free number, or quote online in Spanish. CoberTOUR^{SM} provides Hispanics a personal touch, while maintaining their anonymity in the online environment. This personal touch is crucial in providing the Hispanic consumer with an inviting online experience. CoberTOUR^{SM} is prominently placed on MiAllstate.com and designed to help Hispanics through the process of shopping for insurance.

b. Spanish–English Insurance Glossary
   MiAllstate.com also features a Spanish–English insurance glossary. Insurance has a unique nomenclature, which makes the process confusing for those that are not comfortable with it, especially if they are fluent in English. The Spanish–English glossary provides key insurance terms in both languages and clear terminology definitions in Spanish.

c. Insurance Calculators
   To help Hispanics make educated decisions about insurance, MiAllstate.com makes available 11 interactive Spanish-language insurance calculators. These calculators prove to be invaluable in helping inform key insurance purchase decisions.

d. Educational Insurance Article RSS feed
Another important educational feature of the MiAllstate.com website is a series of Spanish-language, culturally relevant educational articles available via RSS. Four articles are published every month, which cover a wide range of topics that are relevant to Hispanic consumers in a friendly, lifestyle tone. These topics speak to the hearts of Hispanics and touch on subjects such as retirement planning, protection of property and family, as well as auto and recreational vehicle insurance.

e. Teen Driving Section
Comprehensive culturally relevant section of MiAllstate.com dedicated to providing parents with information about communicating with teens about safe driving. The teen driving section of MiAllstate.com also includes a "Parent/ Teen" contract that can be downloaded from the site.

4. *Integration between MiAllstate.com & Allstate.com*
To address family bilingualism and the fact that many Hispanics would use both Allstate's English and Spanish sites, Captura executed a "sister site" strategy in the development of MiAllstate.com. Allstate's English site, Allstate.com and Spanish site, MiAllstate.com, are closely integrated to facilitate a seamless user experience for bilingual Hispanic families. Integration between the sites is achieved by using a consistent design and information architecture, while preserving cultural relevance on the Spanish site. In addition, clear access to each version of the site is provided through a link on the top, global navigation. Allstate.com users can quickly access MiAllstate.com and vice versa. An additional integration tactic that we employed is bi-directional toggle functionality, which allows users to toggle between similar English and Spanish pages, a feature especially useful for bilingual families.

Effect of the Campaign

Allstate's research-driven Hispanic online strategy has successfully achieved the objectives of the campaign set forth above.

Since the sites launch in January 2008, MiAllstate.com has emerged as the best-in-class, culturally relevant, educational Spanish-language insurance website. In 2008, MiAllstate.com was the most-trafficked Spanish-language insurance website and generated strong user engagement, top search engine rankings, and drove incremental sales for Allstate. The following figures demonstrate the successful business results of the campaign against leading Spanish-language insurance websites.

Competitive Qualitative Site Analysis of Leading Spanish-Language Insurance Sites

Site Feature	MiAllstate.Com	Competitor 1	Competitor 2	Competitor 3
Cultural relevance	5	4	4	2
Content depth	5	5	3	4
Educational content	5	3	3	2
Transaction flexibility	4	4	2	2
Total site quality	19	16	12	10

Source: Captura Group Subjective Heuristic Review on January 12, 2009, Scale 1–5

(*Continued*)

2008 Market Share Among Leading Spanish-Language Insurance Sites

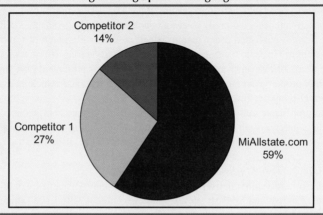

Competitor 2
14%

Competitor 1
27%

MiAllstate.com
59%

Source: Compete.com, 2008 total unique visitors, Competitor 3 not included as data not available.

Search Engine Ranking for Keyword "Seguro de Auto" (Auto Insurance) among Leading Spanish-Language Insurance Sites

Keyword	MiAllstate.com	Competitor 1	Competitor 2
Google	1st	2nd	4th
Yahoo	2nd	NA	NA
MSN	5th	1st	NA
ASK	1st	2nd	4th

Google, Yahoo, MSN, and ASK, Competitor 3 not included as data not available.

End Notes

[1] Gretchen Livingston, *The Latino Digital Divide: The Native Born Versus the Foreign Born.* Washington, DC: Pew Hispanic Center, July 28, 2010.

[2] Ibid.

[3] Presentation of Josh Chasin, Chief Research Officers of comScore to AdTech 2010 in New York City, entitled "Strategies for Advertising Online to US Hispanics: What the Data Tells Us."

[4] Ibid.

[5] *Source*: comScore Custom Study on the US Online Hispanic Market, June and October 2010, persons age 13+.

[6] *Source*: Pew Research Center Report: "More Cell Phone Owners Use an App for That: 59% of All Adult Americans Go Online Wirelessly," July 7, 2010: http://pewresearch.org/pubs/1654/wireless-internet-users-cell-phone-mobile-data-applications. The reader should keep in mind that going online wirelessly according to this study means accessing the Web from any wireless device which could be a mobile phone, a laptop, or other mobile device.

[7] Joe Kutchera, *Latino Link: Building Brads Online with Hispanic Communities and Content.* Ithaca, NY: Paramount Market Publishing, Inc., 2011.

Chapter 10

LATINO CONSUMERS AND THE FUTURE OF US MARKETING

Writing at the end of 2010 the authors contemplate a challenging opportunity for marketers in the several decades to come. The strong, undeniable Hispanic presence in the US should not be perceived as a burden, but as a contributing element to our country's continuing path to innovation and leadership. It will be the fortunate historical development of this young and vibrant cultural group that will inject new vigor into the country. Indeed, the US would be weaker without the energy and entrepreneurship of its stock of Latino immigrants.

Many who have resented the growth of this emerging population will actually benefit from it. Retiring baby boomers will be able to sustain some of their lifestyle in retirement because of the energy of emerging Hispanics. Those marketers that had thought that the Latino market was just a passing historical trend will see their market share and profits decided precisely by these eager consumers. Politicians will strive even harder to speak some Spanish to ingratiate themselves with this deciding constituency. We see trends that will accelerate the importance of the contributions of Hispanics to the greatness of the USA.

Below are trends from preceding chapters that serve as conclusions to this book. These trends paint a picture of the vibrant Hispanic consumer segment which will strongly influence the future of successful marketing in this country.

365

Youth and Fast Growth

As we have shown in this book the youth and family orientation of Hispanics are key engines in the importance of US Latinos to marketers. They represent an important part of the population growth of the country because Latino values are still to have children and enjoy family. They represent a very strong part of the base of the labor force, and clearly of the consumer base. Further, Hispanics are very young. They are about 10 years younger than their non-Hispanic counterparts (27 vs. 37 median age) so they are concentrated in the ages in which they develop their loyalties to brands and ideas. They represent the future, not only in terms of market size but also in terms of the bottom line.

And just being young is not by itself what makes these consumers unique. It is also their youth, their cultural ancestry, and their emerging identity as they develop a new sense of who they are by being here in the US. In all phenomena there are independent and interaction effects. The interaction effect of being young and Latino and also in the process of creating a new identity makes a distinctive difference in marketing. It is imperative for the marketer to understand how this interaction effect takes place and how it can be leveraged to uniquely connect with this important segment of the population.

A More Diversified Cultural Group

While Latinos in general will exhibit youthfulness and still a preference for family life, they will become more diversified due to differences in lifestyle most fundamentally. While most Hispanics will continue to be largely from Mexico, the complexity of the life paths they choose will make them more multifaceted. Gone will be the days in which you could target the majority of Latinos by placing ads on Spanish-language media. Media planning will require more sophistication and knowledge. Still, cultural insights continue to make Hispanics a market, and will likely be effective in connecting with large clusters of Hispanics because of their common cultural upbringing and ancestry.

The choices of lifestyles and the destinies of Hispanics in the US will continue to diversify but will include the influence of their heritage. Thus, while marketers will have to be more specific in reaching out to Hispanics, they will still be able to capitalize on central tendencies of their heritage. That includes the notions of an orientation to the present, collectivism, living with nature as opposed to controlling nature, and many other cultural themes we have discussed in this book.

Culture at the Center Stage

The decade of the 2010s will be the decade of cultural marketing. More anthropologists will be hired to work in marketing organizations. Marketers will realize that asking direct questions from consumers is unlikely to render exciting and promising ideas. It will be the discovery of Latino cultural trends that are included in their lifestyles that will guide the success of marketing efforts. How are values and belief systems reflected in everyday life? Watching consumers behave and consume will guide how the marketer thinks about what will resonate with Hispanics.

It should be obvious that marketing to Latinos is not the only area where cultural marketing will thrive, but Hispanics will exemplify the importance of the trend. They have been identified as a cultural group, and that is something that is more difficult to attribute to other groups in the population, as strange as that may be.

The new generation of marketers will be observing more carefully what people buy, how items are used and worn, and the symbolic use of material and nonmaterial effects. The meaning of using and owning will take new life among marketers. Long and protracted questionnaires will be replaced by proactive relationships with Latino consumers and with all consumers.

Technology and Cultural Change

The outstanding technosocial revolution that the world is experiencing is being reflected by Latinos in the US. As they have adopted new online communication technologies at a faster pace than others, they represent an important indicator of social trends. The adoption of new technologies for expression is an inherent part of the new identity of US Hispanics. Technological innovativeness will create an explosion of Latino expression. As Hispanics are generally expressive, new media will present opportunities for that expression to be more widely shared and more widely emulated.

The influence of Latinos will be felt more strongly for many years to come as they capitalize on technological innovation to make their feelings and opinions known. Marketers will have to pay increased attention to what all customers say online, but in particular Hispanics because they are likely to have a larger share of trendsetters in their ranks.

Crossover Synergies

As we discussed in several sections of this book, the influence of Latinos on the overall culture is likely to increase substantially. It is also likely that Hispanics will adopt more consumer habits from non-Hispanics. This hybridization of culture will make marketing more interesting.

That is why when segmenting, it will be important to segment the marketing target as a whole, and not by ethnicity or culture, but overlaying culture as an important part of what characterizes the orientations of consumers. In this fashion the marketer may discover that common elements of behavioral orientations, tastes, and preferences may be shared by members of different cultures to different extents. A segment that values family as the core of decision making may be strongly populated by Latinos but also by others who share the orientation. That is something we have missed by creating separate segmentations. Further, marketers can more effectively capitalize on shared cultural elements as opposed to having to look at cultural groups as completely separate entities.

Further, as the Latino population of the US continues to increase in size and influence, its impact will be felt in most aspects of life. While current projections by the US Census Bureau and others are that Hispanics will be about 30% of the US population by 2050, these are likely very conservative estimates. Just consider a single cultural group that is a third or more of the population. Latinos will flavor many aspects of life, not only the food we eat. Sheer numbers will energize further change.

A Shift in the Unit of Observation and Analysis

As social media has increasingly demonstrated to marketers, consumers are not isolated entities. It has been somewhat bizarre that we look at consumers as individual actors when the very nature of being human is a collective experience. Without social contact humans are not humans and without social contact consumers are not consumers. Social interaction dictates the outcomes of consumer behavior. This is further accentuated among Latinos who yearn for social contact in a more pervasive way.

We need to start analyzing consumer behavior as group behavior, and therefore our unit of observation should also be shifted to the group. Studying families, friends, acquaintances, affinity groups, and other reference groups will be crucial going forward in the study of consumer behavior. More analytics, like network analysis, will need to be used and developed in order to understand how groups behave. We were impressed years ago by a reference in one of the versions of the book *Diffusion of Innovations* by Everett M. Rogers, that stated that it is weird that social scientist still study individuals when humans are social entities. It included the metaphor that what we do is like what a biologist would be doing if he or she puts a rabbit in a meat grinder in order to study its biology.

We cannot afford to put consumer groups in meat grinders when trying to study their consumer behavior. We need to study consumer behavior as what it is: a social activity. Who talks to whom is a lot more powerful than what individuals report as their sources of influence in a standard survey.

Acknowledging the Supernatural

Latino consumers, like most consumers, are not strictly rational or irrational, they simply put together their ideas about the world depending on many sources of influence in their social milieu and their upbringing. Understanding beliefs about the supernatural and magical thinking can help piece together many behaviors that mystify marketers. Wishes, beliefs, dreams, and aspirations are weaved together on the bases of multiple influences, some of which are metaphysical. Marketers need to understand how these shape human behavior, and specifically consumer behavior.

How do beliefs about nature, and what is beyond nature, affect how consumers think and feel about their existence and role in society? How are consumer orientations and interactions affected by belief systems? How are virtual groups of consumers influenced by their common beliefs in both the physical and metaphysical? Marketers cannot afford to step back from these challenging questions. They are drivers of motivation which affect their consumer behaviors and their relationship to brands.

Gender Role Relations

We have talked about Machismo, Marianismo, and Androgyny. As Latinos develop a new identity, it is important to understand how ancestral tendencies of gender domination are changing and evolving. Is androgyny an emerging trend resulting from the two extremes of machismo and marianismo? How does that affect decision making and consumer choices? How do family dynamics change as values associated with role relations change? These are important ideas to explore in a continued effort to master cultural adaptation and change in a new society. Marketers' awareness of the likelihood of change in gender roles and self-perceptions related to gender is another area of sensitivity for understanding the evolving realities of Latino consumers.

Leadership Trends

As Latinos become more entrenched in US society, their leadership skills will evolve and influence the rest of society. More Hispanics will claim leadership roles in the near future and that will have important implications for marketers in promoting the desirability of their products and services. Understanding polymorphic leadership will become more important as Latinos tend to display this style and to assume it as well to a larger extent than non-Hispanics.

Online and off-line more Hispanics will amass leadership characteristics and will expand their following. Politicians will need to better understand how to communicate with these new influentials. Marketers will also need to improve how they relate to leaders in social networks, and how to assess their impact on even wider groups of consumers.

Use of Time and Space

As part of cultural understanding, marketers will also need to master how different ways of using space and time affect consumer behavior and reactions to marketing offerings. Time and space are fundamental aspects of how people relate to each other. Latino polychronism is symptomatic of service expectations that need to be met.

Marketers will benefit from studying how consumption timing affects the cycle of purchases. They will also benefit from understanding how spatial relationships influence affect and feelings about brands. This book provides guidance for marketers in understanding time and space differences which tend to be particular to Latino consumers as well as research guidance to help unlock cultural tendencies related to particular brands.

Cross-Border Marketing

As brands transcend borders, marketers will be able to capitalize on how Latinos acquire brand loyalties both there and here. Brand perceptions do not have borders but physical products do. As these obstacles are removed, consumers see a more seamless universe of options and consumer interaction across borders. Relatives and friends can give presents across borders and can influence loyalties over time.

The tendency of brands to cross borders will increase as the Internet becomes a platform for sharing and mutual influence. That is why physical borders are becoming obsolete at least in the realm of marketing. Tearing those walls may still be in the distant future, but the psychological and social borders are falling very fast.

Sustainability and Green Consumer Behavior

Latinos will influence the "greening of America" because of their cultural tendency of living in harmony with nature. The conservation of the natural environment is one of the top-of-mind priorities of many Hispanics. In our Multicultural Marketing studies cited in this book we have found that Hispanics who prefer the Spanish language are more likely than anyone else (3.6 in a 0–5 scale) to endorse the notion that "I try to always choose an environmentally friendly option in everything I buy." Hopefully, as Latinos acculturate they will not forget their environmental friendliness. If this attitude is sustained, then Hispanics will likely lead in this important arena. Marketers then will have to look at ways to make their offerings more balanced with the environment and in turn do a better job in serving consumers. As John Gerzema in one of TED's talks[1] argues that value-driven consumption is an asset to marketers as this establishes more long-lasting and beneficial relationships.

Marketing, Empathy, and Ethics

The ethics of modern marketing call for attention to the needs and wishes of consumers as opposed to imposing on them. It just makes business sense to create and reinforce consumer relationships that are based on respect. Cultural sensitivity as addressed in this book is part of that respect.

Hispanic marketing done well should be ethical by definition. Good Hispanic marketing seeks to enhance the lives of consumers. An attempt to better understand Hispanic consumers shows respect for them.

As marketers conduct market research to understand consumers in more depth, and specifically Latino consumers in this case, they get closer to them. Qualitative research is particularly productive in creating closeness. We have heard marketers conducting research with Latinos state their emotional engagement with them when visiting their homes and have seen their faces and expressions in the back rooms of focus-groups facilities. This emotion is associated with a deeper human understanding of the consumer. A marketer who understands the consumer is more likely to do a good communication job, and to think more carefully on how these consumers can better benefit from their products and services. It is symptomatic that the time is ripe for this empathy development. At the 2010 ANA conference in Orlando, Florida,[2] the central theme was purpose-driven marketing which basically endorses a return to basics by deeply engaging consumers and creating a corporate culture of giving back. Times are changing and they are ripe for empathic marketing.

As we discussed, anthropological and qualitative research provides for greater insights. This type of research gives opportunities to observe and live with Latino consumers and becomes a great vehicle for understanding consumers. Market immersion experiences allow the marketer to see, smell, touch, hear, and taste Hispanic culture. These experiences typically include home visits, observation of food preparation, talks with the family, consuming meals at restaurants, and store observations and checks where Hispanic consumers live. There is no better way to prepare the marketer to do a good marketing job and to also do "good" while marketing.

A related approach to getting the marketer closer to the Latino consumer is to create video documentaries based on home and community explorations. These documentaries have great impact on upper management. Such audiovisual tools also help create a deeper commitment to a marketing effort. Marketers cannot stay in their office with spreadsheets and banners[3] and assume they know their consumers.

Marketing is returning to the village that gave rise to marketing but now is at a much larger scale. In that old village the marketer and the consumer interacted as part of a community. Now the village is too large physically for that contact, but new communication technologies and research tools allow for that closeness to be reestablished. Social networks are now an example of how a marketer cannot anymore get away with alienating even one consumer because the word of a faulty product or bad service spreads quickly. They are also an avenue for positive news to move out among social connections. In particular, Latino consumers are prone to share their experiences and that is a threat and also a promise. Marketers that are responsive and attuned to consumer needs do well in the new "global village."[4]

Conclusions

Culture and change are synonymous. By our nature as social beings we are constantly writing and rewriting the essence of who we are individually and as a group. This book on Hispanic marketing has alerted marketers to the shared trends that link Hispanics as a cultural target and to the dynamics of being Latino in the US that increasingly segment it. Hispanics are an important part of who we are as a nation by their size, age, family orientation, and eagerness to contribute to the success of this country. Culturally, they add a new and exciting edge to our national identity. Economically, they bear much of the burden of carrying us forward. Politically, they will shape our future.

Marketers who intend to be successful in their field need to recognize the ongoing cultural shifts in the US and particularly in the largest ethnic segment, the Latino market. This means a marketing mind-shift from a homogenous US focus to a highly segmented national panorama. The good news for marketers is that Hispanics cling to their heritage which makes them approachable as a culture, the challenge is that Latinos are changing their lifestyles as they grapple with what it takes to be successful in the US.

The issue for marketers is both on an individual professional level and on a company-wide level. In order to develop brand relationships with Latino consumers, companies need to move closer to Hispanics internally in their staffing and their cultural awareness, and externally in their culturally informed marketing research and communication. This continuous attention to Latino consumers which is greatly enhanced by technology and the Internet is the only way for brands to stay relevant and committed in their relationships with Hispanics. Hispanics expect and reward brands for their commitment, and notice and appreciate marketing attention with their loyalty.

This book, *Hispanic Marketing: Connecting with the New Latino Consumer*, contributes tools to marketers for understanding and communicating with Latinos. The 25 case studies in this book illustrate how some of the leading companies in the US, their Hispanic agencies, and marketing support services have effectively communicated with US Hispanics. The time is now for marketers to not only learn from these resources, but also find ways to continue to grow in their understanding and relevant communication with this exciting and complex consumer segment. Developing relationships with Latino consumers can be an enjoyable, mind-opening, and career-enriching experience for marketers personally, a competitive advantage for their companies, and a contribution to Hispanics as they continuously enrich who we are together as a nation.

IMPLICATIONS FOR MARKETERS

- Recognize that cultural marketing is the norm of this country and adapt personally and professionally to a more complex and continuously changing consumer panorama.
- Become informed about cultural trends of the Hispanic market as well as other key cultural groups in the US through qualitative research, ethnography, literature, music, and cultural immersion with diverse ethnic markets.
- Combine information about Hispanic consumers directly available on the Internet with culturally sensitive qualitative and quantitative research for your particular brand to inform marketing strategy and communication campaigns.
- Make a continuous effort on a company-wide and individual marketing level to stay current and connected with the changing and complex Latino market.
- Take into account that Latinos are influencing others in the US in a crossover cultural effect. Segment the overall market by lifestyle, and other relevant factors with a cultural overlay to understand how these influences are spreading.
- Develop your cultural marketing and brand relationships with Latinos as well as other cultural groups so that a lasting brand commitment is established and ongoing mutually respectful and beneficial relationships are developed.
- Establish your company, marketing, and professional identities as culturally aware and connected to the influences and trends affecting the US, and to those groups particularly Latinos, which are at the leading edge moving into the next decade.

End Notes

[1] See http://www.ted.com/talks/lang/eng/john_gerzema_the_post_crisis_consumer.html.

[2] See the *Advertising Age* article published on October 18, 2010, with the title "Purpose-driven marketing all the rage at ANA." ANA stands for Association of National Advertisers.

[3] Banners are cross-tabulations that most marketers use to see the numeric results of their surveys and studies.

[4] A phrase borrowed from the book by Marshall McLuhan and Bruce R. Powers, *The Global Village: Transformations in World Life and Media in the 21st Century*. This book was published by Oxford University Press in 1992, after McLuhan died in 1980, and it assembles many of the ideas in his prior work.

About the Authors

Dr. Felipe Korzenny joined Florida State University (FSU) in the fall of 2003. Until then he was principal and cofounder of Cheskin. At FSU he founded and directs the first Center for Hispanic Marketing Communication in the US. This center prepares students to serve the Hispanic marketing industry, conducts research projects, and produces publications to further the understanding of Hispanic consumer behavior: http://www.hmc.comm.fsu.edu.

Before merging his company with Cheskin in 1999 he was president and CEO of Hispanic and Asian Marketing Communication Research (H&AMCR), the company he founded in 1984 to assist Fortune 500 companies in understanding and communicating effectively with the Hispanic and Asian markets in the US and abroad. Now at FSU he continues to conduct research and consults with major US corporations on how to best establish consumer relationships with US Hispanics. He is particularly well known in the industry for the consumer experience insights he has helped generate to position successful products in the US Hispanic market. He has established research traditions and trained many researchers in ethnographic, qualitative, and most quantitative methodologies. A social scientist by training, Felipe has a critical academic perspective combined with a strong business practice.

The experience Dr. Korzenny includes: Food and beverages, finance/banking/credit/insurance, telecommunications, digital technology, entertainment, media, social services, health, education, automotive, and real estate. His contributions have ranged from product development to the elicitation of insights for positioning and to the development of marketing strategy.

Dr. Korzenny holds an M.A. and a Ph.D. from Michigan State University in Communication Research, where he was also a faculty member, and later was member of the faculty of San Francisco State University. He has published six books and almost a hundred research publications dealing with communication and culture.

He is an outstanding and also a distinguished alumni of Michigan State University. He is the first recipient of the Hill Library HispanSource 2005 Award for Outstanding Achievement in Hispanic Marketing Research. Dr. Korzenny is a prominent speaker at nationwide symposiums and conferences on Hispanic markets. His full vita can be found at www.korzenny.com/FKresume.htm, and his blog is at http://felipekorzenny.blogspot.com.

Dr. Betty Ann Korzenny's international experience and passion for cultural understanding have shaped her personal and professional life. She is a native of Troy, New York, and has spent more than 17 years of living and working in other cultures outside of the US. She has pursued her interests in intercultural communication, education and research in Germany, Nigeria, Italy and Mexico, and has worked in the US Hispanic Market beginning with her early research at Michigan State University in the 1970s.

She received her undergraduate degree from Vassar College, and her M.A. and Ph.D. from Michigan State University, all in education. While pursuing doctoral studies at Michigan State University she expanded her cultural interests to include the role of management in bringing about cultural change and innovation in organizations. She lived and worked as a director of research and development in the communication research wing of one of the largest advertising companies in Mexico.

Returning to the US in the 1980s she held key management responsibilities in major corporations for organizational and management development, employee education, and internal communications. She provided leadership in the introduction of organizational innovations, particularly those concerned with customer orientation, for large national companies including two owned by Ford Motor Company as well as Seagate Technology.

In the early 1990s Dr. Betty Ann became COO of H&AMCR, where she collaborated with Dr. Felipe Korzenny to grow the company into one of the leading multicultural research companies in the US. Her responsibilities at H&AMCR included managing the company on a daily basis and working with managers of major Fortune 1000 companies and their ad agencies to shape their approach for developing a deeper cultural understanding of the Hispanic market. As an owner of Cheskin from 1999 through 2003, she continued to play a lead role working with clients in the Hispanic market.

Currently, Dr. Betty Ann is teaching at FSU in the School of Communication where she facilitates graduate students' transition from academia to the professional world. She also provides guidance to the University's Center for Hispanic Marketing Communication. She continues to maintain strong contacts with key players in Hispanic marketing. Her collaboration in writing this book is the result of her long commitment to culturally sensitive customer-oriented marketing.

Index

As this seminal book notes, smart, good business requires rephrasing the question from "How can we translate our ad so it reaches Hispanics?" to "What will be the right motivational appeal to emotionally reach Hispanics?" Fortunately for us all, Felipe and Betty Ann provide solid, well-researched answers. Everything starts with the heart. To cite but one powerful examples from this book, to Anglos, Captain Morgan and his rum works fine, but to Hispanics exploitative pirates mean something else altogether.

Dan Hill, President, Sensory Logic

If you're a marketer looking to better understand the lucrative Hispanic segment, then this book is for you. Felipe and Betty Ann Korzenny take you on a journey inside the mind of the Latino consumer and provide you with the perspective and facts you needed to design more effective and efficient Hispanic marketing strategies.

Gian Fulgoni, Chairman, comScore

Noting that there are over 50,000,000 Hispanics in America is one thing. Understanding how to connect your brand with them is quite another. This book is filled with marketing competitive-advantage built on cultural connection.

R. Barocci, Advertising Research Foundation President/CEO

This book should be on the desk of every marketer responsible for effectively understanding and targeting Hispanic consumers in the US. It's an invaluable primer for those who are new to the market and need to understand the cultural history and dimensions of this population. Those who are well entrenched in this market will find the case studies, practical advice and overall frameworks well suited for further building their business case and exploring new ways to position their campaigns and products.

Tamara Barber, Multicultural Marketing Expert

The Korzennys have beautifully collated and codified the definitive contemporary thinking on Hispanic marketing.

This is not "old" Hispanic marketing but a "new" Hispanic marketing philosophy that demonstrably links how critical culture is in understanding Hispanic's needs and rationalizes why "new" brand marketers must better cultivate this deep culture linkage. **Hispanic Marketing, Connecting with the New Latino Consumer** favors forward thinking marketers who will take the time to dig deep for these Hispanic insights just like the many marketers who graciously "raised the hood" allowing us to peek into how they succeeded in growing their brands so we can all benefit.

Trini Amador, BHC Consulting

This essential manual for the field demonstrates how to navigate and leverage one of the single most impactful demographic and cultural shifts affecting the

US marketplace. The Korzennys' perspective as true veteran practitioners in the Hispanic marketplace and accomplished academics beautifully sheds unique light in this updated edition on a comprehensive array of issues including the most relevant topics discussed in the industry today—from shifting language and acculturation issues to the digital world of Hispanics. Having spent the past twenty years researching cross-cultural consumer differences, I found this a refreshing read. It is equally valuable to the novice and experienced multicultural marketer as the book strikes a strong balance of demystifying the complex Hispanic market and offering guidance on honing skills to think differently and identify culturally driven consumer insights.

Adrien Lanusse, Director of Global Consumer Insights, Netflix

Whether you are a novice or a seasoned practitioner, buy **Hispanic Marketing** today and read it as soon as you can. It's filled with all kinds of practical ideas, tips and tactics (for developing successful cultural marketing and brand relationships with Hispanic consumers) that Dr. Felipe Korzenny and Dr. Betty Ann Korzenny have gathered from years of developing and analyzing Hispanic marketing efforts for multiple industries and organizations. **Hispanic Marketing** will give you a renewed appreciation for and deeper insights into the psyche of US Hispanic consumers, as well as in-depth case studies of successful Hispanic marketing efforts (using all sorts of creative communications approaches and tactics).

Eva A May, President, Español Marketing & Communications

The Korzennys have drawn on their many years of hands-on experience to provide the reader with an in-depth understanding of this diverse market and the importance of understanding it through a cultural approach.

Building on their pioneer work originally published in 2005, they provide richly-detailed portraits of the diverse groups that make up the U.S. Hispanic market while highlighting the shared characteristics that can be leveraged for effective marketing.

Most importantly, the Korzennys provide the reader with a solid conceptual framework to identify and assess the effectiveness of different marketing approaches, and brilliantly illustrate their points with a number of interesting and relevant case studies on how the conceptual framework can be applied on a practical basis.

Carla Briceño, Principal, Bixal Solutions

This is the most complete book I have read to date on the cultural and economic reality of the Hispanic market. It is truly a "must-read" book for anyone in the field of education or marketing communications targeting Latinos. I congratulate Felipe and Betty Ann for making this edition such an excellent resource for those of us involved in the research and analysis of this important market.

Fernando Figueredo, Chair of the Advertising and
Public Relations Faculty at Florida International University

This book is a must read for anyone wanting to gain a deep and nuanced understanding of the new Latino consumer. It is an apt tribute to Felipe and Betty Ann's many years of experience, both as scholars and practitioners in the field of Hispanic marketing. It is, without question, the best book out there on the subject of marketing to Latinos.

David Morse, President and CEO, New American Dimensions

Hispanic Marketing challenges the famous adage that says, "you can't be everything to everyone." Nevertheless, this book has something for everyone. If you are charged with brand management, strategy, analytics or the CMO of your company **Hispanic Marketing** has something for you. The Korzennys continue to lead the way. I continue to be amazed at the passion, dedication and commitment by Felipe and Betty Ann to raise the bar and sophistication level for everyone that is seeking excellence in Hispanic marketing today.

Armando Martin, President, Xledge

Well beyond the statistics in 2010 Census, this new book leverages the Korzennys' deep understanding of the Hispanic culture and market and provides both novice and expert alike with valuable nuggets, practical case studies, and core consumer insights that underpin the tremendous opportunity of the Hispanic market and clearly highlight overall impact on the "now" generation of growth markets.

Cynthia Nelson, President, Todo Bebe

In their lively conversational style, Felipe and Betty Ann Korzenny provide real live case studies packed with practical advice that show you how to develop winning strategies to beat your competitors. **Hispanic Marketing: Connecting with the New Latino Consumer**, Second Edition is your one-stop source for everything you need to boost sales, launch new products, and increase your Hispanic market share.

Charles Patrick Garcia, President, Garcia Trujillo

Felipe and Betty Korzenny have again captured the pulse of the Latino community. Marketing to Latinos is more than conceptual; it's truly understanding the Hispanic mantra.

Rudy M. Beserra, Vice President, The Coca Cola Company

The statistics, forward-looking cultural insights and empirical research in this book provide the marketing analytic community the opportunity to refine how we design complex behavioral models of the Hispanic consumer.

The statistics, forward-looking cultural insights and empirical research in this book provide the marketing analytic community the opportunity to refine how to design advanced behavioral models to better quantify emerging needs, attitudes and purchase behaviors of the critically important and dynamic Hispanic population.

Hoss Tabrizi, Managing Director and Diana Galan, Marketing Analyst,
Strategic Marketing Sciences

Felipe and Betty Ann Korzenny are the preeminent experts on Hispanic marketing. There is research and there is real world experience – nowhere will you find a more practical and salient distillation of what it takes to be successful in the Hispanic market place than in this book.

Michael Durance, CEO, Call Genie